water,
pure and simple

Paolo Consigli (born 1962) is a doctor, psychologist, acupuncturist and practitioner of holistic medicine, and has taught at the Medical Association of Chinese Medicine in Europe. He is the author of a very successful book on acupuncture (*Agopuntura, la più antica medicina ufficiale*) and has written essays and lectured on diverse subjects including humour, postnatal depression, Jewish Thought, Walter Benjamin and Franz Kafka. He lives in Milan with his wife and five sons.

water,
pure and simple

The infinite wisdom of an extraordinary molecule

Paolo Consigli, MD

WATKINS PUBLISHING

LONDON

Distributed in the United States and Canada by
Sterling Publishing Co., Inc.
387 Park Avenue South, New York, NY 10016-8810

This edition published in the UK 2008 by
Watkins Publishing, Sixth Floor, Castle House,
75–76 Wells Street, London W1T 3QH

First published in Italy under the title *L'Acqua pura e semplice: L'infinita
sapienza di una molecola straordinaria* by Tecniche Nuove, Milan
Translated from the Italian by Jeffrey Jennings

Text Copyright © Paolo Consigli 2008

Paolo Consigli has asserted his right under the Copyright, Designs
and Patents Act 1988 to be identified as the author of this work

1 3 5 7 9 10 8 6 4 2

Designed and typeset by Paul Saunders
Printed and bound in Great Britain

Library of Congress Cataloging-in-Publication data available

ISBN-13: 978-1-905857-48-7
ISBN-10: 1-905857-48-9

For information about custom editions, special sales, premium
and corporate purchases, please contact Sterling Special Sales
Department at 800-805-5489 or specialsales@sterlingpub.com

www.watkinspublishing.co.uk

For Alexandra, Natan, Joshua, Dan, Ghidon and Lev

... you will be like a well-watered garden,
like an ever flowing spring
ISAIAH 58. V. 11

ACKNOWLEDGEMENTS

Heartfelt thanks to Fiona Brown and Shelagh Boyd for their excellent editing work, to Massimo Guastini for the title 'pure and simple', and to Tuvia Fogel, agent extraordinaire. My deep appreciation goes to Penny Stopa who kept a patient eye on me to guarantee a happy ending for the book.

I am also indebted to Aldo Bolognini and Ruggero Menegon for their invaluable suggestions, Nadav Crivelli and Haim Baharier for showing me how to delve into the hidden secrets of the Bible.

Thanks to Manuel Manfredi for providing documentation on Louis Turenne, to Rosi Coerezza, Aviad Davidovich, Roberto Germano, Mara Ramploud, Paolo Bellavite and Gianfranco Peroncini for having unearthed helpful source texts on water, and to all those, too many to name, who contributed a drop of their knowledge, insight or counsel to this project.

CONTENTS

LIST OF ILLUSTRATIONS

Illustration Acknowledgements

The publisher would like to thank the following people, publishers and institutions for permission to reproduce their material. Every care has been taken to trace copyright holders. However, if we have omitted anyone we apologize and will, if informed, make corrections to any future edition.

From *Living Water: Viktor Schauberger and the Secrets of Natural Energy* by Olof Alexandersson/Gateway Books, Bath: Figures 1.1, 4.1
Tecniche Nuove Designers, Milan: Figures 1.2, 2.1, 3.3, 4.3, 4.5, 4.6, 5.3, 5.4, 5.5, 5.6, 5.8, 5.9, 5.12, 6.1, 7.2, 7.4A, 7.4C, 7.10, 8.1, 8.3, 14.1
Watkins: Figures 1.3, 1.4, 3.1, 3.2, 4.4, 5.1, 5.7, 5.10, 5.11, 6.2, 6.4, 6.5, 7.9, 7.11, 8.2, 8.4, 12.2, 12.3, 15.3, 17.1, 17.2, 17.3, 17.4, 19.1, 20.1
Institut für Strömungswissenschaften: Figures 7.5, 7.7, 7.8
NASA, USA: Figures 3.4, 16.2
Stefan Muller, Theo Plesser and Benno Hess, Dortmund, Germany: Figure 4.2
James Yorke, University of Maryland, USA: Figure 5.2
From *The Elegant Universe – Superstring, Hidden Dimensions and the Quest for the Ultimate Theory* by Brian Greene/Jonathan Cape, London: Figure 6.3
Office National d'Études et de Recherches Aérospatiales: Figures 7.1a, 7.4b
From *Das Sensible Chaos* by Theodor Schwenk/Verlag Freies Geistesleben, Germany: Figures 7.1b, 7.3
Homer Smith: Figure 7.6a
Netter Collection of Medical Illustrations, Ciba-Geigy: Figure 7.6b
From *The Aquatic Ape Hypothesis* by E Morgan/Souvenir Press, London: Figure 10.1
From *Upon the Face of Waters* by Donald Tipton and Graeme Gourlay/Circle Publishing, London: Figure 11.1
From *Traditional Chinese Acupuncture* by JR Worsley/Element Books: Figure 12.1
From *The Divining Hand: The 500 year-old Mystery of Dowsing* by Christopher Bird/Whitford Press: Figure 13.1
From *La Science et Les Sourciers* by Y Rocard/Bordas, Paris: Figure 13.2
Faustin Bray, website sound.photosynthesis.com: Figure 14.2
www.digibio.com: Figure 15.1
Photograph courtesy of Vittorio Elia's son: Figure 15.2
Gerard Bruneau (Grazia Neri): Figure 15.4
From *Communication between Man and Dolphin* by John C. Lilly/Crown Publishers Inc., New York: Figure 16.1

INTRODUCTION:
IN SEARCH OF WATER

He looked into the rushing water, into the transparent green, into the crystal lines of its drawing, so rich in secrets. ... With a thousand eyes, the river looked at him, with green ones, with white ones, with crystal ones, with sky-blue ones. ... Love this water! Stay near it! Learn from it! ... He who would understand this water and its secrets, so it seemed to him, would also understand many other things, many secrets, all secrets.

HERMANN HESSE, *Siddhartha*

Water is the most common substance on the Earth and yet, paradoxically, also the most mysterious. In fact, for many centuries its true nature remained practically unknown to science, to the extent that the chemist Linus Pauling, two-time Nobel Prize winner, defined water as 'the no-man's land of chemistry'.

We ourselves are 7/10 water, just like the blue planet we live on. But those 7/10 still harbour many mysteries. Not everybody is aware that 99 per cent of the molecules of our body are molecules of water. It forms the better part of the world inside and outside us, which means that, if we want to understand nature – both our own and our planet's – we need to explore water more thoroughly. Human beings are inexorably drawn to water because, through its extraordinary simplicity, purity and transparency, it reveals both the origins and purpose of our lives. The history and the destiny of water intersect with our own – in short, water determines our beginnings, sustains our present, and holds the key to our future.

This book is a journey of discovery into the life-generating forces inherent in and unleashed by water; an adventure during the course of which we will traverse millennia and visit thousand-year-old cultures, each with its own distilled vision of what water is and means. We will investigate water through a deliberately non-hierarchical series of lenses, from chemistry, biology, physics and medicine to anthropology, psychology, philosophy and mysticism, because there is no discipline, scientific or not, for which water is not somehow relevant. Through the fascination of its rhythms and turbulences, water seamlessly brings together science and spirit, technology and humanism, reason and intuition.

This book will also show how water affects our most intimate personal dimension, for better or worse. Water reveals through its own behaviour the principles that move it, what might be called its 'moral values' which we, children of water, would do well to adopt: water teaches us how to live more sensitively, more consciously.

Water, always ready to change, to adapt, to create and transform, is the best guide that nature offers us for understanding how to live with wisdom and serenity, how to achieve a healthy and fulfilling life. First, though, we must understand its movements, its turbulence – as well as the turbulence it provokes within our bodies and minds. When we've understood why water moves as it does, what it's fighting against and what it's striving toward, indeed why it is at all, we will understand a great deal more about our deeper selves.

Much of this knowledge already exists; we simply need to be reminded of it. For many centuries, scholars have sought to penetrate water's nature and origins. A model conceived by ancient Chinese scientists – the familiar yin-yang polarity of energetic forces – turns out to be extraordinarily well suited to understanding the laws that govern the interactions between water and the other forces and substances present in nature. Similar models appear in recent scientific theories.

Water is a powerful force that shapes our planet like a sculptor. Its unstoppable flow transforms mountains into canyons while at the same time providing sustenance to every living organism. What lies within this irresistible power? We will explore the physical behaviour of water, its vibratory structure and ordered flows which are the reasons behind its surprising therapeutic properties.

Water was, of course, a decisive factor in the emergence of a species such as the planet had never seen: *Homo sapiens*. It is to water that we owe the birth and survival of the human race, the most intelligent and self-aware species on the Earth. The illustrious English biologist Sir Alister Hardy was the first scientist to propose the rather intriguing hypothesis that the human species evolved from an aquatic ancestor, an idea that is gaining credence among an increasing number of experts.

As embryo then foetus, we spend the first nine months of our lives like fish in a salty brine, otherwise known as amniotic fluid: every one of us springs from a world of water. It is not difficult to imagine, then, the considerable advantages of waterbirth for both mother and child.

The oceans are essentially a great, wet, omnipresent cradle in which intelligent life was nurtured and grew. The cetaceans, extremely intelligent ocean-going mammals that have lived on our planet for 70 million years, can teach us much about the origins of our own intelligence, and water is the interface between us and them.

Intelligence is the ability to respond to the world in a ductile, inventive way. What could be more ductile than water? It is the intra- and extracellular substance that conducts biochemical and electromagnetic information of every kind for every living creature? Exploring what science knows about the forces inherent in water, we can discover clues as to the mysterious origin and purpose of consciousness, of intelligence.

Religious rites involving immersions and bathing are as widespread historically as they are geographically. The Bible provides frequent and detailed references to ritual baths, intended as the chance to renew oneself, to be 'born again' in both the physical and spiritual sense. Analogously, meditation and identification with water, with the help of psychotherapeutic techniques such as immersion or visualization, can help people face and sometimes resolve psychological problems. Knowledge of water's surprising properties, evidenced in its innumerable therapeutic benefits, will help us to cultivate better our physical, mental and spiritual health.

Today, a new kind of science is taking root – rigorous, attentive to the delicate balances of nature, attuned to the interactions between people and the environment, between people and people. This science, in addition to providing technological advancement, is also committed to building a society that is not only more efficient but more human, more dynamic and more open. Such a society is free, regulated by moral and social values that might be compared to the banks of a river: values that are not artificial boundaries, but creations of the free flow of the 'river' itself.

Scientific theories and discoveries on the one hand, spiritual reflections on the other, reciprocally enrich, indeed complete one another. Together, scientists and sages help us understand our existence, which owes everything to water.

Water is a simple substance, but hardly banal. Guided by its wisdom, we can improve our relationships with ourselves and with others. Let water, with its transparency, purity and simplicity, lead us on a journey to the boundaries of reality, to the twilight zone of pure and simple truth.

PART ONE

WATER AND THE UNIVERSE

Nature always follows the simplest way

ANCIENT CHINESE SAYING

And simple truth miscall'd simplicity

SHAKESPEARE, Sonnet 66

CHAPTER ONE

A UNIQUE AND MYSTERIOUS MOLECULE

Everything originated in water.
Everything is sustained by water.

JOHANN WOLFGANG GOETHE (1749–1832)

Our guide in this exploration of the multidimensional world of water is a man of whom very few will have heard, though in his own time, during the first half of the 20th century, he was known as the 'Wizard of Water'. His name is Viktor Schauberger.

Schauberger was born in 1885 in Holzschlag, Austria, near Lake Plockenstein, to a family descended from the Bavarian aristocracy. He was a naturalist and an inventor of rare perspicacity, who is to be credited with having identified and understood many of the countless eccentricities and virtues of water. As a boy, his stated dream was to become a forest warden like the majority of his ancestors, from whom he learned how to observe and to love nature. As a man he did much more, combining experience with genius to devise extraordinarily original solutions for exploiting water's properties in agriculture, to invent efficient systems for transporting logs and freight down otherwise impassable rivers, and to design special machines for water purification.

The First World War came to a close and Schauberger finished forestry school, whereupon he was hired by Prince Adolf von Schaumburg-Lippe to supervise a mountainous area in Bernerau, Steyerling. It was here that he had the opportunity to observe in greater detail the movement of watercourses, and to consider their relationships with the specific flora and fauna that proliferated around them. The young Austrian quickly realized that there was little correspondence between what he had learned in forestry school and what he was seeing and learning through his own eyes.

Schauberger knew that water tended to flow more intensely in the colder hours and seasons. He liked to recall how his father, also a woodsman, would transport hundreds of thousands of cubic metres of beechwood logs down the river, but only at night and only when the full moon illuminates the river. The reason for water's greater efficiency at night, explained the father with a highly imaginative metaphor, is that the sun's rays make the water 'tired and lazy, so it curls up and sleeps'. By night, however, the river awoke and was better able to sustain the weight of the lumber, even more so during a full moon.

One winter's night, as Schauberger studied the movements of a clear, mountain stream by the light of a full moon, he noticed another curious phenomenon. Certain oval-shaped stones, some of which were as large as a human skull, tumbled on the streambed with a rhythmic motion,

Figure 1.1 Viktor Schauberger

seeming to meet then separate from one another, as if in a dance of alternating attraction and repulsion. Other stones tended instead to float towards the water's surface, as if drawn up by the Moon. Angular or irregular-shaped stones, on the other hand, did not move at all. Schauberger noted that the rhythmic motion overcame gravity, enabling the stones with a uniform shape to climb to the surface.

As we know, if a liquid has a specific weight greater than that of an object immersed in it, the latter will float. A liquid's specific weight increases, however, when subjected to turbulent motion. You can easily see this for yourself by conducting this simple experiment at home: fill an ample pot or pitcher with water and add an egg, then stir the water with a spoon. The egg, of course, floats, for as long as you continue to stir. The natural motion and low temperature of the stream that Schauberger observed helped concentrate the liquid so that the stones were made to float.

Another factor that 'strengthens' water is shade. One day, Schauberger noticed that a natural stone arch which had covered the wellspring of a healthy stream had been removed, and the spring dried up almost completely. Only after rebuilding the arch did it begin to flow again. This, along with his observation of the way that vegetation tends to be distributed along watercourses, led Schauberger to formulate the hypothesis that water is sensitive to shade and to the surrounding flora. Both the curvilinear aspect of most watercourses and the shade provided by vegetation along the banks that protects the water from direct sunlight, ensure its natural flow at a low temperature, which in turn optimizes its strength and load-bearing capacity. 'Water wants to flow this way, curving and creating these shaded banks to protect itself from direct sunlight.'

Schauberger applied his ideas with great success. In the winter of 1918, he managed to transport 1,600 cubic metres of lumber in a single night down from the mountains along a river running through an area considered to be absolutely impenetrable.

Prince von Schaumburg-Lippe owned tracts of forest split by steep canyons. None of the experts had ever succeeded in devising a system for bringing the lumber down to the valley until Schauberger put his theories on water motion to work. Originally excluded from the call for tenders by engineers and hydrologists who thought him incompetent, he was reconsidered when all of the technicians and university professors thoroughly failed to understand the problem, much less solve it.

Beneath the scornful scowls of these experts, Schauberger built a wooden flume whose form, contradicting all logic, was neither rectilinear nor followed the shortest route of descent, but instead zig-zagged meanderingly down the mountainside for some 50 kilometres. The curves of his flume followed the river itself, rather than an abstract geometry, creating a spiral turbulence in water.

Schauberger demonstrated how the biggest logs couldn't make it downriver without cold water; they would invariably jam and back up – precisely what had happened to the technicians who preceded him. An ingenious system of valves allowed Schauberger to release quantities of water from the flume and substitute it with colder water from the adjacent river, thereby calibrating the temperature, in keeping with his conviction that cold water was stronger. He even went so far as to claim that, by cooling the water down, it was reinvigorated, recharged – utter nonsense as far as the 'experts' were concerned.

A trial run failed, and Schauberger concluded it was because the water's load-bearing capacity was insufficient and the flume too steep. But a snake, of all things, provided the Austrian inventor with a great insight the day before the official inauguration: as he studied his flume, he was startled by a snake, which edged into the leg of his pants. He unthinkingly flicked into the current with the toe of his boot. Schauberger was astounded to see the creature easily cross from one side to the other despite the powerful current and steep incline.

Watching the serpent utilize its sinuous, undulating movements to navigate the water's surface, he instantly understood what was missing from his flume. He had to build the curves so that the water passing through them would be agitated in such a way as to mimic the spiralling of the snake's progress.

In short, his system had to imitate natural watercourses even more faithfully: 'Water in its natural state shows us how it wants to flow, and we must obey its wishes.'

To everyone's amazement, the narrow curvilinear flume was a success, and from that moment experts came from all over Europe to study its principles. Logging flumes were built according to Schauberger's directives in Austria, Yugoslavia and Turkey. Elsewhere, people tried independently to imitate his method, and failed. Even for the most advanced scientists, this was all a great technological mystery. Water had always seemed such a simple substance, yet here it was displaying bizarre behaviours that defied every assumption.

Schauberger began observing the movements of fish in relation to those of water, and became the first to demonstrate the connection between water temperature and the behaviour of trout running upstream. Everyone knows that trout and salmon swim against the current to spawn, and the image we have is that of an arduous enterprise. The amazing truth, however, is that these aquatic creatures do it almost effortlessly, mile after mile.

Schauberger explained why. Water of superior quality, the purest and healthiest, has a greater density and runs at the temperature of the so-called 'anomalous point' of 4 °C. It is at this temperature that the fish undertake their upstream run. He conducted further experiments with his assistants. One involved heating the parts of a river where trout tend to swim upstream at the same speed as the current and thus seem 'suspended' in the water. He found that as the temperature rose, the fish darted further upstream to find colder water.

He also was amazed at the ease with which these fish were able to jump waterfalls, observing that they did so with a spiral motion through a conical space created by the rivulets of a vortex. No scientist was able to explain the phenomenon. Schauberger deduced that the natural flow of the water creates an energy field that runs in the opposite direction to the current, and that the strength required to make those prodigious leaps against both current and gravity comes from a force present in the water itself, a confluence of temperature and vortex flow. According to Schauberger, these phenomena are the result of the *cycloid spiral motion* created by the water's turbulence. The fish simply 'ride' this natural countercurrent to facilitate their upstream journey.

Schauberger liked to say that birds don't fly, they are flown by air currents, just as fish do not swim, they are swum. Similarly, the heart does not pump, but is pumped by the continuous flow of blood, an idea that Alexis Carrel, winner of the Nobel Prize for Medicine, had already proposed in 1912.

Schauberger's credo was to understand and imitate nature. We can imagine him listening to water, and what he might have heard: 'Watch how I move and where I go; do as I do and you will choose life; imitate my movements and you will be creative like me …' For decades the Austrian inventor analysed natural creative motion, particularly spiral and cycloid motion. He even built machines that reproduced those movements, with the aim of rendering water more vital.

Experiments conducted in 1952 at the University of Stuttgart confirmed the existence of the flow patterns identified by the visionary forest warden.[1] But it wasn't until the end of the 20th century, with its interest in chaos, vortices and turbulence, that these phenomena became the subject of important scientific research.

We will return to Schauberger's intuitions and discoveries in Chapter 4.

Aqueous Anomalies: Nothing is Impossible

Water is omnipresent on the Earth, and there is no other substance like it, starting with the fact that water is the only compound that is found in nature in all three basic states of matter – solid, liquid and gas. Its form changes with extraordinary ease, and in doing so it absorbs (and contains) an enormous quantity of energy.

Nor is there any other planet like the Earth, still the only watery planet we know of. And there is even more water than one might think. Oceans, rivers and other bodies of water occupy about 70 per cent of the planet's surface, a total volume of more than 500 million cubic kilometres, while an additional 5,000 km³ floats in the atmosphere in the form of vapour. But that's hardly all: the vast majority of Earth's water is hidden beneath the ground. In fact, the amount of underground water is 37 times greater than surface water. One could say that water and the Earth are bound by a sort of monogamous marriage, unique in the known universe.

In addition to being the distinguishing constitutive element of the Earth, water is also an active and powerful substance, having quite literally shaped our planet over millions of years, carving landscapes, sculpting valleys, modelling mountains. It has changed the course of rivers, dragging billions of tons of detritus and sediment over vast distances, constantly redrawing the profiles of coasts and continents. Given time, the delicate caress of water can become extraordinarily powerful.

There are many more proofs of the invincible power of water, and one is its ability to dissolve any substance eventually; its solvent capacity. Nearly half of the chemical elements on the Earth exist in a dissolved state because water is so aggressive that, over time, it can corrode even the most resistant metal. Water can also penetrate living organisms, passing right through them, transforming tissues and solids, softening them.

Through its solvent capacity, water reveals an ethical dimension as well, demonstrating how gentleness paired with constancy can make anything more malleable. Thinking like water, we can learn to tenderize our own character, soften rough edges and aggressive attitudes, both our own and others'. When pushed to the edge of anger, think of the cooling, soothing effect of a cold shower, and you might save yourself and others from a harmful explosion.

Water's erosive action on rock releases minerals and organic compounds that fertilize the soil and nourish plants. When it evaporates, it transfers essential elements such as sulphur and iodine from the sea to the air and thus back to the soil. Even rocks, then, seemingly inert, participate in the vital cycle of life.

This life-giving planetary process is called the *hydrological* cycle, and it is thanks to this that water is able to recycle itself. Oceans, lakes and watercourses evaporate and the water vapour condenses to form clouds, returning to earth in the form of rain, snow and hail; it then either remains on the surface or infiltrates the ground (called 'meteoric water'), creating aquifers that then spring forth through the ground or the ocean floor, perpetuating the cycle.

This planetary flow of water forms and transforms the Earth's crust and makes life possible for every organism, both plant and animal: it is our common source of health and survival. Yet the factors responsible for the presence of water on the Earth are not entirely clear, and it is still a mystery how the amount has remained more or less constant over billions of years.

It was only in 1997 that instrumentation was able to confirm, to everyone's astonishment, what the American astronomer Louis Frank of the University of Iowa had been maintaining for years: every minute, the Earth is bombarded by dozens of tons of water in the form of small comets made of ice – small being a relative term, insofar as they are as big as a house. These fiery aqueous objects appear between 600 and 15,000 miles from Earth at the rate of 5 to 30 per minute, and can be seen from the ground.[2] It is likely that these ice comets have been confused in the past with shooting stars, even with UFOs. They are most visible at twilight or just before dawn, when they superheat and flare up for an instant before disintegrating.

As incredible as it may seem, a million tons of water is hurled at the Earth every day, and no one can explain where it comes from. Yet these big balls of ice are part of our lives. They vaporize upon impact with the atmosphere and therefore contribute to the rain that falls to earth: part of the water that falls on us during a rainstorm and part of the ground-water we drink, is actually extraterrestrial in origin. The Earth is nourished by water from outer space, like a living being quenching its thirst.

Despite the abundance of scientific proof, Frank's discovery was met with scepticism by the majority of researchers, because it forced science to revise assumptions considered certain, but which no longer hold up in the face of this new evidence. As we will see when examining other scientific controversies, ice comets are not the only phenomenon involving water that has sparked endless debate.

Water: the Exception is the Rule

We don't know how water got here, neither do we know all the details of how it works. And it cannot be otherwise, because water epitomizes the mystery of life, which is inherently paradoxical: life on Earth is an exception in the known universe.

Water has unique and surprising chemical and physical properties. Normally, substances become lighter when passing from the solid to the liquid state. Water does the opposite: ice, against all logic, floats.

Habit has led us to think of this as obvious, normal. Yet it is in fact exceptional, because all other solid, liquid or gaseous materials diminish in volume when their temperature is lowered, and this contraction increases density. Gas is lighter than its liquid form, which in turn is lighter than the solid form.

Water defies this rule by becoming less dense as it solidifies. At first it appears to behave like other substances, becoming denser as the temperature drops, but at 4 °C, the unexpected occurs: water decides to change course and begins to expand, becoming even lighter at 0 °C.

It is this kind of behaviour, which we'll call 'anticonformist', that allowed life to be created on this planet. If water did not have this bizarre capacity to expand below 4 °C, ice would sink to the bottom of the lakes, rivers and oceans to the point where every body of water would become permanently frozen from below, the opposite of what actually happens. In fact, the ice that forms on aqueous surfaces prevents the water beneath from freezing.

If water were to behave 'normally', the Earth would undergo temperature fluctuations of hundreds of degrees. Water wouldn't have the ability to store the sun's heat and release it gradually, ensuring a stable seasonal cycle within a temperature range conducive to the development of life. Locked frozen at the bottom of the seas and lakes, water could not evaporate and there would be no rain, no hydrological cycle. In short, the whole Earth would be a harsh wasteland of ice and desert where no living organism could hope to survive.

Other eccentricities of water are its boiling and freezing points. The Celsius scale sets them at 100 and 0 degrees, respectively, which is amazing if we compare water to other chemically similar substances. For all matter, boiling and freezing points increase in direct proportion to molecular weight. By all the laws and logic of nature, with its molecular weight of 18, *water should freeze at minus 100 °C and boil at minus 16 °C!* Again, if water behaved like other molecules, it would boil at arctic temperatures and would only exist as vapour. But that's not all. Usually, the viscosity of a liquid is proportionate to the compression to which it is subjected, but water breaks this rule, too: when cold water is compressed it becomes even more fluid, contrary to the majority of liquids.

Water reaches its maximum density at 4 °C, diminishing on either side of that temperature. This strange behaviour can be explained in part by the degree of 'disorder' of the hydrogen bonds between the molecules. In fact, at 4 °C the increase in kinetic energy apparently 'distances' the water molecules from one another. Schauberger was right to focus on this significant temperature value.

The development of life is possible only if water is present in its liquid state; that is, between 0 and 100 °C. Miraculously, Earth's temperature falls just within this tight parenthesis of 100 degrees, this tiny window of warmth that creates and sustains life. We realize how extraordinary this is when we consider that the interval between 0 and 100 °C is less than 2 per cent of the temperature range of the planets in our own solar system, and that in the rest of the universe temperatures vary by more than 36 million degrees centigrade.

Equally incredible is that the Earth has maintained this same temperature range for four billion years despite the fact that the sun's heat has diminished threefold over that same time period. How? Well, even more incredibly, while the sun cooled threefold the Earth simply became three times warmer, thanks to the effect of heat distribution caused by water. Our life truly does have something of the miraculous about it, built on and sustained by exceptions to the rules, by things that should be impossible.

Every living being, from the simplest virus to the most advanced mammal, owes its existence to this creative anticonformism of water, which has somehow always managed to ensure that every chemical and physical reaction necessary for the creation of our world happened at just the right time and in just the right way.

Water, Heat and Change

Water's ability to absorb heat is responsible for the climate of our planet. We witness this property every day when boiling water for hot drinks or cooking: it takes a long time precisely because of the enormous amount of heat it can accumulate. The metal of the kettle or the cooking pot, for example, heats up and cools down at least ten times faster than water.

A volume of just a few cubic metres of ocean water can store as much heat as the entire atmosphere, and if we consider that the average depth of the oceans is 3.7 kilometres (2.3 miles) it becomes clear how enormously important the oceans are for the Earth's climate.

The water molecule absorbs and releases more heat than the majority of other substances. It is a latent heat that does not generate temperature change, its maximum value being 37 °C.

This is how water maintains body temperature at a constant. Picture a tub of warm water placed in a greenhouse on a freezing winter night: it will give off its heat to the air, warming it, and will ice over only slightly after many hours.

In certain desert environments, temperatures can vary between 50 °C during the day to well below zero at night. Why? Because there is no water to absorb heat when it's hot and to release heat when it's cold. This also explains why people who live by the sea enjoy warmer, more regular temperatures than those living inland, even though both are subjected to the same climatic events.

Water's latent heat causes vapour to condense in the atmosphere, forming clouds, a vital source of heat that directly determines the course of the seasons.

We can get an idea of the enormous potential energy contained in water vapour by observing the spectacular explosions of lightning generated by the dense clouds of a summer storm. The quantity of energy released by a thunderstorm of medium intensity is equal to that of a large atomic bomb. If the effects are less destructive it is only because the energy is less concentrated.

Like humankind, water extends between heaven and earth, tending to draw to itself all that derives from both places so as to elaborate it, like the artist or the craftsman. Solid substances are reshaped by water, dissolving beneath its touch, just as the gases in the air are absorbed by water. Somehow, water knows when there is an excess of carbon dioxide in the air and absorbs it, just as it knows when there's too little, and releases it, creating a seasonal cycle that is fundamental for the growth of the Earth's flora. An additional benefit is that, by absorbing carbon dioxide, water increases its own power to dissolve solid matter.

Water also plays a key role as intermediary and interface: it is a means of communication between heaven and earth, between atmosphere and planet.

Lastly, water is one of the few substances that can act as both acid and base, able to vary its pH without altering its chemical structure. Under certain conditions, this enables it paradoxically to diversify itself, to change itself, to react chemically with itself and reappear under new guises. This capacity for self-renewal and diversification is the secret formula for all evolution and progress.

The Happy Marriage of Hydrogen and Oxygen

The appearance of water on the Earth is probably due to fragments sent here by the explosion of one of the 400 billion supernovae in the Milky Way. After a few million years, when temperatures had fallen sufficiently, hydrogen and oxygen could finally unite in the water molecule, which would have assumed the delicate and symmetrical form of ice crystals and snowflakes.

Hydrogen is the most common element in the universe. It has the simplest and lightest structure of all: a single electron (negatively charged particle) orbiting in a perfect void around a nucleus consisting of just one proton (positively charged particle). Chronologically speaking, hydrogen was the first element to appear in the universe, and as such can be said to be as old as the universe itself. With its single electron and proton, it embodies the essence of all the ineffable 'Unified Theories', both scientific and religious, which lies at the origin of reality.

Atoms need to have their outermost orbitals occupied, and it would seem that they prefer to bond in a 'hetero-ionic' way – that is, with atoms of a different element – to form molecules.

Hydrogen is like a lonely bachelor, driven by an irresistible desire for a partner. Its electron cloud hates being alone, it feels incomplete and will therefore bond with any other electron, even from another hydrogen atom. When this endogamic bond is combined with the exogamic bond formed with oxygen, an atom of opposite polarity, water is the result. And this is one of those marriages that last: *the oxygen–hydrogen bond is one of the strongest that exists.*

One cubic metre of water has 100 billion billion billion (10^{29}) hydrogen molecules. Logic dictates that hydrogen should not be present on the Earth, for our tiny planet doesn't exert nearly enough gravity to hold on to the lightest element in the universe. And in fact, while the Earth was forming, 99 per cent of the hydrogen drifted off into space, the remaining 1 per cent having managed to pair up with heavier elements like carbon, sulphur and zinc. That little bit of hydrogen then waited for the Earth to reach its ideal state of condensation and cooling to divorce itself from the mineral prison of its heavier partners to remarry, this time with oxygen, which up to this point had been absent. Another curious and providential coincidence.

Oxygen is the second most abundant element on Earth, and the third most common in the universe, after helium (table 1.1). It first appeared on our planet between 4 and 2 billion years ago, but only became available in the atmosphere thanks to water. The oxygen we breathe comes from plant photosynthesis, 70 per cent of which is from aquatic plants. Before oxygen had become part of the atmosphere, the first living organisms evolved in water. Only later, when the algae had produced enough oxygen, did the first ozone layer form, opening up the possibility of life on land.

Oxygen is 16 times heavier than hydrogen and has 2 electrons. Like its sociable spouse, oxygen is also eager to partner up with two electrons, whether equal or different.

Water is humble. It seeks out the lowest point and has no form of its own. Behind this modesty, however, lie extraordinary power and elasticity: to separate those two hydrogen atoms from oxygen they must be heated to around 3,000 °C. As the Chinese philosopher Lao Tzu knew, as far back as the sixth century BC, water embodies the ideal of harmony: it is strong precisely because it is so yielding, integral and cohesive, yet ready to be absorbed. It adheres to everything it touches,

Element	Atomic number	Relative quantity in the universe
Hydrogen	1	$2,7 \times 10^8$
Helium	2	1.8×10^7
Oxygen	8	$1,8 \times 10^5$
Carbon	6	$1,1 \times 10^5$
Neon	10	$2,6 \times 10^4$
Nitrogen	7	$2,3 \times 10^4$
Magnesium	12	$1,1 \times 10^4$
Silicon	14	$1,0 \times 10^4$
Fluorine	9	9000
Sulphur	16	5000
Argon	18	1000
Aluminium	13	850
Calcium	20	625
Sodium	11	600

Table 1.1 Relative quantities of the most common elements in the universe

wetting, penetrating, lubricating. It appears submissive, then transforms both itself and that which is not itself. Water seems to be telling us: 'Be humble in cultivating your strength and you will overcome all obstacles.'

Until two centuries ago, water was considered an indivisible element. It wasn't until 1783 that Henry Cavendish stunned the entire scientific community by successfully splitting and resynthesizing the water molecule, combining hydrogen and oxygen. The reason this bond is so tenacious is because the hydrogen atom is so small, causing its nucleus to get extremely close to oxygen's electrons, creating an incredibly powerful covalent bond that is very difficult to break.

The dipole of the water molecule – the positive pole of hydrogen and the negative pole of oxygen – behaves like a bipolar magnetic bar. Hydrogen's positive electric charges and oxygen's negative ones attract each other and form a bond with a stable angle. Normally, molecules align themselves at varying angles, so long as the final alignment is regular and geometrical. Not water, though: once again its anticonformism comes to the fore, in that it always assumes exactly the same alignment.

The angle formed by the bond between the two hydrogen atoms and the larger oxygen atom is 104.7°. This value is called the valence angle. Many of water's unique properties derive from and depend on its asymmetry (figure 1.2). The angle of 104.7° causes the molecule to configure as a fork, the handle of which is the oxygen nucleus, the twin tines the hydrogen nuclei. The whole is immersed in an electron cloud.

When we say that water is a dipole we mean that it's a molecule whose positive and negative electrical charges are set a fixed distance so that the electrons will move closer to the oxygen than to the hydrogen: hence its asymmetry. The molecule has a pole that is more positive, another that is more negative. Schematically, it resembles Mickey Mouse. Around Mickey's chin, the oxygen atom is more negatively charged, while the ears are more positive. This polarized configuration renders the contact surfaces between water molecules quite complex, resulting in something not unlike a tetrahedron, or rather, a pyramid with a water molecule at every corner. Water is, in fact, a liquid crystal.

The static Mickey Mouse model is artificial, of course, because the atomic and subatomic structure of water is vibratory, not solid: it is restless and oscillates continually from one state to another. We must also remember the distances at play: if the nucleus of an atom were the size of a pea, its electrons would be orbiting through a space more than a mile high and wide.

Because of the conjugal loyalty between oxygen and hydrogen, water can do that which for other molecules would be impossible. The asymmetrical distribution of electrical charges makes water a sort of slightly bent microscopic bar magnet. As we know, no matter how many times

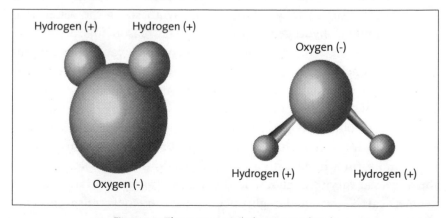

Figure 1.2 The asymmetrical water molecule

you cut a bar magnet in half, it will always maintain opposite charges at its extremities. The same is true for water: it is always constituted by bipolar universes with charges oriented the same way, whether it's a drop of water, a puddle, a river or an ocean.

This property of unvarying bipolarity, regardless of how one cuts a bar magnet or 'divides' water, is called *modularity*. Reality is modular when its sequences and aspect are structurally identical, independent of scale: the microcosm reproduces the macrocosm. Such is the case of water, where the same polarity is maintained no matter how small or how large the quantity, such that a molecule is identical to an ocean.

The dipole of water is a scale model of the cosmology that ancient Chinese scientists constructed around the two basic forces of the universe, *yin* and *yang*. A negative polarity (yin) and a positive one (yang) interact, and from this interaction springs forth the physical and chemical world, also bipolar, asymmetrical and modular. Water, having all these characteristics, is a micro-universe, the embodiment of this interaction of universal forces.

The Hydrogen Bridge: Restlessness in the Void

The elevated electronegativity of oxygen enables hydrogen atoms to trade their own electrons by way of bonds known as hydrogen bridges. The millions of molecules in a drop of water thus combine in a 4 x 4 configuration. Four molecules then bond with the other 16 until they form an elongated pyramid with an empty core that contains no atoms at all. Hydrogen bonds are more numerous when water is in its solid state and are responsible for the six-pointed-star shape of snowflakes. The molecular skeleton of ice delimits yet greater empty spaces, resulting in an expanded and lightweight reticular structure which explains why ice floats.

So far at least 200 different configurations of ice have been identified, varying according to the temperature and pressure in which they are formed. The regular structure of ice carries over into liquid water, though it transforms back and forth at an inconceivable pace: in the liquid phase, crystals of ice are formed and then melt millions of times per second, as if the water 'remembers' which specific type of ice crystal it is supposed to form (we will return to the question of 'water memory' in Chapter 15 when we discuss its electromagnetic properties).

Most people have heard it said that no crystal or flake of snow is the same as another, and that the Inuit have 70 different terms for as many types of snow. Science confirms this common wisdom by organizing snow into six main categories of crystals, each divided into more than 30 subtypes. Snow can also undergo further metamorphoses once it hits the ground, adding yet another four categories to the total.

Hydrogen bonds create enormous empty spaces between molecules, which align themselves in new ways to form snowflakes that are never the same. Water seems to be suggesting a general principle to us here: in nature, *the void is the necessary condition for the creation of new, ever changing forms.* What happens in the empty spaces between hydrogen bonds embodies the enigma of the generative and vital properties of water.

When ice is heated, certain hydrogen bonds are broken and the number of empty spaces between molecules is consequently reduced and water becomes denser, at least in the temperature interval between 0 and 4 °C: the hydrogen bonds diminish but the vibrations of the molecules increase as the temperature rises, as with all substances.

Snow crystals are composed of millions of water molecules that assemble in hexagonal lattices. In addition to six-sided crystals, by far the most common, there are three- and five-sided snow crystals. Form and size depend on climatic and environmental conditions yet to be precisely determined. What is certain, though, is that a snowflake is highly sensitive to variations in temperature: each individual flake is subjected to slightly different microclimatic conditions which condition its configuration.

The hexagonal crystal is one of the two quintessential structures of water, the other being the sphere. A drop of water is a sphere elongated by gravity, while hailstones are formed by spherical layers of ice, like an onion, oriented in different directions.

In the 1930s, Nobel Prize winner Linus Pauling, a chemist, theorized that the laws of quantum mechanics governed the dynamics of the hydrogen bonds between water molecules and the covalent bonds within them. Pauling maintained that there exists a sort of overlap between the two kinds of bonds and that this justified some of water's unique properties, including its special way of bonding with biological molecules which is so fundamental for living organisms.

Pauling's theory was confirmed in 1998 by Eric Isaacs and his team at Bell Laboratories in Murray Hill, New Jersey. Bombarding ice crystals with x-rays, the researchers discovered that 90 per cent of the hydrogen bonds are electrostatic, while 10 per cent interpenetrate with adjacent covalent bonds (with atoms that share their electrons).[3]

The electrons pass from one molecule to another at the speed of light, a critical factor of 'instability' that allows water to interact with biological molecules, creating ever new balances and symmetries. This partially explains the permeability of water molecules in comparison with other substances.

The conclusion to be drawn is that it's best not to trust the atomic models we find in textbooks, flat and static as they are. *Hydrogen bonds are not solid tubes, but restless vibratory entities.* It's difficult to imagine the dynamic reality that underlies the physical world as we perceive it with our senses: who can really grasp the idea of electrons travelling at the speed of light as they pass from one side to the other of the hydrogen atoms of contiguous molecules? Indeed, this happy marriage we call water hides a number of aspects which escape perception and control.

Hydrogen bonds alternate between states of rest and agitation. At room temperature, approximately 86 per cent of water molecules are connected, relaxing and contracting at intervals between a ten-billionth and a hundred-millionth of a second. The sheer number of the bridges between them, along with the inherent sturdiness of the hydrogen–oxygen bond, is what makes water so strong and ductile.

Subatomic physics confirm what Chinese scientists discovered thousands of years ago: the universe is not composed of inert matter, but of fields of force immersed in the void, so powerful and fast as to appear solid and static to our unreliable eyes. The water molecule is made of these force fields. Its dipole vibrates coherently, and its natural distortion forms electromagnetic bonds with other molecules.

The frequency of the molecular vibrations of water changes according to the dissolved minerals present, which explains the different therapeutic effects of waters from different sources. When it comes into contact with different crystals and substances, water changes its 'atomic imprint', which can be perceived with a spectrophotometer, an instrument that measures the luminous radiation emitted by a given material. Spring water seems to have a low incidence of hydrogen bonds compared with tap water, for example. Though this doesn't fully account for the significance of these differences, it proves that water can change its aspect and vibration rate through mere contact with another molecule.

From a Molecule to a Drop of Water

Using laser technology, chemist Yuen Ron Shen and his research team at the University of California at Berkeley identified the molecular structure of the surface of a water droplet.[4] When making contact with air, hydrogen atoms extend outwards from the droplet almost like a man struggling underwater to grab onto something (figure 1.3). The hydrogen atom is therefore capable of interacting with any other negatively charged atom.

It is here, in ionic bonds with other molecules, that water achieves the apex of its capacity for communication and creativity. Unlike covalent bonds and hydrogen bonds, which form part of its structure, ionic bonds (a term deriving from the Greek for 'to go') work with other substances in a reciprocal relationship in which neither part overwhelms or incorporates the other. The two substances in question, water and molecule, communicate with a freer bond. This greater liberty ensures that the dissolved molecules are more available to interact with other molecules. All the most recent scientific literature on water shows that it has an extraordinary propensity for bonding with other molecules, as well as stimulating them to be more available themselves.

When we fill a glass to the brim, we notice that the surface of the water seems enclosed by a transparent membrane that swells above the edge of the glass. Even more conspicuously, when a faucet drips very slowly, the droplet visibly stretches downwards in its effort to remain attached to the faucet. This is known as surface tension, and happens because of the cohesive force of the hydrogen bond.

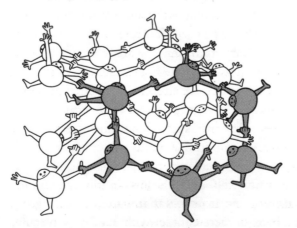

Figure 1.3 As ice, the water molecule bonds with four others in an hexagonal symmetry

Surface tension enables a water droplet, freed from the atmospheric pressure that tends to deform it, to create a sphere which, among all existing forms, has the smallest surface area by volume. A sphere is witnessed when an oyster generates a pearl. Surface tension transforms water into a sort of transparent skin, strong enough for rather large insects to walk upon. This is the same principle that makes it possible for water to transport anything from logs to aircraft carriers.

Water has the virtue of both *adherence* and *coherence*: its molecules tend to cluster together and vibrate in unison. Only mercury is more cohesive than water, but it is not adhesive at all, which is why it doesn't leave the inside of a container 'wet'.

Hydrogen bridges are responsible for another of water's astounding traits: capillarity. This is the tendency that liquids have to adhere to the surface of a material and climb it, in defiance of gravity. The capillary effect is clearest in very thin tubes where, despite the natural tendency to descend, it surprises us with yet another paradox by going up. It is thanks to this miraculous cohesive and propulsive force that blood and other fluids are able to circulate and reach every cell in our bodies. This is the same force that allows plants to nourish their uppermost branches, leaves, flowers and fruits, whether they're 3 inches or 300 feet tall. Put simply, living creatures and plants could not exist were it not for the propulsive force of capillary action.

Which leads us to another singularity that makes water indispensable for life on Earth. When placed inside a pipette no wider than a human capillary, water maintains its liquid state at -8 °C and in some instances even lower. In the vessels of the circulatory system, blood and lymph do not freeze at very low external temperatures, ensuring the passage of nutrients in liquid solution even in subzero climates.

There is one last aspect to consider. People will often casually describe two identical things as being 'like two drops of water'. No simile could be further from the truth. Like snowflakes and human beings, every drop of water is unique and unrepeatable. A droplet is held together by different forces and within each one swims a universe unto itself.

At the 1998 convention of the American Physical Society, David Clary, a chemist from University College, London, was finally able to respond to the eternal question, '*How many molecules are needed to form the smallest possible drop of water?*' The answer: *six*.

Combining lab experiments and computer simulations, Clary discovered that when six molecules bond to form a droplet, something unexpected occurs: from a flat ring of four or five conjoined molecules, the structure of water suddenly springs into three dimensions with the addition of a sixth, forming a round cluster.[5] Interestingly, the fact that the number six introduces a three-dimensional structure was known to the ancient practitioners of kabbalistic numerology, which we'll investigate a bit later on.

After six, these tiny droplets tend not to bond with each other, perhaps because the electrical charge of their surfaces repel them. The factor that influences the size of a water droplet is still a mystery.

In 1997, chemist Richard Saykally of UC Berkeley and his team demonstrated in a study published in *Science*[6] that water can assume the most diverse physical forms. When subjecting it to enormous pressure, comparable to that found in the deepest ocean, its density increases by fully 25 times. This surprising discovery makes the claims of the visionary Schauberger all the more plausible: water changes behaviour and demonstrates new virtues when subjected to even the slightest physical force, such as turbulence and changes in pressure and temperature.

The Water Molecule in Chinese Writing

The ideograms of the Chinese language are graphic images that represent ideas, objects and actions, while at the same time letters and words of the written language. Calligraphy is the most ancient form of Chinese art and the source of all the subsequent major arts (music, dance, poetry) as well as many other creative activities. The visual aims and effects of calligraphy, with its graceful strokes and movements, are both aesthetic and communicative.

Calligraphy mirrors the creative movement of nature, and is its highest expression, for to give a name to things and reproduce them in the same act means synthesizing their essential forces and giving them life. Dipping into the ink, modulating the pressure of one's grip on the brush and choreographing its dance across the paper's surface, affixing the seal – these are the gestures that constitute the creative experience of calligraphy, quintessential union of art and discipline.

We can easily see the importance attributed to water by the Chinese by looking at its importance in their language. Of the 3,650 most common ideograms, fully 146 of them (4 per cent) contain the radical for 'water'. And many of these are verbs, suggesting the extent to which this ancient civilization was attentive to observing all of water's actions, even those less apparent.

The ancient ideogram for the word 'water' (figure 1.4), *shui*, describes a winding water-course, a sort of backwards 'S', surrounded by four curved gestures representing spray or droplets (1 + 4 = 5) which constitute the most vital part. The character is inscribable within an imaginary hexagon, exactly the same geometric configuration favoured by water molecules.

Figure 1.4 The Chinese ideogram for water

The intuitive flair of this sinuous ideogram is remarkable. Not only does it describe a flowing river, it is also an elegant graphic synthesis of the bonds between water molecules: the central stroke (which we can consider a molecule) bonds with the other four molecules to form a hexagonal unit. A modern chemist couldn't have come up with a more suggestive diagram of how water works.

Between Science and Spirit

Science searches for the limits of nature, mysticism its limitlessness; science the drop of water, mysticism the wave ... Together they explore reality, for both science and mysticism are seeking the same reality that underlies matter.

RENÉE WEBER, *Dialogues with Scientists and Sages*

Does life have meaning? If so, what is it? Why did intelligence develop on the Earth? How is it possible that this mixture of carbon, hydrogen and oxygen of which we are made is capable of asking such a question? Everyone has asked at least one of these questions at some point. And since we've seen that water is not just any old molecule but the very essence of life itself, it might help us understand why we exist.

Flowing water is noticed only if it is turbulent: with no rippling of the surface it is simply a monotonous backdrop. So let's try to understand more about water by following its movements. The same approach is used in physics: describe the motion, analyse the probabilistic wave function and the molecules' vibrations.

Western scientists and philosophers have sought for millennia to understand material reality, whether or not it exists at all and, if so, what is the substance that is the foundation of all life. The ancient thinkers of the East, on the other hand, were more concerned with understanding how reality moves and evolves, with the forces that allow all things to develop and change.

Today, the physical sciences no longer search for these foundational elements. Like the ancient Eastern scholars they analyse the processes and dynamics that drive reality, thinking in terms of flux rather than stasis. Our senses show us a world composed essentially of water flux. And indeed 'fluid dynamics' is the perfect metaphor, used long ago by sages and now by scientists, for describing the dynamics of the universe.

The body is itself a flux of chemical and organic processes that continuously replenishes itself. It is not a machine made of inert material as the old mechanistic scientific model would have it. The body has the power to heal and regenerate, thanks to the water fluxes that give it life.

If the flow of water is a metaphor, it is also a microcosm, an ideal model for understanding the nature of the universe and of humankind. And it is a model of behaviour as well: global, ductile and ecological whole, wherein every component, no matter how they are mixed together, shares the same goal, the same direction; wherein every individual atom is an integral part of the all-encompassing fluid that gives their individuality meaning. Water is an ecological model: it generates equilibrium and has the power to harmoniously integrate all things; it is an aesthetic model in that its movement and its rhythms produce beauty. This way of seeing the world is called holistic (from the Greek *olos*, meaning 'all, complete'). The holistic vision unites all phenomena in a single whole constituted by copenetrating parts that interact with and depend on one another.

The traditional Chinese sciences are holistic, based in part on Taoism, as is Indian Ayurvedic science, which derives from Hinduism. Straddling East and West, the holistic vision can be found in the mystical currents of the three monotheistic religions. In secular Western culture, it has been upheld by certain Classical Greek thinkers, by exponents of the Renaissance, by poets, artists and thinkers from all historical periods, and by a number of scientists of our own day.

Science looks for causal connections between phenomena, studying the 'how' but failing to provide a response to the 'why'. This is because science alone can never give meaning to our existence or to the universe. It is easy to touch and feel water, yet impossible to grasp it. We realize this as it passes through our fingers; the scientist when studying its physical and chemical properties. Water is a special molecule, elusive and unique, different from all the others.

By assembling research and insights on water from diverse sources and ways of thought, we might be better able to understand the nature and meaning of our existence on this watery planet, so rich in so many different kinds of intelligence. We will do so by respectfully maintaining the distinction between scientific and spiritual research which, though they can inform one another, must remain autonomous, each with its own dignity.

Scientific thought offers us detailed data on the physical and biological complexity of an infinite reality; spiritual thought offers us the experience of interior reality, of the consciousness that extends beyond the confines of our body. Spirituality needs the rigour of science, for unless it is applied to the concrete details of life it risks being vague, or worse, arbitrary. Conversely, science needs spirituality's ability to extend beyond the limits of the mind, beyond a definition of reality reduced to that which can be counted and measured.

CHAPTER TWO

THE ARCHITECTURE OF IMPERFECTION

Water in its natural state shows us how it wants to flow, and we must obey its wishes.

VIKTOR SCHAUBERGER

The water dipole, with its twin hydrogen atoms on one side and an oxygen atom on the other, is asymmetrically forked. We've seen how this imbalance is responsible for some of the countless properties unique to water – in other words, the remarkable reactivity of the water molecule derives from the bipolarity and imperfect symmetry that make it unstable.

Everything we see reveals the imperfect symmetry of water. All nature is polarized and symmetrical, but in an imperfect way. There is no such thing as a perfectly straight line, nor a perfect circle or sphere in the visible world. Everything is dynamic and tends towards perfection, but there is nothing that can be considered perfectly symmetrical.

On its own, water would not be able to conduct electricity very effectively. But as soon as impurities are introduced, such as a pinch of salt, it is transformed into an excellent conductor. Impurity, then, a form of imperfection, is what makes water such a potent force.

Like water, all the solid movements in nature are formed by three-dimensional networks of atoms that aggregate into crystals. The architecture of crystals depends on their degree of imperfection, or impurity. The presence of even the smallest amount of impurity alters both their structure and their electrical equilibrium: this is what scientists call '*state of defect*', or that which modifies the equilibrium of a substance to render it unstable, which allows it to interact with its surroundings and therefore to evolve.

Impurity can be seen as that 'information' which, when mixed with water, creates new forms and fosters the growth of more 'information'. It is impurity that makes water an electrical conductor and that enables it to assume the form of a droplet. In the same way, impurities render the information of mineral crystals defective, which in turn makes them more open to reconfiguration and therefore to perfection.

Molecular impurity and imperfection enable water to build new forms and vibrations with matter. It is a sort of inorganic vibrational memory. Something similar happens to DNA when the form and substance of the genetic code, through errors and mutations, are altered and lead to new forms of life. From a scientific standpoint it becomes easier to comprehend the vision, shared by many spiritual traditions, of the creation of humankind from a mixture of water and 'dust'.

Paradoxically, it is precisely because of its imperfections that water is driven towards perfection, and is responsible for building the harmony and beauty of the visible world. With simplicity and transparency, the incomplete and imperfect substance we call water seeks an equilibrium that it can only achieve by combining with something impure, something other than itself.

Likewise, it is the imperfection of human beings, also an integral part of nature, that allows us to evolve, working through our mistakes, with the help of others not ourselves. Water teaches us that those who believe themselves to be perfect, or who think that nature exists in a state of acquired perfection, are destined to failure and suffering.

The Bipolar Asymmetry of Water

Geometry is not true, it is advantageous.

HENRI POINCARÉ, mathematician

Let us further clarify the concept of symmetry. By symmetry we mean two things. First and foremost, it indicates something well-proportioned and balanced, whose parts are harmoniously integrated. Symmetry derives from the Greek *sum-metria*, meaning 'the same measure', the right proportion. Symmetry also indicates something more precise involving bilateral correspondence – in other words, the equality of two halves, whether left and right or top and bottom.

For scientists, symmetry means an order, a coherence inscribed in nature that confers beauty, harmony and elegance to the world. One of nature's fundamental symmetries is the simple fact that all basic physical laws are valid in every point of the known universe.

Physicists evaluate their own and each other's theories using not only mathematical parameters, but also aesthetic ones. A physical theory is as valid as it is universal in its application and elegant in its simplicity. One such current theory that responds better than any other to these criteria is superstring theory, also known as M-theory, according to which, subatomic particles are made up of tangles of vibrating uni-dimensional 'strings'.

It is a vision of ultramicroscopic reality that closely resembles the foam of a breaking wave, whereby the entire universe is composed of the totality of spiralling waves of these strings, which allow it to main-tain a regular, symmetrical and coherent structure. Superstring theory, though not yet universally accepted, shows us a universe that reveals in its smallest, most hidden components an extraordinary simplicity and elegance – and perhaps more symmetry than there really is, a subject we'll look at more closely in Chapter 6.

Symmetry-breaking is a concept used in particle physics and high-energy physics. Particles are paired (or coupled), often creating symmetries destined to break, which leads to a change in state known, logically enough, as *broken symmetry*. A concrete example of this common phenomenon can be seen when a container of water is uni-formly heated from below: at a certain critical temperature, before the water begins to boil, the uniformity of the water mass is broken by the appearance of agglomerates that assume a hexagonal convection pattern, interspersed with pentagonal structures. Such a break also occurs when water is frozen, since ice formation is not uniform in every direction. Another example is the magnet, which is the embodiment of symmetry breaking insofar as it tends to be oriented in a single direction.

The imperfect symmetry of the water molecule, with its bifurcated disposition, holds the secret of matter's very existence: instability and imperfect symmetry belong not only to the aquatic sphere, they are the guiding law of the universe since its inception. The universe contains matter as we know it precisely because of its imperfect symmetry. Let's see why.

Subatomic particles are paired: for every particle, there is an anti-particle. The universe produces matter and antimatter, quarks and antiquarks in equal measure.

Quarks combine to form protons and neutrons, which in turn form the nuclei of atoms. Particles and antiparticles are identical. When they meet, they destroy each other in an energy-generating explosion. Taken together, they constitute the 'm' (mass) in the formula $E=mc^2$.

According to the standard cosmological model, in the very first instant of the universe's creation, a.k.a the Big Bang, quarks and anti-quarks collided explosively, transforming themselves into energy while new quarks and antiquarks were formed, exploding in turn. The universe expanded and cooled. Had everything gone according to the laws of symmetry, the universe would have continued to generate radiant energy for as long as temperatures of billions of degrees Kelvin below zero allowed, then it would eventually have stopped, leaving a universe devoid of particles. But that's not what happened. The galaxies, the Earth, we ourselves owe our existence to the fact that, for reasons which are still unclear, there is more matter than antimatter. To put it simply, *the universe is asymmetrical*.

Matter outweighs antimatter by 0.00000000001 per cent, meaning that for every 10 billion particles of antimatter, there are 10 billion +1 particles of matter. An infinitesimal difference, yet at the same time enormous, for it is from those extra particles that all the galaxies and stars and planets and everything in and on them were able to form.

Symmetry-breaking happens when temperatures are lowered. By cooling as it expanded, the universe has become increasingly asymmetrical over time. The water and living systems triggered by this process reproduce the asymmetry of their origins, thereby perpetuating it. This becomes clear if we take that same container of water from the previous example and lower rather than raise the temperature. In its liquid state, the water is distributed evenly in the container, which is why we see a uniform, transparent mass: a symmetry. When the temperature is lowered to 0 °C, the water begins to freeze and solidify. This state transition triggers the breakage of the previous symmetry and solid crystals are formed which are asymmetrical.

Water in its liquid state has a rotational symmetry that looks the same from any angle, while the facets of the ice crystal appear different according to the position of the observer. This applies to all known physical systems. If instead we raise the temperature above 100 °C, liquid water becomes vapour, or gas. The gaseous state is more symmetrical than the liquid one because the water molecules are free to go where they please without having to bond with others (figure 2.1).

In recent years, chaos theory has shown that the same causes can lead to different, unpredictable results, and even more curiously, that symmetrical structures or causes give asymmetrical results. In the world around us, every event entails a certain variance from an originary symmetry. The left and right parts of our bodies are symmetrical but not identical: we use our left and right limbs in different ways, and the left and right hemispheres of the brain are functionally differentiated. Even a drop of water striking a liquid surface produces a cylindrical corona splash that is never perfectly symmetrical.

We live in a dynamic and unstable reality, the underlying premise of which is imperfect symmetry. Like an unbalanced scale or a lopsided ball, it oscillates in synchrony with the rhythm of evolution of the world around us. Water, with its asymmetrical tension between oxygen and hydrogen, embodies the quintessential imperfection striving towards perfection. Imperfection generates an instability wherein everything from subatomic particles to living beings to galaxies is compelled to seek an impossible equilibrium. In this precarious situation lies the secret of nature's evolution, upon which our own spiritual growth is founded.

Figure 2.1 A drop of water forms an asymmetrical corona

Between Change and Permanence

The more things change, the more they remain the same.

ANDRÉ BRETON (1896–1966), Surrealist poet and critic

In ancient China, water was the symbol of change because of its ability to adapt its form to that of the vessel containing it, to change state from solid to liquid to gas in such a tight range of temperatures, to spring forth from the ground and fall from the sky, and to determine huge climatic changes, from droughts to floods. Water is easily transformed, yet it transforms everything it touches through corrosion and erosion.

Chinese symbology uses the dragon to represent mutations in life and fertility because, like life, it originates from water. The dragon is portrayed as emerging in the springtime from the waters of the east and ascending into the sky – the east and spring being metaphors of birth. There is also a dragon that rises from the west, symbolizing autumn and death, who dwells in the darkest depths of the water and is reborn the following spring.

In Chinese natural science, the dragon is humankind's creative life force, fire enclosed by water. It was often depicted with an immaculate pearl in front of its mouth which represented the *Qi* (pronounced 'chee'), the vital force that animates all of nature.

Spheres and spirals, as we'll see further along, are the materialization of the creative and reproductive movements of water. The pearl enclosed in the oyster shell is the solid representation of the sphere formed by a water droplet and evokes sexual and reproductive creativity: the shell itself shares the same form as the vulva.

The cornucopia, or horn of plenty, is at once protuberant like the phallus, but also receptive like the womb and spiraliform like a current of water. It is the symbol of the union of the male and female principles, a source of fortune and fertility. In Greek mythology, the cornucopia belonged to Amalthea, the water nymph who served as nursemaid to the infant Zeus.

Without water, nothing can change. Indeed, what is a waterless desert if not a crystallized landscape, immutable over time? In California's Death Valley, the wagon trails of 19th-century goldrushers and ditches dug by ancient natives are still there, unchanged. The absence of water also comports absolute silence: without it there would be no rustling of leaves, no patter of rain, no chirping of birds.

Water, as represented in the movement of the dragon, ensures that the landscape of this earthly sphere is in a state of continuous transformation. We realize how important this is by looking at the Moon, devoid of water and atmosphere, which still conserves the scars inflicted by meteorites billions of years ago. The Earth would have the same aspect were it not for the transformative capacities of water.

Yet in other ways water is paradoxically the opposite of mutability, for it possesses the characteristic features of permanence. Firstly, the quantity of the Earth's water has remained the same as it was three billion years ago. Since the dawn of time, 200 million cubic kilometres of water have been present on the Earth, continuously moving and changing state – a permanent, and at the same time restless force.

It has been calculated that a drop of water, on average, remains dispersed in the air as vapour for only about 10 days, while it can crystallize in a glacier for 40 years, stagnate in a swamp for 100 years, or hide underground for as many as 10,000. Whatever its destiny may be, however, every droplet goes through the different phases of the hydrogen cycle, demonstrating again *its paradoxical duality of permanence and change.*

In 1994 a group of geologists from the University of San Francisco discovered several water droplets imprisoned in crystals dating back 500 million years. The results of their analysis confirmed that even in concentrations of mineral salts (magnesium, calcium, etc), the water remained unaltered, despite the enormous changes undergone by the Earth's crust. Water is prodigiously stable, if only for the fact that it maintains the salinity of the oceans at approximately 3 per cent. This is one of water's true miracles, since no complex organism and very few cells could survive if that salinity were higher than just 6 per cent. We owe our very lives to the stability of water.

The water we drink today in our homes has been recycled from the oceans, lakes and rivers of the entire planet, probably already having been drunk by humans and animals many millennia ago, just as it is possible that the water molecules that make up our bodies once made up theirs.

As we've said, water also has the opposite virtue, in that it changes form continuously. Its inexorable metamorphosis is perpetuated by the countless natural forces to which it is subjected – the rotation of the Earth, solar energy, gravity, the chemical and geophysical irregularities of the planet's surface – all of which contribute to the incessant change of water's state. The balance of the world's ecosystem depends on this ever-changing behaviour.

Change and permanence go hand in hand where water is concerned: the mutable configuration of a snowflake's structure is inseparable from its fixed hexagonal symmetry, just as our bodies constantly shed and regenerate cells while remaining the same.

Water is a molecule that loves to nuture paradox thanks to its dual nature. It is the incarnation of the infinite bipolarities present in the universe, where the coupling of that which tends towards change and that which tends towards permanence animates everything – the potential energy that accumulates in solid matter is transformed into kinetic energy and vice versa; negatively charged electrons orbit around a nucleus containing positively charged protons; matter bonds with anti-matter, quarks with antiquarks.

As the ancient Chinese naturalists explained with elegant simplicity, water contains within itself the natural balance of two polar principles, the male and female. It is at once *yin* (negative pole) in its tendency towards stability and *yang* (positive pole) in its ability to move, evolve and transform.

We really should be talking about waters rather than water, for it is always different in its flow and its components, yet has remained unaltered for billions of years. The paradoxes are innumerable, but they all point in the same direction: water is a dynamic but coherent whole. Its balance of flexibility and stability is an exquisite metaphor of physical reality, and ideally of our own relationships with ourselves and others.

The Paradoxical Ethic of Water

The paradox is only a conflict between reality and your feeling of what reality ought to be.

RICHARD FEYNMAN (1918–88), winner of the 1965 Nobel Prize for Physics

Water can show us the road to improving our relationships with ourselves and others, all of us integral parts of an imperfectly symmetrical whole, born of the same substance. Schauberger once wrote:

Mankind in the future ... will become the supreme servant and at the same time the lord of Nature ... There will be ample space for everyone who takes part in the whole process of development in the use of raw materials ... Everything emerged from the water. Water, therefore, is the raw material of every culture or the basis of every bodily and spiritual development. The discovery of the secrets of water makes nonsense of every kind of speculation leading to war, hate, envy, intolerance and discord.[7]

Science interprets phenomena in terms of nature's complexity so that it can intervene in the environment in an intelligent way. Through this approach, we can cultivate an ethic inspired by the imperfection, asymmetry and paradoxes of water.

Water reflects our image, which we sometimes hesitate to recognize, for it can be an image we don't like, which seems foreign to us. The myth of Narcissus, who admired his own reflection in the water, shows us how dangerous vanity can be, leading to the worship of empty, superficial beauty. The myth is also fuelled by our atavistic fear of water, source of illusion and distortion, an abyss that separates us from the void, from death.

An Islamic Sufi master, called al-Shibli, is the protagonist in the following parable.

> Shibli was asked: 'Who guided you in the Path?'
>
> He said: 'A dog. One day I saw him, almost dead with thirst, standing by the water's edge.
>
> 'Every time he looked at his reflection in the water he was frightened, and withdrew, because he thought it was another dog.
>
> 'Finally, such was his necessity, he cast away fear and leapt into the water; at which "the other dog" vanished.
>
> 'The dog found that the obstacle, which was himself, the barrier between him and what he sought, melted away.
>
> 'In this same way my own obstacle vanished, when I knew that it was what I took to be my own self. And my Way was first shown to me by the behaviour of – a dog.'[8]

Water is the origin and the goal, and as such it both attracts us and frightens us. Water pushes us to look inside ourselves, to discover things we'd prefer not to see, to face fears that we've carried within us for countless generations. Looking into water shouldn't mean stopping at its surface, but penetrating its transparency and exploring its fundamental nature, our nature.

Water is at once the guard posted at the door of our unconscious, of our hopes and fears and the path of access to it. Like in Kafka's parable, *Before the Law*, we all find ourselves before an open gate guarded by a keeper who frightens us, but it turns out that we ourselves are the only impediment to entering it because, as the keeper finally reveals to the old man, that gate is there for us and nobody else.

The Pure is Born of the Impure

We've seen how water is incapable of condensing into droplets of vapour without the presence of dust, impurities or violent disturbances. Water is 'invisible', and to show itself it needs something other than itself. Indeed, distilled water, completely free of solutes, does not exist in nature.

Every form of water present on the Earth contains hundreds of organic and inorganic substances, from bacteria to nitrogenous compounds, from minerals to metals. A cloud of water droplets can only form in the presence of atmospheric impurities, such as mineral dust, soot and gases produced by plankton. These miniscule solid particles are called 'condensation nuclei'.

Again, pure water needs impurity to fully realize its potential.

In ritual bathing of a religious nature, water is used to cleanse what is considered spiritually impure: for instance, the bodies of those who must be purified. Just as the purity of water is revealed only in the presence of impurity, so must we face the 'murkiness' within ourselves, if we wish to realize ourselves fully.

According to Taoist doctrine, the Tao (or Dao) is the Way, the Ultimate Reality from whence all things come. It is the order upon which and with which the universe is built. It is the principle of harmony that humanity must obey in order to live a good life. Those who wish to live long and well following the Tao must seek to live in harmony with the natural forces that nourish us and with the environment that surrounds us. The Tao is at once a cosmological, religious and ethical concept.

The first and most important classic text of Taoism, the *Tao Te*

Ching ('The Book of the Way and Its Virtue'), compiled 2,500 years ago in China by Lao Tzu (whose name means 'old sage'), has its roots in even more ancient traditions dating back to the Yellow Emperor, Huang Di, who lived between 2697 and 2598 BC. The Chinese consider themselves descendents of Huang Di, the symbol of Chinese civilization, whose *Medical Canon of the Yellow Emperor* is a fundamental treatise on traditional medicine. It is no accident that he was also known by the title of *Lord of the Waters*.

Water is a metaphor of the Tao, inasmuch as it is ubiquitous and shared by all. Water helps us understand what the Tao is and means. The *Tao Te Ching* celebrates the modesty of water which, after having created and nourished all living things, withdraws to the lowest, most hidden part of the world. No obstacle can block it; water unfailingly finds its own path. Water never loses its direction, flowing inexorably toward the ocean with the aim of perpetuating the cycle of wholeness. To follow the path of water, Lao Tzu writes, is to return to one's spiritual essence. In verse 78 of the *Tao Te Ching* it is written that 'In the world there is nothing more submissive and weak than water. Yet for attacking that which is hard and strong nothing can surpass it.'

The coexistence of two opposite poles, the positive pole of hydrogen and the negative pole of oxygen, and the bonds between the molecules, at once strong and unstable, are just some of water's paradoxical aspects. Water is constantly renewing itself, yet it is also a permanent presence. Water excites our senses with its transparency, but also with its opacity – against a sufficiently dark background, it goes from transparent to optically impenetrable, deflecting light away from itself. It's difficult to accept this paradox if we really think about it. Sometimes, however, it dominates our lives, such as when we experience so-called 'extraordinary states of consciousness'. This paradox violates Aristotelian logic, which asserts that A cannot be NOT A. Feeling ourselves to be insignificant and at the same time fully understanding the cosmos, nullifying the self while experiencing ourselves as the entire universe, are some of the characteristics of the ecstatic state that can be reached through hypnosis, meditation and immersion in water, which we'll investigate further in Chapter 14.

In water, mind and matter, motion and rest are reconciled. The paradoxical stability and instability of water is a perfect metaphor of both physical and subjective reality. Lao Tzu taught that water is the unsurpassable master of behaviour: if you wish to be strong, you must know how to bend, how to be flexible. The Zen Buddhist tradition, which is Chinese in origin, uses *koans* as a teaching tool, whereby the master stimulates the disciple by imparting paradoxical riddles that seem absurd, but which contain profound truths about life and the world.

Adapting ourselves with humility to the shape of the container as water does, accepting the equivocations of life – these are the keys to changing the most negative situations from within. Those who express the highest intelligence are those who demonstrate the greatest flexibility. Opposing forces, those that tend towards change on the one hand and permanence on the other, must interact in order for life to be fulfilled. Life is immersed in paradoxes, and if we're not able to accept them, we condemn ourselves to live poorly and die even more so, victims of our prejudices and neuroses. Life, essentially organized matter born of the void, is by nature contradictory.

Sigmund Freud observed that in dreams, water represents our deepest desires and sexual pleasure. Conversely, water is also the substrate of our worst fears: those of drowning, of being unable to breathe, of suffering before death. The paradoxes of water teach us that in order to live we must learn the art of dying, as well as facing every situation with an appropriate degree of humour, for humour feeds on paradox, and without paradox life would be supremely boring. *Water, in a word, is wisdom.*

Water's fundamental role in the life cycle – one need only think of amniotic liquid, of sexual fluids, of the oceans from which all life originated – is by no means antithetical to its role in death. Life and death are inextricable, parts of the same process, as epitomized biologically by the near-death of the birthing infant, and spiritually by the rebirth that comes after being 'drowned' in ritual cleansing.

The image of water and its flow is central to the unconscious that, as clinical psychology has shown, also speaks a paradoxical language. Water in its restful state evokes the silence and calm of contemplation and emotional detachment, while a stormy sea or whitewater river stands for emotional agitation.

The adhesive property of water echoes the noblest of human sentiments, love. Water adheres to everything and invariably adapts itself to the form of that which contains it. Love is the most powerful force we have for perpetuating life. Like water, the paradox of love is its ability to absorb and be absorbed without sacrificing its own identity.

Multiplicity and Community

As in water face answereth to face, so the heart of man to man.

Proverbs 27:19

Water, over time, renders every substance soluble and mixes it with that which it already contains. Solubility, both physical and metaphorical, means the capacity to assimilate anything and everything into a context where all can coexist. This fundamental property of water provides us with yet another model for our own lives – that of the ideal integrated community.

There exists no material that can contain water without surrendering some of its molecules. Even rain absorbs atmospheric gases. The water we drink always contains minimal quantities of molecules from the glass that contains it. However, if we really are willing, we can transform our environment in our image and likeness with our bodies and minds.

Like oxygen and hydrogen, water doesn't like being alone. It dissolves and incorporates everything, then returns it transformed. This is the ideal formula for an open, multiethnic society, which is the opposite of isolationist tribalism, but also of the annihilation of local traditions, or worse still, totalitarianism. The idea of a system that connects individuals in an equilibrium of the specific (i.e. ethnicity, religion, gender) and the universal, based on community ideals that together constitute the nation, is what makes the United States an exemplary country. This is not a partisan political statement, but a point of fact. Since its inception, the United States has been the paradigmatic model of a 'melting pot' operating as a nation.

The food we keep in our refrigerators will dehydrate even if we seal it with an impermeable polymer film. The process takes several days, but it is inexorable. This is because every substance, no matter how impenetrable, must sooner or later relax its opposition and allow molecules of water to pass through. Optically, water appears to adhere to the inside of the container, but it does not submit to it, for at the molecular level it is tenaciously infiltrating it, slowly breaking it down.

Similarly, an open society is capable of absorbing and accepting everything. It is tolerant, but up to a certain point; like water, eventually it will liquidate and destroy that which seeks to restrict it, impede its freedom of expression or isolate it from the world outside its container. And yet another paradox: water, in the natural process of destroying something, is simply preparing it for rebirth in another form.

Water is a source of inspiration for those who wish to live in a free, civil, multicultural and multiethnic society, in that it incorporates everything and respects its diversity. Chemists have discovered that the dissolution of substances in water is a creative process that tends towards equilibrium, towards a higher level of symmetry. The same holds true for the constituents that mix together in any community worthy of being called such.

CHAPTER 3

THE WATER PLANET: FROM ANCIENT CHINA TO THE GAIA HYPOTHESIS

The water of the contingent seas makes the sphere of waters, whose centre is the centre of the world.

LEONARDO DA VINCI (1452–1519)

The Greek philosopher Heraclitus of Ephesus (*c*540–480 BC) compared the universe to a river, the flow of whose waters changed continuously though always appearing the same: 'You cannot step twice into the same river, for other waters are ever flowing on to you.' Heraclitus meant to say that reality, static and permanent to our senses, is constantly changing like the water that flows along a riverbed. By recycling its water, the river renews and strengthens itself. Likewise human beings, despite the continual transformation of our organic makeup, our experiences and our attitudes (or precisely because of it), maintain the same physical and spiritual identity.

Water, mother of all change, has inspired numerous theories of change. Many centuries before Heraclitus, the Yin and Yang School had already classified the mutations of natural phenomena. Reproposed later by Taoism and Confucianism, these ideas constituted the backbone of Chinese thought in every field, from medicine and engineering to geomancy, astronomy and agronomy, not to mention politics and the arts. Today, ancient Chinese science has proven to be as relevant as ever, for certain of its premises are found in the most advanced theories of

Western science. The profound understanding of water's properties on the part of the Chinese naturalists was owed to their meticulous methods of observation, which they began applying more than a thousand years before Leonardo da Vinci, using their results to invent ingenious technologies for channelling water and optimizing its virtues.

In Renaissance Europe, Leonardo was the first great reseacher of the modern era. He was deeply drawn to water, and his observations of it provided inspiration for many of his artistic and technological inventions.

Among the many documents written and illustrated by Leonardo is a treatise on water and its behaviour known as the Leicester Codex (formerly the Hammer Codex). In it, Leonardo alternates between empirical observation, technical applications, philosophical reflections and extraordinary drawings, all in the open spirit typical of the true genius of Renaissance. In Europe, Leonardo was a pioneer whose ideas were way ahead of their time; had he been in China, he probably would have found both audience and fortune even several centuries earlier.

Leonardo maintained that the energy present in the universe, which flows through the Earth and the human body, behaves like the currents of rivers and canals. Five centuries later, Viktor Schauberger identified analogous centripetal, hyperbolic and spiraliform movements: an aquatic environment where these kinds of movements prevail will generate ordered living systems, whereas the contrary centrifugal and dispersive movements caused by heat and combustion will generate disorder, such as that created by explosions and nuclear fissions, which unleash an energy that is toxic to living systems.

Water and Energy in Chinese Science

The Book of Changes (I Ching) says: 'The Heavens created water before all things'. The Taoists say: 'Water is the mother of the Three Sources of Power – Heaven, Earth and Man'.

JIANG JING-YUI (*The Book of Classifications*, 2nd century BC)

For ancient Chinese scientists, an Ultimate Reality subtends the continuous transformations of the universe which they called the Tao (or Dao) (figure 3.1). It is the undifferentiated One, the Origin and Order from whence everything comes. Tao in Chinese also means 'harmony' and 'way of life'. In the worldview of Chinese science, spirit, health and the physical world are simply different aspects of the same unitary principle that is the source of them all.

Figure 3.1 Yin-yang diagram of the Tao

The Tao is symbolized by a fluid sphere divided into two different areas of colour. The bipolar principles known as the yin and the yang, opposite but complementary, are the foundation of the natural world. Yin and yang are represented as two fluid masses, water-like, one white and the other black, or sometimes red and blue. The straight line that would bisect the circle morphs into an 'S' shape, such that the two halves interpenetrate, creating the image suggesting an imminent vortex. From their interpenetration and interaction all the fields of force in the universe (the Qi) are released, including the bipolar water molecule.

Yin and yang are dynamic principles whose power is never absolute but fluctuant – when one grows, the other shrinks accordingly, and vice versa. The universe's tendency to concentrate matter is *yin*, while the tendency to move it and disperse it is *yang*. Yin, the negatively charged feminine principle, is paired with its opposite, the positively charged masculine principle of yang.

Modern science uses a similar model of opposite forces that regulate the dynamics and evolution of the universe: *kinetic energy* (which would correspond to yang) and *gravitational energy* (yin), which bind the constituents of matter. The Qi, or ch'i, is both energy and material structure, just like the forces and particles studied by subatomic physics. In Japan, this energy is called *ki*. In Sanskrit, the life force has a similar sound, *chaitanya*, which isn't far from the Hebrew term *chai*.

The central 'S' of the diagram suggests the phases of an alternating, vortical motion. That which is yin becomes yang, reflecting the tendency of everything in the universe to slowly transform into its opposite. Mass becomes energy, day becomes night, the warm seasons alternate with the cold ones, that which is up tends to come down, that which is on the inside tends towards the outside, and so forth.

Another clear manifestation of this universal law is the way that yang, in the form of light and heat from the sun, increases during the morning to reach its maximum at midday, the same moment that yin, which represents darkness, begins to emerge. Through the afternoon yin augments while yang recedes until midnight, the apex of yin, at which point yang begins to increase again, perpetuating the cycle. Every moment and every phenomenon is an ever-fluctuating mix of yin and yang, in which the prevalence of one or the other is relative and subject to change (table 3.1).

Yin	Yang
Shadow	Light
Night	Day
Water	Earth
Moon	Sun
Feminine	Masculine
Right	Left
Cold	Hot
Heavy	Light
Interior	Exterior
Lower	Upper
Dark	Luminous
Hidden	Revealed
Structural	Active
Descend	Ascend
Interiorize	Exteriorize
Centripetal	Centrifugal
Conserve	Consume
Concentrate	Expand
Condense	Disperse

Table 3.1 Yin-yang polarities

In the diagram of the Tao there are two dots of opposite colour vertically disposed on either side of what would be the horizontal bisector. These dots represent the point where, at the maximum expansion and expression of one of the two principles, the power of the opposite principle is concentrated, ready to sprout and expand into a new cycle. It is the universal concept that anything pushed to excess ends up triggering its opposite.

All the laws of energy are synthesized in this simple diagram. And it is also a valid model for water: it describes the dynamics of all the possible interactions between positively charged hydrogen atoms and negatively charged oxygen atoms. It also offers a compelling image of the fluxes that keep the perfectable symmetries of water in a constant state of oscillation.

The Energy in Water

It is likely that there's a lot of water beneath the surface of Mars, and possible that many eons ago the Red Planet was traversed by rivers thousands of kilometres long. Unfortunately Mars is now too cold to support the full water cycle, so whatever water there is would be frozen far beneath its crust.

Mars is interesting in that water teaches us something even here: in itself, water is not sufficient to ensure the emergence of life. In order for it to be the life-giving force it is on Earth, it needs heat and something that will cause it to move, that impetus of invisible forces we call energy.

In the Chinese language, the literal meaning of the word Qi is energy, with the accompanying shades of meaning like force, gas, breath, life principle. Qi is the most basic and subtle movement and constitutes all things; it is the energy that generates all matter and life in the universe.

The ideogram of the word Qi (figure 3.2) is a synthesis of its meaning. The lower part represents a grain of rice being cooked and expanding in four directions. Rice, the quintessential foodstuff, is energy in its potential state (yin), enclosed in solid matter and liquid water. The three horizontal strokes above describe the movement of the vapour unleashed by the rice: this is the kinetic aspect of energy (yang), the centrifugal energy of expansion which causes water to become gas.

This ideogram shows water in its three states: solid, liquid and vapour. Its synthetic beauty recalls the famous mathematical equation formulated by Einstein to support his General Theory of Relativity, $E=mc^2$: energy is equivalent to mass multiplied by the square of *celeritas* (the speed of light in a vacuum). The speed of light is a constant, while energy and mass are variable yet interdependent parameters that are transformed into one another. Mass, in other words, is nothing but concentrated and solidified energy.

Figure 3.2 Ideogram of the word Qi, or 'energy'

The energy and mass of an object are not separate entities. With Einstein's formula, we can determine an object's energy by multiplying its mass by the speed of light squared. We can also deduce that the faster an object moves, the more energy it possesses, and with this increase in energy comes an increase in mass. Modern physics and ancient Chinese science show us that the concepts of time and space, once considered separate and absolute, are interconnected and relative.

The ideogram of steaming rice is meant to remind us that the impalpability of vapour and the invisibility of the energy create solid reality and vice versa, that energy and matter, regardless of state, are one and the same. Water creates visible matter and transforms itself into invisible force.

Water in the Five Movements

Natural forms are never perfectly straight, particularly rivers. Inspired by their sinuous meandering, the Chinese have always favoured architecture and urban layouts that are curvilinear, with rounded or flared corners, in syntony with the energy fields of living organisms and of the environment itself.

The movements of water have led Oriental civilizations to conceive space and time as being curved, cyclical. And for good reason: the phenomena that flow through space between past, present and future are never aligned in a linear way, but follow instead a spiral movement of perpetual return, much in the way that evaporating ocean water invariably returns to the ocean.

The Chinese conceived the Theory of the Five Movements (*Wu Xing*) in ancient times as a means of codifying the rules that govern the spatio-temporal changes that occur in nature. The practice of organizing reality into units of five dates back 3,500 years to the Shang Dynasty, and reflects the Chinese concept of five directions: the four cardinal points (north, south, east, west) and the centre, which is the point from which we experience the world.

This theory became a sort of measuring stick for natural phenomena in all the ancient Chinese sciences, including medicine. The interactions between the Five Movements are seen from a holistic standpoint, and account for all natural events and phenomena. As figure 3.3 demonstrates, this cyclical spatiotemporal scheme is quite precise.

Nature transforms and is transformed continually, from the infinitely small to the infinitely vast. The Theory of the Five Movements holds that reality, in all its spatiotemporal dimensions, is constituted by five dynamic and interdependent 'agents' (the literal meaning of *Wu Xing* is 'travel'): Water, Wood, Fire, Metal and Earth. Material reality, in both its structure and movements, is very much like the flow of water.

Matter is organized in space in a circular way: four Movements interact with one another in relation to Earth, our vantage point, which occupies the centre. This scheme suggests that our perception and

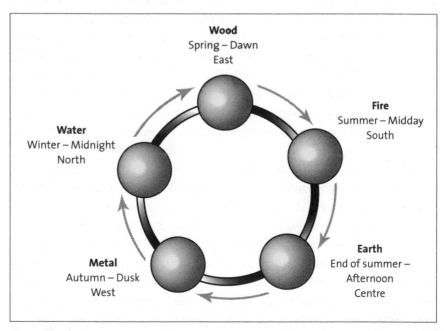

Figure 3.3 The cycle of the Five Movements in space and time

judgement of phenomena are always relative, dependent as it is on our viewpoint, the Earth.

Corresponding to each Movement are precise categories: elements, cardinal points, colours, body tissues, bodily organs, activities, emotions, etc. Living wood is green until it is set on fire, becoming red. Dry earth is yellow, shiny metal is white, deep water is black. As in the theory of yin and yang, the classification of the various aspects of material reality is applied analogically, evaluating phenomena in terms of their individual qualities, such that everything that falls under the category of Water reflects the behaviour of water at every level.

In figure 3.3 we see how the Movements follow one another through time, with the hours of the day corresponding to the seasons of the year, while table 3.2 (*see* page 48) shows further correspondences to organs, colours, flavours, mental processes, and so forth. It also shows how human beings have five seasonal phases: at birth we are soft and elastic like a green seedling (associated with Wood), and then move through growth, maturity, decline and death. The forces that govern the cycles of change in the visible world are reflected in the microcosmic and macrocosmic dimensions as well – the Earth, the human body, the psyche, and every element in nature, from the subatomic to the cosmic. These cycles, it should be remembered, proceed *spirally*, such that a previous cycle is never identical to a subsequent one, just as this year is not the same as the last.

The Five Movements interact according to what might be called a *production cycle* – that is, they stimulate and fuel each other. Wood generates combustion for Fire, which combine to form ash for Earth, which in turn gives forth Metal, from whose rocks comes Water, which then nourishes the planet's vegetation, bringing us back to Wood, thereby completing the circuit so that it may continue, differently each time, but always the same.

The Five Movements also interact by way of a self-regulating control cycle. Wood controls Earth insofar as vegetation prevents landslides and topsoil dispersion; Earth controls Water by allowing itself to be carved into the channels and hollows that contain lakes and rivers and seas; Water controls Fire by extinguishing it; Fire controls Metal by melting it. This reciprocal feedback among the Movements regulates the relationship between natural events and phenomena in an exquisitely designed holistic system that ensures, like the water molecule, the paradoxical coexistence of stability and continuous transformation.

In the Theory of the Five Movements, Water is associated with the

Movements	Wood	Fire	Earth	Metal	Water
Day	Dawn	Midday	Afternoon	Dusk	Midnight
Seasons	Spring	Summer	End of summer	Autumn	Winter
Cardinal points	East	South	Centre	West	North
Weather conditions	Wind	Heat	Humidity	Dry	Cold
Numbers	3+5=8	2+5=7	5	4+5=9	1+5=6
Colours	Blue-green	Red	Yellow	White	Black
Flavours	Sour	Bitter	Sweet	Spicy	Salty
Food	Grain	Corn	Millet	Rice	Beans
Processes	Germination	Growth	Transformation	Gathering	Storage
Odours	Rancid	Burnt	Sweet	Carnal, acrid	Rotten, putrid
Evolution	Birth	Growth	Maturity	Decline	Inertia
Major organs	Liver	Heart	Spleen	Lungs	Yu
Viscera	Gall bladder	Small intestine	Stomach	Large intestine	Kidneys
Sense organs	Eyes	Tongue	Mouth	Nose	Bladder, ears
Senses	Sight	Touch	Taste	Smell	Hearing
Body tissues	Tendons, nails, ligaments	Veins and arteries	Muscles	Skin and hair	Bones, marrow, teeth
Emotions	Anger	Joy	Reflection	Sadness	Fear
Harmful actions	Looking	Walking	Sitting	Reclining	Standing
Sounds	Screaming	Laughing	Singing	Crying	Wailing
Fluids	Tears	Sweat	Saliva	Mucus	Urine, sperm
Pathologic actions	Spasms, cramps	Anxiety	Spitting, belching	Coughing	Trembling
Qualities	Emotivity	Sensitivity	Contemplation	Deduction	Wisdom
Psyche	Soul	Spirit	Logic	Courage	Will

Macrocosm / Humans

Table 3.2 The Theory of the Five Movements and its correspondences

number *six*, the colour black and the moon, which influences the tides and creates the morning dew. Black is not a colour, but the absence of colour, and as such it corresponds perfectly with the colourless transparency of water. Black is also associated with all that is dark and mysterious. Water corresponds to north, to winter and to cold because in winter water expands itself as ice and snow. As for the human body, Water influences the activities of the kidneys and bladder. The sense associated with Water is hearing; the bodily tissue, bone. The sound of Water is the mournful cry (wailing). Its virtue is wisdom. Water nourishes the hair and the head. Its activity is storage.

Thousands of years ago, the Chinese had already grasped one of the fundamental properties of water: its ability to conserve or store substances both material and not. An obvious example is the fact that ice is the best means of preserving vital substances. But this ability to store refers not just to external reality, but also to internal reality: water influences the organization of thought, learning through listening, the formation and conservation of memory. We'll see exactly how later on in the book.

The emotion associated with Water is fear, the primordial fear we carry with us from birth: humankind's greatest obstacle but at the same time, like water, necessary, for it is what keeps us alive. Fear works off our survival instinct and activates our defences. But it can also paralyse us, and over time creates stasis where instead there should be movement. Like water, if allowed to stagnate, fear can destroy life.

The Gaia Hypothesis

The frog does not drink up the pond in which it lives.

INDIAN PROVERB

When the first astronauts left the Earth's atmosphere and saw our planet from afar, they were enchanted by its beautiful blue and white mass, like an enormous drop of water, glowing in the surrounding blackness. With 7/10 of its surface covered by water, our planet would have more aptly been named Water rather than Earth.

In 1972, two noted scientists, the chemist James Lovelock and microbiologist Lynn Margulis, published a paper claiming that the Earth

Figure 3.4 Planet Water

should be considered not an inert rock that happened to support life, but very similar to an immense living organism. This was the earliest formulation of the Gaia hypothesis, also known as the Gaia theory.

The incessant shedding and restoration of cells in living tissue enables organisms to adapt to their environment, instant by instant. Every part collaborates to maintain the dynamic balance of the whole, a process known as *homeostasis*. According to the Gaia theory, the biosphere and lithosphere are analogous to the interdependent organs of a single entity, the Earth, the largest 'living creature' in the solar system. Like all organisms, the Earth maintains its homeostatic equilibrium through physical events and chemical reactions that take place in solution, which is why the integrative function of water is so important to the planet as a whole.

The different parts of the animal, vegetable and mineral kingdoms interact harmoniously with one another, like the organs of a single being. We humans are like individual cells of the tissue mass of humanity, which is part of the organism Earth. Heaven and Earth comprise a single organism that contains humanity, which is in turn like a planet on a miniature scale, at least according the holistic and modular concept of the interdependency of parts that characterizes much Oriental thought and certain mystical and Renaissance currents in the West.

For the nomadic Aboriginal peoples of Australia and for many animist cultures, the Earth is the mother-organism constituted by spiritual entities that reside in specific places. The Earth must be treated with care; in the interest of its health and our own, of its spirit and ours, we should be prohibited from harming it. Rivers and subsidiary waterways are the circulatory system of this single living organism. The mountains and valleys and plains are the surfaces of its body.

Like all living things, water is a self-organizing system: a drop of water is a universe unto itself, containing substances and living creatures, generating and responding to vibrations, perpetuating the same patterns and sequences that we find on a larger scale in our own bodies, in the Earth, indeed throughout the entire universe. Water is the smallest, yet also the most all-encompassing and immanent of universes.

Today the Gaia hypothesis is taken seriously by a growing number of scientists, particularly since the emergence of the mathematical theory of complexity and the most recent research on superorganisms.

A superorganism is an organism formed by a group of individuals whose collective behaviour results in coherent activity that benefits the whole, just as in the traditional definition of a single organism. The beehive and ant colony are the most conspicuous examples of how a group of individuals transforms itself into a complex and self-perpetuating whole, the result of whose labours is greater than the sum of its parts. Social insects create a harmonious whole possessed of an identity and a *raison d'être* that far outweigh those of the individual components. An ant colony, for example, 'knows' exactly how hard it must work to generate the thermal energy necessary to maintain the optimal temperature for reproduction.

All living organisms are organized systems of organs made of tissue, which are in turn made of cells that contain the materials and information necessary to autonomously reproduce, like DNA and mitochondria. Every part of a living organism is composed of water, and is reciprocally interdependent with respect to every other part, such that they are all necessary for the proper functioning of the whole, each one reproducing a pattern of repeated modules on different dimensional scales. By this definition, the Earth is indeed a superorganism. And to understand how it works we need to look at the whole.

The biblical account of Creation and the scientific study of fossils corroborate the same scenario: humankind is the last link in the evolutionary chain that began with water, which gave rise to the plant and eventually the animal kingdoms. Every part of the living organism called Earth shares a common aquatic origin. The evolution of life and intelligence seems to have the purpose of building a world that is ever more symmetrical, ordered, complex and harmonious.

When a new species or a new physical or chemical entity appears in nature, it is by definition superior to the sum of its parts. This same evolution from symmetry to asymmetry also applies to the marriage of hydrogen and oxygen whose child is water, to the collectivity of drones and workers that constitutes the hive, to the system of cells that make up a tissue, to the tissues that form an organ, and to the thoughts and feelings and deeds that make up a person. By extension, it applies as well to a group of people, whether in the form of a sports team or a voting bloc or a nation, who together constitute a mass that can mobilize to achieve a common objective, and whose strength transcends that of the individuals of which it is composed.

Evolution Through Cooperation

There is the unity whereby one creature is united with the others and all parts of the world constitute one world.

GIOVANNI PICO DELLA MIRANDOLA (1463–94)

Water is the substance that ensures the homeostatic equilibrium of the organism Earth, enabling communication between the different organic and inorganic parts that compose it. It is a restless molecule, as the water cycle of evaporation, condensation, precipitation and collection attests. This cycle is essentially the Earth's metabolism, which is also influenced externally by the circadian rhythms of the Sun and Moon (i.e. the 24-hour light/dark cycle) and by the constant bombardment of water-packed 'mini-comets' from outer space.

Leonardo da Vinci compared the Earth to an organism nourished by a vascular system consisting of oceans, lakes, rivers and underground water tables. Our planet is literally drenched in water, as are the cells of our bodies.

Meteorological forecasts are based on what goes on in the oceans, which influence atmospheric events by way of the exchange of heat and water vapour. The oceans interact with one another through the major wind-driven surface currents, which modulate the atmospheric climate.

Water is inextricably bound to the biological world – each owes its existence to the other. The water cycle is regulated by the biological cycles that take place in the oceans. *Clouds exist thanks to algae*, the decomposition of which releases dimethylsulphide gas, which is oxidized by hydrosilicates present in the air and converted into sulphuric acid and methanosulphonic acid. When these gaseous acids saturated with water vapour reach high enough altitudes, they enable that vapour to form clouds.

Every living thing, from the Earth itself to the tiniest single-cell organism, needs to both contain and be surrounded by water. The Gaia hypothesis confirms the intimate reciprocity of the relationship between the climate and all living organisms, large and small. Nature manifests itself through mechanisms of cooperation between entities that only appear to be radically different, but are in fact coextensive aspects of a unitary whole.

On the one hand, neo-Darwinian thought on evolution explains the existence of ordered natural systems as being the result of adaptation through natural selection, i.e. the random mutations of genetic material that provide greater assurance of survival. On the other hand, the Theory of Complexity holds that order is triggered from within the system, and would therefore be a property of the system itself, which makes evolution not so much a question of the mutation of individual organisms as of cooperation between the mineral, vegetable and animal spheres in an integrated planetary process.

This new view of evolution, no longer dominated by the random chance of neo-Darwinism, mirrors the human notion of the ideal society, where cooperation leads to the greater good while also benefiting every individual. Evolution is guided by an intrinsic force that goes beyond individual self-interest or the so-called 'selfish genes'.

Ants provide a helpful example here as well. When the population of a colony increases, the individual ants will spontaneously exhibit new coordinated behaviours to accommodate the change in their numbers – yet another indicator of the role of cooperation in the evolution of the species.

Not surprisingly, the evolution of organisms depends on the evolution of the aquatic environment that surrounds them. This global interaction between the whole and its parts should induce us to be more careful with regard to nature. Those who wish to understand and protect the Earth should adopt the comprehensive attitude of the general practitioner or the holistic doctor as opposed to that of the specialist, mindful that the Hippocratic oath, *Primum non nocere* ('First, do no harm'), is equally applicable to the Earth as to any patient.

~

CHAPTER FOUR

ORDER EMERGES FROM CHAOS

When water is forced into immobility, it transforms from a source of life into a vehicle of death and calamity. Turbulence activates the life-sustaining properties of water and keeps it, quite literally, alive. Two pioneers at the margins of traditional science arrived independently at the conclusion that water, activated by controlled turbulence, can acquire therapeutic powers. One was a German doctor named Christian Friedrich Hahnemann (1755–1843), father of homeopathic medicine, who insisted that the meticulous stirring of his medicines diluted in water conditioned their effectiveness. The other was the Austrian inventor, Viktor Schauberger, who we've already met.

According to Schauberger, water is 'activated' at lower temperatures caused by the shade of surrounding forestal flora and rocks. Up to 4 °C, its dynamic and biological action is at its maximum, decreasing above that temperature, if only for the fact that it allows pathogenic bacteria to multiply more readily. We know today that cold water absorbs more oxygen than warm water: further proof that Schauberger was very much on the right track.

Going against the scientific wisdom of his time, Schauberger was certain that changes in temperature of as little as one tenth of one degree Celsius caused decisive changes in the flow and load-bearing capacity of water. Applying these insights to the wooden flumes he built for transporting timber, Schauberger provoked a reconsideration of Archimedes' law: logs and rocks with a greater specific weight than water floated like feathers.

Because water is so vital to the biosphere, it is important that its natural course is not modified, that it be allowed to maintain its tendency to change direction and form vortices. The water at the bottom of a river is subjected to the constant friction of sediment and detritus and therefore moves more slowly than surface water, creating a rupture in the symmetry of its flow that results in a screw-like motion. Sediment is removed from the outer bank and deposited on the inner one, which increases the curvature, further affecting flow patterns. Once again, water demonstrates its ability to shift suddenly from one symmetry to another, which is the motor of the evolution of living systems.

A 'healthy' river builds its banks laterally and is protected by the vegetation that grows alongside them, while a 'sick' river drags tons of mud and sediment along its bed, raising the height of its banks and eventually disturbing the sea into which it empties.

Schauberger's revolutionary holistic principle was that 'a river should never be regulated by its banks, but rather by its own flow'. Redirecting a river by building straight concrete banks is tantamount to condemning all forms of life both in and near it to death.

Thanks to the success of his ingenious zigzagging flumes, Schauberger was appointed by the Austrian government as an official consultant on timber transport. The appointment generated not a little envy from his colleagues. Vehement protests were voiced by the many who refused to take orders from a nonacademic. Others tried to imitate his designs, but there was always something that didn't quite work, at which point they would reluctantly summon Schauberger to resolve the problem.

This proved too much for his detractors – the case was brought before Parliament, where it was decided that his salary should be cut. Understandably, Schauberger eventually resigned, working through the 1920s and '30s on numerous flume projects all over Europe and pursuing his research, followed everywhere by the ridicule of engineers and scientists.

Schauberger noticed that the characteristics of water changed according to unexpected parameters. He observed, for example, that it is a good sign when the 'tail' of an algae colony points against the current – this means that the latent energy of the water is at the right temperature. When tracts of the river are deforested, he found that this is one of the first parameters to change – the algae either changes configuration or disappears altogether, which results in the river losing much of its vitality.

Schauberger considered water a living organism. He had what would be called today an ecological and holistic approach. Deforestation, in addition to provoking landslides, avalanches and severe erosion, has completely transformed the world's rivers. Water that was once crystalline is now murky, choked with weeds and detritus. The absence of root systems causes them to erode their own banks, which makes them more likely to flood under heavy rains as well as to dry out during arid periods. For this reason, in 1951 Schauberger and his son Walter, an engineer, founded the world's first organization for the protection and regeneration of the forests. They knew then what we can see all too clearly now: deforestation causes water to lose its strength and vitality, just as any organism is weakened by fever.

Understanding and Imitating Water

Schauberger realized that the centripetal, hyperbolic and spiraliform movement of water is accompanied by a decrease in temperature, meaning a contraction and concentration of water molecules, and that this stimulates living organisms. These aquatic dynamics regulate the order of complex systems.

It is possible to reproduce this spiral movement in the laboratory by directing water flow through special conduits in the shape of an antelope horn. Researchers have been surprised to find that the spiral, compared with other forms, reduces the resistance of the container to nearly zero, allowing water to follow its natural course and speed and to flow more freely.

The lone inventor spent many years devising machines that would optimize the energetic capacities of water. He designed a turbine that produced clean energy by way of a system of spiral tubes made of carefully studied materials: the water followed the same movement it makes over the gills and body of a swimming fish. He got some positive results, but in the end was unable to control the emission of energy.

Schauberger considered drinking water pumped mechanically from underground aquifers to be 'immature', since it lacks the vital properties that can only be acquired by completing the hydrological cycle, returning naturally to the surface. Indeed, he thought that this water could be harmful, capable of draining the life force of those who drank it; it was even worse if the water were conducted by metal plumbing, which he claimed 'kills' water's qualities. Waters from above-ground sources have superior qualities of potability. Schauberger discovered that by drinking a litre of this water, which should weigh a kilo, body weight increases by only 300–400 grams; the rest is converted by the body into usable energy.

Another of Schauberger's intuitions was confirmed when it was shown that not only the form and direction, but the material through which water flows makes a difference. Copper, for example, offers less resistance to water flow than glass. So he decided to line only the internal fixtures of the tubing in his inventions with copper or silver so as to help the water to flow as it should.

He was convinced it was essential that drinking water be conducted through wooden tubing, not metal or concrete. The hydraulic efficiency of wood is superior, and a container made from a natural material like wood does not degrade any faster over time than a metal one, particularly if it is insulated externally by a layer of sand.

Schauberger suspected that the disinfection and sterilization of drinking water with chlorine, silver compounds or quartz lamp radiation might have carcinogenic effects. Waters coming into contact with toxic substances, even if purified, would be stripped of their original energy. He also thought that the consumption of fruits and vegetables grown in chemically treated soil could lead to a rupture in the energetic equilibrium of the human organism and, over the long term, to a greater susceptibility to degenerative and infectious diseases. Schauberger predicted that within a few decades a bottle of water would cost more than a bottle of wine: yet another of his prophecies that is well on its way to coming true.

In the 1930s Schauberger patented a device for biologically reactivating water. It conducted the deactivated water along a centripetal spiral route while bringing it to the optimal temperature of *'biological zero'* (4 °C). Minerals and carbon dioxide were also added to help restore the water to its natural state. It was essentially a system that accelerated the steps of nature's hydrological cycle, which from a chemical and physical point of view produced a water with all the characteristics of a mineral water from a thermal spring. The device had an ovoid form, was vacuum sealed, and contained a mechanism that would agitate the water and ensure its proper spiral flow; the number, rhythm and direction of these agitations was of paramount importance.

As we'll see further on, many years later the agitation and succussion of water would play a decisive role in the controversial experiments of immunologist Jacques Benveniste on 'water memory'. Agitation and succussion of aqueous solutions are also essential for the preparation of homeopathic remedies which, once 'dynamized', acquire pharmaco-logical properties. Schauberger thought that the effectiveness of a medication depended on both the kind of *agitation* to which it is subjected and also the *form of the container*, a consideration that manufacturers of homeopathic remedies might do well to investigate to improve the effectiveness of their products.

Scientists who work with chaotic phenomena have difficulty analysing the complex turbulences of water, even those generated by opening a simple bath tap. Water that is forcibly made to flow through pressurized metal tubing moves in concentric circles, and, according to some, tends to become destructured. Unstructured water is character-ized by a missing electron in the outermost orbital of the molecule, while the structured water we find in nature has all its electrons. The potential consequences for our health from drinking unstructured water remain to be clarified.

In 1934 Schauberger had a private meeting with Adolph Hitler, who had been Chancellor for a year. Hitler summoned the inventor to Berlin for a consultation on the state of the nation's rivers. Schauberger didn't hesitate to respond to the dictator with his characteristic directness, telling him that the technologies being used by his scientists would destroy Germany rather than strengthen it. Schauberger's prophecy of the potential fall of the Reich must have been rather difficult for Hitler to reconcile with his vision of it lasting at least 2,000 years. Needless to say, the Führer no longer had much use for Schauberger's consulting services.

But the Nazis did keep an eye on him after the annexation of Austria in 1938. Schauberger built a lab for generating electricity using thin low-pressure tubes, to which no one paid much attention. During the war, however, he was conscripted to collaborate on a project for a 'flying saucer' powered by air and water. Preliminary tests were encour-aging, but the facility that housed the project was destroyed by the Russian advance.

With the end of the war, Schauberger spent the next ten years study-ing the practices of Austrian farmers, seeking to unveil the mechanisms of certain mysterious phenomena connected to the magnetism of soil and water and their effect on the growth and quality of the harvest. In the meantime, he designed a special spiral plough that would improve the productivity of the soil (figure 4.1).

Schauberger authored an essay entitled 'Natural Farming' that is full of interesting material, the fruits of his careful observations of those farmers who reaped the best harvests. For example, he found that to make the soil more fertile, the furrows should never be so deep as to uproot existing vegetation, which served to partially cover the furrows. The results of experiments conducted with special copper ploughs confirmed his theories, but at that time they went against the interests of industry which, with the Austrian government's blessing, encouraged the use of nitrogen compounds for fertilization.

Schauberger, bankrupt and alone, could no longer afford to keep up his research. In 1955 some American investors showed an interest in his projects for machines that would generate 'clean' energy, but he died that same year.

Not all of Schauberger's ideas have been tested, and perhaps if they were to be, some would be proven wrong. But as Stephen Jay Gould wrote, 'Error is the inevitable consequence of courage'. Nonetheless, his theories are still pursued by an increasingly large number of supporters in the academic circles of Scandinavia and the English-speaking world.

Several research institutes in Europe have revived Schauberger's legacy, implementing technological initiatives inspired by his thoughts.

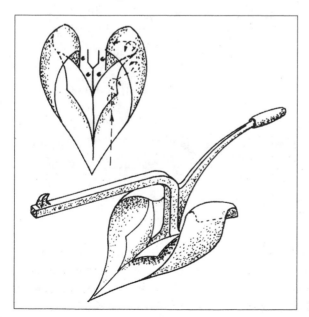

Figure 4.1 Schauberger's spiral plough mimics the activity of moles

Among the more recent such initiatives is that of Wilfred Hacheney, who invented a machine for activating water, a hyperbolic steel cylinder with a funnel-shaped mechanism at its core that causes the water to move in opposing vortices, without creating turbulence. Lab tests seem to show that water subjected to this process accelerates plant growth and, when used to make concrete, increases the binding strength of cement and its resistance to compression.

The Damage Caused by Dams

In another of his prophetic intuitions, Schauberger insisted that the exploitation of hydroelectric resources and the forcible channelling of waterways would end up having disastrous effects on the natural world. The validity of his concern is right before our eyes: once-pristine rivers now accumulate mud and debris, flooding occurs if rainfall levels rise even slightly higher than normal. We are faced with extreme topsoil erosion and the disappearance of arable land, forests and wildlife.

Today, 'official' science has finally acknowledged that meddling with a river's natural course causes the impoverishment of the surrounding soil and subsoil. The American hydrologist Luna Leopold has demonstrated the calamities caused by the channelling and dragging of American rivers. Attempts to regulate flooding have had the opposite effect, increasing the frequency of flooding. The cementification of waterways and the construction of dams have upset the self-correcting mechanisms of living ecosystems. There are approximately 40,000 large dams in the world (15 metres or higher) and more than 800,000 smaller ones, many of which were built in the first half of the 20th century.

The environmental damage caused by dams is incalculable, starting with the loss of terrain, often rich with mineral resources, unique flora and fauna, as well as potential for tourism. Moreover, the bottoms of dams encourage the build-up of layers of decomposed organic matter that can often be toxic which, along with sediments oversaturated with heavy metals, can kill aquatic flora and fauna.

It is estimated that more than half of the fish that once fed off the Pacific coast of the US have disappeared as a result of dam construction. Hydroelectric power has the disadvantage of being considered by most people a 'clean' energy source by comparison to oil and coal, and is therefore regularly classified with other, legitimately green, alternative energy sources such as wind and solar power, when clearly it shouldn't be.

According to study conducted at the University of Hamburg and Baltic Sea Research Institute, a dam on the Danube has caused the proliferation of a type of algae in the Black Sea that kills other marine life forms.[9] This is the result of a drastic reduction of the silicates produced by the natural erosion of the river. To understand the scale of the disaster, one must consider that the Black Sea depends on the Danube for 80 per cent of its silicates.

A sharp reduction in silicates has also been recorded in the Rhine and the Mississippi rivers which, though they are not dammed, have been subjected to modifications of their banks. The Aswan Dam on the Nile has altered the ecosystem of the entire eastern Mediterranean.

The devastating floods in Mozambique in the year 2000 were due to the incompetent management of South African dams: an over-zealous water release schedule resulted in floods that killed thousands and left half a million people homeless. Other areas at high risk of lethal flooding are those downstream from China's colossal Three Gorges Dam on the Yangtze and the Sardar Sarovar and Tehri dams in India. The Sardar Sarovar, in a spectacular feat of recklessness, is built on seismically active terrain in the vicinity of a junction of three fault lines.

There are signs, however, of a reversal of the trend. In 1996, an unprecedented event occurred in Newport, Vermont, which is set on the Clyde River: for the first time in history, a dam was dismantled for purely environmental reasons, foremost among which was the disappearance of salmon from the river. Since then, there has been an intensive campaign underway in the United States to demolish as many dams as possible, particularly those posing the greatest threat to the ecological balance of the surrounding territory.

There is also the fact that it would cost more to repair and maintain existing dams than to remove them definitively.

➤

In 1929, Schauberger patented an apparatus for restoring riverbeds to their original condition that would agitate the water so as to generate a spiral flow along the axis of the current. He offered to rehabilitate the Rhine, but no one listened, as usual.

Given the current situation, it might be a good idea to start listening to him now.

The Ordered Chaos of Water

I am an old man now, and when I die and go to heaven there are two matters on which I hope for enlightenment. One is quantum electro-dynamics, and the other is the turbulent motion of fluids. And about the former I am rather optimistic.

HORACE LAMB, physicist and mathematician (1849–1934)

Computer power and abstract mathematics have laid the foundation for a revolutionary scientific hypothesis known as Chaos Theory. A hidden order in the unpredictability of many sensible phenomena has been discovered between the poles of order and chaos, stability and instability. Water turbulence was one of the principal muses of this theory, albeit an elusive muse. The most brilliant physicist of our time, Richard Feynman, one of the fathers of quantum electrodynamics, admitted that 'What we really cannot do is deal with actual, wet water running through a pipe. That is the central problem which we ought to solve some day.'[10]

The earliest studies of chaos were conducted in an attempt to determine why, in meteorology, physics, chemistry and biology, there exist complex phenomena that do not conform to the standard models of traditional physics. With the advent of quantum mechanics in the 1920s and 1930s, scientists began studying atoms and their constituents with a probabilistic approach. Classic Newtonian mechanics were replaced by a conception of electrons and particles as 'waves of probability'. Today we know that chaos is present in all phenomena, and the Newtonian model, though still used in the natural sciences and in some branches of psychology, has been surpassed.

For decades, science overlooked or pretended to ignore these chaotic natural phenomena: it was impossible to formulate predictive hypotheses because they contradicted the paradigm of a spatially static and temporally linear universe.

In meteorology there are numerous events that cannot be predicted with any real precision, among which are atmospheric turbulence, the motion of the seas and the formation of the aurora by magnetically charged particles. In physics it is impossible to predict with any exactitude the chaotic motion of atoms, gases and particles, disturbances in the impulses of electrical circuits, or even something as banal as how and when a boat will capsize in rough seas. In quantum mechanics, identical causes don't always produce identical effects.

The same holds true for the evolution of populations and demographic fluctuations. In medicine, chaos governs the oscillations in cardiac rhythm, the irregular sequences of the brain's electrical activity and the transmission of nerve impulses. Neither is it possible to predict the progress of epidemics or the dynamics of pathologies like arrhythmia, convulsions, cardiac arrest and the development of Parkinson's disease.

The science of chaos studies complexity and its statistical distortions or, more simply, that which is apparently random. All biological systems constituted by aqueous matter are governed by nonlinear systems. As such, they are chaotic and, up to a certain point, unpredictable. In a paradox that we've come to expect of water, it is this unpredictability that ensures the survival, organization and evolution of these systems.

Thanks to new mathematical models and ever more powerful computers, one can plot a sort of map of disorder and complexity. Chaos theorists integrate data that seem 'incongruous' into a global and holistic vision. In short, chaos science elegantly interprets the relationship between the simple and the complex, between causality and casuality.

Thanks to chaos we are driven to perceive and conceive the world with an increasingly broader view. Chaos is a multidisciplinary subject that generates dialogue among scientists from different fields. Furthermore, chaos also provides certain of them with the chance to delve a bit into the realms of philosophy, even mysticism, for it induces them to address what are basically existential problems: free will, the phenomenological role of consciousness in scientific inquiry, the dynamics of intelligence and evolution.

Chaos dominates the aqueous realm. Let's imagine following a leaf as it floats on the surface of a river: we instinctively know already that it would be impossible to predict its path or destination. Even the slightest variation in the patterns of water flow will significantly modify its trajectory, and each of these slight changes will cause an ever greater number of variations over time. Yet the chaotic sequences created by water turbulence do subtend a kind of order – paradoxically, a complex system triggers both chaos and coherency.

Living Systems Tend Towards Equilibrium

I think we are beginning to perceive nature on Earth in exactly the opposite way we viewed it in classical physics. We no longer conceive of nature as a passive object. ... I see us as nearer to a Taoist view, in which we are embedded in a universe that is not foreign to us.

ILYA PRIGOGINE, winner of the 1987 Nobel Prize for Chemistry

About 60 years ago the Soviet biophysicist Boris Pavlovich Belousov, while studying the citric acid cycle, stumbled upon a chemical reaction that had never before been seen. After preparing a solution of 30 or so chemical substances, he watched as the mixture seemed to take on a life of its own. The liquid began regularly alternating between a colourless state and one characterized by brilliant hues. He noticed that the molecules would often organize into regular patterns in the form of vortices and spirals.

What Belousov had done was to discover the first self-organized periodic chemical reaction. In addition to being macroscopic proof of the existence of spontaneous, self-organized oscillations in water, it also showed that chemical reactions are not always predictable, but are instead an open door to chaos.

As often happens with such discoveries, no one believed Belousov. His work was rejected by various scientific publications and it wasn't until 1970 that a young chemist named Anatoly Zhabotinsky resumed the older man's work and proved him right. Unfortunately, Belousov died before seeing his extraordinary contribution accepted by the scientific community.

The Belousov-Zhabotinsky reaction is a chaotic (i.e. unpredictable) oscillation between two states. For decades chemists refused to accept the possibility because it went against the second law of thermo-dynamics, which states that the universe and every system contained therein are subject to entropy – that is, dynamic differences inexorably tend to even out until reaching equilibrium. A concrete example would be two separate but communicating vessels, one full of water and the other of ink. When the two liquids come into contact, the molecules of one will randomly mix with those of the other, never to return to their original, separate states, eventually becoming a uniform mixture of the two.

The Belousov-Zhabotinsky reaction (figure 4.2) is the first chemical demonstration of order emerging from chaos, a real challenge to the principle of entropy: from disorder are created unstable, ordered, oscillating sequences, significantly spiraliform in structure.

Around the same time, in 1968, Nobel Prize winner Ilya Prigogine was demonstrating how many other autocatalytic reactions are gov-erned by a chaotic dynamic that is far from thermodynamic equilibrium. A few years later, Prigogine concluded that order is reached through fluctuation, and that this is the way organic systems and living beings organize themselves and adapt to change. This enables them to maintain a dynamic homeostasis and also explains their complexity in progressive orders.

An organism is not a static thing, but a process of continual flux with a tendency to cooperate with other organisms in order to create an

Figure 4.2 The Belousov-Zhabotinsky reaction

organized reality and superior symmetries. The idea of the unstable yet ordered network, organized on different scales into microcosms and macrocosms sharing the same structure, is central to the Gaia theory, and can be found in all modular theories, both ancient and modern, including chaos theory.

Living beings are closed energy systems, in that they are self-organized. They are, however, open systems as well, since matter and energy flow through them continuously. Living systems, in Prigogine's definition, are *dissipative structures* because they consume energy through fluctuations in state, thereby building an order. Evidently, chaos always hides a latent order.

The simplest imaginable model of a dissipative structure is that of a water vortex (figure 4.3), like the little whirlpool that forms when we drain a bathtub. The system has a stable form, always remaining the same, but its components are perpetually replaced and are thus never the same, as Heraclitus observed long ago.

Similarly, the aggregate of mass and energy that is the human body maintains its form while transforming itself continually, thanks to the metabolic activity of our cells which destroy and rebuild themselves without interruption. Organisms, explains Prigogine, are stable, but tend towards an ideal equilibrium that they can never achieve. This tendency toward equilibrium drives living systems to evolve and to reach new states of instability.

Figure 4.3 The spiral motion of a water vortex is a model of a dissipative structure

Once again, nature shows us that the life of self-organized systems manifests itself through the paradoxical coexistence of stability and change. Prigogine acknowledged that his theory is inspired by Chinese thought. The Chinese would say that everything manifests itself in structures through which the energetic interactions between yin and yang tend towards the harmony of the Tao. Everything in nature obeys ordered patterns, the aim of which is equilibrium.

Like water, every living being adapts, regenerates and 'updates' itself. We have inherited from water the capacity to preserve ourselves through dynamic equilibrium. Our bodies, like water, are a paradoxical synthesis of permanence and change – we maintain more or less the same aspect over time, and what changes in that aspect derives from the fact that our bodies contain less and less water as we age. The evolution of the species is made possible by the restlessness of water, which gives life the ability to become ever more complex and to strive, albeit unsuccessfully, towards perfection.

A living being is a dynamic whole that is able to function even when something goes wrong, using water as the vehicle of the healing process, regenerating and replacing its own tissues. In short, life's natural tendency is to improve the quality of itself through genetics and behaviour.

Fractals: Infinite Order in Chaos

> Row by row, knot by knot
> trunks upon trunks
> grapes upon grapes replicate continously,
> so is the light within light and my love.
> The miracle of renewal, my sweetheart,
> is to repeat without repeating.
>
> **NAZIM HIKMET**, *Bach's Concerto No 1 in C Minor*

Biologists, chemists, mathematicians, physicists, engineers, doctors and economists have found a surprising order underlying chaos. With the help of computers, they've taken complex mathematical equations, transformed them into digital images, and discovered the fascinating realm of fractals, a term coined by the mathematician Benoît Mandelbrot to describe the gorgeously irregular agglomerations of curves and spirals whose modular geometry is infinitely repeated at every scale.

Fractals are like fantasy landscapes that seem to encompass all of art, science and nature – and in fact they do. They are the branches of a tree, the bronchia of a healthy lung, the lines on the palm of a man or an ape, the path of lightning bolts, the tunnels of an ant colony, a romanesco cauliflower, the contour of a maple leaf. Aquatically speaking, they are the course of a river and the branching of its tributaries seen from a plane, the formation of clouds, the seeping of water through gravel, the crystals of a snowflake.

Everything in nature is organized into repeating geometrical forms: the disposition of molecules, amoeba colonies, beach sand, the stripes on a zebra. In 2006 Richard Massey of Caltech also found that the dark matter distribution in the universe is fractal and some astrophysicists are convinced that the whole universe is fractal.

The property of maintaining a constant modular form at every scale is called '*recursive self-similarity*'. It is a holistic property in that it describes similar microcosms inscribed within similar macrocosms on a scale that runs in all directions to infinity. If we observe an object in microscopic detail, we find an identical formal and sequential aspect no matter how small we go (figure 4.4). By the same token, if we look at successive magnifications of a coastline, we find that its degree of irregularity remains constant at every scale. The world, then, is regular in its irregularity.

An explanatory model of the contour of a coastline, or the architecture of a snowflake for that matter, is offered by Koch's Triangle, a fractal discovered by Helge von Koch in 1904 (figure 4.5), whereby an infinite line bounds a finite area. Complexity is built in a finite space that contains the infinite; the recursive self-similar sequences of fractals enable us to visually grasp infinity.

The modularity of micro- and macrocosms is present in living beings, which are built of organs and tissues that are in turn composed of cells that also contain self-reproducing 'organs' (e.g. mitochondria), which in their turn are made up of smaller components, and so on to infinity.

This same holistic and modular view is found in traditional Chinese science. Thousands of years ago, Chinese medicine determined that the totality of an organism is represented in each of its component parts – the ear, the tongue, the hand or foot – such that observing a part is the same as observing the organism in its entirety, for every single part contains information that is relative to the whole.

We need only examine one area, let's say the ear, to formulate a diagnosis of a person's general state of health, or stimulate an area such

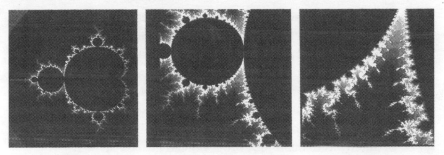

Figure 4.4 Fractals generate new repeating forms at every scale

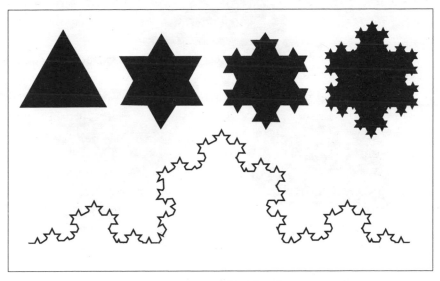

Figure 4.5 Koch's Triangle

as the foot or abdomen to cure the entire organism. The microcosm is like a laboratory where we can analyse and cure the macrocosm. This ancient knowledge was corroborated by the discovery of DNA, which contains all the information for all the functions of the body and is identical in every cell. Observing the human body is like observing the Earth: its forms are like those of rocks modelled by water; its vascular, bronchial and lymphatic systems like the ramification of a river or a tree.

Our bodies are an aggregate of fractals – in addition to the aforementioned systems, there's also the fractal distribution of nerves, of the kidney ducts, and of the dense network of acupuncture meridians which branch out to the junctions between individual cells.

Fractals are also dynamic sequences. The electrical grid of the heart generates a sequence of impulses that follow a fractal pattern. The same holds true for the propagation of electrical currents in the brain, whose synapses – the electrically active bridges between neurons – are continuously formed according to a fractal progression (figure 4.6). Synapses multiply as a result of cognitive and emotive activity as well, which stimulates the production of neuronal material. This construction would go on infinitely, were death not programmed into our DNA.

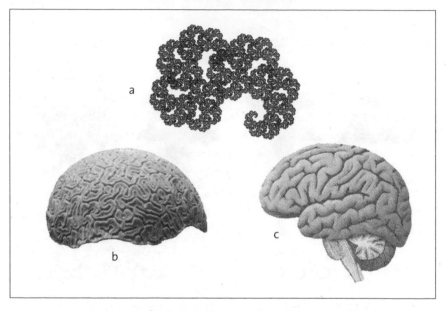

Figure 4.6 a) A fractal, b) a coral formation, c) a brain

The science of chaos demonstrates that nature is not randomly designed and that from chaos there inevitably emerges an infinite order, no matter how difficult it might be to identify. Indeed, this is precisely what science is: the search for order in what seems to be meaningless disorder.

Understanding why mushrooms in a field tend to concentrate in certain areas; why people are more attracted by shiny objects than matt ones, and seem to buy more cars of one colour than another; why a language contains more vowels or consonants of a certain type; why water, in the apparent chaos of its turbulence, tends to build coherent sequences – means understanding the architecture of nature, whose destiny we share.

Order in Entropy

We did not come into this world. We came out of it, like buds out of branches and butterflies out of cocoons. We are a natural product of this Earth, and if we turn out to be intelligent beings, then it can only be because we are fruits of an intelligent Earth, which is nourished in turn by an intelligent system of energy.

LYALL WATSON, *Gifts of Unknown Things*

The course of a chaotic system depends on its initial conditions, for example its position and rhythm of growth. Tiny variations change the direction and destiny of systems which are very similar to one another. For this reason it is impossible for anything in nature to be the same as something else – not the proverbial two snowflakes, not two grains of sand, not two drops of water. A snowflake and a drop of water, though made of the same material, are two entirely different worlds in both aspect and behaviour. To melt a snowflake, one needs 80 times the amount of heat required to raise the temperature of a drop of water by 1 °C.

In the 'globalized' realm of chaos, every event, however small, provokes a chain of consequences that affect the whole. Minor variations can have disproportionately major effects. To use a famous adage, the beating of a butterfly's wings in China can unleash a tornado in America.

Scientists love to look for regularity, reproducibility, linearity and order in phenomena, but in nature the rule is disorder and irregularity. Or rather, chaos insinuates itself into order, and vice versa. According to the second law of thermodynamics, all natural systems tend to progress from order to disorder (entropy). Statistically speaking, disorder is the predominant state in nature, insofar as the number of disordered atomic combinations is significantly greater than the number of ordered combinations.

One would think that there was a greater probability that the newborn universe, expanding and cooling, would have contained a disordered mixture of matter and energy. Yet against all odds, ordered life forms developed – a near impossibility from a statistical standpoint. Though it seems counterintuitive, chaotic systems tend to create more order, more complexity, more intelligence.

And it is here that we find ourselves straddling the boundary between science and metaphysics, which seems an appropriate moment to quote the Bible, specifically the Book of Genesis, which opens with the words:

> In the beginning God created the Heavens and the Earth. And the Earth was Chaos, and void; and darkness was upon the surface of the Deep. And the Spirit of God hovered upon the surface of the waters.
>
> Genesis 1: 1–2

The Bible addresses the cosmological problem of the birth of a chaotic but ordered system (life) in a universe dominated by entropy, and most importantly for our purposes begins by describing the birth of the world with the formation of the waters, which are present during the creation of a chaotic universe still void of form.

In the original Hebrew, 'without form and void' is *tohu va vohu* ('chaos and void'), and it is from this chaotic entity that the progressive organization of creation into something orderly proceeds. Humankind is created at the end of the process, an active part in the construction of order from chaos.

The Hebrew word *tohu* also means 'astonishment, surprise'. Indeed, chaos does elicit a fair amount of astonishment: what other reaction can there be to a chaotic and empty (*vohu*) universe producing an ultimate order, completely free and unpredictable? Here the Bible offers us a valuable suggestion. If we wish to be creative, like God, let us create an empty space inside of us and let it be filled with amazement. Let us allow ourselves to be surprised by life, without hanging on to expectations, and something unexpected will happen: reality will become its opposite and show us its other side, and from chaos will emerge order, from darkness light.

Order was already written into the primordial chaos. The medieval Jewish commentator Nachmanides (1194–1270) explains that *tohu* is an extremely fine nonsubstance, with potential but without form. *Vohu*, most often translated from the Hebrew as 'void', also means 'in it, there is'. In other words, *vohu* is a void that contains potential matter, a concept we also find in quantum physics, where the subatomic void is composed of potential matter. Similarly, the voids created by the aggregation of water molecules make possible the chemical reactions and energy fields that make life itself possible.

Jewish mysticism teaches that God created the world and withdrew, leaving behind an empty space that dilated as He contracted, in which the expanding universe then appeared. This is essentially a description of the state of the universe immediately prior to the Big Bang.

Even after this point, biblical interpretation and scientific theory continue to coincide in rather suggestive ways.

And God called the light Day, and the darkness he called Night. And there was evening and there was morning one day.

Genesis 1: 5

In keeping with the holographic model, the primordial water that preceded the universe was invested with the coherent light of an immense cosmic laser, which created matter and the expanding void from a single point. The Bible gives us a synthetic account of the passage from night to day, from darkness to light, from chaos to order, from the Big Bang to the harmony of life.

The root of the Hebrew word *erev* ('evening') means 'chaos, disorder, mixture', while the root of the word *boker* ('morning') means 'ordered, that which can be discerned'. The Bible interprets the birth and formation of the universe as moving from a state of disorder to a new order contained therein. Evening and morning blend into one another, alternating and interpenetrating like the yin and the yang. Chaos conceals within itself an order which in turn contains elements of unpredictability and improbability but also of a cyclicity that repeats like the morning and the night, every day in a different way.

Nature does not produce the regular forms of Euclidian geometry (rectangles, cones, spheres), only complex structures. As Mandelbrot liked to say, there are no spherical clouds or conical mountains, no circular coastlines or straight lightning bolts. Nature and all it encompasses, including human beings, is never perfectly symmetrical, building instead imperfect symmetries to create an ever more complex order, oblivious to the increasing entropy of the universe.

The unstable and imperfect symmetry of the water molecule is reflected in a visible world made up of imperfect structures that nevertheless tend towards equilibrium, harmony and beauty. Fractal structures repeat, yet every one is different and unrepeatable. Fractals, defined by sameness, are the very essence of uniqueness, unpredictability and therefore of freedom. They are by definition the same, yet paradoxically obligated to be different from others and from themselves. It works for fractals; it should also work for us.

Fractals guard the secret of the development of life from the simple to the complex: the evolution of simple water into single-cell organisms and eventually into us, the most complex and intelligent of life forms. This is how the wavy and vortical forms of nature are organized. This is what drives water to create more order, more complexity, more difference, more information and, by extension, more intelligence.

Water, the Blood of the Earth: Feng Shui

The water that springs from the mountains is the blood that keeps those same mountains living and is the vein that is formed within and across them.

LEONARDO DA VINCI

Over the centuries, Chinese civilization developed the art of regulating the flow of water. It was on China's rivers that the first dams and embankments were built, deviating their courses through a dense network of canals. For millennia, China was at the cutting edge of hydraulic science with respect to the rest of the world.

According to traditional Chinese science, life is not a property that is exclusive to the plant and animal kingdoms, but vibrates throughout the mineral realm as well, in the rocks and sands, in the waters, in the breath of the wind. Their vision was that of a harmonious buzz of concerted activities that together constitute the ecology of life – an idea which is not as abstruse at it might appear: no modern scientist would deny the radioactive 'vitality' of the mineral world and the restlessness of the subatomic particles, and many of them consider the Earth to be a sort of macrocosmic organism.

The Chinese discipline dedicated to the relationship between humanity and its space and time is called *feng shui*, meaning 'wind and water'. Feng shui is a form of geomancy, the art of living in harmony with the Earth while drawing from it maximum material, mental and spiritual benefit. The Great Imperial Encyclopaedia considered experts in feng shui to be true scientists, and for centuries the Chinese people accorded them maximum respect.

Wind and water are the primeval forces that sculpt the landscape and give it life – or better, they are the expressions, made manifest in the landscape, of the Qi, the energy that animates the evaporation of water and returns it, revitalized, to the Earth to be absorbed by living beings by way of air and food. The planet's topography is incessantly sculpted into new forms by wind and water. Feng shui views the Earth as a powerful living being, nourished by water and awakened by wind.

Feng shui studies the circulation of Qi, the invisible energy fields of our planet whose action can be deduced from the movements of matter, waterways included.

For Chinese scholars, the energy of wind and water flows within objects, places, elements and people in a process that can be compared to the basic physics of *energy transduction*. A good example being the wind energy that is transduced into mechanical energy by the blades of a windmill, in turn transduced into electrical energy by a generator, which is then transformed into luminous thermal energy by a light bulb.

All the forces present in the universe are Qi, be they mechanical, electrical, biological, etc. Indeed, the theory of Qi is not unlike the Unified Field Theory. The environmental forces examined by the feng shui master are the same as those studied in the medical sciences (pharmacology, acupuncture, moxibustion), in physiognomics and the arts. In all these fields, the forces to be balanced are analysed according to the yin/yang model.

Two main currents of feng shui practice have developed since its origin in the 10th century BC: the Form School and the Compass School.

The Form School focuses, as its name would suggest, on the conformation of the land and the direction of waterways in order to determine if, where, when and how a particular tract of land can be suited to settlement: in short, its adaptability to provide maximum benefit to the health, happiness and prosperity of those who settle there.

The Compass School analyses the Qi of a place in relation to the people who intend to inhabit it. A magnetic needle is inserted into a complex circular instrument composed of several rings called a compass (not to be confused with the simpler navigational tool of more recent times). In each ring are inscribed different symbols that represent the forces of the physical world. The master conducts complex operations involving temporal and directional parameters, using the movements of the needle to evaluate the energy of the site.

For the last two centuries or so, the Form and Compass Schools have more or less merged, such that today they each use both systems, with the shared aim of understanding the geographic properties and energy fields emitted by a given site and any water that may be present.

The form of a site, the position of landscape elements (hills, waterways, trees, other dwellings) and, in the event that the site is itself an existing dwelling, the disposition of rooms and objects contained therein are observed in order to determine the optimal harmony between all these factors, including the people who inhabit the site, in accordance with the Taoist ethic. For political and ideological reasons, feng shui is not officially recognized by the current regime of the People's Republic of China, but its principles are still used by a large part of the population, particularly in rural areas. Feng shui is widely practised in Hong Kong, Singapore, Taiwan and wherever there are large Chinese communities abroad.

Fascinated by the exceptional aesthetic, functional and ergonomic results obtained with feng shui, many Western architects, agronomists and urban planners are delving into the art of wind and water, drawing upon it to harmonize the formal relationships of urban, rural and interior spaces. Geobiology, a modern discipline that studies the disturbances caused by electromagnetic fields, has proven to be a useful ally. Combined with feng shui, geobiology can help correct the chemical and electromagnetic pollution caused by seismic fault lines, underground aquifers, electrical power plants, home appliances, harmful building materials and radioactive geological features.

The Chinese tradition teaches that a site with good Qi brings three blessings to those who live there: health, happiness and prosperity. It is a good sign if there is water flowing near, beneath, even through the dwelling, though it should be as clean and pure as possible. A stagnant body of water, apart from being a potential source of illness and insect infestation, will tend to cause the economy of the household to stagnate.

Living water, clean and mobile, activates the Qi. Dead water, impure and stagnant, causes the depletion of our Qi, thus damaging our health. Though they used different terms, the ancient Chinese knew that water combines with air and contains the oxygen essential to its purifying properties. When water stagnates it becomes toxic precisely because it is movement that enables it to absorb life-giving oxygen.

The feng shui master's task is no easy one. He must consider the many factors of local and individual biorhythms that can affect the Qi of those who live there, including the cardinal orientation of the terrain and architecture, the location of the areas devoted to sleep and work, the forms of individual environmental elements and the direction of windows and entrances. He then makes a sort of map of the site's energy and identifies the specific adjustments to be made.

Everyone has had the experience of feeling particularly at ease in certain houses without knowing exactly why, while in others we are struck by a strange, inexplicable distress. Feng Shui explains that subtle unease is the result of a Qi that is 'trapped', not allowed to circulate – or, conversely, of a Qi that flows too frenetically. Common sense is really all that's needed to grasp many of the basic principles of feng shui – we know instinctively that building a house by a crystalline stream is wiser than building it next to a swamp. To resolve more complex issues, however, it's best to consult a qualified professional.

Water Dragons

All the rivers run into the sea; yet the sea is not full; unto the place from whence the rivers come, thither they return again. All things are wearisome; man is not able to tell it; the eye is not satisfied with seeing, nor the ear filled with hearing.

Ecclesiastes 1: 7–8

Dragons are mythical, dinosaur-like winged creatures whose sinuous movements are similar to those of water. In many cultures they are a symbol of the rain that brings nourishment and life to the Earth.

In the traditions of Thailand, Myanmar and Japan, dragons are considered benevolent beings that ascend to the sky and, beating their wings and limbs against the clouds, cause the rain. The chimera of Greek mythology can assume many forms, including that of the fire-breathing dragon, the Spirit of the Tempest. The dragon is also the celestial emblem of the Chinese emperor, he who ensures harmony.

For the Chinese, every river, lake and well has its dragon spirit, and throughout the history of the rest of world one encounters similar beliefs regarding bodies of water. The Greeks, for example, believed that nymphs inhabited the sources and courses of water. These nymphs also had a potentially malevolent side, like the sea sirens. It was said that those who looked upon them would fall victim to madness.

It is always a good sign if the form of a hill resembles that of a dragon, and the ancient texts of feng shui place great importance on the way that rivers and lakes flow and meander and descend, and on the configuration of the tributaries that feed and drain them. When these structures are serpentine (like certain fractals), they are called *water dragons*.

The Great Imperial Encyclopaedia contains an ancient text entitled 'The Water Dragon Classic', which evaluates the variety of forms of waterways with the aim of determining the 'energy state' of a given site. The confluence of two rivers is a positive factor in that it indicates a con-centration of forces. Conversely, the point where a waterway breaks off from another represents a dispersion of Qi. A river that descends steeply causes the Qi to flow too quickly, particularly if it does so along a straight path, like the flight of an arrow, which can have a negative influ-ence. The best omen is when a river meanders gently and naturally.

The *Kuan Tzu* is a Chinese treatise compiled in the 3rd century AD, attributed to Kuan Chung, a thinker of the 7th century BC. In it is a theory of the properties of water that brings us back to origin of fractals.

> The Earth is the origin of all things, the root and garden of all life ... water is the blood and breath of the Earth, flowing and communicat-ing within its body as if in sinews and veins. This is why water is said to have a complete sensitivity. It accumulates in Heaven and Earth and is stored there. It springs forth from metal and rock and is concen-trated in living creatures. This is why it is said that water is spiritual. By accumulating in plants and trees, it induces the orderly growth of their branches, it makes the flowers grow in the right numbers and fruit in the right measure. By drinking water, the bodies of birds and animals become big and fat, their feathers and fur become shiny, and stripes and markings may appear there. The reason why living creatures are able to realize their potential and develop normally is that their internal regulation of water is harmonious.

According to the Kuan Tzu, then, water is not only the main constituent of body mass, but 'orders' its biological structure and provides living things with the necessary information for achieving harmony, both physiologically and aesthetically.

This text was compiled more than 1,700 years ago, yet we find it relevant still today, a view of biophysical dynamics that attributes the order of organic systems to the turbulence of fluids. The Kuan Tzu proceeds:

> Consequently, the solution for the Sage who wishes to change the world resides in water. When water is uncontaminated, the hearts of men are upright. When water is pure, the people's hearts are at peace. When a man's heart is upright, his desires do not become dissolute. When people's hearts are upright, their conduct is without stain. Consequently, the Sage governs the world not by taking his teaching from man to man, or house to house, but uses water as his key.[11]

By changing water, it might be possible to change people, for water provides the blueprint and the foundation for the construction of living things in their totality. We are what we drink, one might say, and we're also influenced by the lakes in which we swim and the waterways that pass by our homes and schools and towns. The presence of water, and the quality of that water, conditions our body, mind, character and behaviour.

CHAPTER FIVE

HOW LIFE IS CREATED: CHAOS AND TURBULENCE IN WATER

A drop of water, hanging from a faucet, waiting to break off, assumes a complicated three-dimensional shape, and the calculation of this shape alone ... [is] 'a state-of-the-art computer calculation'.

JAMES GLEICK, *Chaos: Making a New Science*

Water is fertile terrain for the study of chaos. Einstein considered the chaotic dance of fluid turbulence as the greatest challenge faced by classical physics. Still today, scientists are unable to predict its behaviour.

The universe is composed of invisible vibrations and energies. We can neither see nor hear subatomic particles, but we can intuit their behaviour by analysing the shadows and contrails they leave on a photographic plate, or the 'noise' that can be picked up by an electromagnetic instrument. In much the same way, we are able to understand the invisible forces of water, identifying the traces it leaves behind and the peculiar ways in which it is registered by our senses.

Water turbulence creates vortices and spirals which the laws of classical physics are unable to explain with any precision. In his pioneering work on chaos entitled *Strange Attractors, Chaotic Behavior and Information Flow*, American physicist Robert S Shaw addresses the complex behaviour of water flowing past an obstacle. Let's look at what happens when water flows around a rock protruding from the middle of a creek: downstream there appear vortical spires which at a certain velocity are stable; if the current speeds up, they change position, moving from left to right in a chaotic and unpredictable way. Water flow thus becomes a source of continuous information, always new and unpredictable: chaos is creative and generates information.

To prove his theories, Shaw chose a leaky tap – a simple phenomenon, or so it would seem. When a tap leaks, the droplets fall in irregular sequences of longer and shorter intervals. Opening the valve slightly, the motion of the droplets becomes turbulent, even more irregular and unstable, until eventually reaching a chaotic regime. A leaky tap generates new and unpredictable sequences. In this way, water can be said to be creative, a generator of infinite information.

Fluid turbulence, as elucidated in the work of mathematicians David Ruelle and Floris Takens, follows the course of 'strange attractors', or the probabilitistic tendencies from which it is possible to construct fractals. These attractors are repeating figures calculated by computer, the first of which was discovered in 1971 by Ruelle while he was working on fluid dynamics.

The complex behaviour of strange attractors is due to the fact that their trajectory is highly sensitive to the initial conditions. Confined to a finite space, they contain an infinite number of possible configurations. Water motion creates vortical and spiral conformations, similar but never identical, that are described by these strange attractors (figure 5.1).

Figure 5.1 LEFT The Roessler strange attractor; RIGHT The Lorenz strange attractor

Once again anticipating modern science by millennia, Taoist sages studying the hexagrams of the *I Ching* were able to identify repeating patterns in all natural phenomena. Taoist philosophy considers every temporal event as being connected to all others in a spiraliform system of relations, with every cycle resembling the previous one, though never exactly.

The ways in which information is created follow precise lines of tendency that can be studied through the dynamics of water flow, the originary matrix that gives rise to complexity. All research on chaos to date demonstrates that complexity emerges from simplicity. Just as complex structures like fractals and strange attractors are born of simple nonlinear mathematical equations, so is the complexity of living systems born of water, pure and simple.

The laws and equations of fluid dynamics are valid at every scale. A cloud maintains its dimensional characteristics whether seen from up close or far away; without external reference points it is impossible for an observer to determine its distance.

We can imagine the movement of a particle along a strange attractor in this same way: whatever its point of departure, the particle will always follow a similar but never identical trajectory with respect to the previous one. There will be small variations, only apparently random.

The flow of waterways follows these same repeating, yet unrepeatable rhythmic sequences. Such sequences can be favourable or less favourable to biological systems, which require ordered rhythms. Heartbeat, breathing, sleeping/waking and the circadian rhythms of the endocrine system are the 'tides' of the microcosm that is the living being.

Figure 5.2 The Ueda attractor recalls the yin-yang symbol

The Vortex

I run to surpass myself, doubling the passion.
Towing a continent,
with the vague sense that the only true thing
is that self outside myself, that breathes by me.

MAURIZIO MESCHIA, 'Bikila'

Vortices are everywhere. We see them every time we stir our coffee or drain the bathtub. Less readily visible but even more ubiquitous are the vortices that shape the atmosphere, the ocean currents, the planet's flora and fauna, the tissues and organs of our bodies.

One summer night in 1922, while travelling on a ferry bound for the Spanish port of Alicante, the Dutch artist MC Escher witnessed a spectacle that he described in his diary as 'unforgettably beautiful': a group of dolphins swimming alongside the ship, lit by bioluminescent plankton, leaving behind a wake edged in phosphorescent blue. That bewitching vision inspired his celebrated woodcut, *Dolphins in a Phosphorescent Sea*.

About 80 years later, a similar experience led Jim Rohr, a fluid dynamics expert with the US Navy, to analyse the trails left by bio-luminescent organisms on ocean waves. Since these luminous wakes follow the movement of the water, they allow the naked eye to follow its complex and elusive patterns, a little like using fireworks to see the wind. Rohr discovered that the plankton's luminescence increases in correspondence with the speed of the current, and he presented his results in 1998.[12]

Single-cell plankton accounts for nearly all marine bioluminescence. Thanks to these microscopic ocean-going fireflies, sensitive to even the slightest disturbance in the current, scientists are finally beginning to understand the way water moves and the laws that govern whirlpools and vortices. This precious data helps us penetrate mysteries such as the causes that drive the Gulf Stream, so vital to maintaining Europe's temperate climate, how clouds form, and how dolphins manage to achieve such high cruising speeds.

In effect, turbulence governs the whole of nature. By understanding it better, we would know how to pump water or petroleum more efficiently from wells, or how to improve the design of incubators for the cultivation of animal and human cells used in medical research. Unveiling the mysteries of vortices could also lead us to the ideal structures for artificial organs, such as an artificial heart that would impede the formation of life-threatening thrombi. We would also be able to improve the propulsion and manoeuvrability of submarine vessels, and better regulate the performance of the nanorobots currently being developed for medical diagnosis.

If we place a hand in the stream of a running bath tap, we find that large vortices divide into smaller ones. It is a waterfall effect, which transfers energy from larger to smaller scales until eventually reaching the disorganized motion of the molecular level which generates heat. Three-dimensional turbulence is a scientific enigma, in that we still don't know what triggers these fluctuations. These are the inexplicable phenomena known as 'anomalous waves'.

In 1998 Maarten Rutgers of Ohio State University reduced water turbulence to an ultrafine two-dimensional film of soap and water made to flow over a wall.[13] Using a laser detection device, Rutgers confirmed what the American physicist Robert Kraichnan had predicted 30 years previously: small vortices link up with one another to form larger ones in a process that can eventually result in enormous cyclonic storms. This amplification effect, known as an 'inverted waterfall', is visible on the surface of Jupiter in the form of the Great Red Spot, which is probably a two-dimensional vortex. The same principle regulates the immense multiple vortices of Earth's oceans that govern the global climate.

Energy in a moving liquid is distributed in eddies of differing dimensions formed by thousands of spiral arms, the rotational direction of which can sometimes invert. These inverted waterfall spirals are what create the larger stable vortices of the Earth's wind and ocean currents.

In 1993, Phil Richardson of the Woods Hole Oceanographic Institute in Massachusetts conducted a survey of the immense vortical formations of the Atlantic. There are quite a lot of them, around a thousand, with an average diameter of 80 kilometres. Ocean eddies, as they're called, tend to maintain their autonomy, though it sometimes happens that two will join up or one will split. There are also tripolar formations composed of three adjacent eddies with a larger central element flanked by two smaller ones rotating in the opposite direction.

These eddies influence the distribution of plankton and affect the climate. When the warm air from the equator meets the winds blowing in diagonally from cooler areas, currents are formed which cause the waters of the oceans to be pushed westwards. When these fronts encounter a landmass, their path is deviated in such a way as to form circular vortices that spin clockwise in the northern hemisphere and counterclockwise below the equator. This macrocosmic interaction between wind and water – the essence of feng shui, as we'll recall – causes a massive redistribution of heat all over the planet: the best-known example is the vortical front of wind and water from the North Atlantic that powers the Gulf Stream and all its providential effects.

Mory Gharib, an aeronautical engineer at the prestigious California Institute of Technology, reproduced in his lab a sort of miniature Earth. To better understand the formation of the planet's vortices, Gharib came up with an ingeniously original approach, using sound waves to lift a drop of water, creating miniaturized vortices: again, wind and water.[14]

Water is the key to the terrestrial climate, the vault that safeguards its secrets. The study of ocean eddies, even the smallest ones, demonstrates yet again how the invisible events of the microcosm are mirrored in the similar realities of the macrocosm.

The Model of the Vortex

As early as 1867, Lord Kelvin (1824–1907), one of history's most eminent physicists, imagined that atomic motion was vortical. The German physicist Hermann von Helmholtz (1821–94), studying the vortical motion of fluids, became convinced that his friend Kelvin was right, having observed that in the absence of attrition, a fluid can produce stable vortices *ad infinitum*.

Another genius of early physics, the Scotsman James Clerk Maxwell (1831–79), embraced what has come to be known as Kelvin's 'vortex atom hypothesis'; some years later, Sir JJ Thomson (1856–1940), the man who discovered the electron, sustained that the vortex theory of matter was more plausible than the solid particle model, which was in fact later refuted by relativity and quantum theory.

The vortex atomic model fell into disfavour when it was discovered that 'ether', then considered the substance in which atoms move, doesn't exist, and that they move instead in a void and do not need a substance to support their rotation. This discovery, along with the fact that the atom was no longer considered the smallest unit of matter, all but eclipsed the image of the vortex from scientific inquiry.

Since then, we have tended to think in terms of waves. But with super-string theory, the idea that matter moves vortically in order to manifest itself has returned to relevance. According to this theory, the most elementary particles of matter are spiraliform strings of movement – matter is essentially vortical energy, pure movement.

To understand how something dynamic like energy can create some-thing apparently static like matter, try to imagine a ball of yarn formed not by a single filament, but by many short and extremely fine threads, each forming spirals which are then all tangled up with one another (figure 5.3). Though an admittedly simplisitic image, it is nonetheless helpful in showing how energy, through movement, can create matter, and how energy becomes mass. The two directions of the spirals, clock-wise and counterclockwise, echo the polarities present elsewhere in nature, such as the most basic one of negative and positive charge. The image also helps us better understand several rather abstruse quantum concepts, such as the fact that a particle's rotation is intrinsic to the particle itself – in other words, a particle's movement is its essence, and structures its very existence.

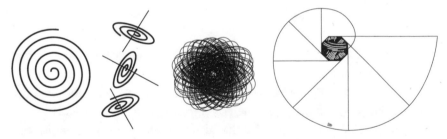

Figure 5.3 A continuous spiral vortex results in a 'spool' of matter

These recent discoveries that matter is motion, energetic activity, confirm what the ancient Chinese sages already knew, and what we our-selves can intuit from the evidence of our own eyes when we perceive a current of water or an ocean wave as being simultaneously in motion and stationary. What we're seeing is that matter and motion are one and the same.

Chaos theory teaches us that when a stationary wave motion encounters an obstacle – the rock in the middle of the stream from our earlier example – a type of wave motion is generated that is at once constant yet which has a new and unpredictable character from each moment to the next. Hiding behind the appearance of stability is variety and change.

Similarly, this aspect of the movement of water lies at the origin of the constant yet unrepeatable forms of living things. It is creative movement that forms water, that gives it direction and compels it to be in a given place; it is movement that informs the strange attractors into which the fractals of life are inscribed.

In a universe dominated by vortical motion and constant change, physicists have identified numerous mathematical constants. And there is also a permanent axis, a constant directional vector that governs that change. The motion of the universe, then, obeys rigorous rules. Permanence is part of change.

The space and time of material reality were created through movement. But what generated that movement in the first place? Certain scientific theories that we'll look at later on posit an unknowable dimension of the universe, such as Bohm's holomovement or the morphic fields of biologist Rupert Sheldrake. This is a territory, however, that science is not capable of exploring fully, and is closer to the religious and spiritual traditions that attribute the creation and purpose of reality to a god or cosmic consciousness.

Evolution by Leaps

When a drop of water detaches itself from a surface, it narrows and elongates into a cylindrical sleeve, at the extremity of which a new spherical droplet is formed (figure 5.4) which then separates entirely. While this is happening, the surface of the sleeve develops tiny waves that move toward the point of origin and transform into spherules. This cylinder also detaches, forming a new, smaller sphere at the bottom and further undulatory movement along the remainder, which recall the forms of Mandelbrot's fractal (figure 5.5).

This is a frighteningly complex event, one that for years no one dared to study. In 1994, Jens Eggers and Todd F Dupont succeeded for the first time, using computer simulations, to establish the mathematical equations relative to the formation and behaviour of a falling water drop. However, we still have absolutely no idea as to why its dynamics should be so complex.[15]

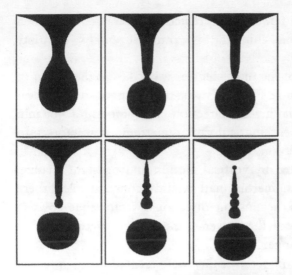

Figure 5.4 A falling drop of water

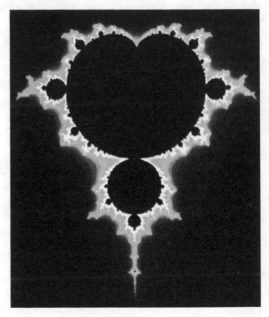

Figure 5.5 A Mandelbrot fractal

The form of the drop depends on the viscosity of the fluid. A team at the University of Chicago headed by X D Shi discovered that the greater the viscosity, the more numerous the spherules that are formed by the sleeve;[16] indeed, their number would increase infinitely were it not for the limits of the atomic structure of matter. In other words, a 'simple' drop evolves and reproduces by creating a fractal – yet another example of infinity within the finite, of infinity within water.

Researchers have realized that water-flows spontaneously change form. Analogously, many structural changes that occur in nature do so not gradually, but by leaping from one state of symmetry to another. Water and nature alike tend to proceed by leaps. Let us look at some examples.

In 1888, French scientist Maurice Couette, wishing to study the flow of water, invented the cylinder that bears his name – essentially a tube containing a liquid, inside which spins a concentric tube of smaller diameter. This device allows one to visualize the layers of liquid in contact with plumbing surfaces, aerodynamic surfaces, the atmosphere, and so forth. If the internal cylinder is rotated at a constant velocity, the uniform flow of the liquid between the two cylinders does not present any pattern at all: it is pure symmetry. As such, our eye cannot perceive it, since it is trained to detect only the imperfect symmetries that give rise to chaotic turbulence.

Something does begin to appear, however, if the two cylinders are rotated at different speeds (figure 5 6) In 1923 the English mathematician Geoffrey I Taylor discovered that if the speed of the internal cylinder is increased, flow is no longer uniform, but interspersed by layers of liquid in which regular and repetitive vortices are generated. This behaviour, called Couette flow, is a partial breaking of the symmetry in the vertical translations, such that from nothing, as if by magic, spiral forms appear. If the speed is increased further, there is progressive symmetry breaking, and unstable wavy vortices are formed; faster still, and Taylor vortices begin to appear, the most turbulent of all.

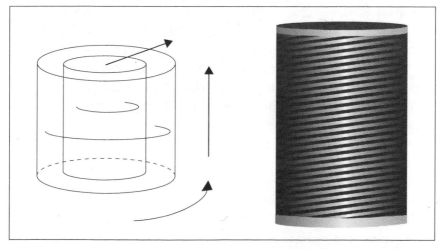

Figure 5.6 The Couette cylinder – Radial direction; Axial direction; Angle of azimuth

When the two cylinders are rotated in opposite directions, a helicoid spiral is formed. A spiral is a breaking of the symmetry of a linear movement. It is a screw motion that rotates around and translates along an axis, creating a new symmetry. Once again, *complexity is born of the simplicity of water*. Movement generates *ex nihilo* new aquatic and fractalic forms.

We find these same kinds of sudden and unpredictable changes at the subatomic level. When electrons are provided with energy, they jump from outer orbits to lower ones, emitting a photon. This wouldn't be all that extraordinary if it weren't for the fact that the amount of time required to make the jump has been measured to be zero – that is, it happens instantaneously, with no intermediate stages.

Another process involving sudden leaps can be seen in the behaviour of dissipative structures studied by the chemist Prigogine (see Chapter 4). In the Belousov-Zhabotinsky reaction we witness an incessant interposing of one symmetrical form with another. The same symmetry breaking appears on a computer monitor when the most minute change in the mathematical parameters of a fractal transform it suddenly into another one entirely.

From the chaos of water comes the order of life. Order does not emerge gradually, but through a series of leaps from one state of symmetry to a more complex one, as if the latter were created from nothing. Nature is rife with examples of this process, jumping from one ordered symmetrical state to another without ever achieving a definitive equilibrium. In effect, the evolution of life on our planet has imitated the radical state changes characteristic of fluids, making new species appear not as gradually as once was thought, but suddenly.

According to the Neo-Darwinists, natural selection is not the result of a plan intrinsic to nature, but of a blind system governed by chaos. Genetic mutations occur randomly, with the 'good' mutations being those which – again randomly – just happen to be best suited to the environmental conditions of the organism. It is difficult, however, to explain the emergence of life and intelligence as a consequence of random chemical reactions. Our universe is too young (just 14 billion years) for such an improbable sequence of events to have already occurred.

British astronomer Sir Fred Hoyle (1915–2001) observed that the probability of a single-cell organism creating itself from a random aggregation of chemical substances is the same as the probability of a tornado passing through a junkyard and building a 747 jumbo jet: it is, to put it simply, statistically impossible. For Hoyle, the universe is governed by what he called an 'intelligent network'.

It is, at the very least, curious that life should have appeared on the Earth so soon after the cooling of its crust and the subsequent formation of water some 4.5 billion years ago. Random chance fails to explain how over the course of the next few million years so many complex and diverse forms of life developed. It has been calculated that, if random molecular combination were the only driving force, the creation of just a simple bacterium would require more time than the universe is likely to exist,[17] compared to which the 14 billion years it has thus far existed are but a drop in an ocean of time.

Neo-Darwinian theory is hardly exhaustive. We still don't know what induces the DNA double helix to create cellular systems at a given moment, following constant growth patterns and expressing traits that have been lying dormant in the genetic makeup of a given species for millions of years.

We are simply unable to explain the enigma of the emergence of certain biological forms and behaviours that seem to have no adaptive purpose. For example, the feet of the more than 500 species of tree frogs are equipped with suction pads at the end of each digit which allow them to climb, hang and leap from branch to branch. And yet all the species of land frogs, whose ancestors never lived in trees, also have suction pads that serve no purpose at all. It is a pre-adaptive trait, as if nature had supplied these creatures with something useful for dealing with trees in the eventuality that it might become necessary for their survival.

Biologist Lyall Watson writes:

Unintelligent selection can only produce random and unintelligent results. But if the system itself has an inherent form, and encourages developments which are appropriate to that form, then fitness for a species or a new mutation begins to mean something more than a slight statistical shift in the odds on its survival.[18]

The potential of human memory has no adaptive value, but has turned out after the fact to be adaptive. The mnemonic and calculational capacities of early *Homo sapiens* vastly outstretched his needs. Yet the brain of a modern-day actor, capable of memorizing hundreds of pages of text, is identical to that of the humans who lived 200,000 years ago, who had no such demands placed on their mnemonic ability. As the

English writer Arthur Koestler pointed out, the brain poses 'the paradox of a gift one did not ask for'.

The battle between Neo-Darwinists, who explain evolution through random errors in the replication of DNA and those who interpret it instead as a process governed by complexity or by an intelligent network intrinsic to nature is still in full swing, and no one can yet lay claim to having solved the problem definitively.

Vortices and Spirals in Nature

*In nature there is nothing outside of force and movement
and everything tends towards equilibrium.*

LEONARDO DA VINCI

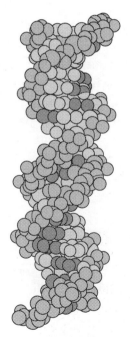

Figure 5.7 The DNA spiral

The spiral is ubiquitous in the universe. The smallest subatomic particles never move in a straight line, but follow elliptical orbits and parabolic curves. At the opposite end of the scale, galaxies like our own Milky Way tend to organize themselves into spiral forms. At both the microcosmic and macrocosmic levels, the universe is vortical. It is no coincidence that the mathematical symbol for infinity is a twisted loop, a self-perpetuating closed curve that is conceptually not unlike the *ouroborus* of ancient Egypt and Greece, the serpent that swallows its own tail, representing the continuous cycle of death and rebirth.

The forces present in the universe favour a helical motion, and the life on our planet developed along the spiraliform lines that can be found in all plant and animal structures (figure 5.8). The vortex we see when draining a bathtub reproduces the analogous structures of DNA, of cyclones, of magnetic force fields and galaxies.

As soon as children have mastered walking, usually between the ages of two and three, they love to play at twirling themselves around till they lose their balance in an instinctive quest to achieve an altered mental state similar to that sought by Sufi mystics and dervishes. It is almost as though human beings are instinctively drawn to the same spinning motion and spiral structures characteristic of the water from whence we come.

Why does nature prefer the spiral, that assemblage of curves which vary in size but never in its modular, self-similar, infinitely shrinkable and/or expandable form?

Over the course of evolution, water has left curvilinear and spiral signs not only on the Earth itself, but both in and on our bodies – the spiraliform meshwork of the osseal trabeculae (i.e. the structural tissue of the spongy part of bone), the sinuous lines of muscle fibre, the whorls of fingertips, the helical twist of DNA, the loopy tangle of chromosomes, even the serpentine movement of spermatozoa.

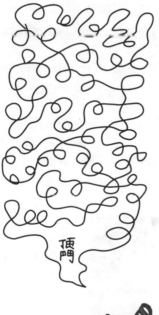

Figure 5.8
LEFT Ancient Taoist ideogram of the yin-yang spiral;

BELOW the spiral structure of proteins

In 1917 the English biologist D'Arcy W Thompson (1860–1948) published his monumental *On Growth and Form* (revised by the author in 1942), considered a milestone of modern biology. With rare erudition, Thompson describes the process of growth throughout nature, in all its variables and constants, using the instruments and principles of mathematics, physics and chemistry of his time.

Thompson examined the way that cells tend to organize themselves into precise and repetitive geometric forms, starting from simple organisms such as jellyfish and anemones which, not insignificantly, have forms similar to those created by water turbulence. He concludes that there exist forces that drive the overall growth of living creatures that originate in the alchemical recipe of water, salts and nutrients.

Thompson is an originator of what is known as *transformation theory*, which holds that species do not evolve through a steady sequence of small changes, but through large-scale transformations that involve the entire organism. As such, it is one of the first theories in the field of biology that could be called holistic: evolution is seen as occurring by leaps – as we've discussed in relation to both nature and human society – involving the system in its entirety, whether organic or social.

The spiral curves found in the most ancient aquatic creatures such as molluscs are the most recurrent forms in nature. The distinguishing feature of these curves is that each is larger (or smaller) than its predecessor by a constant exponential factor (figure 5.9). This formula

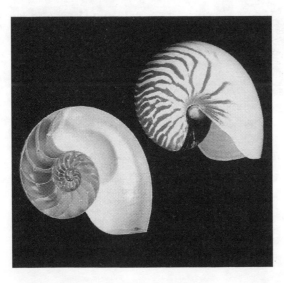

Figure 5.9 The *Nautilus pompilius* is an example of a logarithmic spiral in nature

applies in the same way to the disposition of seeds in a sunflower as to the distribution of stars in a spiral galaxy, each following the same precise mathematical coordinates.

D'Arcy W Thompson studied the growth rates of animal structures, specifically their proportions, correlating them in terms of evolution. What he found was that there are only slight parametric variations between the helicoidal forms of mollusc shells and the curved carapaces of the crustacean subphylum. From this, Thompson deduced for the first time that small variations in one aspect of an organism lead to major transformations of the creature as a whole. This is the same concept upon which chaos theory is founded.

Fibonacci, *Phi* and the Mathematics of Growth

> *To see a world in a grain of sand,*
> *and a heaven in a wild flower,*
> *hold infinity in the palm of your hand,*
> *and eternity in an hour.*
>
> **WILLIAM BLAKE** (1757–1827), *Auguries of Innocence*

Just as pi defines the circumference of all circles, so does another mathematical constant govern the spirals present in nature. Leonardo Fibonacci (1175–1240) was the most illustrious European mathematician of the Middle Ages. Born in Pisa, where he absorbed the Pythagorean and Euclidean traditions of Greek mathematics, he moved to Morocco to study the Arab tradition. Fibonacci is best known for having discovered the linear numerical sequence starting with 1 that bears his name, wherein each successive number is determined by the sum of the two that immediately precede it, as follows:

$$1, 1, 2, 3, 5, 8, 13, 21, 34, 55, 89, 144, 233\ldots$$

The result of the fractions formed by dividing each number by its predecessor (1, 2/1, 3/2, 5/3, 8/5, 13/8...) is a number that tends to grow closer and closer to a constant known as the golden ratio, or phi, whose value is approximately 1.6180339887.

1/1 = 1.000000	55/34 = 1.617978
2/1 = 2.000000	89/55 = 1.618182
3/2 = 1.500000	144/89 = 1.617978
5/3 = 1.666666	233/144 = 1.618056
8/5 = 1.600000	377/233 = 1.618026
13/8 = 1.625000	610/377 = 1.618037
21/13 = 1.615385	987/610 = 1.618033
34/21 = 1.619048	...

Like pi, the golden ratio is an irrational number whose decimal progression continues infinitely. It is an extraordinary number that has intrigued generations of mathematicians and artists.

The golden ratio, once known as the divine proportion, is found throughout the universe at every level – from crystals to black holes, from the reproductive rhythms of rabbits and bees to the spirals that define a pineapple husk.

Organic elements tend to assemble in groups of 3, 5, 8, 13 and so on, following the Fibonacci sequence – flower petals, leaves, conifer cone scales, the spotting of animal hides. Nearly all of nature's spirals tend to grow and multiply in accordance with the Fibonacci sequence or in proportion to the golden ratio. Fibonacci numbers also insinuate themselves, not surprisingly, in the helicoid spirals of DNA. It is also significant that the logarithmic spiral expressed by the ratio 1:1.618034, the only one that extends into infinity, also defines the fractals most commonly found in nature.

Figure 5.10 The Fibonacci sequence related to a human hand

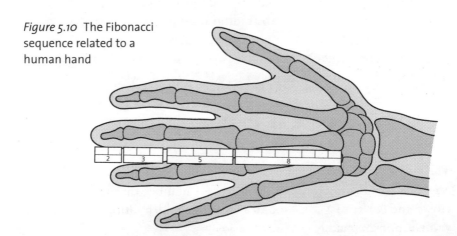

The golden ratio was discovered by Pythagoras (c569–500 BC) and his followers. In 300 BC the Greek mathematician Euclid of Alexandria explained the number in terms of a line divided into two unequal segments (figure 5.11), whereby the ratio of the larger segment to the whole is equal to the ratio of the smaller to the larger segment (a+b)/a=a/b), or to put it another way, a bisected line expresses the divine proportion when the ratio of the lengths of AC to CB is equal to the ratio of AB to AC, where AB is the total length.

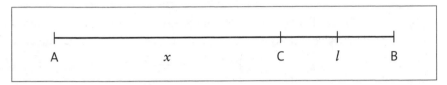

Figure 5.11 Euclid's Golden Ratio

Another fascinating aspect of this number can be seen in the golden rectangle, which is formed when the ratio of base to height is phi:1. If we inscribe a 1x1 square within this rectangle, the remaining rectangle is also 'golden', and so on into infinity. Even more amazing, this progressive subsecting forms the same infinite logarithmic spiral, omnipresent in nature, whose value is expressed by phi (figure 5.12).

Kepler (1571–1630) considered the Fibonacci sequence to be a mathematical symbol of creation and generation. In his treatise, *De nive sexangula* ('On Hexagonal Snow'), he explored the mathematics of hexagonal water crystals and found them to be governed, along with the ternary and pentametric symmetries of flowers, by Fibonacci numbers.

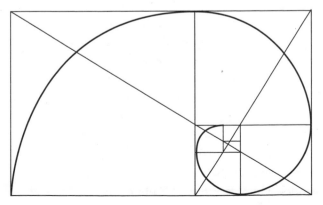

Figure 5.12
The Golden Spiral inscribed within the Golden Rectangle

The dodecahedron, a geometric solid with 12 pentagonal faces, is closely connected with the golden ratio. Each pentagonal face can be divided into three groups of four, which form a golden rectangle. Similarly, the vertices of the 12 triangular faces of an isocahedron create three golden rectangles.

It is thus with mathematical rigour that nature organizes the repetitive sequences, fractals and infinite spirals we find everywhere, including in the behaviour of water. The golden ratio is the foundation of nature's proportions and symmetries. Mathematics ceased being an abstraction with the discovery of 'orders of infinity' and the application of nonlinear equations to chaos theory. As the Pythagoreans and Kabbalists intuited thousands of years ago, mathematics and infinity are written into the very fabric of the universe, as confirmed by the ubiquitous presence of the golden ratio at every level of existence.

The Fibonacci sequence has also been used throughout history by painters, sculptors, architects and musicians, oftentimes without even intending to. From the builders of the Parthenon to Leonardo and Albrecht Dürer, from the Cubists and Futurists to Le Corbusier and Salvador Dalí, the golden ratio has served as the code for unlocking the secret of universal harmony.

Piero della Francesca, in addition to being one of the greatest painters of the Renaissance, was also an accomplished mathematician, to the extent that a treatise of his was incorporated by Luca Pacioli into his seminal *De divina proportione* (1509), a study of the golden ratio illustrated by none other than Leonardo da Vinci.

Debussy appears to have understood the profound connection between water and the golden ratio, as witnessed by the fact that the rhythms and intervals of his water-inspired works – the piano sonatas *Reflets dans l'eau* ('Reflections in the Water') and *Jardins sous la pluie* ('Gardens in the Rain') and the symphony *La mer* ('The Sea') – are structured by the Fibonacci sequence. On a piano keyboard we find the Fibonacci numbers: eight white keys and five black keys.

The golden ratio is the most efficient pattern of growth and it is also the most beautiful. Creative thought moves spirally like water, like the space–time infrastructure that surrounds us. A spiral curves backward in order to move forward. It is never a straight line, nor is it a circle that repeats its form or experience, but a path that paradoxically turns back on itself to memorize and relive past experiences in new, more ample curves. As Oliver Wendell Holmes wrote, 'A mind, once stretched by a new idea, never regains its original dimensions'. The golden spiral is a 'virtuous circle' that illustrates the evolutionary principle of *reculer pour mieux sauter* – that is, in order to move ahead, one should first take a step back so as to get a better perspective on a given situation. The spiral widens *because* it recedes; its eternal return, always the same yet never repeated, is the same as its infinite expansion, like consciousness itself.

CHAPTER SIX

WATER AS A ROLE MODEL OF THE UNIVERSE

Western science is approaching a paradigm shift of new proportions, transforming our concepts of reality and of human nature. Overcoming the difference between ancient wisdom and modern science.

STANISLAV GROF, *The Holotropic Mind*

Modern physics studies the energetic states of matter, meaning that it essentially measures dynamic activities and sequences. Karl Popper, referring to the progressive rarefaction and acceleration of subatomic matter, noted that scientific materialism has ended up transcending itself. In quantum physics, the more one tries to confine a subatomic particle, the faster it moves, as if unrest were a condition of its basic nature. The flows, vibrations and rhythmic fluctuations of water help us understand the realities of submicroscopic matter and energy.

The particles of light that Einstein called 'quanta', today more commonly called photons, are the 'building blocks' of matter and energy, measuring between 10 and 100 million times smaller than the smallest atom. They are essentially vibrations that assume physical form, for at this level, energy and matter are in fact interchangeable.

Reality, for all practical purposes, is vibration, a vortical motion that coagulates into the appearance of concrete matter only to our extremely limited perceptual range. Quanta and superstrings, 'invisible' yet very powerful and very real, are analogous to the Chinese concept of Qi and its Indian cousin, *prana*. Matter is mobile, like a river; impalplable and elusive, like steam. It is, as we've seen, nomadic.

Like everything in nature, we ourselves are made up of vibrations and particles, and as such are instinctively driven to move around, to circulate in the world. A person attuned to his or her own basic nature tends to follow the vortical rhythm of matter – and water, refusing to adapt to imposed spatial limits, evolving past constrictive mental schema.

In 1927 the German physicist Werner Heisenberg (1901–76) formulated his famous 'uncertainty principle', which establishes precise limits for measuring the position of a given particle with respect to its motion. If we know the position of, say, an electron, it is impossible to determine its direction and velocity; conversely, if we know direction and velocity, we cannot determine position. In short, the more accurately we know one variable, the more uncertain the other becomes.

The uncertainty principle sent a shockwave through the scientific community of the period, which operated on the assumption articulated more than a century earlier by Pierre-Simon Laplace (1749–1827) that human intelligence is capable of understanding everything that happens in the universe. Heisenberg showed instead that it is impossible to precisely know the speed, direction *and* position of the basic constituents of reality. As a result, the very foundations of physics had to be rethought, and with them its language, such that scientists began thinking and talking in terms of such elusive and uncertain entities as 'quantum waves of probability'.

Our sensory apparatuses enable us to see the world only as an amalgam of static material objects. In this, we are essentially victims of an illusion that physicists unmasked long ago. In particle physics, neither the present, much less the future can be known. Particles, like water and like human intelligence, are quantum objects with uncertain boundaries and possible behaviours.

The uncertainty of scientists with regard to the nature of quanta is not due to their ignorance, but to the intrinsic nature of quanta themselves. Einstein, contradicting the mathematical evidence of quantum theory, insisted that the universe is governed by strictly deterministic laws. An experiment conducted in 1982 by Alain Aspect and his team resulted in one of the most remarkable discoveries of the 20th century, and proved Einstein definitively wrong: two particles that have at some point interacted with one another will remain interconnected *independently of the distance separating them*. This property is known as *non-locality*.

Bell's theorem states that all objects in the universe are interrelated and mutually influence one another in a non-local way. This seemingly odd theorem has actually been demonstrated: a proton changes state, thereby influencing its corresponding antiproton, which can be located on the opposite end of the universe.

Quantum theory also asserts that subatomic particles do not act in a reciprocally independent way to form a whole, as classical physics would have it, but are instead influenced by the whole – that is, by the totality of the field in which they operate, which is to say the entire universe. The quantum view of the universe has a notable affinity with the holistic, modular view, and as such is in many ways close to Oriental thought: every part contains within itself a complete representation of the whole. In this, the universe is, like a fractal or hologram, infinitely divisible – or, more poetically, like an orchestra, where the meaning and relevance of the melody played by a single instrument resides entirely in its relation to what all the other instruments are playing; to the composition as a whole.

Perhaps some of the otherwise inexplicable properties of water might be explained by non-local events that we simply don't yet know how to see.

The Holographic Universe

Nature uses only the longest threads to weave her patterns, so each small piece of her fabric reveals the organization of the entire tapestry.

RICHARD FEYNMAN

Science's new paradigms often lean on the analogy of water in order to explain how matter and energy move and transform, from the vibration of a quark to the expansion of the universe. At the subatomic level, reality continuously changes state, with the masses of an atom's nucleus dissipating and reconstituting themselves at speeds approaching that of light. It is difficult, to say the least, to comprehend such notions. One of the best ways to understand the wave behaviour of subatomic particles is to study the dynamics of water.

Nobel Prize-winning physicist David Bohm (1917–94) of the University of London, one of the fathers of quantum physics and Einstein's collaborator, developed a theory based on recent discoveries in quantum physics wherein he compared the universe to a giant hologram.

Some physicists have come to see this as more than a mere comparison, and that the universe is in fact a hologram on a cosmic scale. In describing his holographic model and its implications, Bohm often availed himself of aquatic and marine metaphors.

Holography is an advanced photographic process whereby a special plate is exposed to a coherent light source (laser beam) to produce a three-dimensional image, or hologram (figure 6.1). The laser beam is divided in two by a semi-reflective mirror called a beamsplitter, which sends half toward the object to be photographed (illumination beam), while the other half is angled off a mirror directly to the plate (reference beam). Combined with the light reflected by the object itself (object beam), the overlapping, or 'interference' between the various light sources is recorded on the plate. When that plate is then illuminated by a beam of the same wavelength that created it, a hologram is produced. Those who have seen a hologram exhibition know that the resulting illusion of a 3-D object is breathtaking.

According to the holographic model of the universe proposed by Bohm, we perceive three-dimensional reality in much the same way, in that the overlapping of light quanta from multiple sources is what underlies our optical experience.

And here's the amazing thing: if the holographic plate is smashed into a thousand fragments, it would be possible to reproduce the original image in its entirety from every single one of those fragments. This phenomenon challenges the very foundation of the 'part-whole' construct, insofar as the parts, in this case, are the same as the whole. The hologram is thus a very useful model for understanding the holistic and modular nature of the universe which, like the fractured hologram, is a sequence of microcosms contained within macrocosms, infinitely reproducible in either direction.

Bohm is to be credited with having sketched the first outlines of a holistic theory of physics in his book *Wholeness and the Implicate Order*. Our senses perceive only the three-dimensional image of the

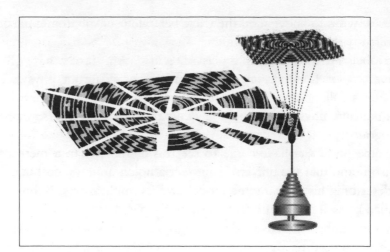

Figure 6.1 Every part of a holographic plate contains all the information of the whole, such that if it breaks, each fragment can reconstruct the entire image

hologram that is, for us, the world. But behind that there is a coherent and unitary dimension – like the light of the laser – that can recompose the entire universe from any one of its constituent parts.

In quantum reality, every point in space is the same, and no single point is separate from any other. Bohm insisted tenaciously on the non-local nature of quantum reality. He called the static and fragmented image of the world generated by our senses the 'explicate order', while the invisible matrix from whence it comes, inaccessible to our senses or to scientific instrumentation (which in the end is inevitably modelled on our senses), is the 'implicate order'.

According to Bohm, the vast reality that lies beyond our senses is an undivided and coherent whole, implicate as opposed to manifest, a reality similar to the continous flow of water that he called the 'holo-movement'. This oceanic process, constant and incessant, is 'enfolded' in the phenomenal world of events and objects, where generally accepted spatiotemporal relations no longer hold any meaning, for, like a hologram, each part contains, indeed is the whole. By extension, every element of the explicate, or 'unfolded' order that we are able to perceive contains all the information of the implicate order.

In a reality governed by Bohm's holomovement, the meaning of each part, regardless of scale, lies in its relation to the larger whole, exactly in the way that the activity of a cell or the organ of which it is part has meaning only in relation to the organism in its entirety, which in turn is utterly meaningless if not in relation to its environment, and so on. The distinction between organic and inorganic matter, or between consciousness and matter, are mere abstractions, since all are part of the inexorable flow of the holomovement.

For Bohm, the tangible reality of our daily lives is not an illusion of which we must divest ourselves, but the curtain that we must pull back to discover the hidden forces that feed it. In the Vedic tradition, the Sanskrit word *maya* (literally 'that which is not') indicates the boundaries of the world generated by our physical senses – or better, the illusion that what we perceive is all there is.

The Vedantic philosophical system teaches that the world does not have an independent existence, and water seems the best model for explaining not only the world we *can* see, but also the world hidden by the veil of maya, the reality that lies behind our illusions. A simple wave, cresting with foam, is a visible expression of a complex of forces that we still do not understand.

The holomovement model elegantly integrates the discoveries of modern physics with the ancient texts of the Vedas and of Taoism, and the mystical traditions of many religions, which unanimously affirm that we are part of a whole that is at the same time entirely contained within us. 'All that the Holy One created in the world He created in man.' (Talmud, Avot de Rabbi Nathan 31)

Everyday material reality – explicate, unfolded, manifest – can only be analysed through mathematical abstractions and probability projections; every measurement, every scientific model, every rational deduction is by definition a creative act, an invention, for the implicate order – i.e. 'real reality' – is hidden. We can only access it through the interior experience of non-ordinary states of consciousness (e.g. mystical trances, meditation, hypnosis) that typically induce a sense of being part of a whole, of the flow of consciousness that is the holomovement.

To make his point clearer, Bohm described the relationship between twin subatomic particles with an aquatic metaphor. Let us imagine, he suggested, a fish in an aquarium, and that we've never seen a fish before, or a video camera. Now imagine viewing this fish by way of two cameras set up perpendicularly to one another, such that we see two images, a frontal view and a side view of the fish. It would seem like two separate, but interconnected creatures, for the movement of one would appear to provoke movement in the other, and vice versa. Since we are unaware of the hidden reality of the aquarium, we would assume there is some sort of communication between the two creatures, without necessarily grasping the fact that they are simply two aspects of a single, indivisible entity.

Bohm explains that this is what happens in the world of particles as a consequence of the paradoxes of quantum physics. Until recently, only the variables of quantum mechanics were considered non-local. With the advent of chaos theory, non-local events began cropping up in biology, medicine and psychology, suggesting that the holographic model is applicable to every field. More and more scientists are coming to view the universe as a totality immersed in the space–time continuum. And though the average person may not have their knowledge or sophisticated instruments, we too can sense, by contemplating the aquatic world in which we ourselves are immersed, the dynamic indivisibility of reality.

The Holographic Brain

... our relations with friends and kinsfolk are in no sense permanent, save in appearance, but are as eternally fluid as the sea itself.

MARCEL PROUST (1871–1922)

The holographic paradigm was also used by Karl Pribram, a neurophysiologist from Stanford University, who likened the cerebral cortex to a holographic device. Pribram was a student of Karl Lashley (1890–1958), the renowned neuropsychologist who discovered that the cerebral circuits responsible for fixing memory activate, to varying degree, the entire cortex. This activation generates interference between the neurons distributed throughout the cortex, creating the holograms that make up our thoughts.

Pribram observed that synapses generate slow wave potentials even in the absence of a nerve impulse, and hypothesized that the parallel development of these potentials causes the activation, continuous but of variable intensity, of the whole brain, as if it were an assembly of holographic plates.

Water helps us understand the holographic behaviour of the brain. Neuronal activity is similar to the flow of a watercourse: just as the stones of a stream bed create turbulences and constantly alter the aspect of the current, so the perceptual data that reaches the brain provokes the fluctuations in neuronal activity and interferences that generate cerebral holograms.

In psychology, literature and the arts, consciousness is often compared to water because of its intrinsic property of uninterrupted flow. Indeed, our thoughts tend to form and dissipate in much the same way as aquatic ripples, waves and vortices.

Our memory creates mental holograms that behave for the most part like stable vortices, though sometimes they surge and become difficult to control or eliminate. Ideas, fears and prejudices catalyse the normal flow of consciousness and cause mental blocks that can thwart our mental growth. We are all part of a single cosmic river, and each of us an amalgam of vortices, unique and differentiated yet inextricably interconnected.

The Swiss psychologist Carl Gustav Jung (1875–1961), working with Nobel Prize-winning physicist Wolfgang Pauli (1900–58), studied the phenomenon of *synchronicity*: the connections between events and/or between the minds of separate individuals in the same instant, even at a distance. Synchronic events are those we often perceive as extraordinary or meaningful coincidences, or whims of fate: the familiar experience of meeting someone precisely in the moment we're thinking about them, the feeling of being connected to distant events, *dejà vu*, premonitions that come true seconds later, or simply being in the right place at the right time. According to physicist F David Peat, synchronicities are access portals, fissures in the fabric of the implicate order.

The psychiatrist Stanislav Grof has drawn inspiration from the holographic theories of Bohm and Pribram to create a theoretical framework for his holistic psychotherapeutic techniques such as holonomic integration, which involves the inducement of non-ordinary states of consciousness through hyperventilation, musical stimulation and massage. Holonomic integration, as the name suggests, involves every part of the organism in the treatment of psychoemotive imbalances, enabling patients to transcend their own spatiotemporal boundaries and access experiences from their most distant past, expanding their perception of the self beyond the confines of the body.

Other types of holistic therapy, such as transcendental meditation, *qigong*, yoga and acupuncture not only stimulate organ and somatic functions, but provoke low-frequency electromagnetic waves in the cerebral cortex, fully visible on an EEG, which activate the holographic functions of the brain.

String Theory: the Foam of the Cosmos

When it comes to atoms, language can be used only as in poetry.
The poet, too, is not nearly so concerned with describing facts as with creating images.

NIELS BOHR (1885–1962), winner of the 1922 Nobel Prize for Physics

Physicists and mathematicians are feverishly scrambling to build a unified field theory that would explain how the universe works. String theory is an important step in that direction.

Physicists recognize four basic forces in the universe: gravitational, electromagnetic, strong and weak force. The particles that govern them are the graviton, the boson and the gluon.

The basic principles of the gravitational force have been known since Newton's apple; we now know that it is generated by the curvature of space–time, meaning that any body having mass tends to curve the space around itself, thereby attracting bodies of lower mass. It was Einstein's general theory of relativity that first introduced the idea that space responds to the presence of accelerating masses by curving around them. The form of space, then, varies according to the objects present. Physicist John Wheeler put it most succinctly: 'Mass grips space by telling it how to curve, space grips mass by telling it how to move.' The Chinese thinkers who built the Theory of Five Movements also understood that space and time were indivisible, and considered space to be curved.

The electromagnetic force is what makes televisions and computers and mobile phones work; it is the power behind a lightning bolt and it flows copiously through our bodies, causing our neurons to fire and our hearts to beat.

The strong and weak forces act at the subatomic level, and as such are nuclear forces. The strong force binds quarks, protons and neutrons, while the weak force is responsible for beta decay, which manifests itself as radioactivity.

Physics has identified numerous basic particles: electrons, quarks, the massless neutrino, and the ephemeral particles created by high-energy collisions such as antiparticles, muons, muon-neutrinos and tau-neutrinos. But for many years now, some of the greatest minds in physics (Heisenberg, Pauli, Dirac, Feynman) have been suggesting that the most basic components of the universe are not particles, but rather something like a 'spray'.

According to string theory, if we examine these particles we find that they are in fact clusters of fine, one-dimensional elastic strings (figure 6.2) that form bows and loops. The differences between the particles depend on the differences in their vibratory resonance. The length of one such string would be about a hundred billion billionths of an atomic nucleus. Strings have been theorized as having open, closed, bow and loop forms.

The ripples that form on the surface of water are the closest thing we have in the visible world to these strings. We might imagine them as filaments that twist like the foam of a wavecrest, which at the ultramicroscopic level would be a quantum foam where space is heavily distorted.

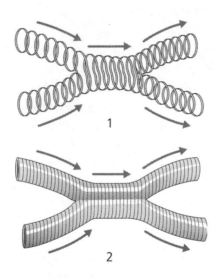

Figure 6.2 Two strings colliding to form a 'bow'

Superstring theory is one of the best candidates for eventually becoming the 'Theory of Everything', the holy grail of theoretical physics. It represents the as yet unrealized possibility of bringing together all the physical laws that govern reality, whereby everything from the tiniest particles to the most massive stars, from the Big Bang to the swirl of the galaxies to the four basic forces would be demonstrable through the same equations and physical principles.

It is essentially a problem of finding a definitive mathematical description that would reconcile two incompatible 'truths': general relativity, which governs the stars and galaxies, and quantum mechanics, which deals with the realm of atoms and molecules. If it turns out to be possible, it would be quite reassuring, for it would give us a coherent and comprehensible universe, the whole of which would derive from string entities which, by combining with themselves in different ways and vibrating at different resonances, would account for the whole of existence and all its apparent variety.

So we can see how modern science, like ancient Chinese science, is moving ever closer to a universe that can be likened to a cosmic ocean, moved by different but harmonious waves and currents, the basic constituent of which is the identical, everywhere. To paraphrase a Taoist saying, 'The two, the three, the ten thousand beings all derive from the One.'

Beyond the Four Dimensions

Edward Witten is a sort of modern-day Einstein. A pioneer of string theory, he is considered one of the greatest contemporary physicists. In 1995 his work sparked what is known as the 'Second Superstring Revolution', an ambitious attempt to unify all five of the string models proposed to date.

A fundamental property of the string theory is supersymmetry, a mathematical principle that combines the vibratory sequences of strings in pairs known as 'super partners', which are differentiated from one another by a half rotation. The existence of super partners may (or may not) be demonstrated sometime around 2010, when Geneva's nuclear research facility, CERN, will have finished building the enormous accelerator known as the Large Hadron Collider.

Witten called this revised and corrected consolidation of existing string theories 'M', which postulates the existence of fully 11 dimensions (10 spatial, 1 temporal). The actual significance of the 'm' of M-theory is a subject of debate among physicists – mystery, 'mother theory', membrane, matrix? No one knows, and Witten is not very forthcoming with explanations.

As chance would have it, the letter 'm' is closely connected to water, insofar as it is considered by a number of mystical traditions to be the primordial sound produced by the universe, as we'll see in Chapter 17.

The first scientist to suggest that the universe has more than three dimensions was the Polish mathematician, Theodor Kaluza, in 1919. In 1925, Swedish mathematician Oskar Klein posited the existence of a fourth, specifically circular dimension. Kaluza and Klein both maintained that in every point of every dimension there is a circular 'extradimension', not unlike a magnifying glass that reveals the dramatic relief and complexity of a woven carpet which, from a distance, appears flat. Its existence is, at this point, purely theoretical, inasmuch as it would not be verifiable with existing maths or technology.

The more we penetrate the subatomic realm, magnifying the details of the fabric of reality, the more we realize that there exists an added dimension. It's like looking at the ocean from an aeroplane: at high altitude, the surface appears flat, while at low altitude we realize that it is in fact rippling with waves which, if we get even closer, are themselves made up of smaller waves and foamy crests. Our grasp of reality depends entirely on the point from which we observe it.

Kaluza figured out that the added dimension corresponded to the mathematical equations that Maxwell had used for the theory of electromagnetism, and was thus able to unify, for the first time, Einstein's theory of gravitation and Maxwell's theory of light. Gravitation and electromagnetism are like undulations in the same spatial fabric. But whereas gravitation is transported by ripples that form in the three standard dimensions, electromagnetism rides on the ripples of the new, curved dimension.

Fifty years later, string theory managed to resolve the incompatibility between quantum theory and general relativity through the discovery of several additional dimensions – fully ten in space, and one in time. In these 11 dimensions, curved and entangled together, ultramicroscopic strings oscillate and vibrate like so many tiny waves on the enormous and apparently flat surface of the ocean.

The three dimensions familiar to us are not actually as familiar as we might think. Rather than planes or lines, they are like great cosmic bedsheets all rolled up, curving into themselves to reach to opposite side of the universe. Travelling through these dimensions, strings alter their vibrations, exactly as the form of a wave varies according to the geography of the sea floor.

To better visualize these wrapped dimensions, physicists use six-dimensional geometric figures called Calabi-Yau forms, named for the two mathematicians that developed them. Figure 6.3 is a representation – though approximate at best, given that it is two-dimensional – of a Calabi-Yau form.

According to string theory, all objects in space, human beings included, move in all ten dimensions and not just in the three we're able to perceive. They are so small that we can completely circumnavigate them without even realizing it. Everything in the cosmos is the product of hidden vibratory resonances that enwrap each other and flow together in a wavy motion similar to that of water. This scenario should sound familiar at this point, in that it shares many analogies with Bohm's notion of holomovement.

Multidimensional strings wiggle through our world, rolling up into tiny and complex forms, constantly transforming and repairing themselves as a result of cuts and tears in their space. It is a world not unlike the ever changing surface of the sea, wrinkled by vortical waves that fold back into themselves in bursts of foam in a continuous, regularly repeating movement that tends toward symmetry and is paradoxally coherent yet never the same.

According to M-theory, the interior of a multidimensional Calabi-Yau form contains spheres on which three-dimensional membranes are 'spread'; these spheres can collapse to form miniature black holes. The membranes serve as a protection against such a collapse, which could irreversibly swallow everything that comes within its event horizon, just like an intergalactic black hole.

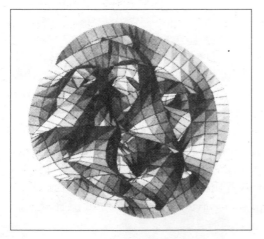

Figure 6.3 Representation of a six-dimensional Calabi-Yau form

Subatomic black holes are even more disconcerting than their more famous cosmic counterparts, for they are without mass. The vibratory sequences of strings, also without mass, would become transmutations of the black hole generated by tears in space, from which would emerge new Calabi-Yau forms.

The largest and smallest objects in the universe – black holes and elementary particles – are not all that different from one another. Indeed, some physicists consider the former to be essentially gigantic elementary particles, yet another instance of the microcosm reproducing the macrocosm. Physicists Andrew Strominger and Brian Greene, along with American mathematician David Morrison, have compared the connection between black holes and elementary particles to the phase transitions of water:

> there is a tight mathematical and physical analogy between such phase transitions and the space-tearing conifold transitions from one Calabi-Yau shape to another. Again just as someone who has never before encountered liquid water or solid ice would not immediately recognize that they are two phases of the same underlying substance, physicists had not realized previously that the kinds of black holes we were studying and elementary particles are actually two phases of the same underlying stringy material. Whereas the surrounding temperature determines the phase in which water will exists, the topological form – the shape of the extra Calabi-Yau dimensions – determines whether certain physical configurations within string theory appear as black holes or elementary particles.[19]

In many ways the physics described by string theory mirrors the physics of holography. And in fact, some of the world's best physicists are working on an attempt at integration that might be the prologue to a third superstring revolution. English mathematician Roger Penrose has proposed a model of space he calls twistor space, in which the strings are complex curved manifolds ('Riemann surfaces') existing in the four standard space–time dimensions. In 2007 Garrett Lisi proposed a unification model alternative or complementary to string theory. Through computer simulations Lisi analysed a complex eight-dimensional mathematical pattern with 248 points; for example, he found that a *hexagonal* pattern predicts the relationships between particles and forces (figure 6.5).

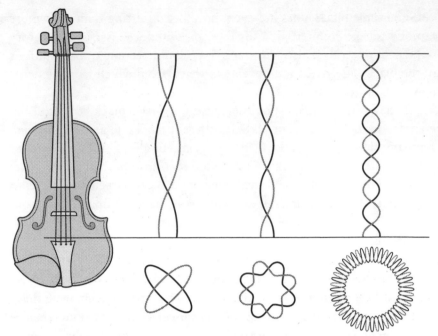

Figure 6.4 Strings and vortices of a violin

As we've seen, chaos theory and quantum mechanics reveal non-local connections at the visible and invisible levels, demonstrating that everything is interconnected and intercommunicating, beyond space and time.

Scientists use the Greek letter psi (Ψ) to indicate psychic phenomena that could be called 'paranormal' such as extrasensory perception, telepathy, precognition, clairvoyance and psychokinesis. For decades now these phenomena have been the subject of proper scientific research, and in some cases their existence has been confirmed with truly astonishing results. For more on this subject, see the work of psychologist Dean Radin of the University of Nevada, the Koestler Parapsychology Unit of the University of Edinburgh, and the experiments we touched upon in Chapter 5 conducted by biologist Rupert Sheldrake.

Among the more intriguing results is that telepathy has been shown to occur independently of electromagnetic phenomena. Subjects are able to obtain information about objects at significant distances and even enclosed in rooms insulated against electromagnetic waves with lead and copper. Our consciousness moves on paths still unknown to us,

Figure 6.5 A hexagonal pattern (also a basic fractal of the water molecule) predicts the relationship between quarks (triangles) and gluons (circles).

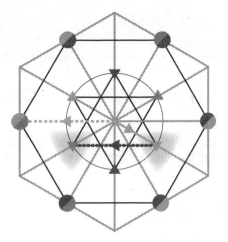

and once again water, with its order and chaos, its simplicity and complexity, can help us understand nature's imponderables. When we fully understand the implications of chaos theory and string theory, we will be able to understand non-local psi phenomena, which continue to remain a mystery.

Journalist Tiziano Terzani, in his book *A Fortune Teller Told Me*, recounts an exchange of views during a dinner in Ulan Bator with an American meteorologist, who made the following rather bold claim:

> "It's already possible to forecast the weather of the next three days with 99 per cent accuracy. The last big step will be to understand chaos theory. At that point, we will be able to do exact long-term forecasting, up to two or three years", he said.
>
> "Still, if it's possible to forecast the weather, why isn't it possible to forecast one's future? We are also made of air, water, clouds, dreams… and depressions," I went on. The meteorologist was convinced that he was talking with a deranged person and perhaps, from his point of view, he wasn't that wrong.[20]

But the American weatherman has failed to grasp an important point. Chaos theory destroyed Laplace's certainty that everything in science is predictive and determined. Meteorologists cannot predict climatic events with exactitude, for the same reason that even the most predictable of human beings is and always will be, however imperceptibly, free and therefore unpredictable.

CHAPTER SEVEN

THE SENSITIVE CHAOS OF WATER

Water flows and streams on the earth as ceaselessly as the stream of time itself. It is the fundamental melody that forever accompanies life in all its variations.

THEODOR SCHWENK

In 1960 the engineer Theodor Schwenk founded at Herrischried, in the heart of Germany's Black Forest, the Institute for Flow Studies, which he then directed for many years. He invented specific photographic techniques to determine and analyse the flows of water, interpreting his data according the theories of the Austrian philosopher Rudolf Steiner (1861–1925).

Years later, the same forms that he had pointed out with his equipment appeared as fractals on the computers of scientists who studied chaos: spiral forms, bell and rose-diamond forms (figure 7.1). The institute in Herrischried has been conducting experiments on water flows for more than 40 years: in the laboratory, in organic structures, in rivers and in man-made water delivery systems. Among Schwenk's different techniques for visualizing water flow were the injection of more viscous liquids like glycerine and the aspersion of fine powders like that from the plant lycopodium.

Schwenk regarded water as a vital and creative element. In 1961 he published a book that anticipated chaos theory, suggestively titled *Sensitive Chaos*, in which he gathered the first data of his researches.

'Sensitive chaos' is an expression taken from the *Fragments* of the German poet Novalis (1772–1801), who defined water as 'sensitive', ready to respond to and create harmony. According to Jacques Cousteau, who wrote the preface, that book was the first phenomeno-logical study on water.

As we have seen in Chapter 1's analysis of the phenomenon of super-ficial tension, water molecule clusters tend to assume the form of a sphere, maintaining a unitary organic structure: the water sphere mirrors the image of the entire cosmos, the microcosm *par excellence*.

When the directional forces of the water sphere combine with gravity, they create an intrinsic spiraliform movement. Schwenk probed the spiraliform behaviour of water in riverbeds: it is a backwash move-ment that mixes the turbulences of the stream. The spirals of vapour rising from a cup of hot coffee or tea look like the laminar, corkscrew flows responsible for the erosion on the bottoms and banks of rivers.

Schwenk confirmed some of Schauberger's observations: water heated by the sun is less dense and forms more whirls than water that flows in the shade. Even in artificial conduits like pipes, or in the rectilinear banks of cement aqueducts water always tends 'to realize itself', to curve rhythmically, fighting whatever prevents it from follow-ing its natural course.

When we hit a billiard ball, it rolls along a predictable line. On the contrary, if we stimulate water with a linear push, it ripples in a myriad of shapes (figure 7.1b). Its transformational drive acts on rocks too: water slowly abrades, grinds and crumbles them into mineral and organic compounds, essential for enriching the soil and nourishing plants; it is a destructive force that water itself controls, building banks around itself.

At the water line, water lifts the sand off the bottom in combs and ridges that responsively affect the coming flow of water: a reciprocal interaction that transforms both of them. We can easily see the power of water movements when we water a garden or wash a car with a hose: if it slips out of our hands, water pressure causes it to flip and fly wildly about, whipping and wriggling suddenly and unpredictably, like a snake gone mad. This is flowing water that transforms itself in a 'plastic animal'.

The blood vessels in the human body develop at the behest of the liquid that contains them. It is the same principle proposed by Schauberger: movement acts upon and builds matter. The heart, formed

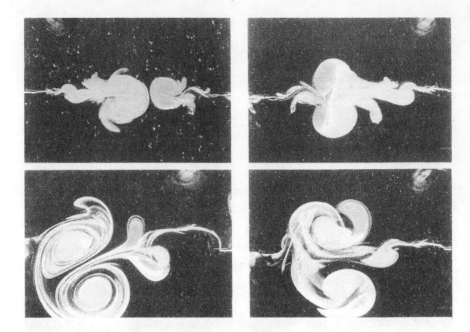

Figure 7.1
ABOVE a) Fractal turbulences produced by the encounter of two liquids;

LEFT b) fractal whirling forms created while moving a stick on the surface of a liquid strewn with powder

by muscle fibres with a spiral design, receives and expels blood: it doesn't pump blood, but *is pumped* by the blood flow.

During the development of the foetus (figure 7.2), the muscle fibres grow along an interwoven spiral, following the movements of the blood, its rhythmical contraction and expansion. Subsequently, the specialized electrical tissue of the heart will govern that rhythm. Every creature passes through an embryonic liquid phase before forming itself into shapes.

Organic tissues assume the shape of the liquid that flows around and within them. It happens in the winding peristaltic intestines, in the twisted renal tubules that filter the body and in the bones: even though they are the most solid part of the body, they undergo a complete cellular turnover in just a few years. We find the same convoluted spirals printed on the barks, venations and trunks of trees and plants, and in the spiral movements of many unicellular organisms.

With its different flows, water directs the formative processes of organisms, distributing energy for their growth. Inside an egg, Schwenk reminds us, the formation of the embryo is supported by the wavy contractions of the amnios that 'massage' and mould the contents of the egg. Here again is the concept of the form born of movement, present also in mystical writings.

The kabbalistic text *Sefer Yetzirah* ('The Book of Formation'), whose paternity dates back to Abraham, father of the three monotheistic religions, describes step by step the divine creation of the world. Creation happened through the 'vocal', vibratory emission of the letters of the Hebrew alphabet and their interaction. The information produced by the emission of letters and words caused the cosmos to emerge: thus, 'In the beginning, there was the Word.'

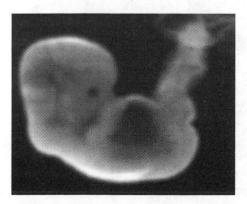

Figure 7.2 The embryo is the materialization of liquid turbulences

In the same way, the first material objects and afterwards the shapes of aquatic organisms were sketched along the molecular vibration of water and its flows: from those that create vortices and waves with their whole body like the jellyfish and the snake, to those that move by way of cilia and fins. The earliest life forms show signs of spiral movements. As an embryo, the human being spends his/her first nine months of life exposed to these directional forces, then following birth tends to 'solidify' more and more. Just as the river creates its own banks in order to limit itself, so the body solidifies to limit an otherwise destructive, explosive vitality. Old age is accompanied by the drying up of the body which, by losing water, exhausts its vitality.

The waves of the sea draw shapes in the sand with harmonious, creative and elegant patterns. The sea's edge is the border zone between two elements: water and earth. Rhythmic waves and streams interact with earth, combining to give life to constant but always new forms.

Water is like a sense organ: it 'feels' whatever force or substance interferes with it and reacts accordingly. When a straight jet of another liquid is injected into it, it forms a bell whose contour curves outward, then back in to create twin rings of spiral motion (figure 7.3), which eventually destabilize and assume star-shaped outlines. We find these

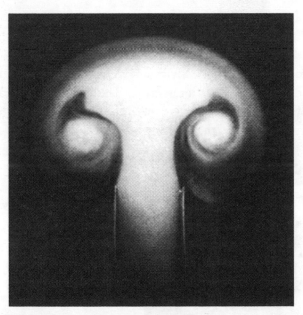

Figure 7.3 A jet of liquid in another liquid naturally creates a symmetrical pair of whirling rings

patterns of fractal forms in aquatic animals such as starfish, morays, snakes and shellfish (figure 7.4).

The biologist D'Arcy W Thompson, discussed in Chapter 5, correlated the ripples and sprays produced by a drop on a liquid to the archetypal forms of sea animals like jellyfish and anemones. In fact, the jellyfish are an accurate reproduction of water turbulences: a pattern of forms springs out of an impulse and movements always derive from unstable forms.

A falling water drop creates a series of emblematic fractals. The impact of the drop makes a hemispherical crater in which the drop expands. The water that is cleared away gives rise around the edge of the crater to a wavy ring and a crown, while inside water flows back from every direction towards the centre of the crater. Here, sufficient force is released to generate a vertical column of water, splitting into suspended droplets which, one by one, will fall and form under the bottom of the crater vortices and whirling rings (figure 7.5).

a   b

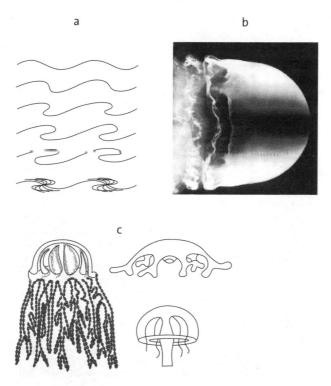

c

Figure 7.4 a) Spirals of water at the water line;
b) a liquid turbulence; c) forms of marine creatures

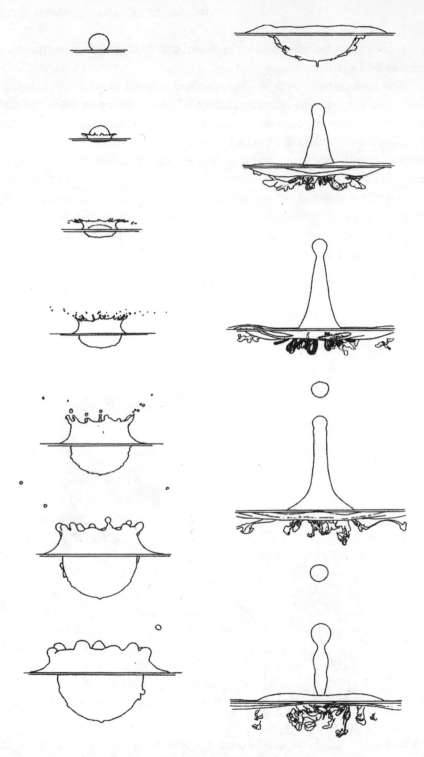

Figure 7.5 Sequence of a falling drop in a liquid, magnified 1.4X

This sequence of the falling drop is also a model of the transformations we experience in our growth to maturity. We would do well to face every exterior and interior problem of our lives like a water drop, diving in, immersing ourselves, getting deeply involved, prepared to recognize and accept the motives behind our wounds and traumas and, by extension, our responsibilities.

Only then can we inscribe a 'crater' inside and outside of us, a wound, an empty space to be filled: the crater means that our actions will leave a concrete trace in reality. From this crater a new force will spring to the top like a crown and will lift us up with it. We will form a new multi-dimensional identity (the suspended droplets at the top) and with our unique and unrepeatable contribution we will overcome gravity. Then we will be ready to fall again, differently this time, leaving further traces, integrating ourselves in the spiritual sea of humanity.

Waves: the Sensitive Boundary

Waves move to different harbours
Through the immense sea of being,
And each with its given instinct that carries it away.

DANTE ALIGHIERI, *The Divine Comedy*, Paradise (1, 112)

It is at the boundaries between fluid surfaces that water shows its greatest sensitivity: the interactions between forces and currents materialize new forms.

The fertilized ovule gives life to an embryo that immediately swells out and folds in on itself. Some cells migrate through a cavity toward the inside in a process called gastrulation. We don't know why it happens. It is not a random process: it happens at a bifurcation point of instability, perhaps guided by chemical instructions or by DNA.

Later on, the various foetal organs are formed by a swelling and folding process, analogous to gastrulation. A multitude of currents, niches and gorges compose the complex structure of an embryo. The replicating cells create folds in their membranes, bending and folding before they split (figure 7.6).

It is very interesting that, from its beginning and during each cell replication inside the embryo, an empty space is created all the time.

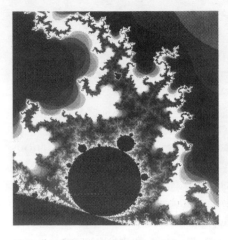

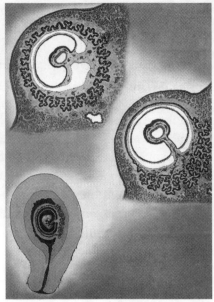

Figure 7.6 ABOVE a) The Mandelbrot set;

RIGHT b) between the empty spaces of the amnios, the first embryonic cells are formed

That empty space is the necessary premise for every development and replication. It is as if nature is hinting that this is the only way to be vital and creative, that we ought to establish a 'border zone', a boundary between ourselves and that which is not ourselves, creating an empty space. In other words, if we want to create something new, we must empty out part of ourselves.

Silence is a sonic void, the precondition for listening and learning, just as the spatial void in a cell or the figurative void in our hearts shows us that, in order to grow, we must fill our gaps and mend our failings. It is the key to freedom and creativity in all aspects of life: travel to the limits of our world and beyond, be ready to give, to renounce something in order to evolve.

Let's go back to the embryo. Gastrulation, the folding process called invagination formed inside the embryonic blastula, is a deviation from the spherical symmetry of the early embryo and is a consequence of the intrinsic instability of ordered organic systems. Instability gives rise to symmetrical and more complex patterns: the embryo is a 'dissipative structure'.

We still find bends and folds, clefts and fissures in the adult body: the lines of the fingertips and toes, the niches of the serous membranes that contain the organs, the crevices that separate the cerebral convolutions, the hidden channels of the acupuncture meridians. Like a hologram, water imprints the three-dimensional image of its own movements onto matter.

Schwenk defined water as nature's 'most impressionable vehicle', sensitive even to the most imperceptible stimulus. It is no accident that water can be heated more easily at body temperature (37 °C): at this same temperature water is most sensitive and atomically 'malleable'. This phenomenon also applies to air as well, which contains water vapour.

A swarm of insects, Schwenk observed, with the cumulative flapping of its wings, creates wave trains that 'sensitize' the air, such that even the slightest sound, like a handclap, is enough to cause the entire swarm to react coherently, as if it were a single being touched by an invisible object. A swarm is an example of a superorganism, made of many individuals who all respond as one. The same thing happens with migratory birds, where the collective motion of wings reproduces the vectorial wave produced in the air by the individual leading the group. On a larger scale, referring back to the Gaia hypothesis, the Earth itself can be seen as an aggregate of interdependent chaotic phenomena contained within a giant superorganism that is sensitive to the tiniest change.

Whether flowing over a river bed or through a pipe, water shows a laminar flux: the water layers at the centre of the current move faster than those closer to the edges. Turbulences appear if there is a big difference in the flow momentum between the banks and the centre; when the difference increases, vortices and whorls form more easily.

Vortices and whorls appear at the boundary between two elements, such as when there is a difference in density between the carriers of the flow. Vortices are also easily formed between two different surfaces in contact with water: for instance, between a moving surface and one at rest, as in Couette's cylinder (see Chapter 5); or between a solid surface and water, or where water flows over small obstacles, like pebbles and stones.

The junction layers between different flowing currents are sensitive zones. They respond to external stimuli by contracting, expanding or creating rhythmical waves. Water is a sense organ, able to react to everything, changing its behaviour accordingly; its aim is to move, so it exploits the empty spaces within and between flows and bounding materials. The secret of the emergence of complexity, information and intelligence is kept in the hydrogen bridges (the intermolecular 'empty spaces') and the border zones between water and that-which-is-not-water.

Water and living creatures constitute a whole which moves in synchrony with itself. Consider that the rhythm of respiration has a fixed rapport with the rhythm of circulation: about 72 heartbeats for every 18 breaths, a ratio of 1:4. The same relationship exists between water waves and air waves: sound moves four times faster in water than in the air.

When a breeze blows over the sea, waves are formed, which Schwenk considered a third element in and of itself, created by the interaction of air and water. On the meeting surface of these two elements, the wave undergoes changes and assumes new forms: it is creative. It bends, curves and folds upon itself, forming empty spaces in the foam, air temporarily trapped by water which, when released, dissolves as vapour in spiral trails.

In 2005 Sidney Nagel, Lei Xu and Wendy Zhang of the Department of Physics at the University of Chicago tried to see if a water drop striking a flat surface produces a splash even in the absence of air. The result surprised them: without air there is no splash. On the Moon, therefore, water poured from a cup would not rebound. New liquid forms are generated only if water meets air: it is feng shui again.

The huge void in which electrons travel around the atomic nucleus is the territory where solid and finite matter is built. The border zones between fluids, between the full and the empty, between different elements or different areas of flux, are the places where life is formed. The creation of empty space, through the folding and bending of aqueous matter, is essential to create living systems.

The encounter between two different media creates a vortex: for example, between a slow element and a fast one, between a solid and a liquid, between a liquid and a gas. And the list goes on: between a hot element and a cold one, a dense element and a rarefied one, a heavy element and a light one (like salt and fresh water), between a viscous element and a fluid one, between an alkaline element and an acidic one.

The flourishing of living forms in these borderline areas recalls the way Qi – energy – springs from the meeting and merging of the two opposites, yin and yang. The yin-yang diagram is a whirling symbol of the formation of matter. The two entities of different 'density' (yin and yang) mix together to create phenomena and events. At every point of the diagram it is possible to reproduce the whole, just like a hologram.

Man is a microcosm of heaven, earth and water. The human brain, superior to that of the other apes, probably started to increase in size millions of years ago in Africa, in a 'borderline' geographical area, an ecosystem at the boundary between dry land, waterways and the sea. When it comes in contact with diversity (of elements, density or content), borderline water becomes sensitive, and from its vortices new forms arise. Schwenk writes: 'Wherever the first differentiations are present the water acts as a delicate "sense organ" which as it were perceives the differentiations and then in a rhythmical process causes them to even out and to merge.'[21]

Diversity springs from complexity: diversity in vegetal and animal species, amongst human beings and cultures, gives the natural world and humanity the possibility to create and to evolve. In nature as in society, order is destroyed when diversity is lost.

Over the years, the scientific research of the Herrischried Institute, led by Andreas Wilkens, Michael Jacobi and Wolfram Schwenk, made rapid progress. This research involved photographing and analysing the forms generated by single drops of water falling into a container full of liquid and glycerine: this method, invented by Theodor Schwenck, is called *Tropfbild* (or 'drop image').

The drops create complex harmonic turbulences, which differ according to the origin of the water. The most pure and vital water forms articulate ripples and vortices, whose shapes vary according to the substances dissolved therein, the material of the pipes through which it is transported, the water-bearing stratum or the stream where it originates. Contaminated water, by contrast, generates simpler and less symmetrical forms (figures 7.7 and 7.8).

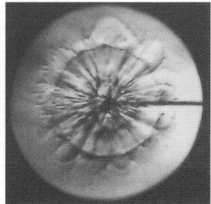

Figure 7.7 LEFT a) Spring water from the Giura River, pure and hard; RIGHT b) drinkable stratum water, enriched with filtered river water (*Tropfbild* method)

It has been noticed that a polluted stream can usually depurate itself just few kilometres beyond the polluting source, and is able recover its original biological features. Thanks to this process of self-depuration, the previously destroyed flora and fauna reappear in the stream, and the water's *Tropfbild* regain in harmony and complexity.

 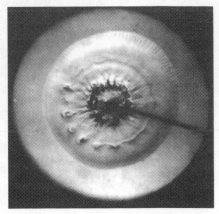

Figure 7.8 LEFT a) Water sample drawn upstream of a wastewater discharge; RIGHT b) water drawn downstream from the industrial emissions in a river (*Tropfbild* method)

Water as a Sense Organ

We always find spiral structures close to or inside the sense organs of animals. Take, for example, the inner ear or the cartilaginous turbinate of the nose. Animal horns often branch spirally from the nasal and ocular area and are an extension of sense organs. The most sensitive tactile zones of the body are the fingertips, where water left its imprint of swirling whorls, just like the rounded ridges of sand we see in shallow sea water.

It is intriguing that it is precisely the fingertips that are used to identify people, separate them out from others, confirming the fact that every person is a unique and unrepeatable expression of our whirling, watery world.

Everything begins with water. Crystallizing, it gives rise to an unstable border zone with ramifications and indentations. These are the fractals we see in snowflakes and along the edges of a falling droplet. Because water is sensitive to change, the unstable and asymmetrical balance of these borderlines stimulates the emergence of life forms, from the simplest to the most complex. It is not a coincidence that the ocean areas most abounding with fish are those on the boundary between different currents.

In the depths of the oceans there are enormous vents. Very hot water and minerals erupt from these underwater volcanoes: it is supposed that the first forms of life developed in such places. In 1999 Japanese researchers led by Koichiro Matsuno of the Nagaoka University of Technology reconstructed in the laboratory a model of these vents.[22] Their study showed that, by introducing the amino acid glycine into an overheated and pressurized room (200 atm.), this amino acid would aggregate into peptides (the so-called 'building blocks' of organic matter). With a certain amount of copper in the water, chosen because there are large quantities of it near ocean vents, these peptides became even longer. Therefore, life could well have sprung out of borderline zones, like the ocean vents, where a thermal gradient is present.

The surface of the water that scientists and poets equate with skin, is in fact like a sense organ, a layer of skin that is the most sensitive part of water. Though extremely thin, it is tough as steel: just look at the size of the ships it can support. In our bodies, the cellular membrane is a similar 'skin', a borderline between cells, where all the most important physiological and energetic exchanges occur.

Thought as Repetition and Innovation

Chinese medicine associates the health of the inner ear with the activity of the Kidney, the organ whose corresponding Movement is Water. Just as water is sensitive to the slightest stimulation from the air (e.g. the rippling of a water surface in response to even a whisper of wind), so is the inner ear supremely sensitive to sounds carried through air. It also serves the essential function of maintaining our sense of balance and enables us to judge spatial depth and the acceleration of our body. The cartilage of the external ear is structured spirally. The inner ear or, more precisely, the cochlea (figure 7.9), is covered by a spiraliform bony structure suspended in liquid.

For Chinese medicine, the health of the brain (or Marrows) depends on the Kidney and on Water. The brain floats in the cephalo-rachidian liquid, which protects it partially from the force of gravity. With its twin hemispheric form and elaborate circumvolutions, it is water's creative masterpiece. The brain's cells, or neurons, are connected by dendrites which branch out like fractals, which are by definition always new, original and unpredictable. It is therefore natural to assume that the mind itself is likewise unique, original and never entirely predictable.

Learning and memory are cerebral activities founded on repetition and, more than reflection, on 're-flexion', in that thoughts renew themselves by continually flexing around themselves. In this sense, thought is just like a whirlpool of water, like a spiraliform strange attractor that turns on itself, ever expanding and ever new.

Healthy thought, whether of an individual or a culture, is founded on spiral repetition, which fosters the fixing of thought in ever more ample and evolved memories. Thought must renew itself, remain open to new interpretations, visions and variations. Otherwise it stagnates in tired, immobile schema, destined, like water that is not allowed to flow, to putrefy and die. Thought must be founded on the memory of past formulations, but at the same time it must be re-elaborated and distilled, for healthy thought is built in harmony with ineluctable change.

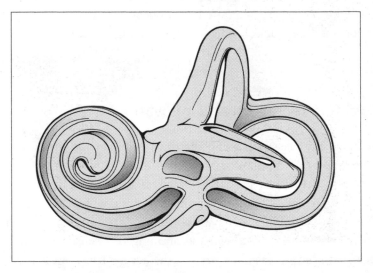

Figure 7.9 The cochlea

One of the ways human thought is expressed is through the larynx, which contains the vocal cords. These produce sound vibrations, transforming the air that leaves the mouth and nose into intelligible language. The larynx is a sensitive boundary zone, like the 'skin' of water. The encephalic trunk is the part of the brain stem that hosts a number of centres for the elaboration of vocal signals entering and leaving the larynx. In cross-section, the larynx and encephalic trunk are extraordinarily similar, like a jellyfish – they both have the indelible imprint that water has left on them over millions of years of evolution (figure 7.10).

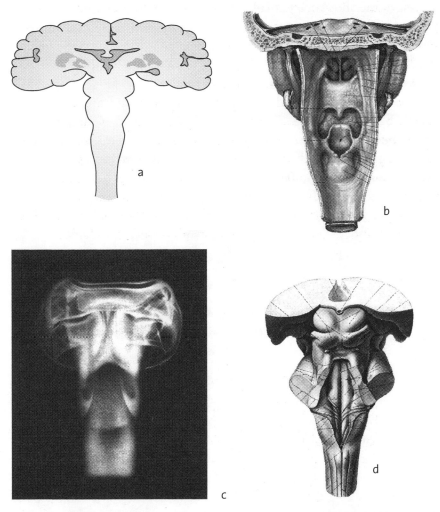

Figure 7.10 a) The jellyfish-like form of the brain in cross-section; b) the larynx; c) liquid turbulence; d) the encephalic trunk

The Bible recounts how God put a soul into the body of Adam by exhaling through his nostrils. From that moment, Adam was able to give names to things and creatures of the world. Adam is the first spiritual being precisely because he was endowed with creativity and and a larynx 'educated' by water to produce language.

Having a soul means being able to give a name to things, to identify and place them correctly with regard to their purpose and their moral value. Naming is producing intelligent language that is capable of distinguishing the functions and qualities of things.

In Chinese medicine, the Heart does more than just distribute blood. It has another fundamental role as the seat of *Shen*, the mental activity that coordinates and integrates the emotions as a whole. It is the supreme commander, the emperor of organs. Language is considered the highest expression of an individual's spirit, and the Heart is what regulates the articulate emission of words.

The Heart is associated with Fire in the Theory of the Five Movements, but it is essential that the Fire of the Heart be contained and disciplined by the Water of the Kidney, which governs the brain, or Marrows, as it's called. For this reason, the Chinese ideogram for the word 'thought' (*Si*) combines the image of a head and the symbol of the heart (figure 7.11).

Figure 7.11 The Chinese ideogram for 'thought'

The language we generate is the product of the Fire of the Heart's emotions and the rational analysis of the brain. The word is thus born of an encounter between Fire and Water, which are irreconcilable only in appearance. We've seen how, in both the realm of the spirit and the basic architecture of physical reality, opposites merge to become one, and the impossible becomes possible.

Native Hawaiians call water *wai*, and consider it the source of all energy. The expression *wai wai* means 'full of energy', while the word *pu'wai* signifies the heart, to be understood as a mass of water and densely concentrated energy.

All of us harbour a fire within us that we must learn how to manage. It is the fire of our passions and impulses, the force that drives us to always want more, to accumulate wealth and power, to experience ever more intense feelings, to achieve success and recognition. This fire, left to its own devices, would lead us only to alienation from the world and from ourselves. It is the fire of self-destruction, one that consumes itself, thereby exhausting our vital energy, which is, in fact, that very fire.

With sensitivity and wisdom, the Water governed by the Kidney can harness this Fire, contain it without extinguishing it, then conserve it for one's whole life in the *Ming Men* of the lower spine (*see* Chapter 12). This is not to say that water should serve to suppress our instincts, but rather to orient them, conduct them towards a constructive expression of lasting values. It is the secret of self-realization for a life that is not repressed, but disciplined, healthy, creative and rewarding.

Water, Moon, Tides

The water on our planet is subject to the influence of various extraterrestrial energy sources, foremost among which is the thermal energy of the Sun: it warms the air to generate the winds that move the waves, and heats the water, giving rise to the all-important ocean currents. There is also the gravitational pull of the Sun and Moon, which are responsible for the tides. These gravitational and electromagnetic forces also influence the liquids in our bodies.

American physicist Edward P Clancy defines the tides as 'the pulse of the Earth'. Like our heart, the Sun and Moon act as hydraulic pumps, stimulating the circulation of the Earth's waters. The force exerted on the tides by the Moon is almost equalled by that of the Sun, for water is also sensitive to the electromagnetic and gravitational influence of sunspots.

The Moon attracts the Earth's waters, causing the tide to rise in those places with which it is aligned, with a delay each day of 48 minutes. The complete cycle of lunar phases, from one full moon to the next, lasts 29.5 days. Twice during the cycle, at full moon and the beginning of the new moon, both Sun and Moon are aligned with the Earth, which causes higher tidal levels than usual, known as 'spring tides'. Twice a month, in the first and third lunar quarters, tidal levels are less dramatic, and these are known as 'neap tides'. Numerous animals, both aquatic and terrestrial, feel their direct influence.

Thanks to Schauberger's observations, we know that transporting logs on a river is more difficult during the new moon, for they tend to get tangled up along the banks. It is also interesting that the most durable lumber is that which is cut in the winter season during the full moon. Underground aquifers and artesian wells are also influenced by the lunar cycle, proving that tidal pull has a direct or indirect effect on all the water present on the Earth.

The cyclical influences of the Moon on living creatures obey the rhythms of the tides. In human beings, for example, the circulation of bodily fluids follows diurnal, semidiurnal and 14-day cycles. There is not a drop of water on Earth exempt from this rhythm, and the life of every marine plant and animal is measured out and governed by the tides.

Without the Moon, life on Earth would have been impossible. The Moon was formed five billion years ago from the detritus produced by the Earth's massive collision with a large celestial body. Four billion years ago, when life emerged on our planet, the lunar orbit was much closer to us than it is today, and the Earth's own rotation was much faster. Because of this, the Earth was washed by massive tides that penetrated hundreds of kilometres inland every few hours, which created dramatic fluctuations in the salinity of coastal regions.

According to the Scottish molecular biologist Richard Lathe, these fluctuations were a determining cause in the evolution of the first biomolecules and the subsequent appearance of life. The tides would have produced the necessary force to repeatedly join and then split the twin strands of early DNA-like molecules. Another expert, Graham Cairns-Smith, agrees that the environmental changes caused by the Moon may have been decisive, though he believes that the first self-replicating molecules were not RNA or DNA, but much simpler structures that arose from the crystallization of clay-based minerals.

Every aquatic creature is sensitive to the tides, from the oyster, which closes in response to high tide, to the convoluta worm, which emerges from the water with the rhythm of the tides to feed on algae. Astonishingly, these small, simple marine organisms evince the same behaviours in the laboratory, even if they've been transported far from the sea to another geographical area entirely, obeying the lunar rhythms of the new site they demonstrate that they are not influenced directly by the tides per se, but by the moon. 'Without a brain or what we could call a memory ... *Convoluta* continues to live out its life in this alien place, remembering, in every fibre of its small green, body, the tidal rhythm of the distant sea.'[23]

The moon is essential for the survival of fish and terrestrial animals such as insects, which synchronize their reproductive and egg-laying cycles with the Moon. Even in the simplest creatures, we find a close connection between the Moon, water and sexual activity. Many clinical and epidemiological studies have likewise demonstrated the sensitivity of the human body and psyche to the phases of the Moon.

Every civilization throughout history has associated the Moon with water, the menstrual cycle, procreation, ritual baths and ceremonial ablutions. The Chinese tradition holds that in ancient times, the natural cycle of menstruation always occurred during the full moon. In newborns the development of the brain, which Chinese medicine associates with water, is popularly thought to be facilitated after conceiving the child on a brightly moonlit night.

The Moon also determines variations in barometric pressure: it has been verified that the heaviest precipitations occur more frequently in the days following a full moon or a new moon.

Many years ago, Giorgio Piccardi (1895–1972), director of the Chemistry Institute of the University of Florence, tested his suspicion that water's basic chemical properties changed according the sequence of lunar months, which vary according to the equinoxes and the 11-year sunspot cycle.

Piccardi had in fact intuited yet another of water's bizarre aspects. Scientists naturally want their experiments to be as reliable (i.e. reproducible) as possible, but water often ends up undermining that. Chemical reactions in aqueous solutions can give variable outcomes, ranging from unpredictable and contrasting results to not occurring at all. Yet when the same solution is placed in a copper-lined container, the chemical reactions take place exactly as they theoretically should, always identical.

Piccardi and his team decided to do a simple test and repeat it three times a day for an extended period. They chose a very simple reaction – the precipitation of bismuth oxychloride, a quite common colloid, in distilled water. A colloid is a substance which, in water, exists in an intermediate state between the solute (ions) and a suspension (particles).

After ten years and 200,000 repetitions of the experiment, the Italian chemist discovered that the variations in the degree of precipitation were correlated over the long term with sunspot activity, and over the short term by fluctuations in the Earth's electromagnetic field. A copper container blocks these influences, and the reactions are stable.[24] These same results were confirmed by a research team at the University of Brussels and the Atmospheric Research Center in Colorado.[25] In addition to providing yet further proof that the water molecule is influenced by electromagnetic fields, Piccardi discovered that water activates in contact with dielectricity and piezoelectricity, which also induce changes in its basic chemical and physical properties. He proved scientifically another important fact that Schauberger had deduced empirically, which is that water's electrical conductivity varies in relation to temperature.

Piccardi's work paved the way for subsequent studies of water's 'memory' – that is, its capacity to change behaviour in response to chemical and physical stimulation.

Activated water, Piccardi said, is like a magnet, in that it can have different properties depending on the thermal, mechanical and magnetic stimuli to which it is subjected, on its 'history' and 'memory' or on its dynamization (homeopathic term for the degree of dilution and succussion of a given preparation). These phenomena are called '*hysteresis*'. Usually applied to magnetic materials, the term also describes water's ability to 'remember' the history of thermic, mechanical and magnetic events it has undergone – an ability that French immunologist Jacques Benveniste was first to postulate, and which has recently been confirmed by the research team headed by Italian chemist Vittorio Elia (*see* Chapter 19).

Water, Moon, Void

We've seen how cells in the replication phase create invaginations in their membranes, which tend to fold back and split much in the way of wave flows. Similarly, it is the empty space that a woman harbours within her body that enables her to create a new being.

In nature, the creative act requires the formation of an apposite void and a stimulus towards change, which come together in a border zone. This suspension between two diverse but contiguous elements provokes a 'leap' beyond the boundaries of either: the birth of something new, be it a replicated cell, an embryo or a spiritual insight. This jump from one state of equilibrium to another is literally a 'leap into the void'. It is a wager like the one constantly made by water, with its willingness to become something other than itself in order to serve a purpose, to sensitize and revitalize itself, to evolve. It is the key offered to us by water to understand the evolution of life, the path that all living things have travelled for billions of years in order to preserve and improve themselves.

We can learn more than that from water. By following its path, leaving a bit of emptiness around and within ourselves, we can extend and sharpen our sensitivity, transform ourselves like a stream of water into a single sense organ and thus expand the range of our abilities and our consciousness.

Nature's law that a creative event demands an empty space is one that applies to our inner life as well. There are moments of crisis that require us to exert ourselves creatively in order to overcome the profound sense of loneliness and frustration that every one of us experiences in varying degree and frequency. Loneliness, the feeling of being separate (and separated) from others, can manifest itself in many ways, from selfishness and arrogance to sadism and its opposite, submissiveness. Yet that very same sense of isolation and emptiness can be used to generate something positive. The frustrations and dissatisfactions we experience in our lives help us to understand that it's time to make a change. To paraphrase the cardinal principle of Alcoholics Anonymous, the only thing we can and must change is ourselves. No excuses, no alibis. Otherwise we are condemned to repeat our habitual, ineffective patterns.

> We shape clay to birth a vessel,
> yet it's the hollow within that makes it useful
>
> We chisel doors and windows to construct a room,
> yet it's the inner space that makes it livable
>
> Thus do we create what is
> to use what is not
>
> *Tao Te Ching*, Verse 11

The sense of emptiness and separation that sometimes insinuates itself between people who love each other can also offer space for creativity.

At certain times, in order to cultivate true intimacy, it may be necessary to pull back and wait, for intimacy is not just closeness, but distance as well, which allows both partners the time and space necessary for self-examination and personal evolution.

Every relationship needs to breathe, to expand and contract, to alternate between separateness and closeness. Parents, for example, need to establish a certain psychological distance from their children. They must understand that, in order to grow and learn to live with themselves and others, children need their own realm of intimacy, their own space, their own secrets.

Teaching is much the same, for in passing on knowledge, the pauses between lessons are as important as the lessons themselves, for they allow the student to absorb and process what's been taught and to then pass it on him- or herself with a new perspective.

Emptying oneself does not mean annulling oneself. Quite the contrary, it means giving space to the expression of all one's potential. It is not imploding into an absolute vacuum, but being aware that within us there is an absence that must be filled. When we have the feeling that something is missing, this is not to be feared, for it means we have room within ourselves for the birth of something else, something beautiful, like a foetus in a mother's womb. It is the equivalent of the artist's 'negative space', the jazz musician's 'afterbeat', the mystic's blissful 'emptiness'.

The Talmud – the nucleus of the ancient Jewish oral tradition, compiled in the 4th century to collect the laws, teachings, parables and debates passed down orally from the time of Moses – recounts the creation of the Sun and Moon (Hullin 60b), and informs us that the two stars were originally identical. The Moon protested that the existence of two equal stars implied that there was one too many. God agreed with the Moon and promptly made it smaller, allowing the Sun to reign during the day. He then compensated the Moon for this forced act of humility by conferring upon it absolute reign over the night, and by making it visible, though faint and small, even during the day.

In human terms, the Moon represents humility, 'making oneself small'. It is the symbol of the resizing of the ego, the shrinking of the Self so as to leave an empty interior space that can then be filled with our creativity. The emptiness and silence ruled by the Moon are the starting point in our quest to understand our destiny and embark on the path to realizing our identity.

The tides of our own biorhythms, governed by the Moon both day and night, help us to complete this creative undertaking with humility and discretion. It is the same creative task that is incessantly performed in the subatomic voids of water and that allows the seas and heavens to communicate. It is a rhythm that is renewed and revitalized every day, the motor behind the evolution of all things, of intelligence and consciousness.

Like the tides, our emotional relationships are subject to highs and lows. Moments of trust alternate with moments of disappointment, joy gives way to sadness, and intimacy to estrangement. It would be so regrettable to condemn ourselves to unhappiness, merely because we are unwilling to accept these alternations and reluctant to try to understand their meaning.

~~~~~

CHAPTER 8

WATER BY NUMBERS

God is a mathematician, and the universe is beginning to look like a big thought rather than a big machine.

<div align="right">

SIR JAMES JEANS, physicist (1877–1946)

</div>

Numbers do exist, and their existence, I believe, is independent of people. In another universe, one without people and without anything we recognize from our own universe, numbers will still exist.

<div align="right">

AMIR D ACZEL, mathematician

</div>

The Greek philosopher Pythagoras (500 BC) and his followers thought that water was 'the first of all things' and that the universe, in its essence, was made up of numbers. Not a bad idea, really, if we think about how important certain mathematical constants are in nature. Mathematics is a valuable tool used by science to explain the universe, and through it physics reveals the processes that underlie reality. With mathematics, scientists have been able to conceive and demonstrate otherwise absurd theories, like quantum mechanics.

Sages and mystics throughout history knew that everything could be understood through numbers, the study of which is called numerology: a set of doctrines that associate every aspect of reality with numbers. In the kabbalistic tradition, the universe was created through the computation of the Hebrew letters, each one corresponding to a numeral. Analogous techniques were devised by the Greeks and the Arabs. The arrangement of the letters in the text of the Torah (the biblical Five Books of Moses) is seen as a sort of code that reproduces the universe in all its spatiotemporal coordinates. In the Midrash, the rabbinic homiletic literature developed in the 4th century AD, it is written: 'The Holy One, Blessed Be He, looked into the Torah and created the world.' Letters, then, are essentially numerals and codes, fluctuating between the physical and the spiritual worlds.

Let's look at two in particular.

Number 6: The Formation of the Visible

Carbon is the fourth most abundant element in the universe and, after hydrogen and oxygen, the components of water, it is the third most important for sustaining life: more important than even nitrogen, which makes up most of the air we breathe. Like water, carbon loves company. It is the only element that can create extraordinarily long chains with both itself and almost all the other elements to form solutes. It has a tendency to bond with two favourite partners, hydrogen and oxygen, but it also gladly bonds with other larger and more complex molecules, including DNA, the most complex of all and the central data bank of life on Earth.

The diamond is the only precious stone to be made entirely of carbon and is the hardest substance in the world. Its hardness derives from the strength of the bonds between the carbon atoms, which also accounts for its seductive brilliance. If we look past the superficial factors of rarity and prestige, the real reason we are attracted to diamonds is the same reason we're attracted to water: we sense their essence, the synthesis between the tridimensional reality of carbon and the invisible life force of water that inhabits it.

It is perhaps worth noting that both diamonds and water are transparent, and that transparency symbolizes truth in all cultures.

The atomic number of carbon is 6. When radioactive beryllium (number 4 on the periodic table) absorbs a helium nucleus (atomic number 2), they form carbon (4 + 2 = 6). The ancient numerological traditions held the number 6 in great esteem, correlating it to the formative processes of matter.

Carbon is the basic building block of all living systems. And yet its formation depends on a fleeting reaction, which is theoretically highly improbable: beryllium has a half-life of just 0.000000000 00000001 seconds, meaning that a helium nucleus has only that infinitesimal amount of time to bond with it. Despite this tiny window of opportunity, carbon is the fourth most abundant element in the universe. And, significantly, it tops the charts as the most abundant element within the temperature range in which water exists in a liquid state – a rather felicitous arrangement, given that their interaction is necessary for the development of life.

We know that water starts to behave as a liquid when it assembles into clusters of six molecules. If we add one molecule of water to a cluster of five, its flat planar structure snaps into three dimensions, resembling more or less a puddle. If you want to get something wet, make sure you have at least six molecules of water.

The number 6 describes the physical dimension of things. The six directions (above, below, east, west, south, north) mark the boundaries of the three-dimensional network of reality. In astrophysics, there are six universal constants that govern the complexity of the cosmos: the N, epsilon, omega, lambda, q and D constants. The basic form of natural solids springs from the hexagon, which is of course a geometric manifestation of the number 6.

The number 6 also figures in the formation of the physical structures that issue from the encounter between water and carbon. It is interesting to note that in ancient Chinese cosmology there is the same association between the number 6, the Water Movement and the processes of construction and storage.

The mathematician Fejes Toth demonstrated that a hexagonal structure, with six corners and with six sides offers the most efficient way to pack the largest possible number of identical circles into the smallest possible area. This is why matter tends to assemble itself in hexagonal shapes: it is simply the most efficient way to occupy space.

When water clusters into solid forms, such as snowflakes, it shows us a fleeting visible symmetry in the form of a hexagon. The hexagonal crystals of snowflakes reproduce the primary structure of mineral crystals (figure 8.1).

Quartz was the first mineral to be called a 'crystal', and is one of the most abundant on Earth. The hexagonal shapes of quartz appear when silica and oxygen atoms aggregate in a stable lattice of about 60° at each

Figure 8.1 The hexagonal crystal of a snowflake

corner. In ancient times, quartz was called 'Holy Ice', as if to confirm a sort of Jungian intuition of the relation of water to solid matter.

A tendency toward hexagonal symmetry is also evident in the animal kingdom: certain species of fish in Lake Huron have been observed to divide their territory into almost perfect hexagonal areas, and bees famously build their hives in hexagonal cells. While it is true that octagonal or tetragonal crystals exist, they are composed of different elements.

Another curiosity: in the Hebrew language, six corresponds to the letter *vav* (figure 8.2), whose primary meaning is the conjunction 'and' – the very essence of the concept of connection. In a sentence, *vav* connects one word to another, the same way that carbon, atomic number 6, connects one element to another. Moreover, this letter can indicate a cause-and-effect relation. Another meaning of *vav*, echoed in its very shape, is 'hook', which suggests linking, connecting. *Vav* also means 'but' and 'or', words with are used to partition, compare and contrast disparate words and ideas.

In the Bible, six is the number of days of Creation, the unit of time in which an abstract idea manifested itself as physical matter. The first word in the Bible is *Bereshit*, composed of six Hebrew letters, which means 'in the beginning', or 'the genesis'. Pythagoras considered six the number of creation, and St Augustine (354–430)

Figure 8.2 The Hebrew letter *vav*

wrote in his seminal *City of God* that 'God created everything in six days because this number is perfect, and it would remain perfect, even if the work of the six days did not exist'.

Finally, the shape of *vav* recalls a pillar, strong and stable, like the 12 main pillars that according to tradition sustain physical reality. A solid cube has 12 edges and 12 diagonals; the number of constellations of the zodiac is, of course, 12.

In what is surely more than mere coincidence, the most ancient Chinese inscriptions known to us are pictograms that represent none other than the number 6 and the word 'divination' – clearly related to the earliest Chinese treatise on divination, philosophy, mathematics and natural science, the *Yi Jing*, better known in the West as the *I Ching*, The Book of Changes, compiled by the Emperor Wen towards the end of the Shang dynasty (1766–1121 BC).

In the *I Ching*, cosmic events are analysed through the detailed interpretation of 64 hexagrams. Each hexagram is composed of six lines in the binary code of a broken line (– – yin) or continuous line (—yang). Their sequence describes the different ways that yin and yang interact with each other and reveal themselves in nature (figure 8.3). In the Chinese tradition, six is the minimum number of lines we can use to

Figure 8.3 The 64 hexagrams derived from the 8 trigrams account for all possible spatiotemporal conditions and events

connect phenomena and express synthetically the manifold manifestations of the energetic events as determined by celestial influences. Hexagrams are symbols of actual spatiotemporal states.

In Chinese numerology, six is associated with the concept of becoming: the hexagrams allow us to predict the possible evolutions of phenomena at both the microcosmic and macrocosmic level. The *I Ching* advises us to look for that which is unchanging in that which changes; basically, it suggests that we look for the permanent laws of cosmos by studying nature's transformations, such as the flow of water.

The form of the number 6 designs a spiral: it is the numerical skeleton of the modular structure of the universe. On both the microcosmic and macrocosmic scale, energy flows along six different levels of depth with different proportions of yin and yang. A microcosm manifests and resonates in a macrocosm through the various combinations of the Six Energies and the Five Movements; the dodecahedron, the solid with 12 pentagonal faces ruled by the golden mean, is the geometrical synthesis of that.

In space, the 5 cardinal points (4 plus the observer) are subdivided into 12 (6 + 6) directions. In time, the Chinese sages measure out the year in 12 Terrestrial Branches with 10 Celestial Stems. The human microcosm has 12 acupuncture meridians of 5 different categories (major, distinct, collateral, tendon-muscular and cutaneous) and 12 articulations (shoulders, elbows, wrists, hips, knees and heels).

Number 7: The Realization of the Living

In the sapiential texts, six denotes the physical dimension of the object, while seven describes the authentic nature of an object, its purpose and its character.

In Hebrew, seven is represented by the letter *zain* (figure 8.4), which follows *vav* in the alphabet. *Zain* is a wavy letter, like a *vav* that folds itself into a spiral to become more fluid, as if transforming into water. With its sinuous shape and curved trajectory, *zain* is a sort of upgrade of the rectilinear, cause–effect link described by *vav*. Its form evokes a cyclical relationship, like a feedback circuit designed to manage information flow.

Zain is inscribed with the order of life formed from chaos, in an incessant exchange of energy and information. *Zain* follows *vav* in the alphabet because their sequence illustrates the spiral aquatic movement that carbon- and water-based living systems must follow in order for intelligence to become possible. By transforming the straight line of *vav* into the more flexible curve of *zain*, the material world becomes mobile, more 'elastic' and 'intelligent'. Graphically, *zain* represents the evolutionary stage following *vav* and the number 6, both of them symbols of the three-dimensional world made of the opposition or union of distinct objects and events. It turns the certainty of *vav* into a question mark, an emblem of the doubt and curiosity that stimulates the expansion of information and knowledge.

Figure 8.4
The Hebrew
letter *zain*

Zain is the letter associated with the evolution of knowledge and memory. When two *zain* are coupled, we obtain the word *zaz*, which in Hebrew means 'to move', 'to shift'. It is a double serpentine that holds the mystery of the transmission of information and the complexity of life. The two *zain* spirals are the graphic equivalent of the DNA double helix, the genetic memory of all creatures. The sinuosity of this letter also recalls the looped filaments of superstrings which, according to the theory of the same name, constitute the entirety of material existence.

The word *zain* can also mean 'instrument of war'. The shape of the letter is like a dagger: a weapon for distinguishing the just from the unjust in order to steer one's life in the right direction. It symbolizes the power to discern the good through one's own insight and conscience.

Another meaning of *zain* is 'penis', the reproductive organ that transfers the genetic information necessary for procreation and evolution, and not just in the biological sense. In Judaism, circumcision is the symbol of the rectification, or better the spiritualization of the sexual and reproductive act. Moreover, the word for circumcision (*milah*) also means 'word', such that we can also read circumcision as a challenge on the possibility that cultural and spiritual conditioning by speech deny the so-called 'selfish genes' their monopolistic sway over our instincts.

For Rabbi Shimshon R Hirsch (1808–88), six is the symbol of the physical and material universe, while seven embodies the creative freedom of the spiritual aspect of nature. Every physical object can be described through the six directions of space, whereas seven is the object's essence, its relation to the whole. Nature, symbolized by the six days required to create it, evolves under the influence of seven, the spiritual ideal of the seventh day. And beyond six and seven lie the creative synthesis and ideal harmony of the physical and the spiritual, represented by eight.

The highest qualities of the human being develop in the realm of seven. In temporal terms, the essence of the six days of the week is realized on the seventh day, the *shabbath*. According to tradition, at the age of 70, when we have completed 7 decades of life, we can achieve full maturity. The Bible recounts how, at the end of the six days of creation, God abstained from any further intervention on the seventh day. In the same way, we are asked to devote the seventh day to verifying what has been built in the previous six days, to enjoy the fruits of our activities with all our senses, intellect and emotions. The seventh day should be an opportunity to pause, to take stock of one's life and the world, to cultivate a harmony with the whole of creation. After the seventh day, a new cycle begins, hopefully better than the previous one.

Chinese culture also associates seven with procreation. It is the number that stands for the development of living creatures, particularly the splendidly integrated system of organic and emotional activities that is the human being.

According to Chinese tradition, an individual expresses seven fundamental emotions: joy, anger, anxiety, concentration, grief, fear and fright. Seven is the multiplier of the female biological cycles (at the ages of 7, 14, 49 years, etc); there are seven endocrine glands. When we include the two meridians along the medial line of the body that send energy to the brain and to the reproductive organs, the major meridians become 14. The Indian tradition identifies seven *chakras*, the energy centres situated on the frontal and medial lines of the body.

PART TWO

WATER AND HUMANKIND

~~~~~~~~~~~~

CHAPTER NINE

THE ORIGINS OF LIFE

Science without religion is lame, religion without science is blind.

ALBERT EINSTEIN

Water holds within itself the enigma of the origins and the evolution of life. It is the first and the most fundamental molecule that scholars of the natural sciences explore, and it is the first physical substance named in the Bible. Even before the advent of science, humans have always sensed that they are defined by water, as witnessed by the cosmological myths of the great civilizations, all of which agree that the universe, and life itself, originated from water.

In Indonesian mythology the supreme god Mahatala spread his ten fingers and posed them on the primordial ocean; from his fingers came some drops which created Djata, the divine virgin, from whom the cosmos then sprang forth. According to the Babylonians, before earth and sky there existed only a vast plain of water. In Greek mythology, Okeanos is the god that created the universe and the other gods. In the Hindu tradition water is identified with Prakriti, the eternal and primordial substance from whence the universe derives. Prakriti activates itself when the equilibrium between intelligence (*sattva*), dynamism (*rajas*) and inertia (*tamas*) is broken, allowing reality to reveal itself in the form of matter. Brahamanda, the primordial egg and source of all energy, is hatched on the surface of the primeval waters of Prakriti.

In the religious poem *Bhagavad Gita*, Krishna states, 'I am the taste of the living waters'. In the New Testament, God and the Virgin Mary are called 'fountain of living waters'. In the Koran it is written, 'Water is the source of all living things'.

For science the ever evolving universe is polarized and asymmetric like the water molecule, it is composed of fractals, whose design follows water's movements.

In Genesis, the first book of the Bible, the birth of the universe, the formation of the Earth and the emergence of life appear allegorically in the same order proposed by scientific theory. Already by the 14th century the Kabbalist Rabbi Itzhak of Acco (1250–1350) had calculated that the universe was 14 billion years old, a number derived from the sum of the seven temporal sabbatical cycles, according to the chronologies in the Bible – an amazing result: it coincides with the conclusions of modern astrophysics.

From the Big Bang to Life on Earth

The most widely accredited theory of the birth of the universe, known by scientists as the 'standard cosmological model', states that at the moment of its creation some 14 billion years ago, the universe was contained in a single, originary point, a state of infinite compression that was then released by an inconceivably colossal explosion, commonly known as the 'Big Bang'. From that moment, the universe has been continually expanding away from the source of that explosion.

The first element to manifest itself in the newborn universe was hydrogen. The velocity of expansion resulting from the Big Bang generated temperatures so high that heavier elements were able to form: helium within the first few minutes, and all the others at certain points throughout the billions of years that followed. The first life forms appeared on the Earth 3.8 billion years ago, not long after the birth of the planet itself, which is to say just a few hundred million years after the cooling of the Earth's crust, the cessation of asteroid bombardment and the appearance of water some 4.5 billion years ago.

Taking account of the fact that water functioned as a solvent in the highly improbable transformation of inorganic compounds into organic ones, it all must have happened within the range of 100 °C that defines water's freezing and boiling points.

Protein synthesis began with very simple substances: carbon monoxide (one atom of carbon paired with one of oxygen), carbon dioxide (one carbon with two oxygen atoms), ammonia (one nitrogen atom and three of hydrogen) and water (one oxygen, two hydrogen).

The first living beings, the prokaryotes, were able to live without oxygen. When certain of them began photosynthesizing, oxygen was produced, enabling more complex organisms to develop, the eukaryotes, which first appeared about 2.7 billion years ago. Subsequently, greater development and differentiation was possible because the Earth's climatic conditions remained relatively stable. And this stability is owed, of course, to water, thanks to the exceptional capacity of the oceans to absorb heat.

The Bible provides an account of the sequence of the development of life forms that corresponds with what we know from geology and paleontology. In the biblical story of Creation, vegetable life indeed precedes aquatic animal life, followed by land-based creatures, the last of which is humankind.

Primordial Waters

Abracadabra

From the Hebrew, meaning 'I will create while I speak'

Knowing where we come from helps us to understand the direction we must pursue. The Bible's aim is to shape human identity, both morally and spiritually, and towards this end it offers a synthetic description of the way the world was created, on the assumption that, by understanding the way the world evolved, we will learn to live correctly.

Moshe Ben Maimon (Maimonides) (1135–1204), physician, mathematician and biblical exegete, wrote: 'The story of Creation is natural science, but because it is so profound, it appears to us as mere parables.' Through the interpretation of Genesis, we can evaluate the role of water in the development of life on Earth from a perspective that is also both scientifically valid and spiritually stimulating.

In the beginning God created the Heavens and the Earth. And the Earth was chaos, and void; and darkness was upon the surface of the Deep. And the Spirit of God hovered upon the surface of the waters.

Genesis 1: 1–2

Right at the very beginning of everything, then, the Bible describes an aquatic Abyss – the 'Deep' – a vast and chaotic primordial place that preceded the formation of the cosmos. From this 'Deep', this abyss, the Heavens, Earth and everything they include were formed. And water is not only the first thing to be created, but it also anticipates Creation itself. We might want to imagine the Abyss as a sort of cosmic tsunami that only the Spirit of God could control.

'Abyss' can be interpreted variously: the primeval mass of hydrogen of the Big Bang, or whatever universe may have preceded the Big Bang. The Hebrew word for abyss, *tehom*, is formed from *tohu* ('chaos') and *mem*, the 13th letter of the Hebrew alphabet which, as we shall see, bears an interesting connection to water. According to the Big Bang theory, the birth of the universe is the result of the steady compression of an inconceivably huge quantity of mass (all that makes up the present universe, in fact) into a single point of infinitesimally tiny size, the ferocious explosion of which would have started the process of the expansion of the universe. This little point of mass would have been so concentrated as to have generated a gravitational force that nothing, not even light, could escape. The stories are familiar: the Bible calls this mass *tehom*, or 'Abyss', and science compares it to a primordial black hole. In the end, they both seem to be talking about the same thing.

Anyway, darkness covered the *tehom* which, according to Maimonides and Radak (acronym used by Rabbi David Kimchi, 1160–1214), consisted in a great undifferentiated mass of water that covered the Earth at the moment of its formation. Rabbi S R Hirsch links it to the root *hem*, which means both 'boiling' and 'pelting of waves'. In any case it is clear that, for the biblical commentators, water was the first element, something that existed before the cosmos, even before light.

Many scientists agree that liquid water existed in the solar system before the Earth was formed. In 2002, salt crystals and water bubbles were found in a meteorite that currently stands as the oldest known material in our solar system, dating back more than 4.5 billion years, when the young solar system was made up of protoplanets and, apparently, salt water as well.

The mystical rabbi Arizal (Itzhak Luria, 1534–72) explains that in order to make room for Creation, God had to 'contract' Himself. The contraction of the Infinite Divine Light anticipated the formation of the

Abyss and the Big Bang, after which the primordial space called *Avir Kadmon*, 'Primordial Air', was formed.

According to Arizal's metaphorical image, Primordial Air was composed of 13 fluctuating *mem* letters (the word 'water' derives from them). These 13 *mem* represent the 13 different primordial states of the water that preceded Creation and constituted the aforementioned Abyss. They hide the secret of Creation of the 13 divine principles of mercy of the Ineffable Name. According to the mystics, they are the origin of all the sublime pleasures that would become manifest during Creation.

In the biblical narration, Creation starts when the Spirit of God begins hovering over the waters, provoking turbulence. It is the Spirit of God that sparks the expansion of the universe and the subsequent appearance of light. Interestingly, this is the only place in the Bible where we find the term 'Spirit of God'.

The word *ruach*, 'spirit', used in the expression 'Spirit of God', also means 'wind'. We find also here in the Bible the generative coupling of water and wind, reminding us of that 'sensitive boundary' between air and water, that creative border zone of the wave where the Spirit of God meets water and generates living forms.

> God said, 'Let there be light,' and there was light. God saw that the light was good, and God separated between the light and the darkness.
>
> Genesis 1: 3–4

The Bible informs us that from the huge aquatic Abyss, concentrated and dark like a black hole, originated the Heavens, the Earth and the separation of the waters, from which life will spring. To ensure the expansion of the universe, first light was created, whose speed is a necessary constant in the transmutations between masses and energies.

The Formation of the Earth

For the land shall be filled with the knowledge of the Lord,
just as the waters cover the sea ...

Isaiah 11: 9

In the Hebrew language 'Earth' is *Aretz*, derived from *ratz*, which means 'to run', 'to hurry'. Rabbi Hirsch explains that in the origins of the Hebrew language, the concept of the Earth as quickly rotating on itself and revolving around the Sun was implicit. Another concept was implicit, too: the matter constituting the earth appears solid, but is instead dynamic, composed of subatomic particles and strings that 'run' and vibrate vortically. These ancient words resonate in harmony with the most recent theories of modern physics.

The linguistic root of 'earth' can also mean 'to compress'. In fact, the earth is condensed energy, the same energy we find in the heavens and in the waters, compressed in the end, concentrated. The Zohar, the main text of Jewish mysticism, ventures to describe the birth of the universe and the Earth with explicit sexual overtones and imagery, similar to those of the Indian Tantric cosmologies.

> When the higher world was filled and became pregnant, it gave forth two offspring at the same time, a male and a female. They were the Heavens and the Earth, in keeping with the supreme scheme. Earth is nourished by the waters of the Heavens that pour down upon it. These Superior Waters are male, while the Inferior Waters are female ... they make their way to the Superior ones, like the woman who receives the man, and makes her waters gush out to meet his, and produce the seed.
>
> Zohar I: 113–14

We can find several similarities between the biblical account of the appearance of water on the earth and the two most accredited scientific theories on the issue.

The approach that today enjoys the greatest consensus in the scientific community states that the Earth was heated up by the continuous impact of meteorites. Elevated radioactivity and an increase in gravitational pressure would have made terrestrial matter more compact, making it possible for water to have formed from that moment on. The planet continued to heat up even more, to the point where it started melting from the centre outwards. Water would have evaporated, dissolving into oxygen and hydrogen, joining the other gases constituting the Earth's early atmosphere. With the decrease of radioactivity, the process of concentration slowed down and the planet started to cool. The gases, now dispersed into space, were replaced by steaming exhalations of water. Afterwards, when the cooling process had advanced far enough to prevent water from vaporizing, a great deluge began that lasted centuries, finally stopping when the clouds became thin enough to float without precipitating and allow the Sun's rays to reach the Earth's surface.

The second theory, proposed by Harold C Urey (1893–1981), winner of the 1934 Nobel Prize for Chemistry, claims that the Earth never melted, but was born cold, and that water emerged gradually from its solid crust. Urey's hypothesis is based on the fact that the terrestrial crust is formed mostly of silicate rocks, namely hydrate crystals which include water molecules in their atomic structure: in keeping with the biblical scenario, Urey maintains that also the Earth's crust was made of water. Intermittent sources of heat, caused for example by local collisions between large masses inherent in the formation of the planet, would have provoked the creation and then the exit of water from its crust. So, like Genesis, according to this theory, water has existed since the very beginning.

The Formation of Humankind

At the beginning of the creation of the world, the praises to the Most Holy, Blessed Be He came only from the waters ... He said: 'If these, that have neither mouth nor the ability to utter a word, praise Me, who knows how much more when Adam shall be created!'

MIDRASH, Genesis Rabbà 5:1

In the Bible, human creation happens through the intake of divine breath of an alchemical mixture of dust and water. In the Talmud, the process is compared to kneading flour with water (Yerushalmi, Shabbat 20). According to the sages, dust represents inert, compliant matter, while water is the active matrix that ensures the dynamicity of change and organic transformation: in other words, the encounter between pure, simple water and the inherent impurity of dust triggers the generative/creative process. In Chapter 2 we saw that it is enough to add impurities to water to change it completely: for example, the pinch of salt that turns it into an excellent electrical conductor. Impurities alter the architecture and electrical balance of the crystals, making them unstable and, precisely for this reason, triggering evolutionary processes.

Adam was basically androgynous. Humanity didn't become itself until he was separated from Eve, and she from him.

A Midrash commentary teaches that, at the centre of the Garden of Eden, guarded by two angels, the Tree of Life stood nourished by all the waters of Creation. The Talmud states, 'all the waters of the world flow beneath the Tree of Life' (Talmud Yerushalmi, Berachot 1a) and derive from its roots. After the banishment of Adam and Eve, the Garden of Eden was hidden in the depths of the earth, and from it four underground rivers branched out, becoming the water sources for the rest of the world. (Talmud, Taanit 10a).

An analogous mystical river is described in the Hindu tradition, and is given the names Ganga (Ganges) and Saraswati, terms associated with the goddess Shakti. One Hindu myth in particular recounts how human awareness was born when a ripple of water, of all things, chose to leave the infinitely vast ocean of eternal, universal consciousness.

CHAPTER TEN

HOMO AQUATICUS: THE AQUATIC APE

Science does not proceed by fitting perfect data to perfect theories.
Science proceeds by ignoring anomalies, in the hope that further
discoveries will enable them to be incorporated into the elegant theory
espoused by the current paradigm.

RICHARD MILTON, *Forbidden Science*

The number of features that distinguish human beings from apes can be explained by a hypothesis that links us in a special way to water. In the very distant past, a peculiar relationship of contiguity and intimacy with water seems to have fostered the appearance of traits that make us different from other species that are similar, but less intelligent than we.

The last ancestor common to apes and human beings lived eight to nine million years ago in the African forests: his descendants split into the progenitors of gorillas, chimpanzees, bonobos and humans. In spite of the apparent differences between human beings and apes, we share about 98 per cent of the genes that code the proteins responsible for the construction and activity of the organism. At present the genome doesn't tell us much about intelligence, and it is no wonder: just consider that there are more genetic differences between similar families of mice than between humans and apes. But it does seem that friend water, here to astound us once again, played an essential role in the development of human intelligence.

Mysterious Origins

During the first three months of life, all human infants are able to do something truly extraordinary: thanks to what is called the *innate diving reflex*, they can swim underwater while holding their breath. As time goes on, children manifest other skills. My son Joshua learned to swim at two years old when his mother decided to let him get out of trouble by himself in the middle of a swimming pool.

Instantly, Joshua summoned up the ancestral arsenal of his aquatic skills and started to swim, submerging his head at regular intervals, with a perfect mastery of his breathing. Children float very well until their third year of life, and should be encouraged to swim by this age so as to pre-emptively eliminate the fears that often prevent adults from enjoying an intimate and complete relationship with water.

This natural and instinctive affinity of human newborns for water makes a good argument for one of the more fascinating hypotheses regarding the origin of humankind, one that paleontologists have only recently dared to formulate: in an era long past, many millions of years ago, hominids lived for an extensive part of their development in an aquatic environment. This phase would have been decisive, says the theory, for the subsequent appearance of *Homo sapiens*.

Most of the earliest hominid fossils have been found around the Great Rift Valley in Ethiopia, an area that was filled by swamps and marshes between six and eight million years ago. Here, the last common ancestor to humans and apes would have had to adapt to a new habitat and to a semiaquatic life. Only after that, when the drier ecosystem of the savannah had stabilized, would the bipedal hominid, now able to transport water, have become a hunter.

Until 20 years ago all the experts agreed that the ancestor of humankind left the forests on all fours to face the open expanses of the savannah, crowded with predators. The adaptation to the new environment made him first stand up and shed his fur, transforming him into a naked biped, and later into a creature intelligent enough to make his own tools.

That was the savannah theory, and for a long time it was gospel. Virtually every scientist in the field accepted it as the point of departure for explaining hominid evolution. It was an hypothesis enthusiastically sustained by famous paleontologists like Peter Wheeler and Raymond Dart, discoverer of the first *Australopithecus* fossils. The theory prevailed for many years despite lack of evidence, until finally being discredited by the increasing numbers of fossil finds: in the end, common sense won out.

The discovery of *Lucy*, the famous hominid fossil found in 1974 at Hadar in Ethiopia, should have been enough to eclipse the savannah theory. Her bones date back 3.5 million years: Lucy was at least partially bipedal and lived in an area of woods and waterways, not on the savannah. Her brain was larger than that of her 'cousins', the apes, although today it would be comparable to that of a modern chimpanzee, whose brain was smaller back then.

For years Welsh writer Elaine Morgan stood firm and alone in her conviction that the emperor, like the human ape, is naked: there is simply not enough scientific evidence to sustain the savannah theory. It finally fell into disfavour in the early '90s, but until then Morgan was the sole voice in the wilderness that was offering an alternative explanation as to what happened to our ancestors during the Pliocene era, between four and ten million years ago. That explanation is called the aquatic ape hypothesis, according to which an aquatic environment would have been responsible for numerous fundamental evolutionary transformations. Indeed, the being we'll call *Homo aquaticus* may well be that famous missing link in the phylogenetic development of humankind, occupying those three million 'lost' years following *Ramapithecus*.

Today almost all paleoanthropologists believe that the last common ape/human ancestor lived in Africa in a 'mosaic' habitat, a patchwork environment of grassy plains, waterways and woodlands. In a sense, this has been a 'velvet revolution', insofar as scholars are ever so gradually modifying the scenario of the early hominid habitat. The model of the 'savannah' became 'savannah mosaic' and then simply 'mosaic', describing a territory where grasslands were dotted by forests. Even so, several facts are left unexplained.

A tribe of apes suddenly 'decides' to change their features, standing up on two legs to become bipedal, changing the direction of body-hair growth and thinning it out to become naked. Add to that a modification of the phonation apparatus: the larynx drops below the tongue so they can articulate more sounds with their mouths and eventually speak. These apes become fatter, stop panting from their mouths, drastically reduce their apocrine scent glands along with their sense of smell. Sebaceous glands appear all over their body, nostrils tilt up. In the meantime they develop a large brain and give birth to offspring with more 'foetal' features that mature much more slowly than those of other apes.

According to the mosaic theory, these features appeared because the hominid had to navigate broad grassy plains dotted with patches of forest. However, it does not explain why not one other species in the same area manifested similar changes. The truth is that the mosaic theory is not a theory at all: it is simply a rehashing of the old savannah scenario, revised and fine-tuned. Talking about 'mosaics' avoids drawing embarrassing attention to the fierce defence of the savannah theory that reigned until just recently. It is not surprising that such a misconception could frustrate the progress of so many scientists for so many decades when we recall that, from 1924 to 1946, Raymond Dart was the only one to maintain that the 'Taung Child' skull did not belong to a chimpanzee.

The prevailing idea in the mosaic theory is that hominids were driven to move occasionally between savannah and forest by the possibility of exploring vaster territories combined with their ability to transport necessities, along with reasons of thermoregulation. Apart from a few negligible fragments, there is no fossil record of the period, perhaps because for all these years scientists have been looking in the wrong place; perhaps that fossil record hasn't been found in the savannah because our ancestors were busy evolving elsewhere, in the marshes.

The German scholar Max Westenhoefer was the first to hypothesize the origin of our earliest ancestors in an aquatic habitat, in his 1942 book *Der Eigenweg des Menschen* ('The Path of Men'). Twenty years later, the distinguished biologist Sir Alister Hardy seconded the idea that the gap in the fossil record was occupied by an aquatic precursor. Hardy had a hunch about it as early as 1930, but didn't dare publish his ideas for fear of being ostracized by the scientific community.

Elaine Morgan reproposed the aquatic ape hypothesis in two remarkable books: *The Descent of Woman* (1972) and *The Aquatic Ape* (1982), updating the subject in the more recent *The Aquatic Ape Hypothesis* (1997). Her revolutionary ideas have been received with haughty silence or summary dismissal of precisely the sort feared by Hardy.

Finally, at the dawn of the 21st century, an old advocate of the savannah theory, the famous paleoanthropologist Phillip Tobias, professor at the University of Witwaterstrand in Johannesburg, invited his colleagues to open their eyes and reconsider the heretical notion that our species was born in water. Tobias is also convinced that hominids, having adapted to a coastal environment, were able to migrate from Africa to Asia and then to Europe *because they could swim*. Marc Verhaegen, a researcher at the prestigious Putte Centre of Anthropological Studies in Belgium, shares the same opinion.

A New Creature Riseth from the Waters

Let's look at the aquatic ape hypothesis in detail. During the period of the 'fossil gap', around six million years ago, our mysterious ancestor – who would later become *Homo habilis*, *Homo faber* and finally, a mere 200,000 years ago, *Homo sapiens* – passed through a semiaquatic phase before returning to live mostly on dry land. This phase allowed him to become bipedal and hairless, definitively abandoning his coat of fur. From that moment forward, an evolutionary process was triggered that would lead him to develop his cerebral mass and verbal ability, distinguishing him in this way from his fellow primates. Living in water contributed, then, to the development of the brain, and therefore of intelligence, language and consciousness.

It is likely that the Rift Valley near Hadar in Ethiopia, where the Isthmus of Afar once separated the Red Sea from what would become the Gulf of Aden, was the cradle of humankind. Not insignificantly, that area, called the Afar Triangle, was under water during the Pleistocene era, and it is there that the oldest fossil of a bipedal hominid has been found. Her name is *Orrorin Tugenensis* (in the local idiom *Orrorin* means 'Original Man'), nicknamed Millennium Ancestor, and she was discovered by a team of French researchers led by Brigitte Senut and Martin Pickford in 2001. The Millennium Ancestor lived six million years ago in a swampy area interspersed with waterways and forests. That she walked on two feet was confirmed in 2004 by the tomographic analysis of her femoral bones conducted by Robert Eckhardt of Penn State University. This is no small discovery, since it had long been thought that bipedalism dated back a mere three million years; the Millenium Ancestor proves that hominids were walking upright fully six million years ago.

The fossil gap between bipedal hominid and modern man is only partially closed by the Millennium Ancestor, however. In the preceding period in which the aquatic ape would have lived, through that of the

Millennium Ancestor and afterwards, an extraordinary leap forward took place: the brain increased dramatically in weight and size, the cerebral cortex became much thicker, and memory and language skills emerged.

Millions of years ago our brain began developing at an unparalleled pace with respect to other species and other organs. In 1999, anthropologists from the University of California at Berkeley announced the discovery of the fossil remains of a hominid they called *Australopithecus Garhi*, 2.5 million years old, carnivorous, with a large brain already a third the size of ours.

Seventy million years earlier, the cetaceans (whales, porpoises and dolphins) had chosen an aquatic habitat. Descending from furry terrestrial mammals, called *Mesonychidae*, they took to the sea to fill a niche left empty by the sudden extinction of reptiles. They adapted to the fixed temperatures of the oceans, developed a thick layer of subcutaneous fat, lost their hair and developed their brain capacity and communication skills.

Twenty million years later, the ancestors of the sirenians, like the manatee and the dugong, a branch of the elephant family, went through the same process. Twenty-five to thirty million years after that, it was time for the progenitors of seals, otters and beavers to break off from the ancestors they share with bears and dogs and take to the water.

And millions of years later, the aquatic ape would do the same thing.

Only the aquatic ape hypothesis can coherently account for all the questions pertaining to the peculiarities of human evolution. Humans are attracted by water, unlike most apes, particularly the chimpanzee who, though rarely inclined to stand on two legs, will do so to avoid getting its arms wet.

Human hands and feet make excellent fins, and could well be the remnants of palmate limbs. In fact, fully 7 per cent of the human population has palmate toes, more commonly known as webbed feet. The skeletal structure of the lateral fins of marine mammals like the Australian whale, the dugong and the manatee is similar to that of the human hand, and the palmate paws of the sea otter have fingers capable of an amazingly strong grip.

The human brain must have begun developing in proximity to water, if not for the simple fact that it needs the fatty acids that abound in fish in order to grow and function. This is probably why the biggest brains on Earth were formed in water: not only the enormous brains of the cetaceans, but also that of the elephant, whose ancestors evolved in the water.

Michael Crawford, a biochemist at the Institute of Brain Chemistry and Human Nutrition of the University of London, and Andrew Sinclair of the University of Melbourne, assert that *Homo sapiens*' large brain is in some way the result of a diet including fatty acids like the docosahexaenoic acid necessary for building neuronal membranes and the arachidonic acid that is a key component of blood vessel walls.

Fish, seafood, turtle eggs and shellfish are foods rich in polyunsaturated fats and short-chain fatty acids, the well-known 'omega-3': these are the building blocks that the brain uses to function and develop. Such a diet would be possible only in a marine or fluvial ecological niche. The human brain would have thus expanded, thanks in part to a new diet that distinguished it from those of other apes.

Why do Human Beings Walk Upright?

Wading through the marshes, the aquatic ape was compelled to stand on its feet to keep its head above water and reserve the possibility of returning to land when necessary. This also left it free to carry out various activities with its forelimbs, so it began lifting objects up to eye-level in order to examine them, which in turn provided further stimulus for developing manual dexterity and hand-eye coordination. This was accompanied by a progressive increase in the size of the cerebral cortex and, consequently, of the skull – though it should be said that the manipulation of objects and tools was a correlative factor, but not necessarily the cause of cerebral development, since whales and dolphins have a much bigger brain than the other mammals, yet their limbs became fins for locomotion rather than fingers for the manipulation of objects.

The bonobo, a primate species discovered only recently, is one of the apes most similar to humans. Intelligent and peaceful, it often walks upright, making it the only other bipedal ape. The bonobo lives in the rainforests of Zaire, where it spends most of the year wading through marshes and swamps and must adapt to seasonal floods. While other primates such as gorillas and chimpanzees cannot tolerate being in water and avoid it at all costs, bonobos, like humans, actually choose water as a recreational environment. It is not unlikely that the aquatic ape lived in a marshy environment similar to that of the bonobo.

Why are Human Beings Naked?

The human being is the only naked ape. Our hair has thinned and shortened so much over the millennia as to be almost invisible to the naked eye. The notion that the human being is the only creature in all the animal kingdom to have actually *lost* its fur to adapt to the scorching sun of the savannah, where a thick layer of hair would have been absolutely necessary to isolate us from the heat and to protect ourselves from ultraviolet rays, is, to say the least, a dubious proposition.

Denudation is instead a standard form of adaptation to water, because in water subcutaneous fat is a better insulator than fur. Since it never completely left dry land, the aquatic ape kept its hair thicker on some parts of the body: head, pubic area, armpits.

Other animals, like us, have left their cumbersome fur behind. In fact, all the hairless mammals are aquatic in differing degree, with the exception of the Somalian mole, which never comes above ground, and some of the pachyderms.

Pachyderms are not necessarily related to each other: the elephant, the hippopotamus, the rhinoceros, the pig and the walrus have in common the significant thickness of their skin, along with considerable weight. Many pachyderms are hairless, and this thick skin covers an even thicker layer of fat. Some of them – such as the walrus, the hippopotamus and the dugong – are mainly aquatic. All pachyderms are excellent swimmers, even though their weight is greater than that of other mammals, since water is the only environment where weight is not a drawback. In fact, the hippopotamus moves with such graceful ease in water as to have inspired Walt Disney to dedicate an entire movement of his masterpiece, *Fantasia*, to this apparently clumsy creature. As mentioned earlier, it has also been proven that a progenitor of the elephant spent a period of its evolution in water.

Like the pachyderms, our skin is thicker than that of all other primates and has a significant layer of fat beneath. Furthermore, like pachyderms, it is furrowed by congenital lines that cover the body surface, the most conspicuous being the whorls and folds of our fingertips.

Alister Hardy observed that the orientation of the hair on the human body is also not casual, but precisely follows the direction and patterns of water flow on the body of a swimmer. In other primates, body hair grows downward, since that is the most effective way to resist rain.

Why are Human Beings Fat?

The human being is the only primate to have an extensive layer of subcutaneous fat, otherwise minimal in monkeys and apes. One needs only think of their offspring: their newborns look like malnourished miniature street bums by comparison to our chubby little cherubs. In fact, all mammals with subcutaneous fat, man excepted, are either aquatic or hibernators (these latter – the porcupine, dormouse and polar bear – store adipose tissue for winter, but their fat is different from ours anyway. For young human females, fat makes up 27 per cent of body weight, while for males it stands at around 15 per cent. Fat is so important that, if a woman loses the equivalent of 10 per cent of her body weight in fat, menstruation stops and she ceases to be fertile.

What evolutionary advantage is provided by fat in an aquatic environment?

In aquatic animals, fat functions as a thermoregulator, since water disperses body heat more rapidly than air. Thanks to our adipose layer, human beings can survive a remarkably long time in cold water. A mantle of furs is a better insulator against extreme air temperatures, while subcutaneous fat is better in water, and also has hydrodynamic qualities. Precisely because humans are suspended between water and earth, 'neither fish nor fowl', we must wear fur in winter and protect ourselves with a wetsuit against extended immersion in water. Today, in our culture of slenderness, fat has become something to reject, but that doesn't change its importance for staying alive in water.

Subcutaneous fat also ensures greater buoyancy, an important advantage for an aquatic ape, and a clear explanation for why its offspring would have a higher proportion of body fat – adults need to dive for food, while babies must be able to float easily and keep warm. If the aquatic ape had sojourned and slept on the trees, as the mosaic model would have it, the increase in weight and fat would have only been a disadvantage.

Human beings and some sea mammals, like the manatee, have another common trait: their females have swollen, floating breasts, whereas female apes and monkeys have flat breasts. Why? Because with a floating breast, a mother can feed her infant while in the water, with no body hair available to grab, babies would resort to the more sizable breasts.

Women Led the Way

The aquatic ape hypothesis attributes an important role to females in the evolution of the species. As both biology and innumerable cultural traditions teach us, women have an intimate and privileged relationship with water. Human females are more glabrous (hairless) and have more body fat than males; on average, they survive longer immersed in water.

Elaine Morgan suggests that females induced males to choose water as a habitat. Imagine a flooded forest or an island far from the coast that was getting smaller as the sea level rose. The ruling males would have placed their trust in the diminishing reserves of their traditional food sources and would have obstinately insisted on those, a behaviour that reflects how, in every society, long-established dominance tends to lead to conservative attitudes on the part of the dominators. The hungrier and more flexibly minded females would have been driven to look for less familiar food sources, eventually finding them in the water.

How and Why we Sweat

Diversely from other primates, the human being cannot pant with an open mouth to disperse heat accumulated by the body. It is thought that the disappearance of panting is correlated with the development of language: if we sweat through our tongues, we wouldn't be able to talk. Moreover, living mainly in water and in the shade of the forests, the aquatic ape wouldn't need to dissipate as much heat as, say, a savannah dweller.

A human being cannot survive if the body's water content is reduced by as little as 10 per cent, while most other species can tolerate a 20 per cent loss. Our species developed a large number of eccrine sweat glands, double the number of the other primates. These glands cover our entire body, and are the most important means of regulating body temperature. It cannot be insignificant that human beings, with this system, regulate body moisture and temperature *like no other land mammal*. Again, in the sun-scorched, arid environment of the savannah, this would have been an enormous disadvantage.

How and Why we Cry

Human beings produce tears to protect the eye from irritation by foreign bodies, wind or toxic vapours, and also as an emotional reaction. Recent research indicates that other animals weep as a consequence of emotional events, although it is rare.

But the most relevant datum for our purposes is the difference between our tears and those of the other primates: theirs contain lysozyme, a bactericidal substance that can disactivate viruses as well, while human tears have a high concentration of immunoglobulin A, enzymes like peroxidase and amylase, and an elevated content of lactoferrine as well, all of which make for much stronger and more concentrated bactericidal and immunizing properties. Furthermore, humans can produce a greater quantity of tears compared to apes. All these characteristics could have appeared as a consequence of the aquatic ape's need to explore underwater with his eyes open, in search of the fatty-acid-rich fish and shellfish which, as we've seen, were contributing so vitally to the extraordinary growth of his brain.

Phonation and Language

What distinguishes us from all the higher terrestrial mammals is the capacity to produce phonemes in an articulated language, which is the main expression of our intelligence. The apparatus we use to emit meaningful sounds is the larynx, which contains the vocal cords. Other animals have one, too, but ours is positioned much lower in the throat. This evolutionary descent of the larynx is what makes it possible for us to speak.

In the other mammals the larynx remains right behind the palate (figure 10.1), except in three circumstances: when panting, emitting vocal sounds, or swallowing. This same feature is present in human newborns, for it is an excellent system of sealed compartments designed to keep the alimentary and air passages separated. As a result, newborns can suckle and breathe at the same time.

But then, when the human infant hits 18 months or so, something unique and unexpected in the animal kingdom takes place: the larynx drops down into the neck, expanding the vocal passage. From an adaptive outlook, this change would have brought only one possible advantage: the ability to produce complex and varied sounds necessary for spoken language. The other primates maintain instead the advantage of drinking and breathing at the same time. Some are intelligent enough to use sign language, and many will emit unintentional sounds linked to emotions, but none can voluntarily control their phonation.

The lowering of the larynx creates several disadvantages for humans. Food can go down the wrong way and mix with the air in the larynx, causing us to choke; breathing with our mouth makes us more vulnerable to bronchitis and pneumonia, because the air is not filtered and heated through the nose. For these reasons, we breathe with our mouths only during physical exertion and when we talk.

Why did our progenitor's larynx descend to a risky and potentially fatal position? Attributing it to language appears to make sense, but speaking was still a long way off. What about a present adaptive need, rather than a future one? The only other advantage of mouth breathing is the ability to quickly inhale a larger volume of air and hold one's breath, both of which are crucial for swimming, especially under water.

The lowering of the larynx gave the aquatic ape voluntary breath control and the consequent possibility of storing oxygen, something the other primates cannot do. On the other hand, we share this ability with all the other non-fish species that submerge themselves in water: the aquatic birds, reptiles and mammals.

Other data suggest that respiration through the mouth is an adaptive function linked to water. Only three other sea mammals present a

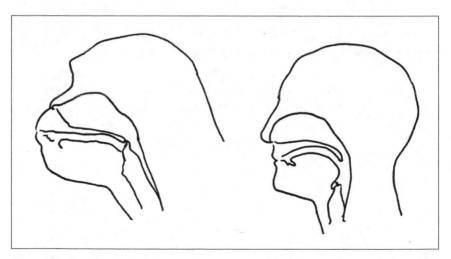

Figure 10.1 The position of the larynx in a gorilla and in a human

descended larynx: the dugong, the sea lion and the walrus. Humans, like all aquatic mammals, have a very developed diving reflex: when we go under water, the heartbeat automatically slows down (bradycardia) and the blood vessels contract (peripheral vasoconstriction). Bradycardia and peripheral vasoconstriction are mechanisms designed to provide an adequate supply of oxygen to the diving animal's brain.

Humans are so susceptible to the diving reflex that we can elicit it by submerging only our face in water. In fact, we can provoke remarkable cardiovascular changes: just 15 minutes a day in the water can reduce heart rate by up to 45 per cent. Other semiaquatic mammals, like the beaver and the otter, show these same physiological responses to immersion.

Water and Language

> *The words a man speaks are deep waters,*
> *A flowing stream, a fountain of wisdom.*
>
> Proverbs 18: 4

The boundaries between water and air, as we have seen, are very meaningful: here, forms materialize from unstable and rhythmical processes. In the same way, the intrinsic instability of marshy and shore environments, by definition a space between earth and water, provided the human ancestor with the impetus to walk upright and to develop the brain and the functions of language. Between water and air, humans acquired their unique, defining faculty: speaking, the exchange of ideas and information from a distance.

Which factor played the main role in the birth of human language? We might think of the need to transmit instructions on the use of tools and instruments, or the necessity of communication among more socially complex groups. But that's not all.

The tendency to make sounds, as opposed to the gestural language used by other animals, could have developed in response to the fact that our ancestors, limbs underwater engaged in the work of keeping afloat, did not have a visible body to communicate with. The face, therefore, became the most expressive part of the body. The aquatic ape had to find new ways of communication, prioritizing the expressiveness of the face. This led to an increase in facial musculature and the range of sounds produced by the larynx, and by the time the upright hominid had returned to land, he was learning how to communicate in this new, verbal way.

Water, then, gave us the basic tools to transmit information, memories, emotions. It led us to create a culture founded on communication.

The intelligent sea mammals, like whales and dolphins, confirm the strong link between water and communication: their language is based on a very complex acoustic apparatus, able to operate over long distances.

Homo erectus, who lived two million years ago, had a skull with a flexed base. This conformation is consistent with the descent of the larynx, necessary for the emission of vocal sounds. In fact, the base of *Homo erectus*'s skull doesn't look like a monkey's, but like a six-year-old child's, fully equipped with the physical qualities necessary for developing language.

Other Support for the Hypothesis

Human beings practise frontal coitus, a position common only to other aquatic mammals: whales, dolphins and beavers. Among the primates, only the bonobo, which lives in a semiaquatic habitat, frequently mates face to face. With bipedalism and the habit of swimming, our spinal column has straightened and our limbs have realigned themselves such that frontal access to the vagina is more advantageous for reproduction.

There is another factor that distinguishes us from our fellow apes: our sense of smell is inferior to at least half of the primate species, which may have something to do with the fact that aquatic mammals are completely without olfactory receptors. The sense of smell is not particularly useful underwater.

Human menstruation follows a cyclical rhythm that roughly corresponds with a lunar month (29.5 days). Many marine species, more so than land-based creatures, have biorhythms that follow this same lunar pattern. The menstrual cycle could be something left over from the tidal rhythm developed by the aquatic ape for the gestation period, a multiple of the menstrual cycle. Furthermore, it would have been essential for parturition that our ancestors knew the tide levels and were able to adapt to them automatically.

The sebaceous glands of apes are few and isolated to specific parts of the body – the eyes, lips and anus – while human beings have thousands of sebaceous glands concentrated principally on the face, head and back. The substance they produce, sebum, is a water-resistant oil. The sebaceous glands of the gestating human foetus are active in all parts of the body, producing vernix caseosa, the oily, cheese-like substance we see covering the body of a newborn infant. The great number of sebaceous glands in humans could be the heredity of the heavy sebaceous activity typical of aquatic apes for protection against overhydration and cold.

In humans, the nostrils are oriented downward, while in the majority of primates they point forward. The position of our nostrils is the most advantageous for swimming with the head forward and for swimming under water.

Another interesting connection with aquatic mammals is blood composition. Because they spend long and frequent periods under water, marine mammals have a low incidence of red blood cells and higher amounts of haemoglobin, the protein that transports oxygen. It should come as no surprise that humans, compared to other primates, have fewer red blood cells and a greater haemoglobin content.

〜

CHAPTER ELEVEN

WATER AND BIRTH

*What does a fish know about the water
in which he swims all his life?*

ALBERT EINSTEIN

The Embryo

There are two fundamental questions that molecular biology cannot answer. The first: how does an aggregation of molecules develop into an embryo, and from this an autonomous living organism? The second: what is consciousness, and what is its relation to the body?

In 1828, the Estonian embryologist Karl Ernst von Baer realized that the embryos of different species looked surprisingly alike. He came upon the discovery when he found two embryos conserved in formalin that he'd neglected to label and was unable to determine whether they were reptile, avian or mammal. Analysing this similarity more carefully, von Baer discovered that in the early phases of embryonic development, all vertebrates are more or less identical, and that only in later phases of gestation does it become possible to discern the identifying differences between classes (fish, birds, amphibians, mammals, etc) and even later the finer taxonomic distinctions of order, family, and so on.

Water is the medium in which everything is born and develops. It is literally the origin of all life, both ontogenetically (embryonic development) and phylogenetically (the history of the entire evolutionary process of a given species). There exists no living thing whose phylogeny does not start with water.

And that includes us. In the foetal stage, the human being is a symbiotic aquatic animal, suspended in a warm, salty liquid that reproduces the hydrosaline equilibrium of the oceans. For nine months we live like marine creatures. The germinal cell, which subsequently becomes an embryo, develops in a liquid medium that later becomes the amniotic sac. Up to the moment of parturition, the human foetus behaves much like a fish, immersed in amniotic fluid and receiving oxygen through the umbilical artery.

The progenitors of all living creatures were aquatic, who only recently (i.e. 400 million years ago, in the Devonian Period) began developing from fish into animals that could survive on dry land. Their evolution led to the first amphibians, then to reptiles, mammals and birds. Later on, some of these creatures would decide to change habitat, such as the bat, which chose the sky, while seals and whales preferred to return to the sea from whence they came, as did the penguin. It would also appear that the precursor of humans returned, at least for a time, to the water.

Haeckel's law, which takes its name from the German naturalist Ernst Haeckel (1834–1919), long stood as one of the foundations of biology: 'Ontogeny recapitulates phylogeny', which is to say that the intrauterine development of an embryo corresponds to the evolutionary history of the species to which it belongs (phylogeny), from microorganism to fish to amphibian and so forth.

In effect, a sperm cell does look quite a bit like a flagellate protozoon, and in the third week of gestation human foetuses do develop brachial arches on the sides of the head which, were we fish, would become gills, but since we're human they're clearly vestiges of a time when we weren't. When the eyes form, the embryo begins to resemble an amphibian, and subsequent developmental phases recapitulate more advanced classes until we become fully human. As we've seen elsewhere, the principle applies both micro- and macrocosmically – that is, to the parts as well as to the whole. When we look most like a fish, our heart has only two chambers, as do fish; when we start looking more like a salamander, it develops a third chamber, like a salamander, eventually arriving at the four-chambered heart characteristic of mammals.

Today Haeckel's law is no longer considered valid, in part because it was discovered some years later that the old fox had manipulated his drawings of embryos to make them support his thesis. The insight that inspired it, however, is not entirely wrong.

An embryo does not faithfully recapitulate the appearance and structure of the animals that preceded it phylogenetically. A human embryo does not pass through the stage of an adult fish, but shares characteristics with a fish's embryonic development – a fine point, perhaps, but important nonetheless.

Ontogeny does recapitulate phylogeny, but not in the schematized way proposed by Haeckel. More accurately, as biologist Lyall Watson has suggested, ontogeny *anticipates* phylogeny: the embryo and the ways in which it develops contain the seed, the meaning and the evolutionary dynamic of the species, wherein we find reminders of our ancestral past, a memory of the species contained not only in the genome but in its very anatomy.

Waterbirthing

Given that our identity is forged in water, it only follows that the healthiest and most harmonic method of childbirthing is one that enables the gentlest possible transition from amnios to air by creating an intermediary 'cushion' of water. Many researchers, midwives and obstetricians have been saying for years that waterbirth is the best way to bring a child into the world. While a relatively new concept for Western culture, it has long been practised by others. Before the missionaries arrived in New Zealand, for example, women from some Maori tribes habitually gave birth in water.

During labour, a primordial instinct is triggered in the mother that compels her to concentrate exclusively on the act of birthing, achieving a unique state of consciousness beyond all rationality. To favour this state, the women of many populations throughout history would separate themselves from the community and retire to isolated places, oftentimes near water, much like a shaman going off into the desert to commune with the spirits. Today, thanks to visualization techniques and hypnosis, something like this state can be reached, and the mother can face birthing with less pain and greater serenity.

Clinical research indicates that waterbirth reduces complications of delivery, the duration of labour and, most importantly, infant trauma.

Water alleviates the force of gravity, which affords the mother greater relaxation during contractions. For both mother and newborn, this near-weightlessness induces a drastic reduction in oxygen and energy consumption and stimulates all the organic functions.

The French obstetrician Frederick Leboyer was the first contemporary doctor to scientifically approach what he called 'birth without violence' and to encourage the idea that the first contact of the newborn with the outside world be with warm water that simulates the uterine environment, thereby making the transition less traumatic. According to Leboyer, a 'nonviolent' birth has not only immediate physiological benefits, but far-reaching psychological ones as well, helping the child later on in life to face difficulty with optimism and self-assurance, and contributing to a perception of the world as a benign, less foreign place.

The number of doctors and obstetricians practising water birth and studying its effects on mother and child increases every year. In the 1980s, at the Pithiviers hospital in France, gynaecologist Michel Odent introduced several techniques involving the use of birthing tubs in an effort to counter the excessive medicalization of traditional delivery rooms. In fact, an alarming increase in both the number of Caesarean births and the use of anaesthesia during labour has been recorded in nearly every Western country.

Odent had noticed that during labour many women expressed the desire to take a bath or shower, so he brought in an inflatable tub and invited the mothers-to-be to use them during labour. He also decided to transform the rooms of the neonatal unit into an environment that would be as close as possible to home, allowing the women to move around and make as much noise as they pleased. Going against existing practice, he also encouraged new mothers to breastfeed their newborns within an hour of delivery and to sleep with them.

With the introduction of waterbirth, Odent succeeded in bringing the perinatal mortality rate below France's national average at the time (nine per thousand) and reduce the number of Caesarean sections by a factor of four (6 per cent). Odent later relocated to London, where he founded the Primal Health Research Centre for the clinical study of the period between conception and the first year of life.

Today in Great Britain alone more than 70 hospitals are equipped with birthing tubs and in 1992 a governmental health committee recommended that all hospitals offer the option of waterbirth. Since then, thousands of women have given birth in this gentlest of ways.

Water Babies

Even better than warm water, specialists agree that the ideal environment for labour and birth is warm *sea* water, as it is similar in density and composition to amniotic fluid. Through the first year of life, infants are able to adapt to water with surprising ease, demonstrating a natural inclination for swimming and an utter lack of fear. Newborns are able to stay underwater for up to 40 minutes while still attached to the umbilical cord, and instinctively know how to navigate toward the water's surface.

The Russian Igor Charkovsky was one of the pioneers of waterbirth in Europe. An expert in physical education, from 1962 to the end of his career he oversaw thousands of waterbirths, many on the shores of the Black Sea. His method involved a series of phases, the first of which was to instil in the future mother a familiarity with water.

Charkovsky was the first to observe that infants smile rather than cry when born in water, and are able to hold their breath for several minutes, even after separation from the mother.

The postnatal part of his programme was very demanding and not without a certain severity, which made him the object of much criticism and contestation. Among the exercises he required were submersion in freezing cold water, postural torsions pushed to the limit of skeleto-muscular possibility, and testing the duration of a newborn's ability to hold its breath underwater. The unorthodox Russian did get some positive results, however, particularly with regard to improving the condition of infants born with congenital psychomotorial disabilities.

Charkovsky's 'shock treatments' were intended to push the limits of survival, to be *near-death experiences* which, according to Charkovsky, would trigger in the infant a mechanism of 'rebirth', a sort of turbocharging of the organism. Prolonged contact with water under extreme conditions, he believed, induces a massive stimulation of the body, which is otherwise unreactive. The consequent regenerative effect should ostensibly be similar to that of the death-rebirth that occurs during parturition, and is also the objective of certain religious and tribal initiation rites.

Charkovsky also maintained that the sensory and intellective capacities of infants who undergo his treatment are significantly superior to the average, and that children trained to play, eat and even sleep in water are more inclined to develop extrasensory abilities for communicating with whales and dolphins.

The Russian's own claims aside, it has been observed by others that children in whom an intimate relationship with water is cultivated are able to stand, walk and speak earlier than their 'dry-born' peers. It has also been proposed that 'water babies' acquire heightened mental and adaptive faculties in specific areas, an hypothesis which, if true, would be yet further proof of the roles played by water in the development of intelligence that we've investigated elsewhere in this book.

Homo delphinus

Many of the waterbirths that Charkovsky conducted in the Black Sea employed the active collaboration of dolphins, whose complex and refined bio-acoustic system soothed them with sounds and ultrasounds, and who helped them to the surface to breathe. Dolphins in captivity regularly and voluntarily offer their assistance in waterbirths in Russia, Australia and New Zealand. Since 1993, the town of Eilat, Israel, has been providing obstetrical services in a pool with two dolphins.

The dolphins direct a barrage of sonic stimuli at the mother and infant: thanks to their sonar, these highly intelligent cetaceans can effectively 'see' inside of our bodies, just like an ultrasound or CAT scan, and monitor foetal activity in the womb.

Australian obstetrician Estelle Myers has conducted a number of waterbirths with the presence of dolphins, and has observed in both mother and child a powerful sense of serenity and wellbeing after the birth. Myers confirms the claims that these infants appear more secure, more gifted and less aggressive than their peers. Numerous scientists and scholars who have witnessed these kinds of 'close encounters' between children of different ages and dolphins (figure 11.1) suggest that the marine mammals could be conveying bio-acoustic information to the children's cerebral cortex, and that this exchange instils in them a profound serenity.

Noted American neurophysiologist and 'dolphinologist' John C Lilly (who we'll meet again in Chapter 16) and English biologist and medical doctor Horace Dobbs have hypothesized that the incessant stream of messages sent by dolphins to human beings are telepathic in nature. Transmitted by ultrasonic waves through the water, they might stimulate similar telepathic abilities in the newborn humans.

Prolonged contact with water over the course of our respective evolutions has given both humans and cetaceans a formidable brain and

Figure 11.1 Dolphins may convey bio-acoustic information to a baby's cerebral cortex, instilling a sense of profound serenity

superior cognitive faculties. These newborns, so instinctively 'at home' in the water and in the company of dolphins, take us back to a forgotten past and remind us that our roots as conscious, intelligent individuals are planted in the water, which is the privileged domain of communion among intelligent species.

In his preface to Theodor Schwenk's *Sensitive Chaos*, Jacques Yves Cousteau describes his first underwater experience:

> My body floated weightlessly through space, the water enveloping my skin … Gravity – I saw it in a flash – was the original sin, committed by the first living beings who left the sea. Redemption would come only when we return to the ocean as already the sea mammals have done.[26]

Perhaps this is why dolphins try so insistently to communicate with human beings. There are those who believe that exchanging information with cetaceans could provide valuable data for the survival of the human species. Dolphins adapted themselves to the water 60 million years before humans first appeared on the planet, so they have much to teach us about living on the Earth and how to make the most of water's capacity to help us develop our mental faculties.

French free-diving champion Jacques Mayol (1927–2001) recounted his extensive experience with dolphins in his 1979 book entitled *Homo Delphinus: The Dolphin Within Man*. Mayol proclaimed the advent of a new human species, born in water and raised in intimate knowledge of it, a human capable of learning from dolphins the secret art of living in harmony with the Earth for many millennia to come:

In many ways these animals are superior to humans, for they require absolutely nothing from us. They need nothing. And what could they need from man if not protection from the pollution of which man is the cause? It is we who need dolphins, and not the other way round. ... What can we teach dolphins that could be of use to them? ... Reading? What purpose could such an elementary system of communication serve if one is able, as they are, to communicate telepathically? Listening to music? The most beautiful music in the world is that of the wind, the tides, the birds, the breath of the sea. Wearing clothes? They have but one skin, perfect for all seasons.[27]

CHAPTER TWELVE

THE WATER WITHIN US

He who takes one life it is as though he has destroyed the universe, and he who saves one life it is as though he has saved the universe.

MIDRASH TANCHUMA, Pekudei 3

There is no part of the body to which water does not have access or play a role. It constitutes 85 per cent of the human brain, 82.7 per cent of the kidneys, 75.6 per cent of muscle tissue, 92 per cent of our blood and 22 per cent of our bones. As for where it comes from, 47 per cent is ingested orally in liquid form, 14 per cent is created by biochemical reactions within the body (cell transpiration) and 39 per cent derives from solid foods.

The fluids that make up our body are a veritable ocean of water and mineral salts. Like the Earth, the human body undergoes a hydrological cycle. Water is released in the form of urine, sweat, respiration and faeces – every day our two million or so sweat glands secrete a half a litre of water, along with salts and urea. Water-based fluids are also recycled back into our bodies – the salivary glands secrete digestive fluids uninterruptedly; lachrymal fluid lubricates and disinfects the cornea every time we blink.

Water never stagnates in our body, nor on the Earth. The 50 kilograms of water distributed through an average human adult are completely replaced 17 to 18 times per year, just as the water in the

Earth's atmosphere is renewed every 12 days and that of the oceans every 40,000 years.

Oxygen and carbon dioxide enter and exit the body by way of the pulmonary alveoli. The oxygen we inhale is transported by the blood through more than 90,000 kilometres of veins and arteries, nourishing cells and enabling them to produce energy. The lungs also use water vapour as a vehicle for the exhalation of impurities and cellular waste products.

Water lubricates the joints to facilitate movement, and cushions the brain from injury. The water in bile transports soluble salts to the intestines which bond with fats and enable the breakdown of enzymes.

The temperature of the water in our body is maintained at approximately 37 °C, which is ideal for the enzymatic activity of our cells. This internal temperature is in turn regulated by sweat – also essentially water – which moistens and cools the body's exterior.

Generally speaking, humans cannot go more than a week without water. If we were to lose just 10 per cent of our bodily water reserves, we'd die immediately. Even a loss of 1 to 2 per cent becomes problematic, and at 5 per cent the skin begins to shrivel, the mouth and tongue dry out and hallucinations set in. Conversely, if we drink too much water, we'd suffer from nausea, weakness, mental confusion, spatial disorientation, convulsions and in some cases even death.

The Body as Aquatic Microcosm

It sounds incredible but 99 per cent of our body is water molecules: the 1 per cent that is left is composed of bigger and more voluminous molecules. Just as the surface of the Earth is covered by 70 per cent water, so the volume of the human body is 70 per cent structured water. Pure and simple water is everywhere. Without it we would never have come to be, nor, now that we're here, could we survive an instant without it.

The salinity of human cell protoplasm and the interstitial fluid in which cells are immersed, nourishing them and allowing them to communicate with one another, is around 0.9 per cent – the same as the oceans from which life blossomed forth some three billion years ago. In a very real sense, we still carry that ocean within us.

Ninety-eight per cent of the atoms in our body are swapped with the outside environment in the course of a single year. We have a new liver every six months and a new skeleton every three. The stomach replaces its lining with new cells every five days, there's not a trace in us of the skin we had a month ago, and even the brain, in its scaffolding of oxygen, hydrogen and nitrogen, isn't the same brain we had last year. Not a moment passes that our body is the same as it was the moment before.

Well before the age of modern physiology, traditional Chinese medicine taught that the human being is a totality of interdependent functions and processes in constant transformation. Eastern medical science compares the human being to a field irrigated by waterways; in India's Vedic tradition, we are a river that flows without changing aspect, incessantly recycling its waters. The human being, in a word, is a watery planet in miniature.

We've already seen how ancient Chinese science is based on a modular, holographic model, which is to say that reality is considered to be a macrocosm that is entirely reproducible in the microcosms of which it is made. Man, specifically, is a microcosm that exists between the macrocosms of Earth and Sky, made up of further, interdependent microcosms: every cell is a planet unto itself, every organ a planetary system, and so forth. Certain zones of the body, such as the ear, the tongue and the radial artery of the inner wrist, are sort of microcosmic maps of all the organic areas. As such, these are essential for diagnosing one's general state of health.

The concept of an 'organ' in traditional Chinese medicine is very fluid. One must take into account the fact that it is not limited to the parenchymatous tissue, but extends to its influence on functions and tissues that may be quite distant, in keeping with the Theory of the Five Movements. For this reason, this chapter will capitalize the initial letter of the names of the organs as a sort of reminder of the significant difference between Western and Chinese medicine.

According to Chinese tradition, many organ functions reproduce external physical phenomena involving water. The organ and viscera located at the centre of the body, the Spleen and the Stomach, represent the Earth. Their role is to collect nutritive substances from food and water, digest them and transform them into vital energy for the entire body.

Moving upwards, the Lung functions as a 'protective cloak' for all the other organs, like the sky protects the Earth. The Lung assumes and vaporises Water, distributing it to all the body's tissues. Like the sky that nourishes the Earth with rain, the Lung distributes the Qi that comes from respiration and digestion along the body's energy channels, or meridians. The Lung protects us from climatic factors such as wind, cold, heat and lack of moisture, just as the atmosphere protects the planet from cosmic rays.

The Liver is associated with Wood – green, living wood – and is responsible for maintaining the circulation of the blood, storing it and regulating its 'tides', or diurnal and nocturnal rhythms. It therefore also conditions the rhythm and quantity of menstrual blood.

Like the subterranean waters of our planet, the Kidney, whose Movement is predictably Water, is the storage tank of the most precious fluids and energies upon which other organs and tissues draw in case of need.

The Heart, associated instead with Fire, heats the body like the Sun with the blood it pumps, coordinating the psychic activity of all the other organs. It is also the centre of Shen, the spirit representing the totality of the psychoemotive activities of individual organisms.

The human body and the Earth are two very similar systems, they're just on different scales. Mont Blanc alone transports some 80,000 tons of detritus away from itself by way of water. The mountain's 'metabolism' is not unlike that of a healthy human who, through the kidneys and immune system, drains itself of huge quantities of accumulated waste and toxins.

A further analogy lies in the fact that mountain waterways extract the energy and trace elements from the rock and store it in their molecular structures, deep beneath the Earth's surface. Similarly, as Chinese physiology would have it, the Kidney sets aside part of the energy supplied by food that is not immediately utilized by the body.

Internal Watercourses: The Meridians of Acupuncture

Traditional Chinese medicine has acquired a deep understanding of the physiology of water and fluids, correlating it with the energetic, biological and psychological processes of the human being. Each organ of the body 'governs' (*zhi* in Chinese), or supervises specific functions. Here the Chinese language reveals its richness: *zhi* means to govern, but it also means 'to regulate water flow', 'to cure' and to 'administer treatment'. *To cure, then, means to regulate the flux of water in the body.* Water is the simplest and most incisive tool that medicine has for diagnosing and curing the body.

One of the most ancient Chinese medical texts known to us, the *Huang Di Nei Jing* ('The Yellow Emperor's Classic of Internal Medicine'), was compiled between the 5th and 4th centuries BC. It records the conversations that the Yellow Emperor, Huang Di (2695–2589 BC) held with his court physician, Chi Po, and constitutes the first systematic treatise on acupuncture and Chinese pharmacology. This book reveals one of the most important medical discoveries of all time: the presence in the human body of an interconnected network of conduits and reservoirs called *jing luo*, or channels and collaterals, also known as meridians (figure 12.1).

The meridians carry Qi (energy), organ fluids and blood to the body's tissues and organs. These channels are found along the spaces and fissures of the tissue at varying depths and are distinct from the nervous system and cardiovascular system. They branch throughout the body in a dense network so fine as to penetrate the spaces between individual cells.

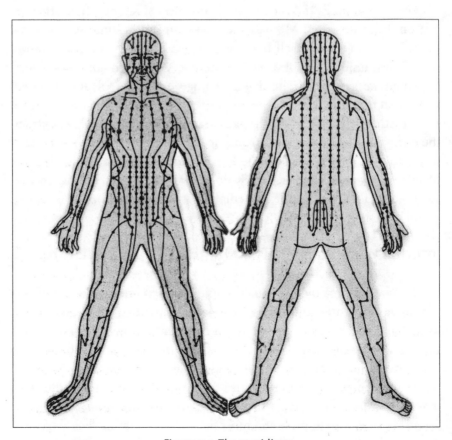

Figure 12.1 The meridians

The meridians connect the organs and viscera to tissue. Along the tracts closest to the surface, running through the torso and limbs, are the points commonly used in acupuncture, each with specific therapeutic virtues. Without a knowledge of the complex physiological theory of traditional Chinese medicine, it is impossible to explain the differentiated effects of each point, even if they are situated on the same meridian or the same dermatome (a cutaneous region innervated by a single spinal nerve).

Meridians, the existence of which has long since been scientifically proven, can be stimulated with a number of therapeutic techniques besides acupuncture. Moxibustion, for example, consists in acting on a meridian with the heat produced by burning the herb mugwort (*Artemisia sinensis*).

For more than 5,000 years, preventive hygiene has been a foundation of Chinese medicine, and in fact the Chinese word for hygiene, *weisheng*, literally means 'to protect life'. The medical application of acupuncture and moxibustion has enjoyed thousands of years of success not only as a curative therapy, but also as a preventive measure, fortifying the body as a whole and impeding the development of illness.

As we've seen, Chinese science considers Qi to be the totality of forces that underlie all the transformations and energetic events in the universe. The human body is part of that energy system and is subject to the same laws. Biological systems, thanks to the electrically polarized water they contain, are immersed in a complex field of multiple forces, including the electromagnetic force that regulates cell function. Any alteration in the flux of these fields can cause disease, which is why a physician must know how these biophysical forces regulate the human organism. Traditional Chinese medicine considers the acupuncture points as spiraliform fields of force through which Qi flows in and out of the body, like a natural spring that both gives forth and receives water: a vortex of energy and matter in perpetual movement.

For more than 30 years these bioenergetic fields have been the object of intensive research, in China and elsewhere, and it has been shown that the meridians mapped by the ancient treatises are fundamentally correct. Innumerable clinical and laboratory studies attest to the effectiveness of acupuncture in treating a great number of pathologies. For several decades now, it has even been used toward analgesic ends during surgery, offering spectacular results.

Meridians are circuits that conduct low-resistance impulses along linear electromagnetic fields with different polarities with respect to the surrounding cutaneous tissue. In 1982, the *American Journal of Physiology* published a paper confirming the existence in the skin of an electromagnetic potential measuring between 20 and 90 mV (millivolts). The electrical resistance values at the acupuncture meridians (10 kΩ, kilo-ohms) are lower than that of the surrounding skin. After stimulation with a needle, the meridian discharges an electromagnetic current of 1 µA (microamperes), which persists for approximately 48 hours, emitting not only electricity but acoustic signals of specific amplitude and frequency.

Like a River Overflowing: The *Shu* Points

Thousands of years ago, the most ancient medical texts compared the meridians of the human body to waterways, connected by tributaries, channels and reservoirs: a meticulous application of the principles of hydraulics, engineering and hydrology to human physiology. Many of the individual acupuncture points use water metaphors to indicate their topographical position and function, with names like Wind Pond, Sea of Qi, Water Passage, Yin Mound Spring.

At every main meridian, each corresponding to an organ, there are five *Shu* points situated between the muscle fibres of the arms and legs. Shu points are like stations along the course of the meridian, and each has specific therapeutic functions. The Shu points of any given meridian are Jing (Well), Ying (Spring), Shu (Stream), Jing (River) and He (Sea). Each is associated with one of the Five Movements.

The Jing-Well point, located at the extremity of the fingers and toes, acts generally on the area closest to the meridian, in much the same way as a well influences the vegetation in the immediate vicinity. At the Ying-Spring point, the flow of Qi in the meridian is faster, reaching maximum acceleration in correspondence with the Shu-Stream point.

The meridian then becomes wider and deeper from the Jing-River to the He-Sea point, the latter of which, due to its greater density, acts directly on the corresponding organ. There are also points of intersection, called *Luo*, which connect the main channel to the rivulets of its collaterals in a fine 'hydric' network of communicating capillary vessels that irrigate the body's tissues.

Stimulation of these points with acupuncture, moxibustion or even simple massage conditions the flux of bodily fluids as well as the dynamic of the energy currents that flow through meridians, optimizing the activity of organ and tissue cells.

Water and Energy in the Human Body

Like the Earth, the human body has its oceans – that is, the four energy centres that correspond to the four seas which, according to Chinese tradition, cover the planet. It is here that the most vital essences and bodily fluids are contained.

In women, one of these seas is constituted by the uterus and a meridian (also present in men) called Chong Mai, or Sea of Blood. The centre of the thorax is the site of the Upper Sea of Qi. The abdominal area below the bellybutton and back through to the kidneys is the Sea of Qi. The fourth sea is the brain, called the Sea of Marrow.

The Kidney is the organ associated with the Water Movement, which is appropriate given that our blood supply is filtered and purified by the kidneys about 15 times per hour (200 litres per day), and that almost all the water circulating in our body is tested, reabsorbed and eliminated by the kidneys.

According to Chinese physiology, the Kidney also governs the genital apparatus and reproductive system – an association that has since been confirmed by modern embryology. The human embryo forms a first set of kidneys in the front-most area of the internal cavity which are very similar to those of fish. After a certain point, these disappear and a new set is formed closer to the spine, and are then transformed into either ovaries or testicles. The tissue of the definitive, functioning set of kidneys eventually develops from cells situated elsewhere.

The relationship of the Kidney to what Chinese medicine considers the Marrows (brain, spinal cord, bone marrow) has also been confirmed by modern science. Consider the hypothalamus, a gland about the size of a hazelnut, located just above the brain stem. The hypothalamus communicates with the kidneys through the secretion of chemical and hormonal mediators that regulate the hydric equilibrium of the body, and it houses the mechanism that stimulates thirst. Through the pituitary gland, the hypothalamus also stimulates the endocrine system, the adrenal glands above all, to secrete hormones such as cortisol, aldosterone and norepinephrine, essential for psychophysical equilibrium and the integrity of the bones.

The hypothalamus is also a sort of command centre for base emotions and instincts (such as the fear and defence reactions) as well as sexual behaviour (arousal, orgasm and ejaculation). As scientific knowledge progresses, the connections between the organs, tissues and psyche identified thousands of years ago by Chinese medicine continue to find confirmation.

The physiological activities associated with the Water Movement have largely to do with storage, as we've seen with regard to the ability of the Kidney to store life energy. Similarly, the brain, nourished by the energy of the Kidney, has the task of storing data in the form of memory. In physics as in medicine, information is organized, ordered energy, while water and the areas associated with it are the loci for communicating and storing that information. Memory is, in a sense, the human being's way of protecting, a bit like a mollusc shell, the energy transmitted to us by our parents and acquired through experience. The Kidney is the storeroom of that energy, of memory, the organic expression of water's capacity to store vital essence.

The physicians of ancient China recognized that one of water's many properties is the ability to transmit, organize and store information. Today, medicine and physics are rediscovering the importance of the relationship between water and memory. As we'll see in Chapter 15, some scientists have managed to demonstrate that water has a 'memory' of its own.

The Door of Life and Memory

There is an area of the body, centred on the spinal column at the height of the kidneys, that the Chinese call *Ming Men*, meaning 'Door of Life' or 'Door of Destiny'. At the heart of this loftily designated area is the acupuncture point of the same name.

According to the *Nan Jing*, a medical text from the first century AD, the Ming Men is the origin of everything that makes up an individual. It is the 'spark' of energy from which life springs, a fire that is paradoxically produced and protected by water. It is this fire that gives us the ability to reproduce and create new life.

The Ming Men acupuncture point, located beneath the second

lumbar vertebra, projects forwards through the lower abdomen towards the navel, the last vestige of the once life-giving connection between mother and foetus.

In the *I Ching*, or Book of Changes, the forces of the universe and their possible combinations in space and time are represented through a simple binary system of a broken line (yin) and a continuous line (yang), grouped in eight trigrams (symbols made up of three parallel yin and/or yang lines) and their possible combinations in 64 hexagrams (six lines).

The trigram for Water (figure 12.2) consists of a continuous line (yang) between two broken lines (yin). Apart from the evident suggestion of a river flowing between irregular banks, it can also be seen as a schematic representation of the two kidneys, which are the yin component of Water, surrounding the yang of the primordial Fire of Ming Men, which represents in turn the generative power inherent in water. Or if we wish, we might even see it as a pair of hydrogen atoms flanking an oxygen atom: the water molecule, with its combustible core, thus represents both Water and Fire.

Figure 12.2 The trigram for Water

The Ming Men is the place where the force that creates the embryo develops from the biological information provided by the sperm and the egg. Chinese physicians call this energetic information *Jing*, or *Essence*. Jing is basically the information that guides the energetic action of Qi and is conserved in the Kidney. There is a distinction between an Essence that derives from the more nutritive and fortifying components of food and water and the Essence intrinsic to the sexual secretions, genetic constitution and the psychophysical traits inherited from one's parents. This innate Essence is stored in the cerebral and sexual structures (ovaries, testicles) governed by the energy of the Kidney, and is what gives the seminal and sexual fluids their fertility.

The origin of matter is Essence. It is the blueprint, the framework upon which life is created. According to Chinese physiology, the embryo develops from the meeting of the Essences of the father and mother, which contain more than just genetic information. To use the analogy of the holographic model, Essence is the interference pattern created by the laser that organizes the matter of the photographic plate into a three-dimensional image.

Essence is the information that underlies matter – the barcode, if you will, from which an individual's energetic state can be determined. Thousands of years before the discovery of the genetic code, the Chinese had already conceived such a code – Essence – as being one of the three building blocks, the three treasures that constitute the foundation of life (along with Qi and Shen, or Spirit). Once again we find that ancient Chinese scholars devised an accurate theory of information in living systems that Western science only began to understand a few decades ago.

Essence is transmitted from generation to generation and can be reinforced or weakened by postnatal events, referred to as 'mutagenes'. In a broader sense, Essence is also the memory we retain of that which precedes us, that which has inscribed itself into our being. And by this it is taken to mean not only the memory processed by the individual, but the shared memory that humanity has transmitted from generation to innumerable generation, and that emerges, in a way that remains unclear, from a holographic matrix of images, myths, fears and desires shared by all humanity, that psychospiritual warehouse that Gustav Jung called the 'collective unconscious'.

In short, Essence is the life-giving principle that impels an organism, in every instant and over time, to continue to exist, to grow, to protect and perpetuate itself. And Essence is preserved thanks to the action of the Ming Men, to the Fire that is ignited by the Water of the Kidney.

Essence is also the informational matrix of the Marrows, which as we've seen are intimately bound to the Kidney by way of the genetic and sexual activities. The Marrows also house the nervous system and the mind, the two other vehicles responsible for acquiring, memorizing and transmitting information down through the generations. Documented physiological studies confirm this connection: stimulation of the Ming Men acupuncture point induces a powerful invigorating effect that influences both the adrenal and pituitary glands.

The Ming Men, protected by the Kidney, is not only essential for maintaining physical and spiritual life, but for ensuring their continuity beyond life through the development of the embryo. This area is not simply a vessel for renewing and replicating life. It holds the very secret of our destiny.

Let's examine the ideogram of these two words (figure 12.3). The radical Ming (life, destiny) on the left is composed in its upper part of two diagonal lines that converge at a single point representing the union of the parents' vital forces as they combine to create a unique and unrepeatable individual.

In the lower part are two characters: on the right, the sceptre-like stroke evokes authority: the king, symbol of stability and the individual's own will, governed by the Kidney. On the left is the square character describing the mouth from which the life-breath originates. Destiny is understood by the Chinese to mean the way in which people develop according to what they've been given by their parents specifically, and by nature more generally, combined with the degree of their determination to follow their own personal inclinations and to cultivate communication through their own energy.

One of the secrets of life can be found in water: if we wish to live long and at the height of our powers, we must follow Heaven, which corresponds to our innate nature, ever aware that we are unique and unrepeatable. And so is our destiny unique, for it depends on our past and the conditions of our present, which can never be the same for two individuals. It is then up to us to take that uniqueness and make something original and creative from it. It is also our individual responsibility to establish a healthy relationship with the Earth through right diet, right breathing and right relationships with ourselves and others.

The word 'Ming' is also found in another expression, *Tian Ming*, meaning 'Mandate of Heaven'. Every individual has his or her own Tian Ming, an inner destiny we must pursue with all our heart if we wish to realize it.

Figure 12.3 The Ming Men ideogram

Memory stores the precious information that has come down to us from preceding generations and transmits it to future ones. It is a store of knowledge with which to understand the past, act on the present, and forge a future to be lived with virtue and wisdom, each according to our talents.

Water, Health and Sexuality in Taoism

Chinese culture holds that the careful regulation of sexual activity can be a valuable means of promoting health and improving one's life. This principle is found in the Bible as well, which associates the cognitive act with the sexual act: the biblical Hebrew word *daat* means both 'to know' and 'to copulate'.

According to ancient Chinese cosmology, the Tao is the point of origin of the yin and the yang, which correspond respectively to Water and Fire. The 'sexual' union of these two opposites, represented in the trigram for Water, is the source of the Five Movements and therefore of all existence.

In traditional Chinese medicine, the seminal fluid and vaginal secretions are 'waters' that provide the impetus for all vital processes, and must therefore be conserved and nourished through proper dietary, physical and sexual education. Over the long run, undisciplined sexual activity, whether it be too much or too little, ends up undermining our psychophysical equilibrium.

Chinese alchemists considered saliva to be the body's own 'elixir of long life', and still today saliva production is one of the aims of energetic disciplines such as *qigong* (chi kung) and *taijiquan* (t'ai chi ch'uan), which also stimulate the secretion of pituitary hormones. Qigong and taijiquan, two of the most ancient of all Chinese martial arts, are characterized by slow, continuous movements that suggest the flow of water, the purpose of which is harmony and balance. Today, simplified popular forms of these ancient disciplines are practised outdoors by millions of Chinese and Western enthusiasts.

The Taoist tradition uses a very apt expression for the female orgasm, describing it as 'high tide', or the 'tide of yin'. One of the lyric forms for designating the sexual act is 'clouds and rain', which refers to

➤

the fluid emissions associated with copulation. From an energetic standpoint, these emissions are a rich and valuable Essence, whose care and conservation falls under the aegis of the Kidney.

In the *Su Nu Jing* ('Classic of the Ordinary Woman'), compiled in the 2nd century BC, the Yellow Emperor is instructed by three courtesans in the sexual techniques that keep the body healthy by cultivating the energy of the water of the Kidney:

> When a man and a woman engage freely in sex, exchanging bodily fluids and breath, it should be like an encounter of Fire and Water, but in such perfect proportions that neither element overwhelms the other. The partners should flow and reflow into one another like the waves and currents of the sea, first in one direction, then another, always in harmony with the Great Tide. In this way the couple can continue all night long, constantly nourishing and replenishing their precious vital Essence and, over time, promoting psychic health and longevity. Without the fundamental harmony of yin and yang, no amount of the highest quality medicines or the most powerful aphrodisiacs will be of any use whatsoever. If the vital Essences are exhausted through excessive emission of semen or through complete negligence, they cannot be revitalized.

~

CHAPTER THIRTEEN

RHABDOMANCY:
TUNING IN TO WATER

The human body is a polarized field crackling with weak electro-magnetic currents powered by ionic cell activity and the acupuncture meridians. These ionic currents run all through us – one need only think of the current generated by the cardiac muscle, graphically represented by an electrocardiogram, or the brain waves we see on an electroencephalogram.

Thanks to its largely aqueous composition, the body is an excellent 'receiver' as well as 'emitter' of electromagnetic waves. The electromagnetic behaviour of water is perceptible to us through rhabdomancy (or alternatively, dowsing, water witching, divining, radiesthesia), which is the ability to detect the presence of water, metals and certain minerals that are otherwise hidden or too distant to see under normal conditions.

Practised since the time of the ancient Egyptians, rhabdomancy (meaning 'to divine with a rod', from the Greek *rhabdos*, 'rod', or 'wand') is still used today by extracting companies to identify underground deposits of metals, petroleum and water. The police forces of many countries avail themselves of dowsing to find hidden corpses or objects, farmers use it to detect subterranean aquifers, and numerous archaeological sites have been found with its help.[28]

The earliest scientific studies of the practice were conducted in the early 20th century in France and Germany, both countries where dowsers were numerous enough to actually have formed professional guilds. Many of them were recruited during the First and Second World Wars for their ability to locate underground tunnels, aquifers, mines and buried grenades with extreme precision.

During the Italo–Ethiopian War of 1935–36, the Italian army was able to survive in that dry region thanks to dowsers who were able to find water sources beneath the soil. In 1941 the Nazis outlawed all rhabdomantic organizations, only to then enlist their members for military service. In the Vietnamese War era, the Americans recruited professional dowsers to teach the Marines how to find the tunnels and weapons caches that the Vietcong had hidden underground. Dowsing is an officially recognized profession in Spain and Russia, where it is routinely used in prospecting, the electricity industry and military operations.

Despite the fact that dowsing has long been a documented reality, scientists who have investigated it over the years have often been subjected to censure. A typical such episode occurred in 1971, when the influential magazine *Nature* published a study of exclusively negative results that 'disproved' the phenomenon, ignoring the protests and research proffered by others demonstrating its validity.

Still today there is an *a priori* scepticism that impedes the diffusion of scientific research on dowsing, such that most mainstream scientists are unaware that this research has ever been done at all. Indeed, the very terms used to define the practice – e.g. water witching, divination – are obstacles to its being seen as anything more than an occult superstition.

In 1957, Yves Rocard, illustrious French physicist and mathematician in the faculty of the École Normale Supérieure di Parigi, conducted in-depth research on dowsing using a proton magnetometer, an instrument that allowed him to register the tiniest variations in what he called biomagnetism and effectively verify the phenomenon of rhabdomancy. In 1983 Rocard published the results of his research in the book *Le Pendule Explorateur* ('The Exploratory Pendulum').

Turning his instumentation to the human body, Rocard found a number of receptor areas sensitive to magnetism that can be activated in different ways after a certain latency period (it is precisely this latency period, which can last upwards of a minute, that would explain the negative results obtained in other tests). Rocard conducted many 'blind' experiments with dowsers, who didn't know who had or had not received magnetic stimulation. It was shown that dowsers are in fact more sensitive than the average person in detecting anomalies in a local magnetic field.

In 1988, a study of more than 500 dowsers, conducted by physicists from several German universities, demonstrated the efficacy of rhabdomancy. Another German study by physicist Hans Dieter Betz of the University of Munich, funded by the German government and published by Stanford University's *Journal of Scientific Exploration* in 1995, presented extraordinary evidence of the utility of dowsing for locating water in arid regions.

The availability of a low-cost method for finding drinkable water is of course essential for the world's poorer countries, where contaminated water is responsible for the majority of disease. Over the course of 10 years, the Munich project drilled more than 2,000 sites in various Asian and African countries. The results were exhilarating: a success rate of 96 per cent in Sri Lanka, for example, by contrast to the 30 to 40 per cent achieved using conventional methods. The role of chance and visual factors – i.e. geological indicators – was considered and excluded, as some of the water strata were in unlikely locations, extremely thin, and lay as deep as 30 metres below the surface. Similar tests conducted in a lab environment gave analogous results, though less spectacular, which suggests that there exist biological factors that make dowsers preternaturally attuned to the biomagnetism of natural water sources.

Certain areas of the human nervous system are in fact quite sensitive to water, and as such are the best means at our disposal for detecting low-intensity energy fields. Approximately 3 out of every 1,000 people are exceptionally sensitive to magnetic fields. But this doesn't mean that the rest of us are insensitive – every human being is innately capable of 'tuning in' to water – it's just that some of us must exercise more patience and persistence to find the approach best suited to us as individuals. We are all potential rhabdomancers, in that we objectively emit and receive, whether we know it or not, electromagnetic waves.

The dowser, or water witch or diviner, as you wish, practises her/his profession using a forked rod of wood or metal, which transmits extremely subtle vibrations to his hands in the presence of water. Not insignificantly, the form of the fork is reminiscent of the 104.7° angle of the water molecule's hydrogen atoms in relation to the oxygen atom. Some dowsers prefer the 'exploratory pendulum' of Rocard's title, essentially a weighted object hung from a string that allows it to rotate freely.

For those who would like to try their hand at dowsing, Rocard advises a string about a metre long and a symmetrical object (crystal, metal, stone) of 200–300 grammes tied to one end. When using a rod, it should be bifurcated, with forks measuring between 35 and 45 centimetres each. Traditionally, only elastic woods such as hazel and filbert were considered viable, whereas nowadays dowsers are prone to use twin L-shaped metal rods that attract or repel one another in the presence of a signal, or rods made from willow, whalebone, even a common wire coathanger. The importance of the instrument itself is relative, inasmuch as some dowsers work with their bare hands. The real instrument, in the end, is our body, which contains innumerable water dipoles that function as magnetic receptors.

Figure 13.1 Dowsing with a bifurcated rod

For first-timers, it's probably best to try divining in a place where you already know there's an underground water source – a public water main, or the immediate vicinity of an artesian well. The rod should be held with the palms facing up and the point directed away from the body.

Remember, though, it's not a question of the instrument itself vibrating or oscillating, but rather of your own involuntary muscle responses to a change in the electromagnetic environment. In other words, don't wait for the rod to move, but for your own body to make it move. If you think you may have felt something, move away, then come back and see if it happens again.

If repeated attempts yield positive results, try looking for water in unfamiliar places to confirm your talents as a rhabdomancer. Make sure there are no cast-iron pipes or metallic structures nearby, for they can compromise your results. At first, detection alone is quite an accomplishment. Professional dowsers, with years of experience under their belts, are able to sense not only the presence of water, but its specific characteristics, such as the size, depth and direction of the source, even the water's potability, hardness and pH.

Another exercise suggested by Rocard consists of walking with your rod or pendulum in the vicinity of an automobile (figure 13.2). Naturally gifted dowsers will feel the vehicle's presence when passing alongside it or just after having passed it.

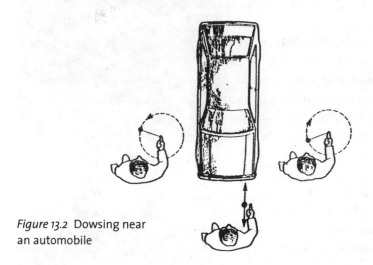

Figure 13.2 Dowsing near an automobile

The Antenna Man

The water molecule dipole reacts to even the most minimal electromagnetic variations and, all the more interesting, water is often found in areas where there are electromagnetic anomalies.

All creatures made of water, from birds to bees to bacteria, are highly sensitive to magnetic fields. Migratory animals of land, sea and sky are also receptive to ultrasounds and the infrared spectrum. Many birds, in fact, have fine feathers called 'philoplumes' which, unlike normal feathers, contain nerve endings, which makes them essentially 'antennae' for detecting and reading electromagnetic fields.

The bodies of many animals contain microcrystals of magnetite, the mineral used to make compasses. In 1983, magnetite was revealed to be present in the brow arch of human beings.[29] Rocard attributes the phenomenon of dowsing, at least in part, to the fact that there are magnetite deposits in the majority of groundwater sources.

Human sensitivity to biomagnetism is due to our body being largely composed of water. We are receptive to terrestrial magnetic and electrical fields, such as natural fluctuations in the layers of electrical current of the ionosphere. From a median value of 0.47 G (gauss), terrestrial magnetism tends to increase towards the poles and decrease towards the equator. Variations in this local field induce a magnetic effect in the human body, detectable through the dowser's rod or pendulum. The natural magnetism of the Earth is closely related to our biological rhythms: the planet's magnetic field pulses between 8 and 16 times per second, in exact synchrony with the predominant electrical rhythms of the human brain.

By extension, we are therefore also vulnerable to perturbations in the electromagnetic environment caused by things like mobile phones, computers, power stations and automobiles. We really should be more mindful of the potentially harmful effects of these by now ubiquitous devices, whose numbers will only increase with time, even if we're still not exactly sure how and to what degree they may be compromising our health.

According to Rocard, when 'magnetic aggression' is artificially increased by a mere tenth of a gauss over normal levels, the body's electromagnetic field is altered in a way that could be damaging, particularly to those more sensitive to such changes. The magnetic alterations in the average Western home are usually below this limit, though they can easily surpass it for those who spend extended periods of time in proximity to artificial electromagnetic sources.

Rocard identified magnetic receptors in the human body in the knees (in the popliteal fossa), the nape of the neck, the inside of the elbows, the heels, between the scapulae, in the lumbar region at the height of the kidneys and in the eyebrows. Alterations in the functioning of these receptors have been recorded in subjects who have undergone trauma, illness or surgery. The removal of a kidney and accompanying suprarenal gland, or even just wearing a steel helmet can diminish our magnetic sensitivity. It has been demonstrated scientifically that the biomagnetic receptiveness of a dowser can be reduced to the point of obliteration by the presence of strong magnetic interference.[30]

The tissues of the sole of the foot are dense with receptors that make them particularly sensitive to magnetism. It should therefore not be surprising that nomadic peoples, whose very existence is often defined by walking, have highly developed rhabomantic skills. The rhabdomancer is attuned to the same forces that the masters of feng shui measure with their compasses and that guide the Australian Aborigines as they traverse their continent, singing. They are the forces of the Earth's 'energy channels', which are in a very real sense a macrocosmic extension of the acupuncture meridians that course through the human body.

Louis Turenne and the 'Universal Pendulum'

Louis Turenne was born in Paris in 1872. At 21 he completed his engineering degree at the most prestigious technical institute of that era, the École Centrale, after which he became a professor of physics, electromagnetism and radiotelegraphy at Fontainebleu.

Turenne liked to tell his students that every man is like an antenna, sensitive to the myriad waves and magnetic fields that surround and pass through him, and that the human nervous system was enough to make anyone, with the help of the right instruments, capable of detecting very weak waves and fields, and even at significant distances.

Turenne's father ran a business that manufactured groundwater pumps and well-drilling and digging equipment. Identifying underwater aquifers and determining exactly where to drill was a task his father entrusted to rhabdomancers and their mysterious hazel rods.

As a child, Turenne wondered what natural explanation lay behind their seemingly supernatural powers, and it was thus that he became the first scientist to study the physical realities of water dowsing. Well before Rocard, Turenne explained that the dowser's pendulum or rod amplified the microcontractions of the hand muscles caused by the neurovegetative system.

From 1910 onwards, he approached the analysis of electromagnetic emissions in a thoroughly original way. Any electric or electronic device creates an electromagnetic field, however minimal, which in Turenne's view obscured the weaker natural waves – not unlike someone trying to hear the sound of the wind through the trees, the flapping of a bird's wings or the babbling of a distant brook while driving a tractor with the motor running, or attempting to observe the night sky while standing next to a floodlight. In order to overcome the obstacle of artificial 'background noise', Turenne set about designing an instrument capable of detecting even the faintest natural wave emissions.

He began to realize that the pendulum, which the official scientific community had determined some years earlier to be a simple and predictable instrument, had instead a very complex behaviour – which, incidentally, made him a pioneer in this field: the behaviour of a pendulum is one of the central arguments of the modern chaos theory's research on complexity. Illustrious predecessors had already conducted important experiments on the pendulum: in 1583 Galileo Galilei articulated the laws of pendular motion; in 1851 Foucault performed his celebrated experiment in Paris's Panthéon, hanging a giant pendulum from the cupola to demonstrate the rotation of the Earth.

It was clear to Turenne that dowsers were more than capable of 'seeing' underground water, yet they weren't always accurate in their description of it – whether is was fresh or salty, clean or contaminated by bacteria, etc. Aware that the information revealed by the pendulum could be conditioned by subjective mental factors, he did his best to eliminate them.

Turenne felt that the pendulum was the best 'impulse detector' for what he called man's 'antenna'. His first design was a small green sphere fixed to the end of a string – green because that is the colour that lies at the centre of the visible light spectrum and because Turenne had also found that it emits a very faint radioactive signal.

But something was missing that would make his instrument obey the laws of electromagnetism while also making it as free as possible from the influence of the operator's mind. He decided to attach two compass needles on opposite sides of the sphere's equator. When the professor tried his new device by hanging it down an existing well, he was puzzled to find that there was no reaction at all. He tried again and again, but what should have been a highly sensitive instrument simply hung there over the well water, inert. He summoned the dowsers who worked for his father, and they weren't able to do any better, nor to explain why this carefully designed device should be the exception to the rule that *any* object hung from a string will exhibit *some* movement.

Turenne wasn't the type to give up easily. He tried a number of reconfigurations, but it wasn't until he moved the tips of the compass needles towards the poles of his green sphere that the pendulum finally responded. After extensive experimentation, he determined that horizontal placement of the magnetic needles made the pendulum receptive only to horizontal 'magnetic' waves, while vertical placement made it receptive to vertical 'electrical' waves. From this, he was able to conclude that water emits only vertical 'electrical' waves and not horizontal magnetic ones.

Continuing his investigations into other elements, Turenne found that the positioning of the needles determined the type of wave the pendulum was able to receive. He classified nine groups of electro-magnetic waves according to their form and direction, all of them far weaker than conventional electromagnetism and not otherwise detectable. He eventually identified the form, height and length of every element in the animal, vegetable and mineral kingdoms, and even ventured into researching the vibratory states of healthy and diseased cells.

In healthy cells, whether human or animal, the pendulum responded only to horizontal magnetic waves, while pathogenic agents and diseased tissue emitted only vertical electrical waves. Turenne also measured and catalogued the harmful waves coming from below the ground, from power stations and cables, from automobiles, aeroplanes and diseased organisms. In this, he was the first to establish the relation between health and the electromagnetic environment in a scientific framework. Every wave carries 'information' that can be beneficial or harmful, depending on the degree of variation from the frequencies emitted by the cells of our body.

A number of famous physicians collaborated with Turenne on his research: Dr Aveline, who brought a statistical approach to the study of the body's interaction with the geobiological context; Alexis Carrel (1873–1944), the famous French physiologist and Nobel Prize winner who worked with Turenne on the radiation emitted by water and its effects on human health; and Professor Nebel, noted oncologist from Lausanne, who analysed the effects of electromagnetic emissions on the formation of tumours, as well as the developing diagnostic and therapeutic methods for degenerative blood diseases.

Like radioesthesia, Turenne's method is based on the principle that every human being is capable of sensing, with the proper instrumentation, vibrational signals – thus the names he used for his method, 'scientific radioesthesia', and later 'radio-disintegration'. Unlike empirical radioesthesia, the operator does not mentally 'ask' the pendulum to move; moreover, Turenne's pendulum stops oscillating when it reaches 'wave saturation', independently of the operator's will.

Over the years Turenne invented other precision instruments for detecting and classifying waves, even at notable distances. He designed what he called 'catalysers': devices capable of fixing the 'information' from electromagnetic waves, which he used towards therapeutic and environmental ends.

There was also a significant commercial value to Turenne's original method of detection: he discovered a gold deposit in Mexico, precious minerals in Brazil and petroleum in Romania on behalf of a government agency. In Morocco, during the period of French rule, he worked with the Ministry of Mining to find phosphates. And of course he found water sources, thousands of them over the course of his life, including the Evian spring in Switzerland, Vittel in France and Sidi Harazem in Morocco.

Turenne and 'Heavy Waters'

Turenne observed a variety of water types and catalogued them according to the height and length of their waves. After years and years of study, he came to the fundamental conclusion that all water, regardless of type, emits only 'vertical electrical' waves, and that it can be made to store 'information' when 'magnetized' with crystals or other magnetic substances.

He maintained that all mineral waters cease giving off vertical electrical waves 24 hours after being removed from the source, no longer providing any beneficial vibrations. Like Schauberger, Turenne considered drinking waters transported through channels or plumbing to be 'unhealthy', since their wavelengths are significantly lower, even if they've been purified, than those of healthy, natural waters. To preserve the salutary benefits of water from an electromagnetic standpoint, he invented special bottle stoppers that maintained its original characteristics. He patiently measured the 'spectrum' of numerous mineral waters and collated their curative powers with their electromagnetic structure.

As early as the 1930s, Turenne had suspected the presence of faint traces of 'heavy' water in the fluids of certain perennial plants, fruit, legumes and other foodstuffs. He eventually identified seven types of so-called heavy water – H_4O, H_4O_2, H_4O_4, H_4O_8, H_4O_{16}, H_4O_{32}, along with another type which he called 'green water'. According to Turenne, every mineral water contained one and only one type of heavy water, while every individual person's electromagnetic constitution had three. From this he concluded that when a person ingests one or more heavy waters that correspond with his or her own, there are significant health benefits. He therefore felt it was essential to determine the three heavy waters specific to each individual so as to be able to prescribe the appropriate mineral waters.

Louis Turenne was awarded France's two highest military honours, the Legion of Honour and the War Cross. The scientific community, however, was a bit less forthcoming with its praise. After the Second World War, he registered his inventions with the CNRS (Centre National de la Recherche Scientifique) and also advised them of the coordinates, dimensions and depth of a rich uranium deposit he'd been studying for three years in the Limousin region. After about a year of bureaucratic stonewalling, the CNRS dismissed his inventions and ignored his uranium find. Turenne turned to the director of the Commissariat à l'Énergie Atomique, Frédéric Joliot-Curie, who did not even deign to respond.

After all he'd done for his country, Turenne was humiliated enough by this rejection that he hardly needed it exacerbated by the fact that, six years later, the CNRS announced that uranium had been found in Limousin, claiming full credit for the discovery. There was some outcry in the press, but it quickly became moot: Turenne died on the operating table in 1954 at the age of 82, and was buried alongside the luminaries of French culture and history in the cemetery of Montparnasse.

In the words of noted editorialist Paul Reboux:

> Louis Turenne was to the study of electromagnetism what Claude Bernard was to psychology and Louis Pasteur to bacteriology. He guided the unsteady first steps of newborn discipline, bringing science and reason and rigour to a practice whose earnest, but too imaginative practitioners had mistaken for wizardry.

The documentation and instrumentation that Turenne and his followers have left to us are considerable. Today, chemists and physicists are finally beginning to study the biological effects of electromagnetic fields at extremely low intensities, particularly microwaves and ELF (extremely low frequency) fields. In Italy, there is an association bearing his name, dedicated entirely to the diffusion of his ideas and methods.[31]

It has been demonstrated that microwave (frequencies between 50 MHz and 700 GHz) irradiation of cellular material causes abrupt variations in its biological properties only when the value of the wave frequency corresponds to that of the specific cell type – a sort of 'on-off' effect that operates independently of intensity since it is in any case well below the thermal threshold, just as Turenne had always maintained.

As for ELF fields, it has been observed that a combination of two parallel weak magnetic fields, one static and one alternating, with an intensity less than 0.1 μT (microtesla) and a frequency below 100 Hz, can provoke a transitory variation in the flow of mineral ions to the cell membranes (the so-called 'ionic pump'), thereby influencing organ and tissue cell function.

The ionic pump can be regulated by a calibrated combination of the Earth's natural magnetic field, that of the cell membrane and artificial generators. The ionic pump is also influenced by the low-intensity, low-frequency fields such as that of the sympathetic-parasympathetic neurovegetative system – the same apparatus that enables us to detect electromagnetic radiation. Louis Turenne beat the scientific mainstream by decades in the discovery of many of what are now understood to be fundamental properties of water. This alone should be enough justification for a more careful look, without prejudice, at his body of work, which could provide important data for the prevention and cure of illnesses with water, as well as expand the frontiers of research on the physical factors that would enable human beings to better attune ourselves to the single most important molecular compound on our planet.

CHAPTER FOURTEEN

WATER AND CONSCIOUSNESS

*Mind is the first and most direct thing in our experience;
all else is remote inference, either intuitive or deliberate.*

SIR ARTHUR EDDINGTON, astrophysicist (1882–1944)

The boundary between physical and mental reality is more ephemeral than ever. Physics with the advent of quantum mechanics, psychology with the study of so-called altered states of consciousness, and chaos theory with the discovery of fractals have broken free of the limits of contingent and mechanistic analysis that once dominated the sciences, unchallenged. Prior to that, scholars contemplated only spatially contiguous events and applied exclusively the principle of causality, building chains that linked cause to effect, extending them in linear succession over time.

Today, consciousness is an integral part of several recent theories in physics, which to varying degrees has embraced the idea that a mental process can influence, as much as a subatomic particle or a physical event, the course of other phenomena and events. Ancient Indian and Chinese science and numerous mystical traditions have always considered intelligence as a property belonging to the entire universe – a holographic intelligence, identical in all its parts, from the smallest to the largest.

Scientific research on consciousness is hardly a new discipline, yet while the connection between observer and observed is by now an established fact in the field of physics, it is all but ignored in biology, where there is great resistance to allowing extrasensory phenomena into the discourse of biochemistry, biology and medicine. Their reluctance is understandable: the study of psychic and parapsychic phenomena generates results that are difficult to reconcile with current theories.

To explore the world, we must immerse ourselves in it as if taking a swim in the ocean, over and through the waves, down to the bottom. The scientific approach is more like floating on that ocean, or at best paddling on the surface. Science analyses that which can be observed, from a position that more resembles detachment than immersion.

The subjective or 'mystical' approach is swimming under water, feeling the sounds of the water blending with those of our body as they reverberate together inside us. It is becoming one with the water, penetrating a more hidden and intimate dimension. These different approaches are not mutually exclusive, but rather distinct yet compatible ways of experiencing and understanding nature. There is no reason why scientific and spiritual research cannot come together in exploring the world we live in and the water that makes up so much of it.

Water and the Brain

The brain is 85 per cent water. And more than any other organ, it lives in an aquatic environment, literally 'floating' in the cephalo-rachidian liquid that protects it from trauma and 'massages' it by penetrating the folds of the cortex and its internal cavities, or ventricles. Looking at the brain, it isn't difficult to see why the Chinese Theory of the Five Movements associates it with Water.

Not only surrounded by water, the brain is also extremely sensitive to it. In the final months of gestation, the foetal brain develops at the breakneck pace of more than 250,000 new cells per minute, the fastest growth rate of any part of the body. Most of this growth takes place in the cortical region, which governs the sensory and motor apparatuses and higher mental functions. The direct contact of the foetus with water – i.e. the amniotic fluid in which it is immersed – appears to favour cerebral development, just as it probably did in the case of our hominid ancestor, whose semiaquatic environment helped him develop a brain as large as the cetaceans'.

Water provides the electrical resistance necessary for neuronal activity – without it, the brain would not function, and we would know neither consciousness nor memory. The neuron, made up of 80 per cent water, is a cell that resembles a swelling water balloon. The brain has about 10 billion such cells, each with approximately 10,000 synapses, which are the junctions that connect them with other neurons. The average person loses 1,000 neurons and therefore 10 million synaptic connections per day, while new cells and connections are formed at the rate of about one every 10 to 15 seconds. And just like the water in a river that is never the same but always a river, human beings, despite this continuous process of destruction and construction, manage to conserve their sense of identity and full awareness of themselves.

The brain is dynamic not only in terms of thought but in its very material structure. Cerebral matter is constantly in flux, creating new synapses, or dendrites (figure 14.1), a term deriving from the Greek for 'tree'. Dendrites, not surprisingly, are fractalic in the structure of their branches.

The neuron is at once constant and ever changing, like water. Consciousness, though immersed in a physical and biological reality in continuous flux, remains remarkably stable. Like a water fountain, our mental and physical identity is a permanent dissipative system, the form and function of which remains constant as the constituent parts are subjected to a massive and continual turnover.

Figure 14.1 Dendrites

The power of the brain is conditioned by how much we use it. When it is damaged and loses neurons in the event of, say, a stroke, the cerebral structure has an incredible capacity to compensate for the functions of the damaged tissue by augmenting and diversifying those of the surviving neurons. While it is true that the brain constructs thought, it is likewise true that thinking constructs the brain, insofar as *mental activity in itself generates new dendrites*. The more complex and varied the mental activity, the more dendrites are formed, such that an individual who interacts with few people will have fewer synaptic connections and thus a weaker brain than someone with complex social and diverse cultural stimulations. What we do and how we interact with the world, depending on the degree of complexity, influences the architecture of the brain, just as physical exercise influences our muscle strength and skeletal flexibility.

The brain is divided longitudinally into two hemispheres, each with specific functions. This differentiation is called hemispheric lateralization. It is only in the higher mammals, those species that evolved in contact with water, that the left and right hemispheres are different in terms of both form and function. The bipolar asymmetry of the cerebral hemispheres echoes that of the water molecule – it is an 'imperfect' symmetry, 'aquatic' in nature, which tells us much about our own type of intelligence.

The left hemisphere is responsible for logical, analytical and linguistic functions – that is, the processes that involve the examination of data in detailed sequence. It also governs the sensory and motor functions of the right side of the body in right-handed people.

The right hemisphere interprets geometric and spatial information and informs analogical and intuitive thought. It analyses data in a simultaneous way, parallel rather than linear. It is the part of our mind that perceives spatial relations, recognizes symbols and synthesizes disparate elements; it has, in short, a holistic vision of things. These functions have been known for centuries by the Kabbalists, who associate intuitive wisdom with the right side of the brain.

The right hemisphere governs primary processes: vestigial primitive thought, instincts, myths and dreams. The left hemisphere supervises the secondary processes of rational analysis of concrete phenomena. The two hemispheres do not, of course, operate independently, but communicate continuously by way of the dense band of fibres that both separates and joins them, known as the corpus callosum. This communication is what gives us a sense of identity, the awareness of a unitary self.

The evolution of the human brain has brought with it a thickening of the corpus callosum and a gradual increase in bipolarization and asymmetry. The more asymmetrical the two hemispheres become, the more they must communicate with one another, which in turn opens up more possibilities for the development of intelligence and, by extension, of human society. In other words, the more the brain imitates the asymmetry of water, the smarter it gets.

The brain is one of the vehicles created by the movement of water to expand and sharpen the intelligence of the universe. Intelligence, however, isn't limited to the brain alone, but circulates throughout our body in a variety of forms.

The Intelligence of the Body

Water is the physical vector that feeds and transports information, making possible the functions of intelligence. With its ubiquitousness and dynamic ductility, water provides an excellent descriptive model for the way intelligence works in the body.

Today, at long last, psychology recognizes the role played by emotions in the expression of intelligence. Individuals are intelligent not just because they have elevated cognitive capacities or score high on a standardized IQ test, but because their emotional quotient (EQ) is highly developed as well. Emotional intelligence is the ability to manage one's own emotions and relationships with others: the ability to sense the difference between annoyance and anger, constructive criticism and cruelty, lust and love – and most importantly, to act accordingly. Water, as we've seen, is at once the source of our most primitive and visceral emotions as well as the quintessential model of evolved flexibility and enlightened cooperation.

Intelligence and consciousness are not 'housed' inside the brain. When we think or experience an emotion, the substances associated with these activities – neurotransmitters called neuropeptides – are not only produced in the brain, but in other bodily tissues as well. Indeed, the flow of neuropeptides involves the entire organism.

Endorphins, for example, are opioid neuropeptides that mediate the transmission and experience of pain and emotions. The cells of certain organs (intestines, kidneys, stomach, heart, skin) contain receptors for endorphins and can also produce them. Receptors are also found in monocytes, a type of white blood cell that works with the body's immune system. As such, all these cells can be said to be 'sensitive' to emotional states, in that leap into action when we experience fear, joy, anguish, satisfaction, and so on. Interestingly, in some nonhuman species it has been discovered that oxytocin, the hormone that contracts the uterus during birth, and vasopressin, a hormone that regulates the body's conservation of water, facilitate the 'emotions' of bonding between mates.

The existence of a dynamic metasystem wherein neurotransmitters, mental activity, hormones and the immune system all work together has long been postulated, and modern medicine has finally acknowledged it in the form of a new discipline called *psychoneuroimmunology*. The ambiguity of the boundaries between mind and body, familiar to ancient science and mystical traditions, is becoming ever more so, across the board.

The heart plays a key role in this dynamic system, as does the endocrine gland, which produces ANP (atrial natriuretic peptide, or atripeptin), a hormone that acts on the kidneys, lungs, liver, small intestine and brain. In keeping with traditional Chinese medicine, the most recent discoveries in the nascent field of psychoneuroimmunology confirm the holistic interconnectedness between the body and the heart, emperor of organs, sovereign of psychophysical health.

Modern physiology has also recently adopted a premise that has informed Chinese medicine for millennia: the 'mind' is not a 'thing' that 'resides' in the brain, but rather a *flow* that *circulates* throughout the entire body. The body, not the brain, thinks and feels as a whole, and this triggers a chain reaction of biochemical responses in every cell, transforming its behaviour, efficacy, even its composition. Intelligence circulates in our bodily liquids, adjusting us by adapting itself, and vice versa. It is the nomadic intelligence of which we spoke earlier, the fluid flux of life itself, omnipresently active, with or without our awareness of it.

The atoms of our body change. Matter mutates. But memory remains constant. Some neuroscientists postulate that the holographic memory of the brain is fixed in the proteic structures of neurons, called microtubules: through the spiral of the proteins and intracellular nucleic acids (DNA and RNA), cells and tissues accumulate memory, perpetually organizing external information while transforming themselves uninterruptedly from within.

DNA is the genetic matrix from which biological matter is formed; a storage tank of memory that is at once permanent and ever shifting. The information contained within the DNA helix maintains a constant identity in each of the billions of cells that make up our body, and is somehow able to both preserve itself and radically evolve – over the course of millions of years in our case, and billions in that of other, more ancient species.

The spiral structure of DNA, the dendritic branching of neurons, the helicoid configuration of proteins and the convolutions of the brain are all simply variations on the vortical rhythms and fractal architecture of water. The structures responsible for intelligence mimic the structures of water, all of them paradoxically stable yet subject to constant recycling of their component parts. The brain and the body and every cell contained therein are eloquent testimony to the marriage of permanence and change that creates and sustains all life.

The Water-like Mind

Psychoanalysis offered the earliest significant speculations in post-Enlightenment Western thought regarding the role of water in mental operations. Freud famously interpreted the presence of water in dreams as an allusion to birth, sex and the unconscious.

We tend to underestimate the events surrounding our own birth because we can't consciously remember them, but they are nevertheless very important for our psychoemotive development. The first to examine that importance was the German psychoanalyst Otto Rank (1884–1939), who in 1929 wrote the classic essay, *The Trauma of Birth*.

Rank pushed Freud's timeline of infant consciousness and sexuality back to the moment of birth, sustaining that the trauma caused by the separation from the uterine environment is the first truly painful, and as such defining experience of every individual's life. Immediately afterwards, when the umbilical cord is severed, the newborn is further traumatized to find himself suddenly forced into tumultuous contact with the innumerable adversities of the outside world – having to breathe, waiting to eat, assaulted by unfiltered noise and light – all of which must feel like nothing less than a jarring nightmare after the aquatic serenity of the womb.

Rank believed that the trauma of separation from the mother at the moment of birth and subsequent attempts to deal with the consequences lay at the origin of infant anxiety and neurosis. For male infants, the problem was the desire to return to the comfort of the womb, with the Oedipal conflict being resolved through sexual union and marriage. For the female, reproduction and maternity were the means of reconnecting, through one's own body, with the lost uterine paradise.

Sándor Ferenczi (1873–1933), another of Freud's disciples, worked in Budapest where he formulated several interesting theories with regard to water and mind. In his 1938 essay 'Thalassa', he seconded Rank in attributing certain sexual conflicts to the traumatic separation from the maternal womb, but went back even further to explore the experience of the uterine world itself.

For Ferenczi, the amniotic liquid reproduces the ocean that our ancestors abandoned millions of years ago. We are driven by a profound, innate impulse to return to the aquatic realm that was the first habitat of our ancestors and the locus of our own first awakening as conscious beings. Ferenczi sensed that rooted in our ancestral memory the human species has an affinity with water: we have a nostalgic desire to return there, a regressive impulse that he called *thalassa*, the Greek word for 'sea'. Ferenczi's vision of the interior world as a reflection of macrocosmic forces seems in many instances to be inspired by mystical traditions.

The regressive 'thalassic' impulse can be overcome by a spiritual effort to abandon the construct of identity, of the separate 'self', immersing ourselves in the ocean of existence. But so long as we remain individuals, we are irresistibly attracted by water, striving by way of sexual ecstasy to return to our aquatic foetal origins – or even, as some have dared propose, to the cellular state. Orgasm brings us to a place not unlike mystical awareness, making us feel part of the cosmic forces that created life from water, identifying with the sperm and the egg and the primordial creative power of the universe.

Subsequent clinical studies have sustained some of Rank's and Ferenczi's ideas, and in a certain sense have even shown them to merit further expansion. The alleged peace and security and cushioned silence of the unborn foetus is, in many cases, as sublime as common wisdom would have it. Sometimes, the lifestyle choices of the mother such as diet and physical activity, not to mention metabolic and stress factors, can make the uterus a less than ideal environment. And as Otto Rank would hurry to remind us, the newborn is hardly a passive witness to his or her own birthing process, which can be a violent, indeed traumatic experience.

The passage through the birth canal causes, even in the smoothest births, significant psychophysical stress which can become, depending on the intensity, the source of profound anxiety later in life.

The most valuable insights relative to this issue have come from the school of transpersonal psychology, the foremost practitioner of which is the contemporary psychiatrist, Stanislav Grof, whose research has helped access and identify the earliest unconscious experience, including foetal memory.

Seeking to penetrate the content of the unconscious, Grof and his colleagues began giving subjects, under close medical supervision, psychotropic substances and hallucinogens such lysergic acid diethylamide (LSD). Later experiments used experiential techniques similar to hypnotism to help subjects relive their own birth as well as to directly face the idea of their own death.

During a transpersonal session, subjects often discover deep connections between the events and circumstances surrounding their remembered birth and the overall quality of their lives, strongly suggesting that the birth experience profoundly influences our personal values, our worldview and self-confidence, our attitudes toward others, the balance we manage to strike between optimism and pessimism – in short, our entire life strategy and ability to resolve problems.

The degree of detail of these memories is often extraordinary. Patients have been known to recall whether forceps or castor oil were used, their position in the birth canal, and complications involving the umbilical cord. Subjects are also able to reproduce in real time the alterations of physiological parameters during the birthing process: tachycardia, increased saliva and mucus secretion, muscular tension, specific positions and movements, even the appearance of bruises and other visible signs.[32] This type of psychosomatic re-evocation is called transpersonal because, while experiencing it, the subject has the sensation of breaking the boundaries of individual consciousness and expanding the confines of the self in space and time. Some subjects are able to describe specific concrete episodes of their foetal lives, while others push their consciousness to events and myths of distant civilizations, both known and unknown.

There also appears to be evidence of access to a cellular level of consciousness, where subjects are able to identify themselves with animals, plants, even inorganic substances. There are those who have 'become' the spermatozoon or the egg at the moment of conception, and have had the insight that contained therein is the entire 'memory' of the universe. Others relive episodes from possible past lives, or from the real-time lives of their own ancestors. And more often than not, these unconscious memories turn out to have an intense relevance for the subjects' own lives.

The common denominator of transpersonal experiences is the identification of the self with a vast cosmic consciousness, a universal mind. It can of course be claimed that these externalizations arc simply the fruit of the subject's imagination; wishful hallucinatory suggestions. But that would not explain the realism and exactitude of the details that these subjects are able to access, nor the indisputable liberating therapeutic effects of these experiences. In any event, what interests us here is the specific content of the imagery encountered in these experiences, which are often connected to water.

No scientific theory has yet been able to entirely explain transpersonal experiences, whether they are evoked by hypnosis, immersion in saltwater isolation tanks, psychoactive drugs or mystical religious practices. But this in no way diminishes their reality or relevance. It simply means that science cannot explain why, regardless of method or culture or final purpose, countless people throughout history have had the same experience of transcending the sense of separate identity and expanding their consciousness into what is commonly described as an infinite cosmic ocean.

It is therefore not entirely rash to suppose that we all carry within us, in the space-time of our consciousness, information concerning the past, present and future of the entire universe, and that we have the potential to access that information. The phenomena of expanded consciousness, if they are ever to be fully explained scientifically, should be examined through holistic and holographic models, which are already intrinsically equipped to accommodate extrasensory experiences such as telepathy, clairvoyance, extracorporeal perception and psychic diagnostics. Telepathy and synchronicity entail non-local connections between mental processes and matter, and do not obey sequential or spatial order as we know it: much like the paradoxes of quantum physics, which physicists themselves are more than willing to admit they cannot grasp. It is thus possible that we can never fully 'know' the nature of these connections except by experiencing them directly.

Non-Ordinary States of Consciousness in Water

Say, you are in the country; in some high land of lakes. Take almost any path you please, and ten to one it carries you down in a dale, and leaves you there by a pool in the stream. There is magic in it. Let the most absent-minded of men be plunged in his deepest reveries – stand that man on his legs, set his feet a-going, and he will infallibly lead you to water, if water there be in all that region. ... Yes, as every one knows, meditation and water are wedded for ever.

HERMAN MELVILLE, *Moby-Dick*

Life begins and ends in the ocean. When we die, we leave our corporeal identity behind. Like the molecules of water that pass through the hydrological cycle to return inexorably to the ocean, so does our identity return to the energy source from whence it comes.

A newborn infant, precisely because of its origins in the universal aquatic matrix, feels at one with everything. In the first months of life, the newborn easily establishes relationships with any and all living things, for the sense of conscious separation between the self and others – the individuality that all too often mutates into a sense of desolation and loneliness in later years – has not yet developed. The infant is not yet concerned about affirming his/her identity, about controlling the present or fretting over the future.

As time goes on, paradoxically, our vision of these things tends to deteriorate: present and future fade into vagueness, while the past remains vivid and real. Elderly people, because they concentrate more on what was than what will be, are the living memory of human society, and can also provide a lesson for living in the present: the wise senior is no longer concerned with developing or asserting the self and focuses more on life's more substantive matters such as family, community, nature and spirit. This attitude helps them prepare for and accept the moment when they will die and return, like our aforementioned water molecule, to the source. Age, in other words, allows us to recover that sense of belonging enjoyed by infants, that feeling of being a part of everything.

William James (1842–1910), a professor at Harvard, was the first great exponent of modern psychology. It was he who coined the expression 'stream of consciousness' to describe the fluid and dynamic nature of thought. The flow of consciousness obeys the same principles as the flow of water. Our sensory perceptions are constantly changing, which is what allows us to be vigilant and responsive in relation to the constantly changing world around us. Just as the 'intelligence' of water derives from its fluidity, so is the intelligence of conscious beings defined by flexibility of thought. Aldous Huxley, in his splendid book *The Art of Seeing*, observed that consciousness is only possible through change; change is only possible through movement. The fact that Huxley was referring specifically to visual perception reminds us of the Couette cylinder, wherein the water becomes visible only when it is set into turbulent motion.

With rare insight for a scientist of his time, James avoided constructing hierarchies and imposing judgements on mental processes. He was the first to clinically study phenomena hitherto limited to the province of religion, such as multiple personalities, out-of-body experiences, trance states and possession. These are the so-called 'non-ordinary' states of consciousness, different enough from the normal waking state to allow access to broader, more 'oceanic' mental experiences and awareness.

All ancient civilizations, including the pre-industrial West, attributed great significance to these states. They were considered a powerful means of accessing the kinds of extrasensory experience that lead to closer contact with nature and with the divine, as well as a shamanic method for diagnosing and curing illness and inspiring artistic creativity. As we'll see in greater detail later on, there are many techniques for inducing such states, from hypnosis to meditation to immersion in water-filled flotation tanks.

Non-ordinary states of consciousness reflect certain paradoxical aspects of water: first of all, they are themselves paradoxical and therefore difficult to accept. Among the typical ecstatic sensations that people experience is that of feeling one's insignificance while at the same time feeling able to understand the cosmos – or to put it another way, the simultaneous annulment of the self and identification with the entire universe. Many physicians and psychiatrists summarily dismiss these experiences as hallucinations or 'depersonalizations', a term for alterations in the vigilant and discriminative state considered 'normal' in psychology.

Yet all of us experience non-ordinary states of consciousness every day, though we tend not to attribute any great importance to them.

Consider for example our nightly dreams, daydreams and alterations of our temporal perception – we all know how time tends to slow down when we're bored and accelerate when we're engaged or amused. Then there is, of course, the virtually universal experience of *déjà vu*, not to mention the telepathic intuitions that many of us have experienced, or the peculiar perceptual state that characterizes authentic artistic creation. These common experiences are simply the hidden face of normality, the unilluminated side of the psychic moon, as it were.

Non-ordinary states of consciousness are among the highest expressions of human intelligence, for they denote the ability to transcend one's spatial and temporal limits. To better understand these phenomena, neurophysiologists have used a number of research tools such as frequency spectrum analysis, thermography, positron emission tomography (PET) – a variation on computerized axial tomography (CAT) – as well as functional magnetic resonance imaging (fMRI).

The frontal lobes of the cortex are the seat of faculties such as intuition, foresight and empathy, while the limbic system contains the circuits that control emotional expression and mnemonic processes. The connection between the frontal lobes and the limbic system is essential for the integration of emotive data and consciousness, as well as for their expansion into what is aptly called 'emotional intelligence'. Indeed, it has been observed that the hypnotic trance state excites the orbitofrontal cortex and certain subcortical areas of the limbic system such as the hippocampus and amygdala.

Non-ordinary states induce varying forms and degrees of the annulment of self, which paradoxically manifest themselves in opposing conditions:

- In response to the sensory deprivation of a flotation tank; in dreams; in contexts of total social isolation such as those cultivated by monks, gurus, lamas, etc.

- In response to intense sensory stimuli such as those induced by mass religious rituals that may or not be characterized by dancing or repetitive chanting; the use of psychotropic substances.

Both the absence and excess of sensory stimuli can provoke non-ordinary states of consciousness. But it is not necessarily always an external agent that causes them; sometimes they occur spontaneously in 'normal' psychic activity, such as artistic creation or intellectual revelation.

Toward the end of the 1970s, physicians and psychologists began taking a serious interest in the subject, first to study the effects of LSD and flotation tanks, later to cure their patients. This research was a significant step forward for the psychological disciplines on both the applied and theoretical levels.

Vortical Forms and Movements of the Mind

UCLA physiologist Ronald Siegel discovered that all 'psychedelic' substances such as LSD and mescaline induce visualizations of four basic forms: spirals, funnels, spider webs and grates. They all echo the natural forms we find in fractals, water flow and the patterns created thereby. These are known as Kluver's 'form constants', named after the German mathematician Heinrich Kluver, who investigated hallucinogenic visualization back in the 1920s.

Particularly interesting for our purposes is the research of biophysicist and mathematician Jack Cowan, who used complex mathematical formulae to demonstrate that Kluver's constants reproduce the forms of heat-driven convection in liquids. The brain and turbulent liquids obey the same mathematical laws. If we heat up a liquid in a pan, as Cowan suggests, we will see honeycomb and spider web forms appear: the same structures may appear while hallucinating. The mathematics of these phenomena is known in chaos theory as broken symmetry. Hence we learn that the brain is intrinsically unstable.[33]

The same forms are found in the art of every ancient civilization, from the natives of North America to Australia's Aboriginal peoples. These universal visual codes, which derive from the movements of water and can provoke intense cerebral stimulation, are etched into the brains of human beings from every part of the world and from every epoch. They constitute a psychic heritage shared by all humanity, perhaps by all the planet's various forms of intelligence. Siegel characterizes these figures as the consonants of a universal human grammar. They are the mental skeleton of the interior images that we project towards the exterior and through which we interpret our perceptions of the world.

In states of consciousness induced by psychotropic substances, the four form constants tend to pulse and/or rotate, continuously in motion like the vibratory and vortical sequences of water. These same images can be perceived when we hyperventilate, when we're hypoglycaemic,

after extensive physical exertion, during migraine episodes, in conditions of sensory deprivation (e.g. flotation tanks) or extreme isolation
(e.g. being underground for extended periods), or during hypnotic
trances and meditation.

The image of the spiral can have negative connotations, evoking
sensations of suffocation or imprisonment deriving from negative
experiences *in utero*. The spiral can also evoke the danger of no way out
of a whirlpool for an organism such as ourselves, accustomed from
conception to associate water with safety and freedom. The memory
we carry of our ontogenetic and phylogenetic past creates in us an
ambivalent attitude of both attraction and fear with regard to spinning
water.

The spiral stirs our fear, but at the same time draws us into its
centripetal vortex. As such, it represents in the unconscious the most
acute anxiety and, conversely, our deepest desires. Yet the spiral also
offers the key to liberation from such conflicts, for its movement is the
quintessence of creativity and its form, governed by the golden section,
is the epitome of the balance present within us and throughout nature.

Meditation

India's ancient schools of yoga (which means 'union' in Sanskrit) developed techniques for achieving non-ordinary states of consciousness
through meditation: their aim is to reach *turiya*, or the 'fourth state
of consciousness'. *Turiya* stands alongside the three ordinary states –
waking, dreaming and deep sleep – and is the most expansive and
profound of all.

Turiya transcends ordinary reality and pervades all things. It is the
communion with the cosmos that allows the mind to repose in silence
and increase its awareness. A similar state is called in Sanskrit *dhyana*,
a term taken from Chinese *chan* (and orginally Japanese *zen*) Buddhism,
which means 'to go beyond'. The Tibetan counterpart to *turiya* and
dhyana is known as *dzogchen*, or 'great perfection'.

The Vedas equate thoughts with ocean waves, for they both come
and go in much the same way, contiguous yet identifiable as being
separate from one another. Meditation helps us to see them as part of
the immense sea of information that is the cosmos. There are many
different traditions of meditation, and many techniques within each,

some esoteric and demanding, others more popular and 'easy' (e.g. the transcendental meditation phenomenon of our own day). The practice of meditation does not have a precise geographic origin, insofar as virtually all of the world's spiritual traditions have developed forms of it, for the most part independently of each other.

Many people know that there's nothing better than a soothing bath for relaxing after a day of stress and work: they intuitively understand that the presence of water in our external environment influences the internal state of our body and mind. For traditional Chinese and Ayurvedic medicine, a state of deep relaxation on the part of the patient is ideal for curing any illness. Even the simple visualization of water has the power to relax us, as demonstrated in the Chinese technique of *qigong* (breathing and energy exercise), in clinical hypnosis and in transpersonal psychotherapies. Elsewhere, the visualization of water and/or direct contact with it is commonly used in religious initiation rites and meditation as a vehicle of spiritual enlightenment.

Water facilitates meditation because it brings us to ourselves, for it is both our origin and our physical essence. It invites us to explore ourselves within, to make our minds more fluid. It encourages us to accept ourselves for what we are and to improve on that, without trying to be something or someone else.

Change is oftening frightening to us. Everything seems so fleeting in a material reality that tends inevitably toward decomposition, yet to which we are viscerally attached and wish could be permanent. The more we look for certainties, the more we condemn ourselves to uncertainty. The secret of life lies instead in cultivating within ourselves a sense of permanence that is paradoxically founded on change, on the continuous renewal of thought, experience and judgement.

There are those who consider meditation a sort of escape from reality, when in fact it is a detachment from an exclusive concern with the material world – which all of the world's spiritual traditions consider the single best way to alienate oneself from the true reality. When we become too attached to material goods, we escape from ourselves. We end up fixating on superficial questions of success or power, neglecting to cultivate our inner selves in a responsible and creative way.

Meditation is a means of becoming mentally present to ourselves, here and now. Thanks to the hectic rhythms and sundry preoccupations of our daily lives, the natural human state of being present to oneself has become, ironically, a non-ordinary state. Marco Valli, an Italian psychotherapist specializing in the meditation techniques of Tibetan Buddhism, offers an example of how water can inspire us:

> In the Tibetan tradition, the symbol of enlightenment is the lotus flower. The lotus is a water lily, whose blossom floats on the surface, nourished by roots anchored in the mud below. It is a symbol of spiritual work: by plunging our roots into the muck of our neuroses and daily reality, we can flower. The juice of life is extracted from the mud […].
>
> A great river flowed powerfully down from the mountains, displacing boulders and carving valleys in a race to the sea. Then one day, in this resolute quest towards its goal, the sea, the river reached a desert, a vast expanse of sand. The river tried to cross it, but the sands absorbed it. It tried again, and was again absorbed.
>
> While the river sought desperately to devise a way to overcome the obstacle, the sands whispered, 'Let yourself go, disappear, become vapour and let yourself be transported by the wind over the desert. This is the only way to cross it, for any other way will turn you into a swamp, and you will die.' […] Whereupon the river stilled itself, the desert sun evaporated it and lifted it into the sky, the wind carried it over the desert and made it fall as rain. The river was reborn and was now able to reach the sea.[34]

Paramahansa Yogananda, one of the first to bring yoga to the West, recalls in his autobiography what his master, Mahasaya, once told him:

> My master always asked me to meditate whenever I saw an expanse of water. Here its placidity reminds us of the vast calmness of God. As all things can be reflected in water, so the whole universe is mirrored in the lake of the Cosmic Mind.[35]

In the Hindu tradition, there is a field of invisible intelligence that permeates the entire universe called *Brahman*, which means 'great' in Sanskrit. According to an ancient Indian saying, a man who has not found Brahman is like a fish that has not found water, which is to say that this invisible intelligence surrounds us just as water surrounds a fish – it's just a question of being able to recognize it. It is only by facing the tempest of life, casting aside our fears and prejudices and embracing

Brahman, that we can build a vessel in which to cross the ocean of our space-time to achieve a full consciousness.

There is a Hindu myth that describes how human consciousness began as a breaking wave that decided to abandon the sea of eternal, infinite awareness. In another water metaphor, the Tibetan tantric tradition compares the mind to a small puddle, isolated from the vast ocean from whence it comes.

Through water's example, we can correct that which isn't functioning properly in our lives, returning to the ocean of intelligence that is within us and around us. To do so, we must accept all our feelings and experiences, even the negative ones: for to overcome them we must first understand them, after which they can serve as a springboard to jump higher towards ever more elevated emotions and states of mind.

Hypnosis

Popular culture has conditioned us to associate hypnosis with the showy bravura of tuxedoed magicians or, alternatively, with the mysterious, often malevolent mind control exercised by witches, wizards or aliens over unwitting victims. These are nothing more than rude caricatures. Hypnosis is in fact a psychophysical state that can be induced or self-induced in various ways and to varying degrees, and in the majority of cases, without coercion.

Another myth that needs debunking is that hypnosis has anything at all to do with 'sleep'. Actually, it is the precise opposite, a state of hyper-vigilance. Hypnosis induces a non-ordinary state of consciousness known as a trance. Depending on the subject and the technique used, it results in an alteration of the sense of self and the perception of space and time.

Around the mid-20th century, hypnosis began to be used towards therapeutic ends. Psychiatrist Milton H Erickson (1901–80), father of modern hypnosis, provides the clearest and simplest definition: the hypnotic trance is a condition wherein attention is focused on one's own interior world (in this, hypnosis is not unlike meditation).

The hypnotic trance can be induced towards medical ends to foster relaxation and generate positive behavioural changes that augment the subject's communicative potential. It is a process through which the individual is provided with control over his or her very self. The amplification of the senses that accompanies hypnosis is made possible, paradoxically, by the temporary displacement of self, or rather, that which we believe ourselves to be.

Hypnotic induction is achieved through a series of suggestions that give the subject access to an unconscious mental realm much more vast than the conscious one. Induction is like a drop of mental water which, by falling onto the mind's surface, expands concentrically in widening rings, reorganizing it.

A similar state can be reached in a flotation tank, and to a certain extent in ritual bathing. When immersion in water is combined with the interruption of access to external sensory stimuli, states of consciousness can be triggered that are yet further dissociated from the habitual perception of space and time. As mentioned earlier, a possible consequence of this is the divestiture of the normal, and therefore limited sense of identity, such that the subject has the perception of being absorbed into something larger, a sort of temporary death of the ego.

Because the ego is what we think we are, it follows that its annulment might constitute a premise for freeing ourselves from counterproductive habits and ideas, from illusions and restrictive judgments. The fact that this annulment is temporary enables us to bring back the insights gleaned from our unconscious mind to explore beyond our self-imposed limits, to reconstruct and simplify our conscious self. Hypnosis is neither showmanship nor sorcery, but a valid means, like meditation, of overcoming our own limitations.

Water and Psychotherapy

Carl Gustav Jung was first to posit the existence of primordial elements in the unconscious common to the artistic, oneiric, and mythological production of all civilizations throughout history. He called these elements archetypes, which he saw as being stored in a collective unconscious, a great reservoir of creativity shared by all human societies.

The collective unconscious is the psychological correlate to the ocean. It is the holographic psychic substrate that connects the individual to the group, just as water is the denominator common to all living beings. Water is, to use another Jungian concept, the 'synchronic' substrate *par excellence*, for it encompasses everything and is the matrix that both stores and transmits information from person to person down through the generations. The collective unconscious precedes and exists independently of the unconscious content of the single individual, just as the liquid in which the encounter of sperm and egg takes place precedes the formation of the embryo.

In his 1964 book *Religions, Values and Peak Experiences*, American psychologist Abraham Maslow analyses the first clinical studies ever conducted on spontaneous mystical states – the so-called 'peak experiences', which can be defined as ecstatic transpersonal states of the 'oceanic' sort, where the subject experiences a sense of fusion with the universe, of belonging to the cosmic whole. Prior to Maslow's work, psychology tended to lean on the Freudian notion that mystical and peak experiences were simply the expression of unresolved conflicts in the individual's psychosexual development.

Maslow's research showed instead that peak experiences are not pathological at all, but rather expressions of an authentic tendency toward self-realization. Challenging the psychological wisdom of the day, Maslow asserted that human beings have needs and values that are higher and nobler than the impulses and drives expressed in normal daily life. Mystical experiences have enormous therapeutic potential, for they can serve as a gateway to the satisfaction of higher needs and the achievement of true mental health.

With the 1960s, psychology as a discipline began accepting and examining the great potential of spiritual phenomena toward therapeutic ends, and became more inclined to acknowledge the importance of approaches that had earlier been dismissed: Jungian analysis, Reichian bioenergetics, Assaggioli's psychosynthesis, Erickson's hypnosis and transpersonal therapy were finally being taken seriously. To better illustrate their more holistic views, they employed concepts from apparently unrelated disciplines such as quantum and relativity theory, system and information theory, even holography. One conviction they all shared was the rejection of the idea that the mind is limited to the brain.

When properly stimulated, the mind is capable of embracing all that exists in space and time. It just needs to be coaxed toward greater elasticity, so as to stretch beyond the limitations we tend to impose upon it. As the English psychiatrist R D Laing observed, 'Mystics and schizophrenics find themselves in the same ocean, but the mystics swim whereas the schizophrenics drown'.[36] In fact, the origin of many mental and somatic disorders is traceable to just those kinds of imposed limitations. Pathology appears when body and mind fail to integrate, and when the individual is unable to integrate with the world.

We mentioned earlier the psychiatrist Stanislav Grof, founder of the transpersonal school and first to do extensive studies on the effects of lysergic acid diethylamide, or LSD. His research, initiated in the 1960s in Czechoslovakia and later in the United States, showed that LSD, administered with expert guidance, unlocks mental potential that can be beneficial to the patient's psychophysical condition.

Using LSD in low dosages, Grof was able to access unconscious autobiographical material that the patients themselves had never examined. Over the course of the therapy, patients would retrieve images of their forgotten past experiences from early childhood, even the intrauterine foetal stage. Increasing the doses, patients were able to relive their own birth, providing such detailed and heartfelt descriptions as to challenge the suggestion that they were merely projections. Memories of 'past lives', of deaths and rebirths and mythological imagery were common as well. Most significantly, in the majority of cases, the longstanding symptoms for which the patients had come to Grof for treatment disappeared after a relatively brief time.

After the use of LSD became illegal in 1966, Grof achieved similar results with a method of his own invention, which he called 'holotropic breathwork'. This is a technique for inducing a non-ordinary state of consciousness through breath control, ambient music (including the sounds of flowing water), massage and artistic expression. This is of course a very different approach when compared to classical psychoanalysis, which strives to protect and reinforce the patient's ego. Transpersonal psychotherapy is concerned instead with creating a support structure that enables the patient to transcend the limits of the ego.

American psychiatrist Brian Weiss has documented numerous cases of patients who, during a hypnotic trance, have been able to provide detailed accounts of 'past lives'. Grof met with the same results in hundreds of cases, and it seems that some of the factual data from these memories, whether his own or his patients', were checked and verified.

When patients regress to the infantile phase, they evince gestures, facial expressions and neurological reflexes typical of that age, such as the sucking reflex and the Babinski sign (dorsiflexion of the big toe, fanning out of smaller toes, normally present only in newborns).

Furthermore, while in these states patients can sometimes assume the same pathologies and alterations that had accompanied their birth or other traumatic events in the very tissues of their bodies. These astounding results show that memory is recorded even at the cellular level, and can be reactivated in the aqueous environment in which cells function.

The re-evocation of intrauterine life may be accompanied by a sense of ecstatic oneness and by oceanic visions. Patients often identify with aquatic life forms such as whales, dolphins, fish, jellyfish, even algae. Identification with inanimate objects has also been reported, foremost of which is water, in the form of a flowing river or a wavy ocean. When the intrauterine experience has been negative, however, due to the risk of abortion, for example, or to uterine toxicity, the image of water is associated with the threat of contamination, and the ocean thus becomes a dark and frightening place.

It is hopefully becoming clearer that our unconscious mind is not limited to the Freudian model of an individual's repressed memories, but is rather an extension of a greater intelligent network that transcends space, time, material reality and selfhood.

The Floating Scientist

To learn to swim, you have to get in the water to actually experience it.

MILTON H ERICKSON, MD (1901–80)

Psychiatrist Milton H Erickson, the father of medical hypnosis, used to say that learning through experience is better than learning consciously. You can learn all the movements of swimming while you are lying on your belly on a piano stool, concentrating on rhythm, respiration, the movements of the head, arms and legs, but when you get in the water you are just splashing around. You have to learn to swim *in* water.

Ken Russell's 1980 film *Altered States* tells the story of a scientist who, closing himself in a flotation tank after having taken a powerful psychoactive drug, experiences extremely intense hallucinations which lead to a series of bodily transmutations that gradually turn the scientist into a true prehistoric hominid. The screenplay – somatic mutations aside – is inspired by the life of the American neurophysiologist John C Lilly, who passed away in 2001.

Considered the first expert on sensory deprivation, Lilly was also a pioneer in dolphin behaviour and language, a topic we'll investigate in detail later on. It was this aspect of his career that inspired another

Figure 14.2 John C Lilly

film, *The Day of the Dolphin*, starring actor George C Scott.

Lilly worked as a neurophysiologist at the prestigious National Institute of Mental Health. In 1954 he designed history's first isolation tank: a cylindrical container in which the subject floats in water maintained at a constant temperature, in absolute silence and darkness, breathing through a mask to ensure the least possible sensory stimulation.

It was assumed that without sensory stimulation, one would end up simply falling asleep. Lilly showed that the exact opposite was true: floating in the water of the isolation tank, one 'forgets' one's body and the normal vigilant state becomes much more acute, making it possible to concentrate more easily on one's mental activity. The loss of contact with sensory reality, the near total absence of gravity, of visual, tactile and acoustic stimuli amplifies the sphere of consciousness and provokes a profound sense of relaxation.

In his autobiography, Lilly recounts his experience in the third person:

[The scientist] discovered that two hours in the tank gave him the rest equivalent to eight hours of sleep on the bed. The two hours were not necessarily spent in sleep. He found that there were many, many states of consciousness, of being between the usual wide-awake consciousness of participating in an external reality and the unconscious state of deep sleep. He found that he could have voluntury control of these states; that he could have, if he wished, waking dreams, hallucinations; total events could take place in the inner realities that were so brilliant and so 'real' they could possibly be mistaken for events in the outside world. In this unique environment, freed of the usual sources of stimulation, he discovered that his mind and his central nervous system functioned in ways to which he had not yet accustomed himself.[37]

Floating in an isolation tank is a bit like navigating the unexplored oceans of the mind, enabling us to experience things quite different from concrete day-to-day reality. By simulating the nine months of foetal isolation, it brings us back to the origins of our existence.

Today there are many types of flotation tanks, though most share the same basic features: water, about 30cm deep, heavily salinated with

Epsom or crystal salt to facilitate floating; air and water temperature at 33 °C; humidity as close as possible to saturation level; a small air circulation pump; total darkness. It is important that flotation sessions are supervised by qualified professionals who understand the effects and potential consequences, for not everyone is capable of entering into the proper mindframe. In the majority of cases, maximum wellbeing is achieved only after a number of sessions.

In normal conditions, 90 per cent of our nervous system is dedicated to managing our faculties of spatial orientation, gravitational balance and the processing of sensory data. It is therefore not difficult to imagine the dramatic change undergone by the nervous system when we absolve it of having to worry about any of those things. In a flotation tank, space, gravity and the body disappear from our perception, leaving the enormous power of our nervous system to dedicate itself to the mind alone.

As one might expect, this more or less total sensory deprivation provokes intense brain activity, including certain areas that are normally silent in conscious life. If expertly guided, one can arrive at what Lilly called the 'metaprogram', a higher state of awareness that allows us to transcend our conscious identity and its accompanying disturbances and complexes that impede mental development. With long-term practice in flotation tanks, one can achieve an expansion of consciousness similar to the *satori* of Zen Buddhism, the *samadhi* of the Hindus, the *devekut* of Jewish mysticism and the 'state of grace' sought by Christian mystics.

Immersion in water also stimulates the areas of the brain connected to pleasure and affectivity, which is only natural, insofar as water is the 'mother' element to which our species owes its existence and entrusts its survival. Immersion is most often perceived as a positive experience, though it can be unpleasant, depending on the psychoemotional history of the individual. If a person has had a traumatic experience related in some way to water, flotation might provoke a negative reaction at first. But with proper training and compassionate supervision, immersion can become a positive experience.

Among the more felicitous effects of this experience is the dissolution of the distinction between matter, energy and consciousness – which is to say, essentially, the transcendence of space and time. If you ever get the chance to use an isolation tank, you may wish to think upon this before asking yourself: 'Once I have disposed of seemingly important aspects of my formal identity – my social status, my ethnic group, my profession, my family role – who am I really? Where does one's sense of self come from? In how many different ways can my experiences be perceived? How can I get rid of the physical limitations of the tank?'

Death and Rebirth in Water

In religious initiation rites, symbols and events connected with sexuality, birth and death often overlap. As Hermann Hesse points out in his novel *Narcissus and Goldmund*, sex, birth and death are all accompanied by the same facial expressions, moans and wails. Death is essentially being born into a new life, the leaving behind of one reality for another, in both material and spiritual terms. At the most literal level, birth and death overlap in that parturition is potentially lethal for both mother and child.

An acquaintance of ours from Chapter 11, Igor Charkovsky, the controversial Russian pioneer in waterbirth, devised risky treatments for revitalizing handicapped infants, using water and extreme physical and thermal conditions to simulate the near-death state of the birth process, including abrupt immersions in freezing water and the forcible twisting of joints and limbs. Incredible as it may sound, his treatments significantly improved the psychophysical condition of his diminutive patients.

Likewise, sex and death are often interconnected. In French, the word for orgasm is *petite mort*, or 'little death', an expression that captures the temporary annulment of the sense of separate identity that one experiences during climax. Sexual congress, in order to be enjoyed to the fullest, demands the obliteration of the ego, a melding of one's self with someone else's, a transitory 'death' of the 'I' that culminates in orgasm.

Strange as it may seem, certain people experience intense sexual excitement from extreme physical pain. The erections and ejaculations commonly presented by victims of torture or hanging, as well as the voluntary practice of autoerotic asphyxiation are just a couple of demonstrations of the extent to which sex and death are contiguous. It is no accident that the cerebral centres of the limbic system responsible for our aggression and self-preservation instincts are located close to the areas dedicated to the processing of sexual arousal messages.

The connection between sex and birth is obvious in the causal sense:

new life is created through coitus. Less obvious is the fact that, in some cases, mothers who have just delivered their babies experience sexual arousal from the stimulation, though largely traumatic, of the uterus and vagina. Sexual excitement has also been observed during transpersonal sessions where the subject relives his or her own birth.

Floating in an isolation tank can elicit powerful extracorporeal perceptions, such as the feeling of leaving one's body and seeing it from a distance. Similar experiences are reported by hypnosis subjects and by those who have been in a coma or have had close encounters with death, as well as during transpersonal therapy sessions, mystical ceremonies, shamanic rituals, rites of passage, episodes of spatial clairvoyance, and the like. In varying degrees, all these experiences elevate the state of consciousness, induce a deep sense of relaxation and psychophysical wellbeing. They also have been shown to strengthen the immune system, and are therefore useful in treating a range of illnesses.

Where there are birth, death and sexuality, there is water. As we'll discuss further in Chapter 18, which deals with ritual bathing, water blurs the distinctions between self and not-self, between matter and energy, between right and wrong. Immersing ourselves in water, we can create our own completely new universe, or, to put it another way, discover the universe within us.

CHAPTER FIFTEEN

WATER, INFORMATION AND MEMORY

Where is the life we have lost in living?
Where is the wisdom we have lost in knowledge?
Where is the knowledge we have lost in information?

TS ELIOT (1888–1965)

When we hear it said that we are 'inundated by information', we immediately think of external stimuli such as the mass media, the internet and other forms of human communication. But the ubiquitousness of information runs far deeper than just that.

Deriving from the Latin verb *informare*, meaning 'to give form to' or 'to put in order', information operates at every level of existence. Subatomic particles, as we'll recall, are organized quantities of energy that produce information. The ordered structures of crystals are information. The more elaborate structures of all living things are information. Within our own bodies, the constant exchange of information between genes, hormones, neurotransmitters and the immune system is what keeps us functioning and alive.

Information is not to be confused with mere data. It is rather the transmission of messages endowed with meaning. Information is organized energy that communicates something about itself, and the world is a system of interconnected information. We see ourselves, other people and our environment as separate things in order to function effectively in the practical realm of daily life. But this way of seeing can also become an impediment if it is our *only* way of seeing, making us blind to the true nature of the world.

Seemingly inanimate objects, from the ripest fruit to the hardest stone, have their own ordered structure, radioactive evolution and vibratory resonance, and are constantly absorbing and organizing information. A rock crystal doesn't just lie there looking pretty: it generates its own current, known as piezoelectricity. The geometrical ordering of the crystalline silicon used to make microchips is what makes it possible to store such inconceivably vast amounts of information in such a small volume.

Water consumes and conquers rock, and so it is that the image of a static, inert world, meaningless and governed by chance, is giving way to a vision of the world as a coherent flow of information, a totality of vibratory interactions that oscillate between stability and instability.

The more we feel ourselves to be part of a totality, the more information and, by extension, the more meaning we find in the world. We are connected to everything, animate and inanimate, by way of a continuous flow of information from countless sources, all of which serve to augment the quantity and quality of messages which, if we open ourselves to receiving them, share a single theme: we are an integral, interconnected and therefore responsible part of this planet, this universe.

Today the concept of information is being applied as an interdisciplinary bridge between a wide range of scientific fields, from biology, physics and engineering to IT, psychology and medicine. We still don't know, however, how the mind could emerge from the brain. But perhaps that's because there's a fundamental flaw in our assumptions about the mind and thus in the way we frame the question. The mind is not, it must be remembered, confined to the brain. It is immanent in the physical body, and at the same time capable of transcending it in space and time through thought, which has no spatiotemporal boundaries.

According to particle physics, it is the observer who determines the occurrence of a quantum event. John Wheeler, eminent physicist from Princeton University, explains that 'Observer participancy gives rise to information; and information gives rise to physics'. The universe was born of information; material objects are merely a secondary manifestation.

The mechanistic and reductionist premises of morphogenesis,

accepted by the majority of scientists, are limited to studying the formation of living systems through DNA and protein synthesis. This view does not explain, however, why or how matter manifests itself in specific forms. It fails to show, for example, why proteins develop in their characteristic spiral folds and not in any of the infinite other possible configurations. It does not explain why proteins form, of all things, cells, nor why from these cells anything so complex as organs and tissues, or so preposterously unlikely as autonomous beings should result.

When a molecular biologist studies gene activation, it's a bit like a structural engineer studying a building: he looks for the way that genetic material is constructed – its bricks and mortar and the interdependencies thereof. What he tends to overlook, however, is the question of why that building has a certain form and not another, and for what reason it was built there and not somewhere else – in other words, is it a dwelling? A school? A church? A military bunker? And so on.

Embryonic development poses problems that have yet to be resolved. It has been observed that a frog embryo in the early stages, if cut in half, will form two separate individuals. Further along in its development, if we cut the part that is destined to become an eye in two parts, both will become complete eyes. Even more amazing is the fact that those same eye cells, if transplanted to the embryo's hindquarters, will become a kidney rather than an eye. This suggests that the embryo follows an established plan from the earliest moment of genetic differentiation in the semifluid state, even when radical external disturbances are introduced.

A few scientists have sought to explain these apparently deterministic forces, notably Harold Burr, professor of anatomy at Yale University from the 1930s through the late 1950s. Burr recognized the presence of bioelectrical fields in all living matter, both animal and vegetable, which he called the L-field, or life field.

Burr explained the differentiation and specialization of embryonal cells as follows: those cells that belong to specific areas of the life field invariably tend to assume, because of their position, specialized forms and functions that are regulated by the field itself. Genetic material, he postulated, is guided by this faint electrical field in the selection of traits to be manifested at the cellular level.

More recently, English biologist Rupert Sheldrake has hypothesized the existence of what he calls 'morphic fields' which, unlike Burr's L-field, are external to physical matter. A second postulate of Sheldrake's theory explains the organization and development of matter through the principle of *formative causation*. Taken together, we can sum it up as follows: the forms of self-organizing systems are modelled by morphic fields operating outside of space and time which 'regulate' everything, from the smallest particle to the largest systems – atoms, molecules, crystals, cells, tissues, organs, organisms, societies, ecosystems, planetary and star systems, galaxies. The organization of morphic fields encompasses all levels of complexity, like a sort of repository of material memory, external to manifest reality, with which it interacts by way of 'morphic resonance'.

When a piano tuner strikes a tuning fork of a specific pitch, it causes only that note to vibrate, leaving the others unaffected; this phenomenon is called resonance. In much the same way, the impulses generated by specific energy fields induce the activation of the genes to which they are 'tuned'. Morphic fields, then, are the information clusters that regulate the ordered networks of living systems through their internal memory. It is as though every object in the universe is connected by something like a collective memory to every object of the same type – a connection that is reinforced by the continuous presence over time of such objects. The enrichment of this 'memory', according to Sheldrake, is what drives and determines the acquisition of new evolutionary traits in living systems, whether at the atomic or galactic level.

Matter, as we've seen, tends to manifest itself in repetitive, fractalic sequences, which are correlated to the forms and movements of water and compatible with Sheldrake's notion of morphic resonance. Going back to the example of crystals, their present form – among the most elementary of all structures – is determined by crystals of the same type created in the past. How? Because earlier crystals generated morphic fields which then functioned as a code for configuring new, similar crystals. The same holds true for living matter – the oaks and ants and crocodiles of today simply follow the tendencies established by all the individual oaks and ants and crocodiles that preceded them. This might sound like Darwinian evolution at its simplest, but it's not.

Sheldrake maintains that the embryo follows a predetermined plan of growth and differentiation, tutored by its own specific morphic field (it should be pointed out that 'morphic' refers, of course, to form, which is why Sheldrake's theory uses 'morphic fields' to describe the forces that shape the evolution of biological entities, while 'social fields' shape social organization, 'mental fields' influence the mind, and so on).

Sheldrake's intriguing vision, while still controversial, is founded on a holistic paradigm that has been duly tested and published in reputable scientific journals. It should also be noted that he has collected enormous quantities of data and personally conducted innumerable studies on phenomena such as telepathy, premonitions and the feeling of being watched.[38]

What his work shows is that it is easier for subjects, both human and animal, to learn things that other subjects have already learned. The acquisitions that a species has made in the past, Sheldrake asserts, influence the morphogenetic fields of that same species *regardless of spatial proximity*, thereby ensuring the evolution of the entire group.

Another phenomenon that suggests the existence of such 'fields' or 'resonances' is the rise in intelligence quotient (IQ) test scores in recent decades across much of the globe, known as the 'Flynn effect'. Sheldrake's theory is also reminiscent of Bohm's idea of holomovement: not only in principle but also in the fact that it is shared by a rather limited number of fellow scientists due to its distance from the neo-Darwinist paradigm favoured by the majority, according to which differentiation and evolution are governed by random selection and have a purely genetic basis. Neo-Darwinism does not allow energy and biochemistry to coexist, which is perhaps why it fails to explain what drives differentiation and specialization in identical cells.

Following Sheldrake's reasoning, we might suppose that the information stored and exchanged by living aquatic systems, from droplet to ocean, is inscribed therein by an external source from another dimension, a wellspring of memory, that we are not yet equipped to measure or explore, but which substantial scientific data suggests may indeed exist.

Water and Memory

Telling the facts accurately is not the same as telling the truth. Telling the truth means trying very hard to get the deepest meanings hidden behind facts.

RABBI MENACHEM MENDEL of Kotzk (1787–1859)

Flowing water has no form of its own; it is ephemeral and cannot be grasped. Analogously, whenever we humans have thought we have grasped and understood the reality that surrounds us, it runs through our fingers and eludes us. Scientists did not want to believe that the improbable flumes built by Viktor Schauberger could transport far more lumber than traditional structures. Before and since then, other anomalies in water's behaviour have led the scientific powers-that-be to cry 'Impossible!'. So numerous are these anomalies that water has become the focus of some of the scientific community's most lively debates.

Water is everywhere, including in our language: an argument 'holds water' or is 'watertight' if it can't be refuted; we're 'in hot water' when we've made a blunder, and 'in deep water' when there's too much to do and not enough time to do it, which means you must try to 'keep your head above water'; if a problem is resolved and all parties are satisfied, it's 'water under the bridge', and so on. The ubiquitousness of water in all aspects of our lives makes us take it for granted as nothing particularly special, and we end up forgetting its innumerable virtues and unresolved enigmas. To paraphrase Ivan Illich, ours is the epoch of the 'waters of oblivion'.

We've seen how, from the physical and chemical point of view, water is hardly a substance to be taken for granted, but rather unique and often astonishing. The French immunologist Jacques Benveniste (1935–2004), along with his collaborators and what has become a growing number of scientists, was among the first to characterize water as a solvent capable of being biologically activated even in the absence of solutes. This contradicts one of the fundamental assumptions of biology: a solute must be present in a certain concentration in order to be biologically active. However, some physicists have hypothesized that water, under specific conditions, has the ability to retain a sort of 'vibrational memory' of the substances with which it comes into contact. If this were true, it would be proof of the effectiveness of homeopathic remedies, which are obtained from agents diluted in water at such infinitesimal concentrations as to no longer be detectable. Benveniste's research in precisely this area created quite a controversy in scientific circles – one that's still a long way from being resolved.

The Benveniste Affair

You could write the history of science in the last 50 years in terms of papers rejected by Science or Nature.

PAUL LAUTERBUR, winner of the Nobel Prize for Medicine 2003

(*New York Times*, 7 october 2003, his work rejected by *Nature* in 1973)

Biologist Jacques Benveniste was a highly respected researcher, among whose numerous contributions was the discovery of the platelet activation factor (PAF), an important mediator in inflammations and allergic

reactions. In 1985 Benveniste published a study in the *British Journal of Clinical Pharmacology* on the capacity of a homeopathic remedy, Apis mellifica, to significantly reduce the activation of basophils, a type of white blood cell. In 1987, he and Elisabeth Davenas reported in the *European Journal of Pharmacology* the results of a study where high dilutions of homeopathic silicea were shown to activate macrophages, which play a key role in keeping the blood clean and the immune system effective.

The following year, in the June 30 issue of the English journal *Nature*, Benveniste published the

Figure 15.1 J Benveniste

results of research conducted by his team at INSERM (Institut National de la Santé et de la Recherche Médicale) in Paris, one of France's principal research institutes, along with three other teams in Canada, Israel and Italy.

The authors had caused human blood serum, which contains high quantities of white blood cells, to react with type E immunoglobulin (IgE). These antibodies work by attaching themselves to basophils and waiting for an attack from an allergen (e.g. mosquito saliva, pollen, dust, etc), at which point the IgEs trigger the degranulation of the basophils and the release of histamines, the substance responsible for the reddening, swelling and itching typical of allergic reactions. Benveniste's experiment consisted quite simply in placing serum (containing basophils and IgE) in contact with an anti-immunoglobulin E solution. As expected, the resulting reaction released histamines, triggering the basophil degranulation.

What was extraordinary about the experiment is that the histamine release took place even when the anti-IgE solution was extremely diluted with distilled water, reacting 40 to 60 per cent of the time even when the high dilutions approached homeopathic levels at which point the solution could no longer be chemically active. The results were anomalous to say the least, in that the reaction took place in water alone, since the dilutions were well below the Avogadro constant – the number below which there can no longer be any molecules of solute present.

In other words, anti-IgE solutions which no longer contained even a single molecule of anti-IgE nevertheless triggered a response from the white globules, as though the solution contained the 'ghosts' of the original molecules. With chemical action being necessarily ruled out, the researchers hypothesized that the water was somehow able to record and transmit information, probably electromagnetic in nature. This property was later dubbed 'water memory'.

Benveniste's work was thoroughly documented, but the conclusions were too unsettling for the mainstream scientific community. For two years the study was kept 'on hold' by the editors at *Nature*, who eventually published it, though reluctantly, on the grounds that it had passed the journal's peer review process. However, John Maddox, the editor-in-chief, took pains to distance himself from the article, accompanying its publication with a rather nasty note.[39]

The discovery put two centuries of chemical theory in doubt, so the avalanche of protest letters came as no surprise. It is clearly impossible, they argued, to trigger a known molecular reaction in the absence of the molecules that cause it. Pressured by the outrage in the scientific community, Maddox took an unprecedented measure, hiring two professional 'debunkers' to get to the bottom of the matter, as though Benveniste's work were some sort of cheap magic trick to be unmasked.

Maddox also insisted on personally inspecting the lab, and eventually appointed himself to the 'fraud squad' he'd hired, made up of former researcher Walter Stewart and an ex-magician by the name of James Randi. Stewart, who had accomplished nothing of note as a scientist, was an expert in scientific hoaxes, while Randi spent his time exposing the magic tricks of his former colleagues and anyone who claimed to have paranormal abilities; Randi had gained a certain renown by unmasking some of Uri Geller's telekinetic feats. None of the three, it should be noted, were immunologists.

The three investigators went to Paris, and for four days watched Benveniste's team repeat the experiment again and again, getting positive results the majority of the time. On the fifth day, the investigators decided to try it for themselves and came up with a negative result. Unconvinced by the statistically positive cumulative results of the previous four days, they decided to publically denounce Benveniste's conclusions, the fruit of years of intensive and conscientious work by researchers in four nations, as unfounded.

On 28 July, 1988, *Nature* published Maddox's account of the inspection under the title '"High-dilution" experiments a delusion'.[40] In a spectacular act of scientific censorship, Maddox stated that Benveniste had been unable to repeat the experiment successfully, that Stewart and Randi had found numerous irregularities in the lab procedures, and that he himself had discovered that the Frenchman's research had been funded by a company that manufactured homeopathic remedies – this latter being of especially questionable relevance, given that the vast majority of conventional medical and drug research is funded by pharmaceutical companies.

Benveniste was allowed to respond to the article in the same issue, where he did admit to certain methodological errors that may have affected the statistical results, though not the principle. After characterizing the climate of tension and intimidation created by the investigators, he wrote: 'All in all, the judgement is based on one dilution tested on two blood samples in awful technical and psychological conditions.' But there was nothing he could say to save his reputation; the official scientific community had pronounced its sentence, case closed. It didn't matter that other research teams had independently achieved the same results in Canada, Israel and Italy. Benveniste became an object of scorn bordering on viciousness, and his brilliant career came to an abrupt halt.

Maddox was right in noting that not all the experiments were correctly analysed from the statistical point of view, and Benveniste acknowledged that some of the researchers knew the contents of the samples, and that the results were therefore susceptible to confirmation bias, albeit minimal. Benveniste launched another research cycle, this time labelling the samples with codes so that their contents would be unknown to the experimenter, and also hired a well-known biostatistician, Alfred Spira, with whom he presented a new study at the 1991 FASEB congress (Federation of American Societies for Experimental

Biology). The new research confirmed that highly diluted solutions can be biologically active. But after the *Nature* fiasco, no one was much inclined to side with the ostracized Benveniste. Predictably, the new study was rejected by both *Science* and *Nature*, which took issue with the statistical validity of the results despite the presence of Spira and the use of automated, statistically controlled equipment.

The experiment was later confirmed by other independent French pharmacological teams on other biological models, such as the stimulation of a perfused guinea pig heart and the use of cadmium to inhibit lymphocytic proliferation.

In subsequent studies, Benveniste discovered a key factor in the fixing of molecular memory: *the success of the experiment seemed to be influenced by succussion* – that is, by simply agitating the test tube.[41] Highly diluted solutions reproduce the biological effects of the agent molecule only if the container is shaken or tapped, in keeping with Hahnemann's theory of homeopathy developed nearly two centuries earlier. Benveniste's study, published in the acts of the Paris Academy of Sciences, negated the hypothesis aired by some critics that succussion triggered an oxy-reduction effect, which by itself would be able to biologically activate the dilution.

Physicist Jean Jacques, specialist in molecular interactions at the Collège de France, showed that any biological effect from high dilutions can be achieved only when the primary solution contains a substance capable of activating basophils. Benveniste took his own research further when, together with a group of physicists from the NCSR, he found that biological action of the highly diluted histamines can be annuled by exposure to an electromagnetic field of 50 Hz, thus confirming the electromagnetic nature of the phenomenon.

Even four years after the *Nature* controversy, the residual unpleasantness was such that Benveniste had to leave his post as director of the immunopharmacology lab at INSERM, after which he took on the directorship of the privately funded Digital Biology Laboratory in Clamart, just outside Paris. A few months before his death, an American company signed a contract to develop one of his 'digital biology' patents.

Water memory has remained a thorny argument, but continues to be investigated. In 1993, *Nature* printed the results of a study on the subject that had come up negative. Other researchers have obtained results similar to those of Benveniste: in 1998 Jurgen Schulte, professor of applied physics at the University of Technology in Sydney, published a collection of fundamental studies on high dilutions in aqueous solutions. In 2004, a team of French researchers once again demonstrated the activation of basophils with high dilutions of histamines.[42]

Studies of the physical processes of water memory have continued as well. In 2003, Swiss chemist Louis Rey published an article in *Physica A* on the use of thermoluminescence in confirming the existence of water memory. The author compared the hydrogen bonds of common water with those of heavy water (which contains deuterium, an isotope of hydrogen) and with samples of homeopathic remedies. The thermoluminescent signatures of the hydrogen bonds were different for the three types of water, suggesting that water memory most likely depends on the vibrational frequency and configuration of hydrogen bonds.[43]

Benveniste's controversial research revealed that water contains a specific electromagnetic 'code' that is stored and transmitted by hydrogen bridges. Under the right conditions, water can be manipulated to retain the electromagnetic information left behind by substances in solution that are no longer chemically present. The reasons for this are not entirely known, which accounts for the difficulty in reproducing the phenomenon in less than ideal conditions.

The Million-Dollar Dare

Vittorio Elia is a research chemist at the University of Naples, where for more than 40 years he has been studying biological molecules in aqueous solutions, and has published more than a hundred papers in the most important scientific journals in the field.

Using state-of-the-art equipment, Elia's team analyses aqueous solutions subjected to succussion and graduated dilutions ranging from 1 per cent to the infinitesimal concentrations used in homeopathy. *In fully 92 per cent of their tests*, the chemicophysical properties of the water were affected, independently of potential disturbances from external impurities. These are incontrovertible results, and they confirm the validity of Benveniste's work and the specificity of homeopathic remedies.

Among the alterations documented by Elia and his team are excess heat, changes in pH, and variations in both electrical conductivity and electromotive force. Moreover, lower vapour tension values were recorded in ultradiluted solutions of water and sodium chloride (salt).

Figure 15.2
Vittorio Elia

Elia recently measured the movements of water molecules, calculating the dielectric relaxation time with nuclear magnetic resonance technology. Having ensured that the allegations of confirmation bias that had beleaguered Benveniste could not be made here, the research team was justifiably delighted to find that the movements of homeopathic water turned out to be more ordered than those of other solutions.[44]

Elia's team uncovered another aqueous anomaly, having observed that *time* and *volume* are additional factors that can alter the chemico-physical properties of homeopathic dilutions. In 2005, another team of researchers discovered that water congeals at 18 °C when reduced to 1 nanometre in size. A possible explanation takes us back to Prigogine (Chapter 4) and his theory of 'dissipative structures': homeopathic water would contain molecular aggregates that are out of thermody-namic equilibrium, and that these clusters dissipate radiant energy from external sources.[45]

The ultradiluted solutions studied by Benveniste and Elia are just such 'dissipative structures', which emerge from the normal state of chaos of ordinary water to organize themselves in a more ordered way; succussion is what triggers the spontaneous formation of these struc-tures, this new dynamic of order. For every X quantity of dissipated energy, an equal quantity of dissipative structures is formed, with volume as a mitigating factor: smaller volumes tend to have a higher 'concentration' of dissipative structures than larger ones.

Temporally determined changes, on the other hand, might be due to variations in the number and dimensions of the dissipative structures.

In any event, we can conclude that highly diluted aqueous solutions present measurable chemical and physical properties that vary according to the processes they have undergone, the specific solute used and the amount of time transpired. All of this proves beyond a shadow of a doubt that water does indeed have memory.

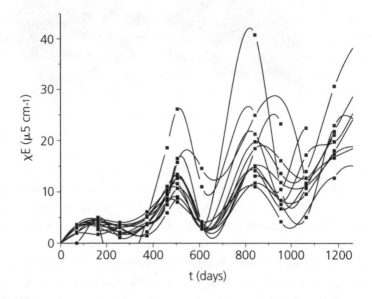

Figure 15.3 Each curve describes variations over time of the specific excess conductivity χE (μS cm-1) of several homeopathic dilutions made from an Arnica Montana mother tincture. This dependence on time cannot be explained by classical chemistry or physics. The graph also shows how the pace of variation and maximum peaks are similar in all the dilutions. (*courtesy V Elia*)

Some years ago, James Randi announced that he would give a million dollars to anyone who could demonstrate the effects of homeopathic water. In 1999, Elia took up the challenge and has presented his work every year since then to Randi and his associates from CICAP (Italian Committee for the Investigations of Claims of the Paranormal). He has repeatedly invited them to analyse and reproduce his results on homeopathic water and has been deliberately ignored each time. Unfortunately for Elia, for science and for all the people that might benefit from homeopathy if the stigma of pseudoscience were once and for all removed, the former magician's million-dollar dare turns out to be nothing more than bombastic showmanship, designed as an instrument of propaganda against homeopathy.

Scientific Theories on the Memory of Water

Nothing is too wonderful to be true if it be consistent with the laws of nature.

MICHAEL FARADAY, physicist and chemist (1791–1867)

A scientific theory of the transmission of biological information through water would provide a key to explaining a number of other vibratory mechanisms involved in the creation of life.

It is easy for biologists to lose sight of subatomic reality, for the scale of their world is cellular; at its smallest molecular. Therefore, it is understandable that they might tend to see anomalies at that scale, in reality caused by subatomic activity, as being the result of experimental or interpretive error. The massless neutrino, for example, is not their concern, and indeed would make no sense had their physicist colleagues not demonstrated its existence; the same holds true for the quark, the smallest particle yet discovered, which is actually a vibration capable of transforming itself into matter.

The idea of a vibration that creates matter is accepted by physicists but is considered by biologists, who deal with the chemical interactions between molecules, to be outside their purview. Biology has not yet addressed the real implications for molecular biology of quantum theory, which is not unlike studying an automobile without opening the bonnet to examine the motor. Benveniste's work showed that water is likely to be capable of 'quantum behaviour' at the subatomic level. The fact that biochemical reactions can occur in the absence of a chemical cause seems impossible, yet it happens. Let's look at a few examples.

Many people manifest allergic reactions at the mere thought of contact with an allergen. The act of thinking and the memory of past contact can trigger molecular reactions apparently from 'nothing'. Similarly, people who have suffered severe trauma need only remember the cause and the same neurovegetative, endocrine and immunitary reactions unleashed by the traumatic event are triggered (production of adrenaline, cortisol, interleukins, neuropeptides, etc). Thought and memory can create new configurations from the molecular 'broth' of which we are made. The problem is that we don't know how it happens.

Benveniste's research demonstrated certain singular properties intrinsic to biological water and the importance of movement in activating them. Any good bartender knows that shaking a cocktail changes it fundamentally, improves its quality, just as Schauberger and Schwenk knew that certain movements made water more vital while others rend-ered it inactive, even harmful.

Water, as we've seen, is never identical to itself, in the sense that water from two different sources can differ in any number of ways. For example, rainwater from a thunderstorm and rain that falls during a full moon have different spectroscopic signatures. They are literally different substances from a physical and electromagnetic standpoint, with distinct properties, information and behaviours.

We might compare two water molecules of different origin to two identical computers loaded with different programs – though they share the same hardware, they perform different functions. This could explain the therapeutic results achieved by homeopathic physicians with highly diluted solutions of biological substances. It would also explain why some studies, though certainly conducted by serious and conscientious scientists, have not shown any evidence of water memory.

Homeopathy uses active principles in dilutions which, from 12 decimals (12 CH) upward, no longer contain a single molecule of the original principle. Yet homeopaths regularly prescribe centesimal, even millesimal dilutions. According to homeopathic theory, for a remedy to be effective it must be succussed – that is, agitated and thus 'dynamized'. In other words, it must be subjected to a physical rather than chemical action.

The more diluted the remedy, the more potent its action – the precise opposite of what happens with conventional drugs, whose potency is in direct correlation to its quantity. Classical chemistry and biology, for the reasons articulated above, are simply unable to explain why this should be so. For now, we have only the documented proofs from scientists like Benveniste and Elia, and the innumerable cases of positive results at the clinical level, since the first study published in 1994 in *The Lancet*, which shows that homeopathic remedies have greater therapeutic efficacy than a placebo.[46]

Just around the time when Benveniste was publishing his results, Emilio Del Giudice and Giuliano Preparata, theoretical physicists at the University of Milan, were working on a descriptive model of the molecular vibrations of water called the theory of superradiance, or the theory of electrodynamic coherence. The Italian scientists postulated a magnetic memory of water powered by coherent molecular vibrations, wherein water molecules oscillate 'in phase' with their own internal electromagnetic field. Under certain conditions, they proposed, these molecules could conserve the magnetic memory of specific biochemical information that had been 'recorded' during contact with other molecules (the presence of coherent electrical vibrations in infinitesimal solutions had been confirmed at the University of Montpellier using microwave and Raman spectography equipment).

Del Giudice and Preparata's study, with their colleague G Vitiello, published by the prestigious *Physical Review Letters* in 1988, proposed an innovative model of the electrical dipole of the water molecule.[47] Their research started with quarks, which are contained along with other particles in atomic nuclei. No one had yet been able to separate them, and modern physics was unable to explain this powerful cohesion.

The dipole of the water molecule is configured asymmetrically, and as such it emits, not unlike a transmitter, electromagnetic waves of variable frequency. The classic telescopic tube model of the bonds of the water molecule is misleading, for it does not explain a number of water's properties, and moreover fails to consider the laws of quantum mechanics. Despite the illusion of static solidity, the constituents of matter vibrate continuously, oscillating between a stationary and excited state.

According to Maxwell's equations, electromagnetic radiation is not a local phenomenon, but one that is propagated at great distances, as

Figure 15.4 Giuliano Preparata and Emilio Giudice

well as in a vacuum. Del Giudice and Preparata applied these equations to solid and liquid matter. When water comes into contact with other substances, its molecules align themselves in phase, in much the same way as the photons produced by a laser beam. This enables them to emit electromagnetic waves that are unique to the active substance in question, even when the substance is removed; the water retains an electromagnetic trace of the now absent substance, and is thus able to transmit its biological information.

The theoretical model devised by Del Giudice and Preparata takes its name from the phenomenon of superradiance, which occurs when water molecules are subjected to an electromagnetic field capable of keeping them in phase. In a superradiant state, the molecules oscillate in unison, and it is this that constitutes the coherence to which we've been referring as 'water memory'.

If the water dipole is exposed to an energy flux within a certain range of frequency and intensity, as commonly occurs in biological systems, all the molecules begin vibrating at the same frequency. The incoming energy, instead of going through the process of thermalization (absorption followed by rapid dissipation), continues to resupply that single vibrational state.

Electrodynamic coherence was first studied in the field of laser physics. A laser is a paramount example of coherence, in that it produces an exceptionally intense and concentrated electromagnetic field in a tight range of frequencies. In the case of liquids such as water, the electromagnetic field, rather than being released externally, is trapped within reactions known as coherence domains, wherein the atoms move collectively, governed by a phase generated by the atoms themselves – another of nature's many self-regulatory mechanisms.

Matter is organized in 'informed' electromagnetic fields – coherence domains – in order to create ever more complex material structures. Water is the ideal medium for achieving this end.

Alongside the order of coherence is the disorder of the gaseous realm, of isolated atoms subjected to a chaotic regime of collision, thermic fluctuation and entropy. Order and chaos coexist, and living matter is a synthesis of both. In the interstices of *water's coherence domains*, the dissolved molecules, initially noncoherent, assemble into coherent clusters which are then able to attract other molecules with which they are in phase.

Water can be induced to simulate all frequencies because its coherence domains are formed by relatively small clouds of electrons. The density of this electromagnetic field depends on its wavelength. The molecules are protected in the coherent phase by a 'shell' of powerful hydrogen bonds; the noncoherent near-gas phase, on the other hand, is responsible for their thermal and solvation properties.

This would explain why 'biological water' (water containing organic macromolecules) behaves differently from ordinary water. Biological water freezes at -50 °C and has a much lower dielectric constant (5, as compared to 80) and therefore is much better at transmitting electrical forces; it also has a lower diffusion velocity through magnetic field gradients.

Del Giudice and Preparata hypothesized that the interstitial liquid and cytoskeleton – that is, the web of polar macromolecular filaments present in organic cells – form a sort of transmission system for these coherent waves.[48] In 1996, a group of Chinese physicists published measurements of the dipolar structures of water that closely resembled those presented by the Italian pair.[49]

'Memory' means affixing something stable within a vibratory domain that is in constant motion. Again, as we saw in earlier chapters, water's permanence is born of change. In an orchestra, a given note is always the same, regardless of how many different instruments might play it, and it is this consensus that gives the orchestra coherence. Analogously, water and a given solute play the same 'note', which is what keeps the molecular vibrational frequencies stable.

In recent years new theoretical models designed to explain water memory have been proposed. Cyril Smith of the electronic engineering department of Salford University studies water's responses to magnetic fields and has hypothesized the existence of a helical structure – a possible prefiguration of DNA? – that is capable of recording and 'remembering' the frequency to which it is exposed. According to Smith, the helix forms when a quantum of magnetic flux induces pentagonal clusters of water molecules to wrap around themselves like wire around a spool to create a sort of molecular solenoid which would thus generate a continuous electromotive force. Similar models have been proposed by others: Julia Goodfellow of the department of crystallography at Birkbeck College in London and theoretical physicist Lynn Trainer of the University of Toronto. Martin Chaplin at the South Bank University in London proposes a clustered network of hydrogen bonds with cavities enclosing small solutes. These are 280-molecule icosahedrons, namely three-dimensional hexagonal shapes made of many small triangles.

According to the hydration sphere model, water molecules assemble in a spherical cluster, while the clathrate model has them folding around an internal cavity, creating a skeleton of hydrogen bridges that can assume diverse three-dimensional configurations.[50] Cancer cells apparently, contain less clustered water.

A study published in *Nature* in 1997 indirectly confirms the existence of the coherence domains postulated by Del Giudice and Preparata. Spheres of a neutral material, polystyrene, with a diameter of 0.5μm were magnetized with a negative charge and then suspended in water. The researchers expected the spheres to repel one another, being of the same polarity. To their surprise, when the spheres reached a critical number they suddenly attracted one another and formed clusters. At the individual level, the spheres do indeed repel one another, yet in an aqueous environment their negative charge is overridden, causing them to attract. In other words, there exists a *'density threshold'* that alters basic magnetic behaviour.

This was the first time that scientists had observed a natural phenomenon transform into its opposite, passing from individual to collective behaviour. The ancient Chinese, consummate experts in polarity, taught that yin, when it reached a certain threshold, became yang, and vice versa: the excessive expression of one polarity transforms it into its opposite, just as the night is darkest before the dawn; just as an exceedingly cold object feels hot to the touch; just as a pendulum is sent forcefully in the opposite direction at the immobile apex of its swing; just as a highly diluted poison becomes homeopathic medicine. We saw a similar oscillatory phenomenon in the dissipative biological systems studied by Prigogine in Chapter 4.

Water's unique properties seem, for this and other reasons, to derive from electromagnetic forces that differentiate one water from another, such that some become therapeutic and others harmful, even in the absence of chemical reactions. Electromagnetism also explains how some substances that are toxic in weighted doses can become beneficial in homeopathic dilution.

The human body is an organized aqueous structure, influenced by dynamic gravitational fields (the lunar cycles), electromagnetic fields (metals and minerals), bioenergetic fields (organic substances) and coherent domains, whether harmful or beneficial, whose vehicle is water.

Quantum Water

In his final years, Jacques Benveniste investigated the possibility of using an electronic medium to record the electromagnetic information codes contained in water of organic origin. The idea is not as far-fetched as it might sound – atoms and molecules do, after all, emit specific vibrational frequencies that instruments such as the radiotelescope are able to capture, even if they were emitted billions of light years ago. Similarly, molecules exchange information and instructions by way of these frequencies, which should therefore be detectable. As Benveniste put it, certain types of water behave, under certain conditions, like the laser beam in a CD player, capable of reading and transmitting coded information.

Life depends on these exchanges of signals between molecules. For example, when we are angry or afraid, the adrenal glands release adrenaline and send it to specific receptors on specific cell membranes, 'instructing' them, and only them, to make the heart beat faster, to contract the muscles and blood vessels, etc. The nature of these molecular signals remains unknown to biologists, precious few of whom are even asking the question.

Benveniste was among those few, seeking the answer in the electromagnetic fields produced in organic water and cell cultures, experimenting with their electronic transmission with a variety of instrumentation and media, including the Internet.

Benveniste was able to capture the wave forms of the electromagnetic fields emitted by more than 30 substances (antibodies, antigens, bacteria, pharmacological and physiological agonists, etc), recording them digitally (at 44KHz) and memorizing them on a hard drive. And sure enough, Benveniste's reproductions of biological electromagnetism triggered the same effects as the original substances.

To make sense of these discoveries we must once again turn to quantum physics. According to quantum theory, subatomic objects are not separate, as one is tempted to imagine. Every particle is 'entangled'; everything is connected to everything else. Be they quarks and neutrinos, bodies and minds, everything interacts through entanglement. The quantum connections that are established within an organism and those between separate organisms explain the extraordinary holistic properties of our planet's water-based life.

The molecules of biological systems resonate with one another in specific ways, like a tuning fork tuned to a specific note that resonates with the string assigned to that note. And just as another tuning fork of a different shape can also make that same string resonate, so can different molecules resonate together. Turenne's theory on the electromagnetic resonances transmitted by organic water has returned to relevance. A number of other studies have been conducted in recent years on how the quantum properties of water allow it to transcend its own chemistry, which is what makes life possible. For DNA, proteins and cells alone cannot create life. As Felix Franks of Cambridge University memorably said, 'Without water, it is all just chemistry. Add water and you get biology.'

The key factor seems to be the hydrogen bridges between molecules. These bridges are at least ten times weaker than the oxygen-hydrogen bond within the water molecule, but this apparent handicap turns out to be an advantage, enabling water's structures to resist compression and operate in continuous transformation, bonding and breaking and reconfiguring with ease.

Hydrogen bonds behave this way thanks to one of the most bizarre of all quantum phenomena, known as *zero-point vibrations*. The zero point belongs to Heisenberg's famous uncertainty principle, which states that it is impossible to precisely calculate the total energy of a system at a given moment. Even if the entire universe were to freeze and its temperature was at absolute zero, zero-point vibrations would still be active, driven by energy from the resulting void.

These vibrations are what determine a higher cohesion between water molecules, and they are essential to life. If we substitute hydrogen with its isotope deuterium, we get 'heavy water', which is poisonous: it has the same chemistry as ordinary water but it is without zero-point energy. As scientist Rustum Roy says, it is absurd to think that chemistry is everything. Take carbon, for example, whose atoms can make graphite or a diamond. Roy and his collaborators at Pennsylvania State University have shown that, through successive succussions, water can reach localized pressures of 10,000 atmospheres, changing its properties all along the scale. Water is very cohesive: considering its boiling point value, it should have a tensile strength of a thousand atmospheres! We should break our head trying to dive in it: instead, we splash in water. Why? Because on the one hand the coherent domains are impenetrable to external molecules, ions and magnetic fields: they are, say, hard like glass, protecting their messages. On the other hand, the noncoherent phase is a gas of free molecules: swimming in water is like swimming in a pool full of polystyrene granules or little glass balls.

Another nonchemical, purely physical phenomenon is *epitaxy*, where the atomic structure of a compound is used to imprint the same structure on others. In the computer industry, epitaxy is used to 'grow' perfect copies of crystal semiconductors without any chemical transfer whatsoever.

Similarly, water uses a kind of epitaxy when it bends amino acids to form the proteins essential for the construction, defence and replication of cells. In 2006, biophysicists Florian Garczarek and Klaus Gerwert of Ruhr University Bochum witnessed an astounding feat of water memory while studying a protein called bacteriorhodopsin, a component found in the membranes of certain cells.

Bacteriorhodopsin contains water, the hydrogen nuclei of which emit protons, which then photosynthetically alter the electrical charge around the protein, effectively turning it into a little battery, or 'proton pump'. By exposing the bacteriorhodopsin to infrared rays, Garczarek and Gerwert were able to break the hydrogen bonds of the water trapped inside, which triggered a chain reaction of events. Fragments and clusters of water molecules began interacting to continue the interrupted proton transfer process, while the amino acids began to curve, trapping the water to form proteins through a complex quantum process. Their experiment demonstrated the emerging fact that 'intraprotein water molecules are as essential for biological functions as amino acids'.[51] In other words, the *quantum properties of water are what make life possible.*

The same quantum effect of water occurs in DNA, which must twist and curve in a highly complex and precise way in order to synthesize proteins. How is it possible that proteins can fit so well into such a complex form as DNA, which we'll remember is not only helical but so densely tangled that it would be a metre long if stretched from end to end?

Scientists have realized that DNA is biologically active only if surrounded by water molecules. Here's how it works: when a protein approaches the DNA, the water molecules between them abruptly stop vibrating. Then, as demonstrated by simulation software developed by Monika Fuxreiter at the Institute of Enzymology in Budapest, the partner protein uses the 'interfacial water' as a sort of messenger, sending it across the intervening space with instructions to break the DNA strand at specific points, whereupon the water bonds firmly with the DNA, transferring the data from the protein. The implications of this are enormous: not only does water clearly have memory, but a memory sophisticated enough to communicate with DNA, the most complex molecule in nature: a feat by comparison to which memorizing the information from a homeopathic agent is mere child's play.

Another intriguing discovery made by a group of scientists at the University of Nebraska revealed that ice, when subjected to extremely high pressures and temperatures, assembles in a way that is remarkably similar to the characteristic double helix of DNA. This suggests that proteins may be synthesized by a matrix intrinsic to water that guides the construction of their multispiral form.

These extraordinary mechanisms can only be explained by quantum electrodynamics (QED) and the theories deriving from it, such as the theory of coherent dynamics described earlier.

Water's Sensitivity to Information

Japanese photographer Masaru Emoto works with water from a variety of sources, freezing it for three hours at -20 °C and then analysing it with magnetic resonance instruments. The purest waters from uncontaminated sources present beautiful hexagonal crystal structures under the microscope, much like snowflakes. When the water is polluted, purified with chemical substances or collected in a seismic zone just prior to an earthquake, it does not form crystals at all.

More fascinating still, if water is exposed to melodic music or positive words (e.g. 'love', 'thank you', spoken or written, in different languages), it forms harmonious, mostly symmetrical crystals. If instead it is exposed to dissonant sounds or aggressive words, the crystals take on a deformed, chaotic aspect and eventually disappear. Placed near a computer or television, the crystals generally tend to break down, but can reform or dissolve completely in function of the content.

The photographs published by Emoto are extraordinary testaments to the sensitivity of water, they show how its molecular clusters are influenced by something as apparently ineffable as a word written on a page and placed near the container, as if it had a conscious soul.

➤

However, these fascinating revelations have to be confirmed through fully controlled experiments.

We are 70 per cent water ourselves, and Emoto is convinced that the water in our bodies undergoes the same reactions as his samples when exposed to positive or negative stimuli, thus conditioning our psychophysical health.

Emoto's experiments seem to show us once again that water is highly sensitive to information, and that its electromagnetic properties are ductile, ever ready to change or disappear at the slightest stimulus, be it physical, chemical or emotional.

It is difficult to fathom the full implications of these phenomena, but one thing seems certain: the equilibrium of the water within us can be influenced by the quality of the information it receives.

The Possible is Not Always Reproducible

There is no such thing as a logical method of having new ideas, or a logical reconstruction of this process ... Every discovery contains an irrational element or a creative intuition.

KARL POPPER

Extraordinary claims must be backed up by extraordinary results. It is absolutely right to demand clear and definitive scientific proof of phenomena like water memory which, if true, threaten to unseat the predominant scientific theories. The problem lies in being able to control the conditions necessary for reproducing a phenomenon that is inherently elusive and not entirely understood.

In nature, nothing is completely reproducible. Science must rely on the generalizations of statistics to distinguish what is true from what is not. The usual reason that natural phenomena cannot be perfectly reproduced is an imperfect control of laboratory materials, methods and conditions. The water molecule is an organized chaotic system that is extremely difficult to tame. The main characteristic of chaotic systems, as we've seen, is unpredictability – that is, a tendency to give different results due to any minimal change in the multiple parameters involved.

Another factor affecting reproducibility is the unconscious influence of the experimenter. The image of the detached, objective scientist is a myth. While it is of course the aim of every good scientist to be as objective as possible, the best ones know that any interpretation of results, including one's own, must take into consideration the specific conditions of the lab in which a given experiment is conducted and the unconscious preconceptions and methodological habits of those who perform it, for these things constitute potential obstacles to objectivity. And this is as true for Benveniste as it is for his detractors.

In science it is best to guard against excessive zeal, as it is likewise with regard to excessive hostility. An a priori negative attitude, however well hidden, can cause an experiment to fail, for even the littlest things can make a difference in the outcome. In the laboratory, there is indeed some truth to the 'power of positive (or negative) thinking' – believing something will happen sometimes makes it happen. Subjectivity, even in the absence of manipulation or intentional negligence, has the power to trigger changes in natural phenomena. Just think back to quantum physics, where the observer is an indispensable parameter and consciousness is an obligatory variable in every equation.

Quantum theory has helped us to understand that the universe does not operate mechanically, and the observer is not a detached bystander but is instead both the subject and object of a given experiment. Quantum phenomena occur only when observed in a certain way. Light can be a packet of photons or a wave, depending on how the experimenter decides to observe it.

In medicine, there are mental factors as yet not fully understood that can lead to the healing of even the most serious diseases. One of these is the 'placebo effect', where a patient, by believing he will heal, in fact does. Researchers tend to consider this merely an element of disturbance in the analysis of objective data, but in reality the placebo effect is as amazing as it is potentially valuable, and represents one of the highest expressions of human creativity. If the underlying mechanisms of this phenomenon were investigated rather than dismissed, it would open a whole new frontier in the understanding and treatment of all human disease.

Mnemosyne: the Aquatic Origins of Memory

... the river is everywhere at once, at the source and at the mouth,
at the waterfall, at the ferry, at the rapids, in the sea, in the mountains,
everywhere at once, and ... there is only the present time for it, not the
shadow of the past, not the shadow of the future ...

HERMANN HESSE, Siddhartha

Mnemosyne, the Greek goddess of memory, was one of the 12 Titans born of Uranus, god of Heaven, and Gaia, goddess of the Earth. She and Zeus gave birth to the nine Muses, each of whom presided over one of the arts and sciences. Mnemosyne used to gather her nine children and tell them about all that had happened since the beginning of time. The nine Muses listened, enraptured, and transformed their mother's tales into poems and songs so that they might better remember them.

Mnemosyne is closely associated with water in Greek mythology. She was the spring of remembrance that bore her name, in which all souls were immersed before assuming human form on the Earth. All the past memories of every soul were washed away and remained stored there in Mnemosyne's spring. Those who drank these sacred waters expanded the boundaries of their consciousness by taking in the immensity of all lost memory, crossing the threshold into complete knowledge of the past and future.

Mnemosyne gave to Hermes the lyre and a soul, a reflection of ancient Greece's understanding of the connection between soul, memory, creativity and the rhythms of nature and their shared origin in water. The name Mnemosyne lives on today in the word 'mnemonic', and she is the symbolic image of a contemporary 'myth' – that of the memory of water, capable of absorbing and safeguarding all the information of the universe.

Until recently it was thought that the mnemonic traces impressed in our brain were permanent, and that with a bit of effort we could recall any memory more or less exactly. But new research has shown that memories are never retrieved in the same way. When an experience is fixed in the memory, the synapses expand and fill with receptors and neurotransmitters to ensure an optimal connection. After a few hours the neurons begin to physically grow, forming the dendrites that consolidate the mnemonic data, using proteins to build new circuits. At this point, the data is now able to migrate. If the memory is recent, it ends up in the deepest parts of the brain, such as the hippocampus. As the days and weeks pass the data migrates further, eventually settling into the larger expanses of the cerebral cortex.

In 2003 a group of researchers from the Universities of Montreal and New York discovered that the fixed and stored memories of lab animals can be cancelled if they are recalled and then fail to be reconsolidated, suggesting that even our most hardwired long-term memories are not immune to interference, even loss. A clear example is the frequency with which eyewitnesses to criminal events contradict one another, or recall their own accounts differently with the passage of time.

DNA testing reveals that many prisoners have been unjustly convicted of serious crimes on the basis of eye-witness accounts, the importance of which is consequently dwindling in criminal trials. Any psychotherapist knows that some patients unconsciously embroider actual traumatic experiences with details and episodes that never happened. This is not to say that memory is untrustworthy, but rather that it is extraordinarily dynamic, always adapting itself to our needs.

If we picture the face of a person for a first time, the next time it will be similar, but not the same. *Retrieving a memory is invariably a creative act.*

Fred Gage, a neurologist from the Salk Institute for Biological Studies in California, conducted a study in a university hospital in Sahlgrenska, Sweden, that was the first to demonstrate that human adults are capable of generating new nerve cells,[52] providing hope for victims of what was always thought to be irreversible nerve tissue damage. This process, called neurogenesis, takes place in the hippocampus, which also happens to be one of the brain's main centres for learning and memory. This capacity of the memory centre to produce new neurons is further confirmation that memory is not something permanent, cemented in immutable strucures, but a dynamic process subject to continuous re-elaboration. In this sense, memory is like flowing water, never repeating itself in exactly the same way.

The more often we retrieve specific memories, the more they are consolidated. Their quality, associations and emotional impact, however, can change. Neither does our perception of ourselves remain fixed; it never corresponds to the same identical engram (the biochemical 'structure' of a memory trace). And it is right that it should be so, given that the rest of our water-based bodies recycle billions of cells every day. The configuration and number of synapses in the brain change continuously: time passes, and imperceptibly changes who we are.

The purpose of the brain is not to preserve memory, but to integrate newly learned data with old. Rather than being conditioned by our memory, like a microbe or migratory fish, it is we who do the conditioning, and this is an enormous advantage for human beings. In this sense we should be thankful for the fact that our memory is not an infallible instrument, but rather a flexible one, receptive to reinforcement and transformation. This new vision of human memory opens the door to therapies that can liberate people by transforming even their oldest, most traumatic memories into something positive, or at least something they can more easily live with.

Perhaps herein lies a key to understanding why experiments on water memory are so difficult to reproduce. Every sample is different because every context, every experimenter, is different, and therefore the memory of the dissolved substance will be consolidated in response to those factors.

Potential differences between solutions of the same liquid are taken into account by homeopathic theory, according to which minimal variations in the number and type of dilutions and succussions confer different, in some cases even opposite therapeutic properties to the solution. If the succussions are not performed correctly, the solution can be rendered totally inactive. Moreover, if it is exposed to even a very weak electromagnetic field (e.g. from a household appliance), the solution may deactivate or change the 'code' of its electromagnetic memory.

Memory as Matter

The cells in our body contain a number of components endowed with memory – DNA, transmembrane hormone receptors, peptides – which act as chemical messengers for the immune and nervous systems, both inside and outside the cells. Memory is not restricted to the hologram of the brain, but is immanent throughout the organism, another example of which is the way the immune system 'remembers' the antigens that have visited the body in the past.

The DNA double helix winds spirally around itself, like the electronic circuit of a television or radio, or like a solenoid. It is tempting to think that this distinctive form is designed to enable DNA to 'tune in' and resonate with the coherent impulses emitted by the water molecules which, as described earlier, make DNA replication and protein synthesis possible.

A cell is basically a membranous sac full of mineralized water. Endrocrinologist Deepak Chopra rightly points out that 'Memory must be more permanent than matter. What is a cell, then? It is a memory that has built some matter around itself, forming a specific pattern. Your body is just a place your memory calls home.'[53] Molecular biology helps us grasp the paradox that it is consciousness – intelligence + memory – that gives rise to organic matter, and not vice versa, and the notion of organic water as a receptacle of memory begins to seem less abstruse.

Plants have memory, too. In 1982, an interesting study was conducted at the University of Clermont on *bidens pilosa*, or hairy beggartick.[54] When the seedlings in the test group had developed the first two symmetrical leaves (cotyledons), the researchers punctured one of them four times, then after five minutes pruned both cotyledons. Twenty days later, these plants showed differences with respect to those in the control group, which had not been punctured. In the case of the latter, the cotyledons had an equal probability of developing a main branch on either side. The test group, on the other hand, having been given only five minutes to consolidate the memory of injuries admin-istered nearly a month earlier, showed a marked tendency to develop branches on the opposite side of the punctured cotyledon. So it would seem that even plants, in their own way, have what we might call 'childhood memories'.

Trees produce substances such as tannins and pheromones which they use to communicate with one another through the air. If one tree is attacked by predatory insects, for example, it will send a message by wind to warn other trees of the danger. This extraordinary form of individual and collective awareness can also involve other creatures, such as bees during pollination season. Despite their lack of a nervous system, plants have the capacity of both memory and communication. Information, its retention and transmission are present in every form of life that depends on water, from the simplest bacterium to the tallest redwood. The more we discover about water, the less surprised we should be that information lies at the root of all life, within the very water that sustains it.

The fact that water acquires new properties in the absence of new molecules makes perfect sense in the context of quantum theory. In the words of physicists Paul Davis and John Gribbin: 'One of the more bizarre consequences of quantum uncertainty is that matter can appear out of nowhere.'[55] The same applies to energy, which can appear from nothing and disappear just as quickly. The 'void', in reality, isn't as empty as one might think.

Experiments have demonstrated the presence of activity in the quantum void – specifically, the spontaneous appearance of short-lived 'virtual' subatomic particles, such as when two protons are made to collide in a particle accelerator, creating 'pions'. Matter constitutes less than 1 per cent of the universe; all the rest is void. And when we break down matter into its smallest components, what do we find? Yes, the void.

This is why physicists think of matter not as something you can hold in your hand, but as a dynamic void: it does not exist in any fixed way, but has only a statistical tendency to exist. The void should not be confused with nothingness. According to quantum theory, nothingness does not exist *per se*, for there is always the possibility that a particle can be created at any moment (by 'moment' we're talking on a scale of trillionths of a second!). As the Buddha said, form is emptiness and emptiness is form. The same thing happens in the formation of an embryo: the boundary zone between the lining of the uterus and its cavity is like a void, and it is there that life is constructed.

The void is the substrate from which information is given forth. And the void within the water molecule is like a bottle that washes up on the beach: it appears empty, but inside there is a vital message waiting to be read.

Naming the Heavens and the Waters

> *Praise Him, you heavens of heavens,*
> *And you waters above the firmament!*
>
> Psalm 148: 4

In the biblical story of Creation, light and darkness appear on the first day. Genesis describes the second day as follows:

> Then God said, 'Let there be a firmament in the midst of the waters, and let it separate between waters and waters.' Thus God made the firmament, and separated between the waters which were beneath the firmament and the waters which were above the firmament. And it was so. And God called to the firmament Heavens.
>
> Genesis 1: 6–8

After separating light from darkness, God differentiated the 'lower waters' (liquid) from the 'upper waters' (vapour); the heavens are made of rarefied water.

Midrashic commentators explain that the upper waters represent the masculine element – the fecundative source of dew and beneficial rain. The lower waters form the oceans, rivers and underground aquifers, symbolizing the feminine element – passive, receptive, formative. Echoing the bipolar principle of yin and yang, opposite yet one and the same, the Talmud says that the difference between the two waters is finer than a hair. Their union creates life, while their separation brings death, just like the Earth's life-sustaining hydrological cycle, any alteration of which would lead to the irremediable disturbance of the entire planetary ecosystem.

The Bible concludes every day of the Creation with the formula: 'God saw what he had made, and it was good;' that is, every day but the second. The Midrash explains that on this day, the separation of the waters created strife, the first fracture in the world, a separation more necessary than 'good', for it was an expression of conflict between two vital, inseparable principles and at the same time indispensable for the evolution of the cosmos (positive, negative – yin, yang). This opposition contains a destructive seed that must be controlled. Differences and divisions are not good per se, but can become good when we appreciate the specific different roles and places of everything and everyone in this world. It is by emulating the upper and lower waters at every level that we can find the key to life, prosperity and harmony.

The Creation story proceeds with the formation of the sea, the cradle of life and the first creative act spurred by the union of the upper and lower waters. It is written in the Talmud that 'every drop of rain that falls from above meets with two drops of underground water that rise toward it.' (Taanit 28) We find the same generative process of the joining of the two waters in the coupling of living creatures. Uniting the masculine and the feminine means fostering life and growth; creating and evolving are only possible when opposites are joined as one.

For the Kabbalists, the meeting of the upper and lower waters transforms the vitality of water into wisdom. The downward flow of the former represents the intrinsic intelligence of the cosmos and divine revelation; the upward flow of the latter symbolizes our subconscious, that which is hidden in the depths of the psyche, afraid to reveal itself yet at the same time longing to do so. The union of the two waters also has ethical implications, in that it represents the capacity to distinguish that which is positive, ordered and spiritual from that which leads to separation and destruction.

'And God called to the firmament Heavens' (Genesis 1: 8). In the mystical texts the expression 'heaven' is ambiguous, and sometimes indicates God himself. In the macrocosmic sense, the 'firmament' is the entire universe, excluding the Earth; heaven indicates the atmosphere, dense with water vapour that filters the light of the Sun and transmits to Earth all the vital forces of the cosmos. At the microcosmic level, the firmament corresponds instead to the creative void within the water molecule, repository of all the information necessary for creating and sustaining life.

The medieval commentator Rashì (1040–1105), referring to the Talmud (Hagigah 12a) points out that in the Hebrew Bible the firmament is called *shamayim*, a word that breaks down into *sham mayim*, meaning 'there where waters are'. Rabbi Ben Nachman (also known as Ramban, 1194–1270) suggests instead that the word for the firmament is composed of *shem mayim* ('the name of water'). Heavens is the name of waters. What might that mean?

Ramban is telling us that the firmament, heaven, *shamayim* is the space created within the waters to conserve the names, i.e. information: it is the space in which memory is constructed. By creating an empty space within this firmament, the upper and lower waters acquired the capacity to receive, retain and transmit information, and thus to form material reality, from the micro- to the macroscopic. If we accept Ramban's reading of the root meaning of *shamayim*, then the Bible may be the earliest text that alludes to water's ability to memorize information.

The space between the waters contains the information that gave rise to differentiated matter. This capacity to conserve 'names' and to express the molecular vibrations that give them voice constitutes what we've been referring to throughout this chapter as the memory of water, the creative force that underlies and informs the material world.

The idea that the heavens express 'the name of waters' brings us to the intimate relationship we're learning to see between water, memory and language; between the creative act and the word. Water encompasses the firmament, figuratively and literally, microscopically and macrocosmically. It contains within it a space charged with meaning, a memory in the true sense of the word, that harbours the master code of creation.

This space is called in Genesis *shamayim*, or alternatively *rakia* ('open space'), a term that contains the words *reik*, meaning 'void', and the letter *ain*, formed by two eyes joined by a trunk, symbol of the union of the bipolar principles of visible reality.

Biblical commentators concur on the fact that the firmament was created on the first day, but that it took physical form only on the second. The firmament is the 'solidification' of the waters, the filling of the void with names – i.e. the bits and bytes of information necessary to complete the Creation. In the Zohar, the firmament is considered a 'third world', suspended between the heavens and the Earth.

Ramban points out that the firmament was the first substance that God created from nothingness, and that it must have been like a tent stretched between the waters, separating them. For Rabbi Hirsch, the term 'firmament' derives from *rakà*, which means 'to extend' or 'expand', like metal hammered into ever thinner and wider sheets. The firmament is the rarefied space within the cosmos of water: it is the apparent void.

The empty space described in the Bible coincides with the quantum void of subatomic physics. It is at once the celestial space that assigns the different waters a name and a precise function, and the space between their molecules, which is named according to the 'sounds' (vibrations) and meanings it can contain. It is the code for the creation of matter and life.

Rashì writes that the ancient word for the firmament could also be composed from *esh mayim*, or 'fire and water', which would confirm the biblical account of how God combined fire and water to make the heavens. The image brings to mind the phenomenon of minicomets, those fiery spheres of ice that constantly bombard the Earth, exploding in the atmosphere and transforming into rain. Here again we find a biblical reference that meshes remarkably with the most recent and mysterious scientific discoveries.

On the human scale, Rashì's commentary recalls a similar 'fire' contained by 'water': the energy centre known in Chinese medicine as Ming Men, the Gate of Life, associated with Heavens and with the name, identity and personal destiny of every human being.

~

CHAPTER SIXTEEN

AQUATIC INTELLIGENCES

*With a big brain, survival in the sea seems to be easier
than survival on land.*

JOHN C LILLY

For more than 40 years, John Lilly studied the bottlenose dolphin
(*Tursiops truncatus*) in the Virgin Islands, Florida and Hawaii,
having recognized their exceptional abilities from the outset. Through
his research on sensory deprivation in water (see Chapter 14), Lilly
sought to identify the states of consciousness that dolphins could have
developed and to determine whether interspecies communication with
humans would be possible.

The most voluminous brains on Earth are found in the water. Whales
are the largest living creatures, with the largest hearts and brains. Of all
marine mammals, only the cetaceans – dolphins, porpoises and whales –
have brains that surpass the linguistic threshold of 600 to 700 grams. A
dolphin's brain weighs 1,600g on average, by comparison to the 1,400g
of the human brain (figure 16.1); the brain of the great whales can weigh
as much as six times our own. Among land mammals, only the elephant,
whose ancestors were aquatic, has a bigger brain than ours, though this
is more a function of the creature's great size and extraordinary capacity for acoustic reception than of cognition *per se*. Cetaceans are the

oldest forms of advanced intelligence, having appeared some 60 million years ago, quite a stretch by comparison humankind's meagre 200,000 years on the planet.

It is impossible to correlate mammalian brain size and intelligence with any real precision. However, rigorous studies of cetacean cognition show intelligent behaviour and a capacity to learn that are in some ways 'superior' to our own, methodologically faulty though the comparison may be. Nonetheless, it is revealing.

Intelligence is generally defined as the ability to communicate and to overcome one's spatiotemporal limits. Our cerebral cortex contains frontal, temporal and parietal associative areas that govern the higher functions of communication, memory and the processes for elaborating complex sensory and motorial data. The development of these associative areas correlates with the expression of integrative activities such as language, motivational thought, and a relational grasp of the past (memory) and future (planning). In dolphins, these associative areas are four times more extensive than a human's, even though their cerebral cortex is thinner than ours.

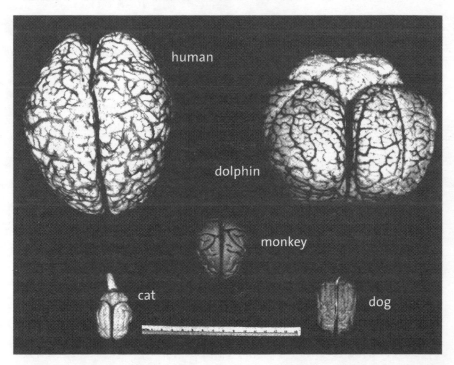

Figure 16.1 Comparison of the brains of a human, a dolphin, a monkey, a cat and a dog

By comparison, the chimpanzee, in addition to having a much smaller brain than ours, also presents a relatively poor distribution of associative areas. Think that a 40-ton shark has a 100-gramme brain, while a 40-ton whale has a 9-kilogramme brain – necessary for cognitive elaborations and communication.

Intelligent Behaviour in Dolphins

Francis Crick (1916–2004), winner of the Nobel Prize for his contribution to the discovery of the DNA double helix in 1953, postulated that life began in a sort of 'primordial soup' made up of hydrogen, ammonia and methane, and he turned out to be more or less right. But this still doesn't tell us how matter was able to organize itself to the point of becoming self-aware.

Intelligence is present in other animal species, though it mustn't be compared to ours. In fact, intelligence studies based on an anthropocentric model were abandoned when scientists realized that animal intelligence depends on their circumstances and biological imperatives, which differ from species to species.

Animal intelligence – or rather, intelligences – evolved in different ecological niches, and the structures of animal nervous systems vary greatly from one species to another. It is therefore relatively futile to impose any absolute hierarchy of parameters for 'superior' or 'inferior' intelligence.

Many people are amazed to learn that cephalopods – octopuses and squid – are intelligent animals, with complex visual, tactile, gustatory and olfactory systems, not to mention an extraordinary sense of hearing. These creatures have complex brains and show a rare capacity for communication and learning. Anyone who has been scuba diving knows how difficult it is to orient oneself underwater and to estimate the depth of one's position, tasks which octopuses handle with ease, while squid are able to communicate through subtle manipulations of body colour.

These abilities alone are surprising for invertebrate animals, so try to imagine the scientific community's astonishment when in 1992 a group of researchers in Naples, Italy, announced that an octopus had learned to choose a red ball over a white ball by imitating another octopus.[56] Observational learning is a faculty that had heretofore been considered the exclusive domain of the higher vertebrates – many mammals are entirely without it. Today there is no longer any doubt that cephalopods are capable of observational learning, considered by many as an essential step toward conceptual thought.

Cetaceans, like humans, are equipped with a highly sophisticated sonic communication apparatus and a bona fide language which they use to exchange complex underwater messages. Water is the ideal medium for the propagation of acoustic impulses, inasmuch as sound travels through water four and a half times faster (1,540m/sec) than through air. Cetaceans communicate with each other over vast distances, reaching hundreds of kilometres for some whale species.

A dolphin's sense of taste is particularly well developed. Its skin is approximately six times more sensitive than ours to touch and pressure, which makes sense: it has been shown that prolonged contact with water *increases cutaneous sensitivity in humans.*

Dolphins in captivity engage in lengthy sexual foreplay before coupling. As with humans, coitus is voluntary and not governed by the seasons. In the smaller cetaceans, gestation lasts ten months and the mother nurses her young for one to two years. Young dolphins already have excellent control of their vocal apparatus at nine months of age and are able to compose complex signals. By comparison, human children, whose brain is the same size as that of a newborn dolphin (about 700g), begin emitting voluntary vocal sounds around the sixth month of life. Cetaceans have a strong and long-lasting sense of belonging to the group and a remarkable sense of creative play, which they carry well into advanced age.

Over 60 million years of evolution, cetaceans have developed a very elaborate acoustic reception apparatus. The language of dolphins is composed of complex sequences of whistles, clicks and high-frequency vibrations. Their capacity to transmit, receive and process acoustic information is as much as 20 times greater than our own. Their visual capacity, though just one tenth ours, is sufficient for orienting themselves outside the water in relation to the Sun, Moon and stars.

Dolphins are thinking beings. At an international conference on dolphin linguistics held in 2000, biologist Louis Herman from the University of Hawaii in Honolulu demonstrated that dolphins are the only known animals capable of understanding a set of complex human phrases.[57]

Though they're surely intelligent enough to communicate with us, the differences in our perceptual organs makes it rather difficult. The frequency spectrum of the human voice is very limited (between 100 and 3,000 Hz) and is often inaudible to dolphins, whose vocal spectrum ranges from 1,000 to an amazing 80,000 Hz (our auditory perception stops at 20,000 Hz). And let's not forget that the higher the frequency, the greater the number of impulses and therefore the quantity of information that can be transmitted per second.

Dolphins have developed their intelligence despite a lack of prehensile limbs. During the evolutionary process, their limbs were replaced by beautifully engineered fins that allow them to swim at incredible speeds. This is why they have neither constructive capacities nor means of transport nor external cultural expressions (books, films, etc). From an anthropocentric standpoint, this might seem a strike against any claims as to their intelligence.

But let's try looking at it from their point of view. Dolphins live in water, which is the best medium for transferring information and electromagnetic waves of any kind aside from light. They have no reason to build anything or to use intermediary structures in order to sustain their species and way of life. 'Cultural' exchange is entrusted to their capacity to transmit large quantities of acoustic information, quickly and over great distances, to their young, who efficiently store this cultural data using the hyperdeveloped associative areas of their formidable brains.

Research conducted by the University of Hawaii and the Kewale Basin Marine Mammal Laboratory in the US confirmed the conclusions drawn by Lilly from the data he compiled on dolphins in captivity:[58] their behaviour attests to a complex mental life and an evolved perception of reality. Deprived of freedom or a family member, or trapped in a situation with no means of escape, dolphins will sometimes consciously resort to suicide, singly or in groups, as we witness occasionally in 'beachings', or strandings. These tragic events, which sometimes involve many dozens of animals, are not entirely understood. While some interpret them as a desperate SOS directed at humans, a plea to stop destroying the ocean's resources, it is more likely that at least one of the causes is connected to geomagnetic anomalies that confuse their echolocation sonar.

Intelligence is correlated to molecules, but not coincident with them. The amount of DNA in a lily is 100 times greater than in a human being, yet flowers are clearly not more intelligent than us by any standard, anthropocentric or not. The DNA in two species of drosophila, or fruit fly, differs much more than ours does from that of a chimpanzee. If intelligence resides in molecules, it is in the molecular structure of cells, in the intervals between molecules, those empty spaces we discussed earlier on that hold the secret of water's unique properties. The evolution of intelligent species can be compared to the development of a fractal triggered by the oscillation of a water molecule until arriving at the primates and the cetaceans.

But the exploration of intelligence must also take into account that which lies beyond the animal kingdom and delve into nature at its most microscopic level, where physicists routinely speak of the 'intentional' behaviours of subatomic particles. Intelligence is intrinsic to nature, and knows no bounds in the universe.

Communicating with Dolphins

One of the major lessons of evolution is that large brains survive only in concert with one another and with the planet ... If, eventually, we can comunicate with them [Cetacea], we may find the ethics, laws, and facts that they have discovered, which have allowed their survival ... to continue their evolution to larger brains and larger internal realities.

JOHN C LILLY, *Between Man and Dolphin*, pp 92–3

Following in the wake of Lilly's pioneering research, a number of scientists have continued to investigate the possibility of communicating with dolphins. If such a meeting of the minds were possible, humans and cetaceans could significantly improve one another's conditions, though on this point the dolphin seems more open to dialogue than humans, reluctant as we are to descend from our anthropocentric ivory tower.

Dolphins adapt better than we do to interspecies communication – when they come into contact with a human, they make an effort to communicate in a different way than is normal for them. When a dolphin encounters a human being, it spontaneously imitates human speech in the air rather than the water, and what's more uses its blowhole, not normally a transmission apparatus, to make low frequency sounds that humans are capable of hearing rather than using mouth and tongue to make sounds that would be inaudible to us. This alone shows us the dolphin's predisposition to learn a foreign language.

For a number of years now people have begun exploiting the communicative potential of dolphins towards therapeutic ends. Struck by the positive effects that contact with wild dolphins produced in subjects suffering from depression, English doctor and biologist Horace Dobbs launched Operation Sunflower in 1987 under the aegis of the International Dolphin Watch, organizing what can only be called interspecies therapy sessions between humans and dolphins.

American psychologists Betsy Smith and Patricia Hindley of Simon Frazer University in Burnaby, British Columbia, along with numerous other therapists, obtained surprising results with programmed encounters between dolphins and autistic children. Since 1988, at the Dolphin Research Center in Marathon Key, Florida, neuropsychiatrist David Nathanson of Miami International University has been using captive dolphins to treat brain-damaged and disabled children. Marianne Kligel, a psychologist at the University of Florida, has obtained encouraging results with a group of adolescents with social and behavioural disorders. Related research on the effects of 'delphinotherapy' is also underway in France, Australia, Mexico, Israel and Honduras. In Italy's Cinque Terra Park in Liguria, a dolphin therapy centre for autistic children has been in operation since 2003.

Human beings perceive a world of light and form, while dolphins live in a realm of sound and echoes. After decades of research, Lilly came to the conviction that dolphins use their vocalizations to create a three-dimensional nonvisual world, a *vocal hologram* that they're able to convey to one another.

It is likely that the communicative gifts of dolphins have something to do with the electromagnetic stimulation of the ultrasound signal emitted by their sonar apparatus, which hits anyone swimming nearby. These sonar impulses may stimulate neuroendocrine structures like the hypophysary-hypothalamic system to secrete psychotropic substances such as melatonin, cath-ecolamine and other neurotransmitters. Moreover, neurophysiological studies conducted at the Academy of Traditional Chinese Medicine in Liaoning Province[59] confirm the therapeutic efficacy of sonic stimuli directed at the acupuncture meridians, which is explained by the fact that these meridians correspond to the areas of the body where electromagnetic waves are most concentrated and flow fastest.

Scientists have discovered that dolphins are highly cooperative, and actively cultivate a group mentality. Every dolphin always knows where every other member of the group is. Dolphins cooperate to search for food and help one another in case of injury or danger, and even help humans in emergency conditions, demonstrating an extraordinary degree of group coordination. In Africa and Australia certain coastal tribes like the Komilaroi of western New South Wales have been fishing alongside dolphins since the dawn of humankind, using a sort of extrasensory communication cultivated through ritual. The Aborigines of Arnhem Land and Groote Eylandt on the northern coast still conserve legends about the souls of the dead being accompanied to heaven by dolphins; they also count among their members special individuals known as 'dolphin dreamers', capable of communicating telepathically with these extraordinary creatures.

Australian Aborigines call their sixth sense the 'strong eye', which they use to establish telepathic contact with humans and animals of other species. Among the tribes of the northern coast and islands of Australia is one that considers the bottlenose dolphin its totem, which is to say the ancestor from whom they descend. The initiation rites for the shamans and leaders of the tribe include entering a hypnotic state to learn the telepathic language of dolphins. The shaman is often considered the reincarnation of a dolphin, and as such is seen as the authority on dolphin language.

In 1997 a group of neuroscientists from the University of Iowa published a paper in *Science* on research that confirms the importance of intuition for making experientially based decisions, by contrast to conscious, rational reasoning.[60] They found evidence that the exercise of the intuitive faculties activates the ventromedial area of the prefrontal cortex, located just above and exactly between the ocular orbits – that is, in precisely the position where so many cultures locate the 'third eye'. This same area is quite developed in dolphins, especially the bottlenose. Many people, scientists and laymen alike, who have spent any time with dolphins in the wild have experienced their telepathic ability to understand our deepest feelings.

Earlier we touched on the relationship between water, electromagnetic phenomena and biological organisms. *All living things*, including bacteria and insects, *react to magnetic fields*. It is thought that fish have a magnetosensitive apparatus, which isn't hard to imagine when we think of how a school of fish responds instantaneously to the slightest external stimulus as if it were a single being. Thanks to the magnetite crystals in their bodies, cetaceans are able to orient themselves by 'reading' the Earth's magnetic lines of force, a process greatly facilitated by the fact that salt water is such an excellent conductor.

As research brings us closer to understanding the electromagnetic memory of water, perhaps we will someday understand if and eventually how the vibratory characteristics of the water molecule contribute to the development of cetacean intelligence, and if in fact water serves as a library of information legible to them. Part of their large associative cortical mass may turn out to be dedicated to deciphering certain kinds of molecularly stored information. As things currently stand, however, this remains a tantalizing hypothesis.

Cetaceans possess the oldest evolved mind. The remote origin of their species suggests that they may have survived this long because of their 'wisdom'. We can witness aspects of this wisdom in their effort to communicate with humans and to help us when we're in danger, despite the fact that we continue to be the greatest threat to their own survival – many thousands are killed every year by fishing and pollution.

Dolphins don't kill each other, if we exclude the only episode ever documented, which occurred as a result of pathological behaviour provoked by eight years of forced seclusion. The instinct to cherish the lives of one's brethren, written into the dolphin's very genetics, is apparently an evolutionary trait still absent in humans.

Dolphins are also thought to possess 'spiritual' inclinations and a biological predisposition to achieve transcendent states of consciousness. If so, the fact that they essentially live in an immense isolation tank where they can relax and 'meditate' as they please might be a contributing element. Perhaps some of the secrets of the powers and intelligence of dolphins are hidden in the unique properties of water: its ability to transform and conserve, to absorb and be absorbed, to heal and nourish, to conduct and impede, to dissolve and create, to adhere and repel, to store information in its molecular structure, to propagate ultrasounds, to cushion blows, and last but not least, to function as a 'sense organ'.

Many of the most important spiritual traditions associate water with wisdom, which dolphins seem to have inherited from water itself. The secret of their intelligence, like that of our own, lies in the possibility offered us by water to transform ourselves physically, mentally and spiritually.

Children of the Sea

From thence we came.
Eternal mirror
where inverted architectures
tremble and welcome
the featureless father of light.
Where your face new and old transfigures
and dreams of having once known
the exquisite oscillation of existence.

MAURIZIO MESCHIA, 'Acqua'

A number of Babylonian and Mesopotamian myths recount how cetaceans were the founders of civilization as we know it, and how whales taught human beings the laws of recurring cycles. In what is probably a reference to dolphins, an ancient Chaldean text reads, 'man on the Earth was never worthy of the love shown him by his blood brothers of the ocean depths'.

Mesopotamia, a region that corresponds roughly to modern Iraq, owes its name to the confluence at its heart of two rivers, the Tigris and the Euphrates. On these fertile plains stood the city of Ur, birthplace of Abraham, patriarch of the Jewish, Christian and Muslim civilizations. Abraham was one of the most profound and original thinkers of his time, and the wisdom of the tradition to which he belonged has come down to us through the talmudic and kabbalistic texts.

A passage from the Babylonian Talmud reads:

Dolphins grow and multiply like human beings. Who are the dolphins? Rav Judah says: 'children of the sea'.

Bechorot, 8a

The literal meaning is clear: dolphins and humans resemble one another in their physical and social behaviour. But according to esoteric interpretation, the text alludes to something deeper. The Zohar, the most famous of kabbalistic texts, posits that when the Bible uses the expressions 'to grow' and 'to multiply', as in God's divine injunction to Adam and Eve in Genesis 1, 28 (usually translated as 'be fruitful and multiply'), it refers the more profound sense of 'growth' – that is, the cultivation of intelligence and wisdom.

If dolphins 'grow and multiply like human beings', this means that the authors of the Talmud already understood that dolphin intelligence develops in much the same way as our own. According to Rav Judah we should show dolphins the same respect and affection we reserve for children. It is probably no accident that dolphins tend to establish preferential relationships with newborns and children, for they are more elastic in their approach to learning, more open to new experience, and generally do not manifest the stiff reactions of defensiveness or aggression typical of adults.

The Hebrew term for 'human beings' (*benè adam*) means literally 'children of man'. According to tradition the child of man is he who speaks, or better, he who says the right thing at the right time, who speaks with relevance and wisdom. The masters of the Talmud understood, then, not only the similarity of human and dolphin intelligence, but the latter's exceptional ability to communicate. Indeed, dolphins are described in the Talmud as 'sages of the sea', endowed with intentionality and conscience.

The medieval commentator Rashì comments on the talmudic text with an intriguing statement that changes the meaning rather radically: 'Dolphins grow and multiply *from* human beings', rather than *like* human beings – quite a surprising substitution, if only for the fact that it is the only instance in the entire Judaic tradition suggesting the possibility of offspring from the sexual union between two different species. And while we know perfectly well that humans and dolphins cannot in fact mate, it is nonetheless interesting that it should ever have been thought possible.

Some scholars interpret the change of preposition from 'like' to 'from' in this and subsequent commentaries as an error of transcription. However, it should be pointed out that Rashì is known for his ability to shed new light on a text by reinterpreting a single letter, which leaves open the possibility that by making this distinction, Rashì intended to teach us something about the nature of the relationship between man and dolphin that would otherwise have been obscured.

In that case, the Talmud would be referring to an intimate dialogical relationship of interdependency and deep spiritual affinity between the two species – which connects back to the hypothesis of the aquatic ape, or more specifically to the possibility that our aquatic ancestors lived for a certain period in close contact with other intelligent water mammals. If nothing else, this would help explain the abundant mythological literature that links us to these animals, dolphins in particular.

Rashì is careful to point out in his commentary that the word 'dolphin' translates into French as *sirène* – that is, an aquatic being with human features, a 'child of man'. The universal image of the siren is of course associated with invisible sources of danger – the siren seduces, causes reasonable men to take leave of their senses, draws distracted mariners into the howling maelstrom. She represents the maelstrom of the soul, the terror of losing control of one's rational self, the absorption of one's identity into the void. We feel a similar mixture of fascination and fear towards the dolphin, whose intelligence seems in some ways so close to ours, yet so foreign and mysterious. The dolphin's irrepressible sense of spontaneous play embodies everything we ourselves wish to be and at the same time fear. Falling for the siren, or cavorting with the dolphin, means sacrificing rational control and, more frighteningly, our sense of our importance as individuals.

The Talmud does not only sustain the possibility of communicating with dolphins, a concept we find in Aristotle and Pliny and confirmed by modern science. It also contemplates the possibility that a human-dolphin union (not necessarily sexual) would generate a new and more evolved being, something like the *Homo delphinus* described by Mayol (see Chapter 11). Dolphins are indeed 'children of man', as evidenced by their overwhelmingly obvious desire to communicate with us, which would be far easier for us to see if only we were to free ourselves for a moment from our anthropocentric presumptuousness.

Another story that takes us back to the common origins of humans and dolphins survives in the legends of the Aboriginal population of Australia's Groote Island. It tells of how the earliest ancestors, the Indjebena, were special dolphins, precursors of both modern dolphins and humans. Their leader was called Dinginjabana. His companion, Ganadja, had learned from the shellfish – the wise Yakuna – all the wisdom of the oceans, and as such spent a great deal of time with them. Dinginjabana, jealous of his lady, instigated a war between the dolphins and the shellfish, the latter of whom formed a reluctant alliance with the tiger sharks, scourge of the seas. Together they massacred all the dolphins along with their leader, Dinginjabana. The Yakuna managed to save Ganadja from the sharks, however, protecting her with their shells.

At war's end, Ganadja, desperate and alone, the last of her kind, discovered she was pregnant, and a few months later gave birth to a son whom she named Dinginjabana, in honour of his father. The young Dinginjabana grew larger and stronger than the others of his now extinct species, and became the progenitor of modern-day dolphins, which explains why they are no longer afraid of tiger sharks. Meanwhile, the carcasses of the slaughtered Indjebena washed up onto the land. Once they dried and hardened, they were reborn as human beings.

The Aborigines of Australia constitute the oldest continuous culture in the world. They have been there for tens of thousands of years, and consider themselves the first humans to have appeared on the Earth. And their collective memory, preserved in their myths and legends, remembers still an originary connection between man and dolphin.

Moving on to other parts of the world, the Vesu people of Madagascar attribute their origin to the union of a fisherman and a siren, while the Maori of New Zealand continue to recount an ancient legend where the spirits of the dead, before reaching the ancestral home of Hawaiki, pass first by Cape Reinga at the northernmost extreme of the island, where they travel down into the earth through the roots of the pohutakawa tree, then enter the ocean to become dolphins. They then swim for about 400 miles to the Three Kings Islands, the final departure point into other dimensions.

Whales and the Leviathan

A passage from the Zohar (3,10a) commenting on Psalm 104 describes intelligent creatures living in the depths of the sea. The protagonist of the tale is Rabbi Nehorai (literally 'the rabbi of light'), a master of the Talmud of the second century AD:

> *O Lord, how manifold are Thy works!*
> *In wisdom hast Thou made them all:*
> *the earth is full of Thy riches.*
> *So is this great and wide sea,*
> *wherein are things creeping innumerable,*
> *both small and great beasts.*
> *There go the ships:*
> *there is that Leviathan,*
> *whom Thou hast made to play therein.*

> Psalm 104

➤

Rabbi Nehorai the Elder embarked one day on a sea voyage. The ship sank during a storm and all the passengers drowned. Thanks to a miracle, he alone survived and descended to the bottom of the sea and found an inhabited land where he saw strange human beings ... They recited prayers, but he was unable to understand them. Thanks to another miracle, he succeeded in returning to the surface. He said: 'Blessed are the just who study the Torah and who know the deepest mysteries. Woe be to those who oppose them and do not accept their word.' From that day forward, every time he would go to the house of study and hear the explanations of the Torah, he would cry. When asked why, he replied: 'Because I was sceptical of the words of the rabbis. I did not believe in the existence of the seven lands inhabited by beings different from us. Now I fear the judgement of the next world.'

The Book of Genesis (1: 21) describes the creation on the fifth day of the *taninim gedolim*, enormous monsters that commentators have identified variously as dinosaurs, whales or a mysterious marine creature of cosmic dimensions known as the leviathan. Tradition teaches that the female of the leviathan will be the 'nourishment' of the righteous at the end of time (Talmud, Baba Batra 74b) – an image of hope that perhaps alludes metaphorically to the wisdom that cetaceans will pass on to the humans of the future, if and when we are ready.

Rabbi Nehorai discovers a civilization different from his own at the bottom of the sea. Recalling it later, he bursts into tears, and thanks to these tears, which taste of the sea, he is better able to see his own destiny, one that is directly tied to that of the intelligent creatures of the water.

Whales have been living in the water for about 50 million years, and over the course of that time they have learned to follow the rhythm of the currents and move without hurry over their annual migratory routes that cover the distance of an entire hemisphere (coincidentally the dimensions of the mythic leviathan), invariably curvilinear and cyclical like the flow of water, never straight. The words 'whale' and 'wheel' share the same origin: whales are like wheels of the sea. Rabbi Nahman of Bratslav (1772–1811) once said: 'The Whole Creation is like a wheel that turns and sways ... everything cyclically rolls.'

In describing the evolution of creation, the Talmud uses the formation of clouds as an example. Clouds are the product of the evaporation of the salty water of the oceans, which is sweetened by its ascent into the sky. This transformation serves as a metaphor for the incessant cyclical evolution of creation in its drive towards perfection. Scholars and sages of the past, well before modern physicists confirmed it, knew that the world is continually renewing itself at every moment. Human beings can participate in this renewal, and help perpetuate the harmony already inherent in the universe.

Intelligence is Nomadic

Yet, in the East, they still preserve the once universal concept: that wandering re-establishes the original harmony which once existed between man and the universe.

BRUCE CHATWIN, *The Songlines*

Water is nomadic and urges us to wander, to follow its flow. Some civilizations are indeed founded on the mobility of water: mobilizing themselves in accordance with water rendered their cultures dynamic. A nomadic culture knows how to move around, having mastered all the rules and secrets of the journey. It moves not because it lacks a sense of belonging to a particular place, but because its sense of belonging encompasses the entire world. Being nomadic means being prepared to pack up and take away everything that one is and has, at any moment. Nomadism is not, however, blind. Just as water inexorably flows to the sea, so does the nomad know that he will end up in the place he was destined for, and then perhaps yet further beyond it.

High intelligence is also nomadic, inasmuch as it is the capacity to adapt thought and action to changing circumstances. It is knowing how to transmit knowledge elastically and by any means, being able to learn from everything and everyone, leaving one's own habits open to the outside and permeable to otherness – all the while maintaining one's identity distinct and intact.

The nomadic mentality develops through the preservation of the opposing tendency: the conservative power of the status quo, from which it builds and safeguards a tradition that is maintained over the course of the generations. Here again we find the dynamic coexistence of change and permanence. That which is inherently renewable must paradoxically be conserved. Knowledge is a good example, in that it is on the one hand a fixed body of accumulated wisdom, yet on the other hand it is worthless if it is not questioned and spurred toward change. This isn't a matter of the virtue of doubt for its own sake, but of the continual quest to approach, albeit asymptotically, the Absolute.

Hindu tradition dictates that holy beggars, the *sadhu*, should strive to emulate water, moving continuously so as to avoid mental stagnation. Significantly, the bodies of the sadhu and newborn infants are not cremated as all others are, but entrusted to the river. The wisdom of the Vedas, of the Taoist texts, of the Scriptures and the oral traditions of many cultures is founded upon this common definition of knowledge as being intrinsically receptive to progress.

Driven by the constant questioning of itself, nomadic intelligence pays attention to the tiniest details, never taking an argument or event at face value. Like water, it infiltrates the lowest and darkest places, where life's most precious values reside, often hidden, among that which is humble, small and overlooked. We would do well to emulate this kind of intelligence, which is the intelligence of nature itself – penetrating, oscillating, always calling itself into question.

Water is a nomadic substance *par excellence*. With its ceaseless creative flux and the vibrant asymmetry of its molecules, it has neither a permanent dwelling place nor a fixed structure. Everything is transported and cleansed by its current. The more dynamic intelligence is, the less likely that it will be entrapped by repetitive circuits and inflexible schema; by adapting its strategies to the immediate circumstances, it finds the solution. Nomadic intelligence is like a fractal, regular yet unpredictable, always expanding like a spiral and always creative.

Among the many attributes assigned to water by the Chinese theory of the Five Movements is the storage of memory and the exercise of will: this is the secret of all the traditions based on the *repetition of never repeating themselves*. Our aquatic progenitors, thanks to the close contact they had with the inherent dynamism of water, made an enormous qualitative leap in terms of the development of intelligence. The same holds true for the nomadic intelligence of the cetaceans.

Intelligence is nomadic and ductile precisely because it is a direct consequence of the mobility of water itself.

Over the millennia, numerous civilizations have enriched humanity through oral transmission of information. The Aborigines of Australia, the Masai, the Native Americans and, prior to the age of written language, the Indian, Chinese, Jewish and many other civilizations have rich oral traditions, limiting the written word to the necessary minimum so as to ensure the elasticity of thought and dialogue.

The Aboriginal oral tradition can be traced back 40,000 years. Quintessentially nomadic, the Aborigines have never developed a written culture or an artisan tradition that went beyond what a person could carry from one place to another. Their worldview is based not on possessions, since the more one possesses the less capable he is of moving; what matters above all material things is instilling a healthy and harmonious relationship with the spirits of the Earth.

Knowledge of the realm of the spirits who created the world is passed on, generation after generation, through songs. At the time of creation, which they refer to as the 'Dreamtime', the spirits wandered the world until each of them found its place of destiny, where they burrowed into the earth and made their dwelling. Through their dreams, the spirits brought the landscape to life and gave names to each place, leaving their imprint on the land.

The dream is the origin of time and space for the Aborigine, the place from whence the spirit comes. The dream refers to places that bear the names of plants, animals, constellations; on long journeys, the Aborigines sing these dreams as navigational soundings to orient themselves in the territory, of which they feel themselves an integral and inseparable part. By singing or drawing their dreams, they commune with the spirits of the ancestors and enter into an ecstatic trance, wherein they become one with the universal spirit. And this is also where they receive the necessary instructions for living correctly.

In making the chanted word into a map of their world, the Aborigines are effectively using the same method as dolphins: localization through vocalization. The word and the song are the instruments of communication, perception and interpretation of the world. The image of this world in Aboriginal culture is like a full repertoire of vibrant symphonies, of chanted stories and dreams that resonate everywhere and in everything.

Not surprisingly, analysis of the melodies of these songs shows that they are essentially acoustic reproductions of geographical fractals, such that two men from different tribes standing on opposite sides of the continent would be able to decipher a melody sung by the other and understand its geographical meaning even without understanding the words.

The Way of the Word

Language, as Aldous Huxley observes in *The Doors of Perception*, is the product of the wisdom of previous generations. When we learn a language, we inherit a bit of that wisdom. The wisdom of the Chinese people, for example, resides in the afterimage of its ideograms, while that of the Aborigines resounds in the echo of its songlines.

The Aboriginal *tjurna djugurba*, or 'footprints of the Ancestor', also means 'Way of the Law'. 'It would seem there exists, at some deep level of the human psyche, a connection between "path-finding" and "law".'[61] *Tao*, in Chinese, means both 'way' and 'order'; the Hebrew word for law, *halachà*, derives from the verb root 'to walk'.

In Aboriginal cultures, to live harmoniously one must move through nature while recounting its spiritual history. The Tibetan word for human being, *a-Groba*, also means 'wanderer', he who migrates. The Hebrew word for Hebrew, *ivrì*, refers to 'he who passes over the water-way'. One establishes a permanent personal identity by following the flow of things: our home, the blue planet, moves with us, as does the culture we carry within us.

Chatwin points out that 'nomads have been the driving force of history, if only because the great monotheistic faiths, without exception, arose from the pastoral world'.[62] The Bible teaches that the right to live on one's own land can be earned only by humanizing it, for otherwise it will devour its inhabitants. The word for Earth in Hebrew has its root in the word for 'to run'. To keep pace with the Earth, we must move with it also intellectually.

All of the world's spiritual traditions affirm that consciousness is inscribed in every aspect of the physical universe. Every one of us, depending on our existential or religious orientation, can attribute varying degrees of consciousness to visible and invisible reality: from the mineral to the human, from the smallest subatomic string to the largest galaxy-swallowing black hole. Consciousness manifests itself in the

Figure 16.2 A spiral wheel galaxy

universe in different hierarchical degrees, though it isn't easy to detect in our chaotic and entropic world. But behind this apparently opaque veil lies the nomadic intelligence of the cosmos, or what Bohm called holomovement. Consciousness is everywhere, we just have to look for it.

At the beginning of time, in the first instant of the Big Bang, the matter that today makes up our brains was formed. The material substrate of our minds was born with the universe, which since then has been in constant movement and expansion. Billions of years later, the vibrations of those first atoms reorganized and became the human word.

The mind, too, is nomadic and can expand, like the universe. It's up to us to exploit its potential and push it to its limits, which are those of the universe itself. In order to feel itself part of the intelligence of the universe, the mind needs to be nourished by movement, be it from one point of view to another, from one state of consciousness to another, from the intelligence of one species to another.

CHAPTER 17

THE MYSTICAL TRADITION AND THE MYSTERIES OF WATER

In his memoirs Viktor Schauberger recalls that one day, while he was testing a method for transforming black water into crystalline water, he was visited by some elderly Austrian Jews. His guests asked how he had learned this purification technique based on the movement of water. They told him that a similar method had been handed down through the ancient esoteric tradition, but the details had been lost.

A famous passage in the Talmud tells the story of four great masters who dared to enter the 'mystic orchard' of Pardes ('paradise'), a truly risky undertaking. Of the four sages, only Rabbi Akiva left unharmed: 'He entered in peace and departed in peace,' says the Talmud. The other masters met instead with dire fates: Elisha Ben Abuyah entered the fire and became an unbeliever; Ben Azzai entered the earth and found death; Ben Zoma entered the air and went mad.

The Zohar tells us that Rabbi Akiva was spared because he knew all the secrets of water, and was the only one able to access the deepest kabbalistic teachings, which reveal the most mysterious aspects of the Bible.

We've seen how physics shows that microcosms replicate macrocosms, and vice versa – a subatomic particle conceals within it a black hole; a molecule of interfacial water carries the entire genetic identity of a human being, and so forth. Similarly, a letter of the alphabet can reveal the syntax of the cosmos.

According to the Vedas and the Bible alike, matter originated from the interaction between vocal codes and a primordial aquatic matrix, while the Kabbalist sages claim that God created the world through the interactions and combinations of the 22 letters of the Hebrew alphabet. Creation, in any case, is not a circumscribed past event – all the components of the universe are in a state of continuous renewal and transformation, exchanging messages and information at every level.

Language is the vehicle we use to learn and share information. In the kabbalistic tradition, the letters of the alphabet represent what remains of the infinite light that filled the universe before the divine contraction that made room for Creation. The letters are legible traces of those sparks from which everything was forged. In the Hebrew alphabet, a letter has an intrinsic spiritual and generative force to which it alludes with its sound, its form and its numerical value. The indi-vidual letters that make up a word also express the essence of the thing they name.

The mystical Jewish texts recount how God created the world by combining these letters. Likewise DNA, the genetic code present in various forms in all living creature, basically recombines the four letters A, T, G and C (which designate the nucleobases adenine, thymine, guanine and cytosine) to create amino acids and enormous quantities of protein. The genetic information inherited from the past finds expression in the multiple recombinations of the 'letters' of a code.

Nucleic acids and proteins are codes, while organic molecules are letters. Their combination is a form of language, necessary for the existence of things like stars and planets and living beings in our universe, which would otherwise be just atoms and void. This is more than just an analogy. Scientists who work with the catalytic enzymes in organic metabolic processes refer to them as access codes and compare them to letters and words. And of course there's mathematics, the code that has allowed physicists to penetrate many of the universe's greatest mysteries.

The Kabbalists believe that the Bible contains secret messages, hidden in the blank spaces between the letters written on parchment, like the void between the waters during creation. DNA has a similar void, in that 98 per cent of its information is actually genetic detritus, indecipherable and apparently meaningless. But we have learned not to be fooled by the appearance of emptiness – it is likely that what looks like genetic spamming actually serves a recombinant function for the 2 per cent of DNA that synthesizes proteins, though why there should be so much of remains a mystery to science.

The Secrets of the Hebrew Letter *Mem*

> *He caused the letter Mem to reign in Water,*
> *tied a crown to it,*
> *and combining it with the others*
> *formed the earth in the world,*
> *cold in the year,*
> *and the belly in man, male and female.*

Sepher Yetzirah 2,5

Sepher Ha Bahir, the 'Book of Brightness', is the oldest kabbalistic text that has come down to us. Published in 1176, it is attributed to the tradition of Rabbi Nehuniah Ben Ha-Kana, a Talmudist of the 1st century. A section of the book is dedicated to the birth of the universe. In particular, it explains the meaning of the 13th letter of the Hebrew alphabet, which holds the secret of water. 'What is *mem*?' it asks. 'Do not read *mem*, but *mayim* (water).' (1,85) The letter *mem* takes its name from the word for water, *mayim*, and represents the masculine and feminine waters that were separated at the beginning of Creation.

Graphically, *mem* is written in two ways (figure 17.1). The open form with the split in the lower left corner is the feminine principle, and is written this way when it appears at the beginning or in the middle of a word. The closed form is the male principle, and appears only at the end of a word.

Figure 17.1 The Hebrew letter *mem*

The form of the open *mem* represents the maternal womb, enclosing the empty space in which life is created, but with an opening towards the outside from which it can emerge. Depending on which commentator one reads, the closed *mem* can be interpreted as the protected womb of pregnancy.

The two forms of *mem* also refer to two states of water, with the open *mem* representing the water that springs forth into the external world and flows on the surface, while the closed version corresponds to the lakes and aquifers that lie beneath the ground.

It is also a symbol of the unconscious, the 'womb of the mind'. In its closed form it is the sealed reservoir of unconscious that we can open and make accessible by training our intuitive faculties and interpreting our dreams correctly. The unconscious is a doorway to the infinite that our mind hides and that we must learn to open lest what lies behind it remains forever unknown to us.

The Kabbalist treatises associate *mem* with the uterus, with birth, with change, and with the water of the ritual bath. When *mem* is the first letter of a noun, it becomes a locative prefix (something like 'from'), indicating where the preceding word comes from, signalling the movement that starts from the origin, both spatially and temporally. *Mem* is about origination, about where things come from. It is the mother letter, the mother water.

In Hebrew grammar, *mem* is also the desinence of the present tense – an allusion to the fact that change can only be brought about if we concentrate our energies on the present.

We've seen how water, both despite and because of obstacles such as gravity, tends to form circles and spirals. A drop of rain is a sphere elongated by gravity, and expresses water's tendency to assemble into a unit, a whole. Likewise, the contained, circle-like form of *mem* offers us an image of the enormous forces at play in the boundaries between the physical, biological and spiritual dimensions.

Water in Hebrew Writing

Written phonetically, *mem* is formed by two *mems*: '*mm*' (as vowels are not written in Hebrew). If we place a yod, a floating apostrophe-like letter, between these two mems, one open and one closed, we get the word *mayim*, or 'water' (figure 17.2).

Figure 17.2 The Hebrew word for water (*mayim*)

The word for water is an ideogrammatic synthesis, suggesting with its feminine *mem* an openness to multiplicity, while the *yod* indicates its connection to a single creative principle and the final masculine *mem* signals a sense of containment and unity. The structure of the water molecule – two atoms of hydrogen and one of oxygen – is represented graphically in the same way: the two *mems* being hydrogen, the *yod* oxygen.

The grammar of the word for water is also instructive. *Mayim* is in fact a substantive plural, dual, with no declensions – dual because water is bipolar; plural and undeclinable because no water is the same as another, because it is multiple and indivisible.

The dual form of *mayim* also alludes to the Genesis Creation story, when the two waters – upper and lower, masculine and feminine – were formed. Water expresses the bipolar essence of reality. Everything in nature is generated by pairs of forces or elements; individualism, in the sense of separateness, is not tolerated by the universe.

Everything tends to couple with its complementary opposite in a dynamic process that evolves towards an increasingly complex order. Spiritually speaking, the masculine part of water refers to the capacity for active change (yang) and the feminine part for receptive change (yin). The upper waters, according to the Kabbala, correspond to the higher state of enlightened consciousness; the lower waters to the realm of instinct and unconscious desires. The Kabbalists believe that water that springs from the ground, and as such is simultaneously both subterranean and surface water, prefigures the day when the upper masculine waters and lower feminine waters will reunite, erasing the separation between heaven and earth.

The Hebrew language speaks not of water, but waters, always in the plural. For water is not a neutral, undifferentiated fluid, but contains multiple realities – mineral salts, life forms such as bacteria, soluble metals, vitamins, proteins, etc. Water is – or rather, the waters are – the very essence of diversity.

Like other Oriental traditions, Jewish thought often makes use of analogies to interpret reality. Water holds the secret of multiplicity and diversity, and the Hebrew language reflects this by pluralizing masculine nouns with a suffix formed by the letters *yod* and *mem*, which on their own make *yam*, the word for 'sea'.

The word *mayim* can also be read backwards (*mem yod mem*), which makes an especially poetic analogy with the fact that water, like the reality it represents, tends to be cyclical, symmetrical and repetitive, much in the manner of the fractal sequences produced from chaos. In the Kabbala, water is associated with formation, which is not the same as creation *ex nihilo*, but rather the dynamization and configuration of elements and energies into a living thing.

We've seen how a *yod* preceding a *mem* makes the word *yam*, meaning 'sea'. If instead we replace the *yod* with *aleph*, the first letter of the alphabet (which also corresponds to the number one), we get *em*, or 'mother'. The Hebrew language associates water with maternity and birth, with the origin of life from a single source. It is thus only fitting that a variation on the word for 'sea' should be 'mother'.

In Latin-based languages, the semantic kinship between 'mother' and 'sea' (*madre/mare* in Italian, *madre/mar* in Spanish, *mère/mer* in French) finds correlation in the physiological and environmental affinities they share, both of them saltwater cradles in which new life is incubated and from which it emerges. It is clearly no mere coincidence that the sea is the ideal environment for giving birth, for becoming a mother.

Openness and receptivity are specific properties of water, and of both mothers and newborns as well. Indeed, the receptivity of the human brain is at its maximum when the child leaves the mother's womb.

Water as Womb

The womb safeguards and nurtures the foetus. It is the centre where life is created and received. According to traditional Chinese medicine, it is here that the most precious Qi and Essence reside. Deep inside the abdomen at the height of the uterus is an epicentre of energy accumulation that the Chinese call *Dan Tian*. It is regulated by the Kidney, which we'll recall is the organ associated with the Water Movement. The Kabbalists also locate the corporeal expression of water at this very point.

In the Chinese language, the word *bao* indicates origin, the matrix that shapes and nurtures something very precious. Its ideogram bears an extraordinary resemblance to the letter *mem*, and shares many of its meanings (figure 17.3). *Bao* means 'to surround, to embrace', in the sense of protection and sustenance. By adding the radical for 'flesh' to *bao*, we get the word 'uterus', whereas if we add instead the radical signifying the act of construction, we have the word for 'cooking', 'cook' and 'kitchen'. The womb, like the hearth, is a place where something vital and new is created and transformed.

And it is other things still. In both the Chinese and Jewish traditions, it is the locus of our base animal appetites, foremost among which is the sex drive, the core of our greatest creative and life-giving potential, which we must learn to harness and guide in a positive direction – physically, ethically and spiritually.

Figure 17.3 The Chinese word *bao* (left) and the Hebrew letter *mem* (right)

Mem can also have negative implications, as in its association with the Hebrew word *mum*, which means 'defect', suggesting a state where emotivity and instinct remain trapped within us. Water can be a negative force as well, particularly when it is not allowed to flow, whereupon it stagnates and becomes a vehicle of *mum*, of physical and moral contamination.

The womb (or in the case of males, the lower abdomen), site of our highest physical and spiritual potential, can paradoxically also become the 'lowest' part of us from a moral point of view. The masters of both the Jewish and Chinese traditions teach that it is always necessary to start from the bottom if we wish to be elevated toward to a nobler level. Take rainwater, for example, which falls from above. Though pure, it is insipid, devoid of the numerous therapeutic virtues of waters from underground thermal springs that originate from below. Likewise in the spiritual dimension, in order to rise from a state of *mum* to that of *mem*, one must pass first through this 'lower' phase: to grow spiritually and live life fully we must face the worst parts of our character, our most base desires, and try to redirect them toward higher, more positive ends.

The Hebrew word *emet*, which means 'truth', is composed of the first letter of the alphabet, *aleph*, followed by *mem* and *tav*, the last letter. Again, we see how the very structure of Hebrew words embodies their meaning, for what is truth if not the inclusion of all aspects of reality, from A to Z, first to last? *Emet* can be broken down into *em* ('mother') and *met* ('death'), another beginning and end, because truth is measured by the life that begins in the maternal womb and ends in the mortal tomb. *Mem* is present in both components of *emet* and, most significantly, is situated in the middle of *aleph* and *tav*, which represent the two spatiotemporal limits of birth and death, between which *mem*, like the needle of a scale, balances the truth. The Hebrew *mem* and the Chinese *bao* symbolize the threshold that connects life and death, which everyone must cross. It is up to each of us to decide how.

Silence, Sound, Mantra

The 'water letter' guards the mystery of all mysteries: the origin of life. The open *mem* refers to that which is revealed by the universe; the closed form represents all that is hidden.

The sound 'mm' is often the first vocalization that an infant is able to pronounce distinctly, usually at around seven months of age. In the Sepher Ha Bahir, it is written that *mem* is 'silent'. Indeed, it is a sound and a letter that emerges from silence, from a closed mouth and sealed lips; it is the hidden word, the nascent meaning, the sound of silence that signals the beginning of the discourse of creation.

The sound of *mem* corresponds to a similar primordial sound common to several mystical traditions originating from the Indian Vedas (Hinduism, Buddhism, the Tantric and Kundalini schools of yoga): *om*, surely the best-known of all mantras.

A mantra is a sacred word that is repeated during meditation. Vedic mantras are the primordial vocal impulses that organize the forms of creation, constituent parts of the cosmic order – just as Hebrew letters are considered the vocal code that the Creator uttered during the act of Creation. In both the Vedic and Hebrew traditions, the Creator effectuated his Creation through speech – by pronouncing their names, forms emerged from chaos. Also, for today's science, the universe started with an originary sound – the 'Big Bang' that is still detectable as a background noise.

The power of the acoustic vibrations of a mantra comes from the fact that they reproduce the primordial sounds uttered by the Creator to form the cosmos. The vibration *om* is omnipresent throughout the universe. When it is pronounced, the forces of creation, conservation and destruction are activated.

The Vedic *om* is composed of three parts: 'ah', the initial sound from the throat as the mouth prepares to form 'oo', which then closes on 'mm'. The Hebrew counterpart is the mute sound of the letter *aleph* (number one), followed by *vav* (number six), pronounced together as 'oh-oo', completed by the 'mm' sound of *mem*. This sequence of three letters makes up one of the secret names of God.

This is the origin of the word *'amen'*, which is spoken in response to Jewish and Christian prayers. *Amen* is composed of *aleph-mem* (which means 'mother') and the letter *nun* (pronounced 'nn'), which literally means 'fish', the exemplification of life emerging from water. *Nun* corresponds to the number 50, whose significance comes from the Fifty Gates of Understanding described by the Talmud (Rosh Hashanà 21b) and the Kabbala (Zohar 2,115; 3,216), or the 50 ways for escaping the boundaries of our narrow mental habits. The root verb of the three consonants *aleph-mem-nun* means 'to believe, to have faith'.

In the Indian tradition, Veda is the universal awareness that precedes existence, the knowledge that was ensconced in the shell (*shanka*) of Vishnu. In that same shell was hidden the sound *om*, the 'aquatic' essence from whence came the Veda. The shell has a spiral structure, in keeping with the form of the human ear, which is able to receive sound precisely because of its form.

Mem and *om* resonate with the centre located in the core of the womb, which harbours the foetus in the same way that an oyster does a pearl. According to mystical tradition, contemplation of the sounds *om* and *mem* revitalizes the energy centre that the Chinese call *Dan Tian*, which corresponds to the sixth chakra of Vedic spirituality. Stimulation of the acupuncture points situated around this centre restores the deep energy of the entire body, particularly the ovaries (or in men, the testes), thus strengthening both the psychophysical barycentre of the person as a whole as well as his/her reproductive health.

The form of the letter *mem* resembles the profile of a mouth, wrapping itself around an empty space in a gesture of pronunciation, as if to express the content of consciousness. In many of the world's languages, the 'mm' sound is the basic component of an infant's name for its mother, and as such is the sound of almost every human being's first attempt to articulate a word. It is the origin of language, the first vocal intonation that arises from the aqueous reservoir of the body, the first act by which we demonstrate our capacity to express our own will and mind.

Mem is the first sound produced by the universe, just as hydrogen is the first element produced by the Big Bang. The closed mouth, preparing to pronounce 'mm', symbolizes the silence that preceded the birth of the cosmos. *Mem is the silence of water*, the humility with which it creates everything without drawing attention to itself.

Leaving spiritual metaphor aside for a moment, scientists have discovered that water actually does make a sound, and that it permeates the entire planet. Junkee Rhie and Barbara Romanowicz of UC Berkeley have shown that the attrition of water masses with the atmosphere and the ocean depths produces an imperceptible murmur whose wavelength ranges from 2 to 7 milliHertz; it is most intense in the North Pacific during winter and in the South Atlantic in summer, and tends to be accompanied by strong atmospheric disturbances.[63]

The silence of water runs as deep as the nucleus of the living cell and the empty spaces of the DNA molecules that occupy it, soundlessly producing thousands of life-sustaining proteins every second. The closed form of *mem*, the letter of silence, is the graphic representation of that cell, as well as of the 'box' that protects our watery brain in a cushion of yet more water, from whence comes the linguistic impulse that is then emitted by the vocal cords, in turn enclosed in the *mem*-like box of the larynx.

The word is mediated by the movements of the heart, enclosed by the thoracic cage. The Kabbala associates the upper torso with the first letter of the alphabet, *aleph*, whose numeric counterpart is 1, symbol of unity and wholeness. The thorax is where the emotions of the abdomen and the rationality of the brain come together. It is the space where the heart and spirit reside, where the breath of life powers the enunciation of the word.

The Number 40

Like the wake of a ship just gone,
thus do we see the hidden face of God.

GERALD L SCHROEDER, physicist

Every Hebrew letter has a corresponding number. The number 40 is the numerical value of the letter *mem*. In the Bible, 40 is associated with dynamic systems related to water, appearing in the rhythms of the forms that evolve towards complexity and spiritual perfection.

Let's look at just a few of the many possible examples: the Great Flood, essentially a ritual cleansing by water to purify humanity of its immoral conduct, lasted 40 days; Moses spent 40 days on Mount Sinai before receiving the revelation; the journey of the explorers sent by Moses to spy on the land of Canaan lasted 40 days; the negative report they brought back is what caused the Jewish people to wander the desert for 40 years; and it was 40 days that Jesus battled the temptations of the devil. Moreover, the minimum size required for a *mikveh* (ritual bath) is 40 seah (unit of volume). Forty years of peace distinguished the reign of Solomon, author of three of the most spiritually elevated books of the Bible: the Song of Songs, Ecclesiastes and Proverbs. According to the Talmud (Niddah 30a–5b), it is after 40 days from the date of conception that the embryo begins to leave behind its liquid state and assume human form.

In nature, 40 is the number of weeks of human gestation; once having given birth, the mother goes through a critical period known in earlier times as 'quarantine', literally '40 days', during which she must be carefully monitored for potentially dangerous physical and psychological alterations (this is the origin of the modern sense of quarantine, which has come to mean the isolation of an infected host).

In the Talmud it is written that 'forty is the age of understanding' (Avot 5,21): Abraham became fully aware of God when he was 40 years old. Elsewhere it states that we are not capable of comprehending the intentions of our masters and the wisdom of their teachings before 40 years of age (Avodah Zarah 5b). The Talmud also considers 40 a crucial number for consolidating memory: 'If one reviews a subject 40 times, it becomes securely embedded in the memory, as if it were transformed into a tool,' (Pesachim 72a).

This number captured the attention of English physicist Paul Dirac (1902–84), winner of the 1933 Nobel Prize for his work on the ratios of subatomic and cosmic quantities. As an exponent of 10, the inconceivably high resulting number – 10 followed by 40 zeros – recurs significantly in the universe. It is approximately the age of the universe expressed in nuclear units, and also the number of charged particles contained therein. Moreover, the ratio of the electromagnetic and gravitational forces between a proton and an electron has a constant value of 10^{-40}.[64] The total mass of the universe doubles the exponential factor to 10^{80}, a number also encountered in expressing baryonic mass.

When Dirac realized the amazing recurrence of 10^{40}, he said, 'such a coincidence, we may presume, is due to some deep connection in Nature between cosmology and atomic theory.' Dirac and Sir Arthur Eddington (1882–1944) attempted to formulate a theory that would explain these suggestive coincidences between quantum and cosmic realities, but were unable to arrive at anything concrete.

Antennae and Dewdrops

One of the esoteric methods for interpreting the Bible is *gematria*, which consists in the analysis of Hebrew words by calculating the sum of the numerical counterparts of each letter. Words or sentences with the same numerical value share a close spiritual connection. The gematric value of the word for water, *mayim* (*mem* + *yod* + *mem* = 40 + 10 + 40) is 90, which corresponds to the value of *zade* (figure 17.4), the 18th letter of the Hebrew alphabet, pronounced like the 'ts' in 'itself'.

Figure 17.4 The Hebrew letter *zade*

Zade has a dipole structure that reproduces that of the water molecule and echoes an antenna and the forked dowsing rod used by rhabdomancers. The antenna-like projections of the number 90 and its corresponding letter *zade* represent the reawakening of consciousness, of the capacity to attune oneself with the aquatic reality that permeates and surrounds us. In the Talmud, Rabbi Yehuda states that it isn't until the age of 90 that one can achieve the ideal concentration for prayer and meditation (Avot 5,20).

Ninety is also the numerical value of the familiar word *manna*. The Bible recounts that manna – a sort of crystallized transparent dew with nutritional value – fell from the sky for 40 years to sustain the Jews as they wandered the desert.

Dew is condensed atmospheric water. During the night, plants emit heat. As their surfaces cool, the water vapour in the surrounding air condenses faster than it can evaporate and clings to these surfaces, forming the gem-like droplets we see on certain mornings, adorning everything from grass, foliage and spiderwebs to windscreens and, less felicitously, bicycle seats.

In a very real sense, there is an invisible network of rivers flowing through the sky: the volume of water vapour transported by the winds during the course of a year is something in the vicinity of 20,000 cubic kilometres. When air rises, it cools and expands, eventually reaching a point where water vapour condenses into tiny droplets which assemble into visible form as clouds. The dew that collects on the ground, then, is the sky made visible. Once again, we see how that which is apparently inconsequential, formed down below in the silence of the night, allows us to understand the immensity and grandeur of the higher plane.

In China, farmers used to collect dew by leaving mirrors out in the fields overnight. Thousands of years ago, the Jews would irrigate their crops by placing piles of stones nearby that would cool during the night and collect dew, which would then run into the soil during the day. Still today, in Israel's Negev Desert, trees and plants are irrigated by collecting enormous quantities of dew on long sheets of plastic, which is then directed through perforated tubes to the crops. Because dew is nearly as pure as distilled water, it is ten times more effective than rainwater in rinsing away excess mineral salts that accumulate in the soil.

Dew symbolizes the purity and refinement of the physical and spiritual worlds. For the Chinese, dew (*Lu*) is the symbol of the grace, hope and generosity that flows from on high, because the quantity of dew is always greater in precisely the hot, arid areas that need it most.

According to biblical tradition, manna was created from the 'upper waters' at the end of the sixth day in order to feed Adam and Eve, both bodily and spiritually. Manna was to be the heavenly dew that would nourish the righteous in the world to come, where peace, justice and love would reign. According to the Talmud (Shabbat 88a), a similar

Dew of Resuscitation will one day come to raise the dead, an event awaited by Jews and Christians alike.

The *Tao Te Ching* (verse 37) also describes a utopian future where humankind will live harmoniously in a state of *wu wei*, or 'non-action', without intruding upon the laws and rhythms of nature. 'A sweet dew would descend to nourish the earth,' and the people would 'seek the wisdom of the Tao, just as all rivers flow to the great sea.'

CHAPTER 18

WATER AND HOPE:
THE RITUAL BATH

Water purifies the body and renews the spirit. Anyone seeking a place and the means of spiritual growth will come upon water in some form. Religious devotees from all over the world make pilgrimages to sites where sacred waters flow, to pray, to be baptised, to witness miraculous events, to die. The famous waters of Lourdes attract hundreds of thousands of Christian faithful every year, and there are hundreds of other sources of sacred water in Europe alone.

The Christian tradition of baptism derives from the ritual bathing practised by early Christians in keeping with the dictates of Jewish law. The word itself, from the Greek *baptizô*, means 'to be immersed'. Let us now look at some of the meanings of the purification ritual that lie at the origins of baptism.

In discussing the chemical and physical characteristics of water, we discovered that water appears to us in liquid form only when it contains impurities such as dust particles. Water is visible and palpable, then, only when it is 'contaminated' by a foreign substance. Impurities are also what make water an excellent conductor of electricity and vehicle of electromagnetic information.

All solid elements contain impurities. In mineral crystals, for example, impurities alter their electrical equilibrium and create a condition of instability. This 'state of defect' is responsible for the formation of different minerals, and in the case of crystals, the generation of the 'information' that drives the process of evolution: a sort of inorganic memory. The same holds true for our own genetic code: over time it has undergone mutations, 'errors' caused by irregularities in our DNA, which are precisely what allowed us to evolve.

Water plays a similarly critical role in spiritual evolution as a means of eliminating personal impurities. Human beings, made largely of water ourselves, can elevate our moral and spiritual condition only by addressing the evil (i.e. the impurities) within and around us. The evolution of nature and of the spirit follow the same laws.

A fundamental teaching of all the great religions is that every physical act has a spiritual counterpart. By physically immersing oneself in water, one's soul is immersed in an analogous spiritual bath. As such, immersion in the *mikveh*, or ritual bath, is central to the practice of Judaism, just as the baptismal font is to Christianity.

In Judaism, the mikveh is more important than the place of prayer, the synagogue itself. Indeed, a Jewish community can only call itself such if it has its own ritual bath: it is the first structure that a community must build.

At the end of her menstrual period, every woman is obliged to immerse in the mikveh before she can have sexual relations with her husband, also to establish an interior bond with future offspring from the moment of conception.

Observant Jews go to the ritual bath without necessarily having a specific obligation – at Rosh Hashanah (the Jewish New Year), before the fast of Yom Kippur (the Day of Atonement), or on the eve of Shabbat (the Jewish day of rest, observed each Saturday) to attune themselves with the holiness of the seventh day. Some especially devout mystics will bathe in the mikveh on a daily basis, while betrothed couples immerse to prepare themselves for the wedding.

Immersion is not merely a symbolic gesture – one cannot simply dip one's feet or hands, but must submerge the entire unclothed body underwater at least three times. The rite must be conducted with great care and precision, and it must be done only in water that comes from a natural source, be it rain, river, sea or spring. Furthermore, it is forbidden to channel the water using any system involving human intervention. We'll recall that, according to the ancient Chinese theory of the Five Movements, Metal generates living Water when the latter comes from a spring, and that in nature it is the metal-rich rock that mineralizes water, rendering it active and vital. For this same reason, the Jewish ritual bath must contain water of natural origin and be situated at ground level or below.

The Hebrew word *mikveh* means not only 'ritual bath', but 'gathering together', and appears in the Bible on the third day of Creation.

> Let the waters under the Heavens be gathered together unto one place, and let the dry land appear.' And it was so. God called the dry land Earth; and the gathering together of the waters called he Seas.
>
> Genesis 1: 9–10

During the creation of dry land, the waters had to be gathered in a ritual bath to allow them to spring forth from the earth. This primordial ritual bath was essentially the womb of all the forms of life on the planet.

The Talmud (Bechorot 55a) states that all the waters of world come from the river that originated in Eden, the spiritual source of all waters. By extension, immersion in any of the rivers and seas of the world have the power to purify, for it brings us back into contact with Eden.

According to biblical prophecy, when the messianic times are upon us, humankind will live on a planet similar to the Garden of Eden, where all 'impurity' shall be banished from the world (Zechariah 13,2). This means that every source comes from a single source and flows back to it. In the Judeo-Christian tradition then, water, paradoxically the quintessence of plurality and multiplicity, also represents the highest affirmation of the Unity and Unicity of God, humankind and all of creation.

He who immerses himself completely in water, without the possibility of breathing, completely divested of any garment or object that might stand between himself and the water, entrusts himself entirely to the Creator. Laying bare all that one is and has, both inside and out, is the necessary condition for achieving a state of purity, ephemeral as it may be.

The Pure and Simple Water of Eden

Ritual purification is by no means the same thing as hygiene, which is an external condition indispensable for physical health. Ritual bathing is instead a means of re-establishing a state of purity similar to that which existed at the beginning of Creation, when the divine spirit hovered over the waters.

According to the biblical account, before Adam and Eve ate of the fruit of the Tree of Knowledge, evil dwelled only in the serpent. After their act of disobedience, good and evil began to interpenetrate and become difficult to distinguish from one another. From that moment, humankind found itself constantly exposed to an evil often hard to detect, and consequently became a vulnerable and mortal creature.

In the Eden before the fall, evil was a force external to man and therefore easy to avoid. Once original sin exposed man to evil, everything in the world became in a sense mortal, destined to erode and decay, thus putting the divine plan at risk. Death distances us from the hope of eternal life, and as such generates impurity.

According to the Bible, everything that is susceptible to death or comes into contact with death is potentially impure. Cadavers, animal carcasses, even living human beings in degraded condition transmit their impurity to everything they touch. When a man ejaculates or a woman menstruates, they become susceptible to impurity, for ejaculation and menstruation constitute a loss of organic material that is no longer vital: sperm, blood cells, the uterine decidua, the unfertilized ovum.

Human beings are easy prey to impurity, for in our 7/10 of water there lurks an unhealthy resistance to change, a destructive instinct, an impulse toward death, an urge to transform everything into material objects without life or purpose. We have a tendency to give importance only to that which can be consumed, beyond which lies death and the meaningless void.

Humans are a combination of 'dust and water', of permanence and change. When we ignore our own fluid dimension, the part of us subject to change, our gaze is limited to look upon death, and there is only permanence: 'for dust thou art, and unto dust shalt thou return,' (Genesis 3:19). This state can be remedied only through water, the source of all that is vital and creative, both phylogenetically (the world was created from water) and ontogenetically (living cells, including the human embryo, are born and grow in a liquid environment). Immersion is therefore a way to be delivered from our contact with death, to be pure and creative like God.

Everything that lives and grows is intrinsically pure. Everything that causes impurity is related to death, and therefore to the imperfection of man. Water and everything that arises from it, including human beings, can be vehicles of purity or impurity. The closer one approaches death, the greater the likelihood of being contaminated by the idea of death, of becoming impure, of losing sight of one's inner strength.

Impurity is the spiritual exile from the experience of the divine. In order to find the way out one must follow a very precise path that leads to an unsettling truth: to reach the good and separate it from evil, we must necessarily come into contact with the latter.

Through the ritual bath, sexuality, birth and death find a common ground and meaning. The act of purification through immersion is a concrete annulment of identity, a temporary death which paradoxically becomes a means of denying death. The ritual bath is a rite of passage that requires us to nearly die, holding our breath underwater in a sort of dress rehearsal for the real thing, for the transition from the material world into a dimension that is no longer physical.

Rebirth and transformation are the results of this 'death' by immersion. Ritual bathing means returning to the uterus and then re-emerging at the boundary between water and air, what we've called water's 'creative zone'; it means leaving behind pain, hostility, sin, obsessions and accumulated errors in order to create oneself anew.

Water is the surface that reflects our own image, which must be erased until we re-emerge from it with another image. Immersion is part of the process of rebirth, which can only take place with the cancellation of an existing identity: life is thus born from death, this is how nature improves itself. We find this same principle of renewal and liberation in many of the world's spiritual traditions, both Eastern and Western, from Christianity to Islamic Sufism, to Hinduism; it is the dissolution of the self in the Tao, or being 'beyond that which is within'; it is the *Tat Tuom Asi* ('you are that') of the Upanishads and the Vedantas.

An analogous concept has inspired a number of currents in the field of psychology: transpersonal psychology, Fritz Perls' Gestalt therapy, Arthur Janov's primal therapy and the psychosynthesis of Roberto Assaggioli. The aim of psychotherapy is to create a support structure within which the ego, or rather, that which we believe ourselves to be, can be transcended. The death of the ego and the consequent experiences of union thus become a new source of strength for our personal identity.

The isolation tanks we talked about in Chapter 14 can also be used for a similar preparation for death. When we immerse ourselves in such a tank, completely separated from normal sensory reality, we have a rare chance to 'die' before actually doing so, floating in a zone suspended between external reality and a new interior reality. In this way, immersion can be a way to exorcize not just the fear of death, but fear in general.

When we realize we've committed serious mistakes, Rabbi Shlomo Carlebach (1926–95) used to say, it's as if we are half-dead, condemned by the past, by regret and a sense of guilt that paralyses us. The water of the ritual bath serves to revive us, to help us accept the idea that our mistakes can be overcome and that we can re-emerge as a new person. Carlebach believed that a kiss is a precious and vital gift, like a little ritual bath – by giving someone even that tiny trace of liquid, it is as if we are giving them life.

We experience a similar 'miracle' when we manipulate medicinal substances. Properly diluted in water, a substance can acquire new therapeutic properties, as is the case with herbal infusions, whereby the toxic substances contained in the plants are eliminated, or with homeopathy, where poisons are diluted in water and transformed into remedies. In the same way, immersion allows us to 'correct' a state of spiritual imperfection and, returning across the border between water and air, gives us a new chance to express all of our positive potential.

In addition to mortality, there is another consequence of man's fallen state after being expelled from Eden: the fact that we must sweat for our food. This, in essence, is the eternal conflict between the individual and the world that surrounds him – a conflict that often generates suffering and explodes into acts of violence.

Metal can be transformed into a tool, an instrument for working and earning one's daily bread. But it is also from metal that arms are made. Metal is a sign of civilization or barbarianism, depending on the use to which it is put, and as such perfectly represents the coexistence of good and evil in the world.

In the Jewish tradition, just as religious conversion is effected through the ritual bath, so does water spiritually convert metal. This is why all pots, dishes and utensils used for cooking and eating must be immersed in the ritual bath before using them (Numbers 31: 23). The Bible requires that metal receptacles be purified in the ritual bath in order to correct metal's ambiguous nature as vehicle of nourishment and instrument of war. By immersing metal utensils in water, one makes a commitment to use them for constructive and life-sustaining purposes. As if intuiting the scientific discoveries of millennia hence, the ancient

Jews chose water, the universal solvent which from a molecular viewpoint dissolves all metals into active ions.

The Bible recounts the story of how the Universal Flood swept across the entire world, causing the annihilation of all the animal species except for those protected by Noah on his ark and, of course, all the aquatic species. Water protected the creatures living within it, for they were not corrupted.

The word *mikveh* has yet another meaning in addition to 'ritual bath' and 'gathering together', and that is 'hope'. This meaning derives from the fact that it offers something that seems an impossible dream: rebirth. Hope resides in the paradox of being able to be reborn after having already been born, in the miracle of a man knowing he has done wrong and having the chance to change. Repentance is equated with immersion in the open sea, whose waters rise to the heavens as vapour, and all the world's great religions agree that an act of genuine repentance is always accepted from on high.

The amniotic fluid is the 'ritual bath' of the human foetus, the creative vessel in which an eventually autonomous living being is formed. The womb is also the most responsive and receptive part of a woman, the place where she makes room for someone not herself. Pregnancy is indeed the contraction of one's own territory to make space for another, much like God, who according to Kabbalists had to contract himself to make space for the cosmos.

Creation means renouncing the focus of attention on oneself, forgetting oneself, imploding and then projecting beyond, towards an identity not one's own. The kabbalistic texts define the Hebrew letter *mem* as 'the letter of simplicity'. The simplicity of water lies in the liberation from the roles and attitudes we construct and the possibility of returning to our true essence.

Immersion in the ritual bath means dissolving oneself spiritually in the realm of change, suspending one's ego, which is an element of permanence. The changes that the body undergoes in the course of a lifetime render us transient, but they also allow us the chance for spiritual renewal – that is, to rectify evil and to transcend our physical death. It is a constant process, supervised by that divine spirit that continues to hover above the surface of our internal waters.

Water and Wisdom

Words are as deep waters, and the wellspring of wisdom a flowing brook.

Proverbs 18:4

The universe is the product of the emission of 'words', of 'mantras'. The primordial aquatic matrix is also a vocal matrix.

Water contains the seeds of wisdom and creativity. Wisdom is the art of being creative in a flexible, differentiated way. Like water, wisdom has no form: the creative act invades interiority and indiscriminately inundates everything, not needing a preconstituted form.

It's interesting to note how close the phonetic-syntactic link between water and enquiry can be in a number of languages. *Mai* in Arabic and *maim* in Hebrew derive from *mah* ('what?'). The Latin *aqua* contains the query *qua*, 'what?' In German, *Wasser* has the same root as *was* ('what?'). Even the English water sounds very much like 'what'. At the graphic level, the addition of a single line to the Chinese ideogram for 'water', *shui*, transforms it into the ideogram *yong*, or 'eternity'. If instead a cross is added, it becomes *qiu*, meaning 'to ask, inquire, supplicate'.

The essence of water is wonder, for we do not really know what it is. Water is an unknown entity, asking to be deciphered, challenging us to interrogate and interpret it.

And we start by wondering how water could be so abundant on the Earth yet so rare in the universe. Water provokes us to look for the meaning of its existence in its very scarcity. Water encloses the question within its structure. It creates a place inside itself, an empty space, a void to be filled with names. And here one finds the silence necessary for listening to the questions and working out the responses.

The question mark, the written symbol that signals the end of a question, describes a sinuous, curvilinear, spiraliform path: the graphic expression of the mystery of the spiral motion we find in water currents. Just a coincidence? No, it is not. The self-reflexive curve of the question mark evokes the figure of a man who, humbly folded in upon himself, seeks the answer to the eternal question, 'Who am I?'

The reply is the silent listening of one who is not satisfied by an answer based on appearances, on one's occupation or role in society. We must transform ourselves, body and soul, into a question mark in order to see things in a different way. When a person is immersed in water, he renounces his ego and asks no longer 'Who am I?' but rather 'What am I?' Surrounded by water there is no breath, just as it was for all of us in the uterus. By immersing ourselves in the undifferentiated 'what?', we enter a realm that bridges the boundaries between life and death, a necessary step for anyone who seeks spiritual and material freedom, for the secret of knowledge lies in the formulating of good questions rather than good answers.

The numeric value of the Hebrew word *mah* ('what?') is 45, the same as the word for 'human being' (*adam*). Like water, the essence of humanity is to ask, which itself means to both doubt and listen. If humankind were to stop asking and wondering, it would stagnate and die. Humankind, to maintain itself as such, must turn itself into a question mark.

Scrambling the Hebrew letters of the word *hochmà* ('wisdom'), it becomes *coahmà,* which means 'the strength of "what?"'. Wisdom is the strength to respond to a question with another question. There is a Hassidic parable that tells of a master who asks a question but receives no answer. A century later, in another place, another master asks another question and receives no response. What he does not know is that by asking his question he was responding to the first.

The strength of 'what?' is the essence of wisdom. The sage is one who asks how to connect one's own questions to others that have been formulated in the past; one who evolves through continuous interrogation of the surrounding world, of the established rules and how they should be interpreted. Water teaches us to accept the doubt we harbour within us, for it is there we find the secret of our evolution into conscious beings.

Wisdom means building an active and meaningful life which, like water, has a direction and an incessant flow. Interrogation is the wisest and most creative force, both in us and in w(h)ater. Wisdom is intuitive acumen rooted in emotional balance, in the abliity to give and to share: a quality known today as emotional intelligence. Wise are those who avoid contaminating their own pure and simple human essence, who do not presume to be something other than their true Self, or something more or better than others.

The evolution of one famous character from Greek mythology takes place in water: Ulysses, who undergoes his crisis of identity among the currents of the sea. The journey by water that he makes from Troy to his native island of Ithaca represents the transformation of a brilliant, yet proud and vain man into a wiser one, his awareness sharpened and his Self purged of pomp. Travel educates: being a nomad helps one grow.

During his journey Ulysses must face the cyclops Polyphemus, son of Poseidon, god of the sea, and in the battle with the monster his name becomes No-Man. Ulysses strips himself of his identity and his name to save himself and be transformed into a new man. At the end of the Odyssey he reaches home, the point of origin of his wanderings, and there he realizes that he is now more present, in himself and in the world, finally free from internal ghosts and false certainties. The long journey through the realm of water has changed him, made him stronger and wiser.

His battle with various forms of water – waves, storms, mirages – brings him within an inch of death. But the greatest danger comes when he meets those perilous creatures from the aqueous depths of the sea, the Sirens, symbolic incarnations of his own deepest and most self-destructive instincts.

But Ulysses confronts them directly. He does not repress their seductive call, the call that provokes dark urges of aggression and masochism, tempting one to believe that all is for nought and that the best thing to do is abandon oneself to the fog. He has himself tied to the mast, but he does not plug his ears. He listens to their call, elaborates it, challenges it and resists it. This is the only means he has of understanding who he is, of taking that next step on his interior journey, a challenge that we all would do well to accept.

Towards Foetalization

Human infants learn to interact with water before they're even born. Aquatic mammals and land mammals with aquatic ancestors have the longest gestation periods of all the creatures on the planet. Dolphins give birth after about 10 months, humans 9, elephants 24, and whales between 11 and 16, depending on the species.

Creatures with prolonged foetal phases are also the most intelligent, and once they're born they continue to evince many physiognomic traits and behaviours typical of a foetus. The features of an adult human resemble those of an ape foetus much more than those of an adult ape, for example. In humans, as in the ape foetus, the weight of the brain with respect to the rest of the body is very high. Moreover, the spinal column forms a 90° angle with the head, and another 90° angle with the urogenital canal. This conformation is what allows humans to perform coitus in the ventral position.

The foetal period and infancy of humans calculated together are longer than those of any other land mammal. In this, humans can be said to tend toward 'foetalization', insofar as we mature very slowly over time, prolonging the phases of growth and of full physical, mental and sexual development. Other characteristics of human foetalization include minimal brow protrusion, scarcity of body hair, pale skin tone among many races and delayed dentition.[65]

Foetalization coincides with an increase in aquatic features and a parallel development of cerebral mass. The brain develops faster in the foetus, perhaps because of the movement of the aqueous fluid in which it lives.

Oddly, the development of the most intelligent organisms requires the presence of unstable equilibria, of imbalanced 'immaturities' which stimulate them to gradually reach a higher order. The evolution of intelligent beings, then, seems to be correlated in some way with a prolonging of the aquatic life inside the uterus and with the persistence of foetal immaturity even after birth.

The Jewish tradition classifies entities that can never be considered impure: living animals, growing plants, objects in the course of construction, and last but not least, water of natural origin. All of these things are connected by the fact that they are growing, evolving, subject to continuous change.

The concepts of growth and incompleteness are associated with spiritual purity. In the biological sphere, we've seen how the extension of the developmental phase of certain species corresponds with the emergence of more complex and intelligent structures, which is to say that the more time we spend immersed in water, the more time and opportunity we have to expand the qualities unique to evolve as intelligent beings. Spending time in water and with it, and accumulating meaningful experiences from it is a way of remaining 'foetal' and evolving to our full potential.

CHAPTER NINETEEN

WATER AND MATTER

All biological structures contain the package of information that constitutes the genetic code. DNA provides the raw materials for the extraction of chemical energy and the production of proteins necessary for the growth, sustenance and replication of cells.

For every living thing, animal and vegetable, DNA produces the same 20 amino acids. Logic dictates that the DNA code should be different for each form of life, yet it's not. This remarkable structural constancy of DNA belies the notion that living systems are the product of a random aggregation of molecules, and reinforces instead the hypothesis of a single source of origin for all known forms of life.

The four nucleotides of DNA are made up of more than 30 atoms. Working in their aqueous medium, these nucleotides have managed to create the units of information we call genes. And they've done so in such an incredibly short period of time as to decimate any statistical probability that the process could be random. In his book *Genetic Takeover and the Mineral Origins of Life*, Graham Cairns-Smith, professor of chemistry at the University of Glasgow, estimated the probability that the construction of DNA could have occurred randomly is equal to that of rolling a single die and getting a six 140 times consecutively. To do so, one would have to roll at least 10^{108} times, which is a far greater number than there are electrons in the entire universe. Or, to get a sense of the immensity of the number, if you had been rolling the die once per second since the Earth was formed 4.5

billion years ago, you'd only have rolled it 1,000,000,000,000,000,000 (10^{15}) times.

In the organic world that has evolved from water, information is also transmitted by chemical substances other than DNA – proteins, antibodies, neurotransmitters and hormones. The chemical message, moreover, is not the only way in which data can be transmitted, nor is the quantity or complexity of information transmitted necessarily determined by 'higher', more sophisticated organic substances. We've seen how inorganic material like crystals can carry information, and then there are of course man-made vehicles like books, magnetic tape, microchips and so on.

It is by now universally accepted that the mind can act upon the body, causing it to be ill or healing it. Which is to say that the mind has the power to act upon matter, something we would do well to keep 'in mind', as it were. Gregory Bateson (1904–80) was perhaps the first scientist to hypothesize the existence of mental functions in animals, plants and, to a certain degree, even inorganic matter. *The rudiments of memory are found in crystals*, which are well known as energy transducers. Quartz crystals specifically are more like condensers, in that they able to store energy and discharge it later, very much like a primitive memory apparatus. In fact it was with crystals of silicon that humans created transistors, semiconductors, electronic memory and artificial intelligence programs. Silicon crystals change their structure every time current is passed through them, becoming increasingly more responsive to changes in the environment. Similarly, the spiraliform proteins in our cells can be said to behave like semiconductors, acting as a support for cellular memory.

Every crystal and every rock has its own repeating reticular structure, a specific way of organizing and evolving. Water is a crystal in liquid form, and its molecules are organized in tetrahedric pyramids with triangular bases.

Everyone is willing to acknowledge that rock can exercise a certain influence on our bodies. Some have an elevated capacity to store and emit energy in the form of radioactivity, prolonged exposure to which, depending on the intensity, can produce genetic mutations and/or promote cancerous cell growth.

Minerals, which of course form the Earth's innumerable types of rock, condition the health of our cells. Certain mineral ions govern the intense exchange of information between the intra- and extracellular environments. Trace elements are essential catalysts for enzymatic processes. Mineral salt crystals have a variety of specific therapeutic effects, as demonstrated through thermal cures and the incorporation of mineral integrators into the diet; both recognized and scientifically valid therapies. Other more elusive electromagnetic phenomena can be detected only under particular conditions due to the limitations of current scientific instrumentation.

Just as we can be influenced by inanimate objects, so can we influence them in subtle ways. Crystals create and replicate themselves spontaneously, swallowing up other molecules as they do so. These same processes occur in the cells of our body, and are the molecular fluctuations that are responsible for our sensitivity to the slightest variations in the environment, such as in local electromagnetic fields, for example. It could be these processes that allow us to access extremely low-frequency signals produced by organisms and objects outside the range of our 'cruder' senses.

Rocks often have the capacity to elicit a powerful emotional and psychological response from us, gems being the most obvious example. We experience similar sensations when appreciating the differences between an authentically antique piece of furniture and a perfectly good contemporary reproduction, even if we're not experts. We also might feel vague intimations in certain places which we later discover to have been important in the past, or in the atmosphere of certain houses that seem to communicate something indefinable about their history and inhabitants. In some cases these 'signals' are scientifically detectable. The megalithic site of the Rollright Stones in Oxfordshire has been shown to emit seasonal signals, particularly at dawn, that could be picked up on ultrasound detectors and Geiger counters by scientists, such as Don Robins, who have convincingly excluded the presence of radiation leaks or random background noise.[66]

All of this brings us into the delicate territory of distinguishing between indisputable physical phenomena like radiation and emanations, and physical but not necessarily quantifiable phenomena, which somehow carry *meaning*. The examples cited above show that places 'charged' with a significant past, whether felicitous or sinister, can sometimes influence people who are completely unaware of that past. Objects have the same power, even on people who are not superstitious or have not been conditioned by the suggestive influence of preconception or expectation. In all of the world's civilizations there is the deeply rooted belief, though largely buried by the pragmatism of the modern era, that human beings can tune in to the 'consciousness' of rivers, animals, the wind and mountains. For many religions, especially the so-called 'animist' ones, even rocks and stones have a sort of consciousness.

There have been numerous 'accidents' reported in Australia, the victims of which were killed or injured by the sudden dislodging of rocks or boulders in places considered sacred by the Aborigines, who have a notoriously intimate relationship with their land which has all too often been violated by European colonists. In fact, there have also been many reports of buildings, bridges, roads and ships built in sacred areas which, during the course of their construction, seem to have incurred a rate of deaths and injuries significantly above the norm.

In 1992 the biologist Lyall Watson published a collection of accounts of the influence over time and distance on human affairs of inanimate objects such as rocks, mountains or personal possessions that seemed 'impregnated' with a sort of memory, or consciousness: a lost object, such as a ring that fortuitously reappears years later in the belly of a fish ordered at a restaurant nowhere near the place it was lost; religious statues that secrete tears or blood; medicinal stones or good luck charms whose history (e.g. the fact of having passed through the hands of someone in particular) seems to have endowed them with an intrinsic power. In cases like these it is clearly difficult to separate the anecdotal from the verifiable. However, there is some compelling data that induces one to suspect that a kind of extrasensory communication between humans and inert matter might be possible.[67]

Some of these phenomena are connected to the presence of water. Poltergeists, for example, while usually associated with surges in local electromagnetic fields capable of affecting household appliances, or with the displacement of objects as if under their own power, often involve liquids such as water, blood or tears that spontaneously flow, sometimes for days on end, in homes or open spaces or, as mentioned earlier, from statues. When every possibility of chicanery (or of perfectly comprehensible chemical reactions) is excluded, it usually turns out that there is at least one individual close to the phenomenon whose psychic state is sufficiently perturbed to unleash a poltergeist. They are often children or adolescents undergoing intense emotional stress.

Objects themselves do not have magical powers. These events depend on the relationship that is instilled between one or more persons and a given object; it is the emotional tension between the two that animates the inanimate and makes it 'speak'.

Most bookworms know that there is a peculiar communication between people and books. When researching a particular subject, it will often happen that the first volume you see on the shelves of a library or bookshop turns out to be precisely the one you're looking for, which might then even fall open to the exact page that interests you. This is what Arthur Koestler called the 'library angel', and many people have encountered it. Equally inclined to attest to the mental connection between humans and certain objects are the numerous archaeologists and paleontologists who, against all odds and guided only by intuition, have discovered artefacts buried in the most remote and unlikely locations.

It would seem, then, that there exists a sort of 'object memory' that our minds are capable of sensing, and that a process related in some way to the properties of crystals might be involved. In any case, there is a key, a mechanism for entering into contact with inert matter, as demonstrated by the incontestable fact that people are able to recover from grave illnesses without medical intervention, even those diagnosed as 'incurable', through the action of the conscious and/or unconscious mind on organs and tissue.

Something similar occurs in cases of people with the extrasensory ability to make quantitative and qualitative evaluations of objects that are not otherwise perceptible through mental analysis alone. This is known as psychometry, which allows people to identify the contents of a closed container or the presence of materials like metal or water beneath the ground. Psychometry also extends to the ability to perceive the history of an object by simply holding it in one's hand. Psychometric ability is more pronounced in certain individuals, but it is likely that all of us have it to some degree, at least potentially.

Speaking to Stones

Tremble, O earth, at the presence of the Lord,
at the presence of the God of Jacob,
who turns the rock into a pool,
the stone into springs of water.

Psalm 114

The presence of water is often decisive for establishing a connection between the human psyche and inorganic matter. Some biblical passages directly address the role of water in the transmission of information between human beings and inanimate objects.

The most important prophet in the Bible is Moses, whose name means 'he who was drawn from the waters' (Exodus 2: 10). Moses led the Jews out of Egypt to the Land of Israel, and it was he who, according to tradition, transcribed the Pentateuch under divine dictation.

His sister was Miriam, whose name means 'bitter waters', and the commentators teach that it was the presence of Miriam and Moses that ensured the Jews their miraculous supply of water throughout their 40 years in the desert. Moses and Miriam quenched the thirst of an entire population: their individual power was amplified into a collective dimension.

A trope common to many religions is that of 'walking on water', which is a way of describing the transformation from an individual form or condition into something universal and shared. In the Hindu tradition, Nârâyana is one of the names of Vishnu and means 'he who walks on the waters'. The Bible tells of the prophets Elijah and Elisha, shamans with the thaumaturgic ability to walk on water. Then there's the well-known episode in the Gospels where 'in the fourth watch of the night Jesus went unto them, walking on the sea'. Jesus' mother, it is interesting to note, is called Maria, the Latin translation of the name Miriam.

Water is at the centre of another famous biblical account, the story of Miriam's well, that takes place toward the end of the Israelites' 40 years in the desert. Miriam's well is not merely a source of drinking water, but the source of the prophetic teachings, the origin of creative thought. Whoever drinks the water drawn from this well becomes wise. When Miriam dies, survival becomes an issue, for there is no more water, no access to the information of life, intelligence and wisdom. The population is thirsty, so God instructs Moses how to draw water from a rock:

> Take the staff, and you and your brother Aaron gather the assembly together. Speak to that rock before their eyes and it will pour out its water.
>
> Numbers 20: 8

Moses did not follow the instructions to the letter. Instead of speaking to the rock, he struck it with his staff, and only a few drops came out. Striking it again, the water came forth copiously. Despite the fact that he had circumvented orders, the water flowed after his second attempt because, according to a commentary on the Midrash, God decided to intervene so as to spare Moses embarrassment before his people. As a consequence, however, he lost his right to enter the Promised Land.

Why did Moses choose to disobey direct instructions from God, having been told to speak to the rock, not to strike it? The fact is that a similar episode had occurred 40 years prior, at the beginning of the journey, when Moses had been ordered to strike a rock with his staff (Exodus 17: 5). This time, however, the spiritual message was more demanding: the Israelites were no longer to rely on the kinds of miracles granted them at the beginning of the journey, such as the parting of the Red Sea. The time had come when everyone had to take responsibility for their own destiny, 'activating' the waters by themselves.

The Bible wants us to understand that a man of Moses' spiritual stature was capable of speaking to a rock and that the children of Israel could learn to do the same, and it is for this reason that his equivocal response was such a grave transgression. For here the Bible shows us the ideal way to 'get water from a stone', metaphorically speaking – that is, how to extract information and wisdom from inert matter.

The prophet's error can also be interpreted from a 'rhabdomantic' standpoint, in that he failed to use the staff correctly. Perhaps to find water Moses should have 'interrogated' the rock rather than strike it, a bit like the rhabdomancer interrogates his surroundings with a dowsing rod or pendulum.

In order to extract information from inert matter we must talk to it, enter into contact, create a syntony with it. How? First off, by considering it not just a dumb rock but crystallized information. The world appears to be dualistic – yin and yang, water and rock – but there is an underlying unity to everything. *All is information, all is One.*

Even a spiritual titan like Moses had his flaws, just like the rest of us. The Bible shows us that it is error and imperfection that enable its characters to develop their virtues. Moses, we'll recall, had to deal with a stutter, a rather large handicap for a leader whose job was to teach and command an entire populace.

The rock that held the reservoir of information (i.e. water) within it should have been solicited with words – Moses' (and our) weakest faculty. It is the most difficult creative task demanded of human language. In order for the word to stimulate the stone, for dialogue to cushion internal and external conflict and violence, it is necessary to build a collective context wherein everyone does their part. Dialogue and peace become solid and real when both sides commit to relaxing their resistance. Otherwise they remain mere words, arid and empty.

Toward the end of his life, Moses realized that there are different ways to transmit the word and to correct his stutter, to coax water from stone and to give meaning to existence. Empathetic, perhaps even 'telepathic' communication with inert matter becomes possible and necessary for the survival of humankind.

What is the lesson of this story? That miracles can't be forced. Nature is in itself miraculous – we've seen as much in examining the exceptional chemical and physical properties of only one of its myriad substances. We must instead learn to speak to nature, understand it so it might then show us its miracles. Wisdom is knowing which questions to ask and how to ask them. In nature, this corresponds to the emission of water from inert matter. Thanks to the action of the word on hidden water, it becomes possible to transform the inorganic into the organic, to invest everything that exists with life.

The Zohar (4,16) compares words to rock, and water to silence. Water, as we've seen, is the universe's first murmur, the 'mm' that broke the cosmic silence. And silence is the antechamber of the word, the empty space that allows the word to be heard, without interference.

Speaking to stone means addressing oneself to an apparently inert world with a query, and preparing for an unexpected response. It is the difference between the twilight of a civilization that idles in wait for miracles from on high and the dawn of one that is aware of the fact that it lives in a world of probable events governed by an often unpredictable order, a world that can change as a result of the smallest act of will. If we make the effort to communicate with the inorganic realm, making the most of all our faculties, water will provide the information we seek.

In Hebrew, *davar* means both 'word' and 'thing'. Word and thing are two faces of the same reality, for inanimate objects speak – though it is admittedly not easy to decipher their messages. The material world is a code whose elements are things, a code we can access and decipher through the word, informed by the science and creative communication that constitute human knowledge.

Talking to rocks would seem the folly of a madman, a paradoxical enterprise at the very least. The biblical tradition tells us that it is instead the door to wisdom, the passage from the question of life's meaning to its inherently unpredictable response. We've seen how today's physicists describe a universe that is not a set of 'tangible' material structures, but is rather composed of minuscule vibratory entities that resemble strings which augment the complexity of information, and of probable events that mutate and evolve uninterruptedly. And what is the word, if not a vocal vibration, one that shapes the world in accordance with the perceptions and intentions of he who utters it?

Whether we're aware of it or not, human beings play an active role in the construction of the cosmos and the expansion of the consciousness, intelligence and information contained in the universe. We can participate more actively and consciously in this adventure of creation if we learn to communicate at all levels, *'speaking' to the inanimate world around us* and making it speak to us, thereby giving greater meaning to our place in the universe. We can be creative only if we are free to forge our personal destiny, in harmony with our surroundings, both organic and inorganic.

Intelligence needs experience in order to become wisdom. And wisdom needs the word in order to be transmitted. According to the Kabbalists, the word ensures the existence of the world. For the Australian Aborigines, the word, in the form of ancestral songlines, expresses the will to transform matter. In theory, there is nothing in the world that cannot be accessed by the word. It's just a question of practice.

Water and Rock

The Earth stands upon columns supported by water found in the mountains sustained by the air enclosed within the storm that God holds in his arms.

RABBI JOSE BEN HALAFTA (2nd century)

Water flows in and through rock, extracting traces of the material of which it is composed. When these mineral ions come into contact with water, they activate and transmit information, messages if you will, which in turn reorganize the configuration of the water molecules.

When this water is absorbed or ingested by living things, the mineral ions it carries and the information contained therein become fundamental parts of the cells of these organisms.

The interaction between water and rock modifies the chemico-physical characteristics of both. Water is therefore not a passive solution with respect to rock, but an active chemical agent.

The pure H_2O structure does not exist in nature, since water always bonds with other substances, integrating them into the empty spaces of its vibratory 'net'. The mineral salt content of a given water depends on the conditions and length of time it has been in contact with which kinds of rock, and is therefore highly variable. But the differences between waters are not merely a question of chemical composition. The many curative properties of thermal waters, particularly those collected at the source, cannot be explained exclusively by known chemical and physical parameters.

We know that three quarters of the planet's land surface was formed because sedimentary layers of compressed material were massively displaced by water. With time, water transforms everything, destroying the hardest rock, yet also capable of constructing the most unimaginable marvels, of revitalizing that which seems inert.

In the *Tao Te Ching* (Verse 78) Lao Tzu writes:

Nothing in the world is as soft and yielding as water,
Yet in dissolving the hard and inflexible nothing can surpass it,
For they can neither control nor do away with it.

The soft overcomes the hard,
The yielding overcomes the inflexible;
Every person knows this,
Yet no one can practise it.

Lao Tzu teaches us that careful observation of the nature of water is essential for spiritual reawakening. It is a simple prescription for those who feel lost, without any purpose in life, drowned by existential doubt: establish a relationship with water. Explore reality, and through the wisdom of water, learn to recognize its unitary nature, one that includes the organic and the inorganic, the material and the mental. See the interdependency of water and rock; use the word to penetrate the matter of the world, the heart, the mind; embrace the realm of the senses and feel how it connects to the all-pervasive wisdom of the universe.

Even something as apparently lifeless as rock contains the secret of how both the biological and cultural 'codes' of living beings are manifested and passed on. The imprint of the information carried by water continues to exist in an apparently empty space, just as the individual and collective memory that parents pass on to their children lives on even after they have left this world.

In Hebrew, the word for 'benediction' is *brachà*, which derives from *brechà*, meaning 'water pool' or 'conduit of water'. Rabbi Levi Meier teaches that there is a way of being, an ethical code, a 'conduct' that can transform us into 'conduits' of positive energy flow, rendering us *brachà* – a benediction – for the world around us.

The Water in the Well

The origin is the goal.

KARL KRAUS

Many wells, lakes and rivers are destinations of religious pilgrimages. In the past, they were considered the dwelling places of spirits, elves and nymphs. Religious buildings such as cathedrals, churches and temples, rather than being built in new locations, were often built on top of existing ones because of their proximity to surface or subterranean water sources.

The attraction that water exercises on our unconscious is tangible in the innumerable wishing wells and 'lucky fountains' around the world. From the Fountain of Trevi to the reflecting pool at the local shopping mall, people's instinct drives them to offer the water something valuable and personal, be it a coin or a message, in a gesture that creates a bond, a virtual bridge between the water and our hidden desires.

Then there's the irresistible impulse we never outgrow to skip stones across a pond, the pleasure of watching hard, heavy rock contradict our sensory expectations by bouncing over soft, pliant water like a tennis ball over asphalt. Water's myriad and astounding properties trigger in us the unconscious desire to return to the place from whence we emerged, and this is because we are very much an active part of the continuous and ordered aquatic flux of our planet.

Water hygiene was a concern of the Chinese since the dawn of their civilization. At Handan, ancient wells were discovered dating back to the 4th century BC, seven metres deep and two metres wide. The Chinese considered well water to be healthier than water from streams, lakes and ponds. During the Warring States period (475–221 BC), a book on wells known as the *Guanzi* was compiled, illustrating the various sanitary measures and procedures for digging wells and keeping them clean. By the 3rd century AD, the Chinese had established a specific day of the year that was dedicated to the cleaning of wells and replacement of their waters.

The smallest nucleus of a community in ancient China consisted of eight families, which shared a plot of land at the centre of which was a well. This is the origin of the ideogram for 'well', *Jing*: to all appearances a tic-tac-toe grid, but in fact a closed central area surrounded by eight open rectangles (figure 19.1). The image communicates an important concept: the people of the village will leave their open rectangles, either by moving away or dying, but the central, empty space of the well always remains. It is a guarantee of stability and sustenance for all who live around it and all who will eventually replace them. But it is important to note that the quality of the well depends on the moral quality of the group that surrounds it, for the well is, by definition, a collective resource, and the individuals in that collective must therefore know how to respect it and share it, putting personal and contingent interests aside in favour of the common good, which of course then returns full circle to become the good of each individual.

Figure 19.1 The Chinese ideogram for 'well' (left) and the *I Ching* hexagram number 48 (right)

In the *I Ching*, hexagram number 48 is the well. It is formed by the trigram of Water on top and the trigram of either Wind or Wood on the bottom (the reader will recognize here the twin concepts of Wind and Water from feng shui, the ancient Chinese art of revelation and manipulation of ambient energy). The hexagram is a synthetic image of fresh, flowing water, continually renewed, the antithesis of stagnation, powered by the wind and conducted by wood, transformed into a vessel by cupped human hands.

If we interpret the lower trigram as Wood, we have the image of a bucket drawing water from below, a type of water with dynamic potential, one that can become a source from which everyone can draw, thanks to the positive intervention of man. Or it could be a tree that siphons water up from its roots into its trunk and branches, a potent water, rich in minerals from the soil and strong enough to defeat gravity. The *I Ching* teaches that:

> The town may be changed,
> But the well cannot be changed.
> It neither decreases nor increases.
> If one draws the water off,
> the jug must be raised from the bottom.
> If the rope is too short,
> Or the jug breaks against the walls of the well,
> the goal will not be reached.

It is important that the well is used correctly, that it is not abused. When drawing water, one must be sure that the bucket is not overfilled, and that it does not bang against the walls. When manipulating nature, the utmost care must be taken.

Another interpretation of this hexagram equates well water with the mind, both of which risk contamination if not treated properly – the well by mud and impurities, the mind by unresolved conflicts and repressed passions. Freud's symbolic interpretation of dreams sees the well as the site and vehicle of unconscious instincts and desires. There can be a negative side to this image, insofar as the well can represent that which is dark and murky and which must be conducted to the surface.

The digging of a well is also an illuminating metaphor: to reach the water that lies below, one must concentrate, dig hard and deep. One must persist, just as when exploring the depths of the mind – without drawing up too much at once, separating the clear from the murky.

The mind, like water, must be lifted up slowly, handled with calm yet left free to flow and act, maintaining them both, mind and water, useful and clear. The hexagram urges us to exercise prudence, to address problems one at a time, always evaluating the damage we might cause to others. As the Taoist master Hua-Ching Ni comments, 'If one cannot reach the well's depth, perhaps it is one's own shallowness that keeps one from tasting the sweet water.'[68]

The well often appears in the Bible at crucial moments as a powerful catalytic force in human relationships. They are always sites of encounter and conflict, cementing love and friendship or confirming irreconcilable differences. Isaac, Jacob and Moses all met their future wives for the first time, falling in love at first sight, beside a well. The well is the place where the spark between soulmates is struck, uniting them to create new love and new life that will extend into the future. Joseph was dumped into a well by his brothers, which was, not insignificantly, dry. The well is the place where we manipulate water and measure our values, for better or worse, in relation to others.

The Master of the Well

Language creates: by virtue of nomination, as in Adam's naming of all forms and presences; by virtue of adjectival qualification, without which there can be no conceptualization of good or evil ... I believe that this capacity to say and unsay all, to construct and deconstruct ... makes man of man.

GEORGE STEINER, *Real Presences*

Abraham is the patriarch common to all three major monotheistic religions: Judaism, Christianity and Islam. The book of Genesis recounts the story of Hagar, one of Abraham's concubines, who bore him a son called Ishmael, progenitor of the Arab people. Hagar was the daughter of the Pharoah, who had offered her to Abraham when he came down to Egypt.

As Ishmael grew, he and his mother began to develop a reputation for immoral and disrespectful conduct, especially with regard to Abraham's wife, Sarah, and his son Isaac, whom the Pharoah's daughter treated as 'commoners'.

God convinced Abraham to banish Hagar and Ishmael from his house. Halfway through their journey, they found themselves in a brutal desert of rock and sand. Dying of thirst, they came upon a well, which they'd almost passed by, thinking it yet another mirage. An angel sent by God opened Hagar's eyes to the reality of the well.

Abraham had banished Hagar for the disdain she showed towards

Sarah. Princess Hagar was convinced that destiny is fixed and irreversible, that those who are born noble remain noble, and those who are commoners are duty bound to submit. With the typical insolence of the aristocratic mentality, Hagar believed that reality has an immutable structure and that life follows a predetermined destiny from the moment of birth.

Lost in a desert of stones, Hagar was compelled to rethink these assumptions. She realized that reality is mutable, and that one must change with it in order to become an active part of it. The stones of the desert seemed inert and immobile, yet they hid a well, the water that creates life and generates the transformations of the world and everything in it.

In the house of Abraham, the princesses of Egypt were divested of their property and titles, for the heirarchy there was no longer based on bloodlines, but on a new morality, the foundation of which was the need to create a sort of interior desert, an empty space which could then be filled with meaning. It took a life-threatening emergency to awaken in Hagar the awareness of this desert within, the empty space that equalizes everyone, princesses and plebeians alike, and the consequent ability to recognize the meaning – i.e. the well – hidden therein.

Unfortunately, it often happens that the most important lessons are learned through suffering. The only thing we can do is transform it in into an opportunity to better ourselves.

Maintaining and drawing sustenance from the well within us is an art – the art of thinking and acting correctly. Rock and water, of which the well is the synthesis, teach us that reality changes continuously, and requires our contribution to its creative rhythm.

Further on in the Bible, Abraham fell into a dispute with the king of the Philistines, Abimelech, when the king's servants took possession of a well that Abraham's men had just finished digging. According to Rashi, who quotes a 4th-century midrash, when Abraham approached the well with his flock the waters rose, and when the Philistines saw this they recognized that the well belonged to him. Later on, Abraham gave seven of his sheep to the king to demonstrate that the rising of the water did not depend on the animals. Henceforward the site was called Beersheba, 'the well of seven'. 'And Abraham planted a grove in Beersheba, and called there on the name of the Lord, the everlasting God.' (Genesis 21 33)

The well is the site upon which monotheism was first proclaimed, the principle of One God, of a Pure and Eternal Spirit, Creator of all things.

The well is the place that instructs a new way of relating to others and to the waters: namely to whatever inspires wisdom.

The Philistines learned from Abraham that the foreigner and the outsider merit the same respect as one's family or neighbour, for we all come from the same source and, so long as we respect one another, draw from that source to the benefit of all.

Isaac, Abraham's son, also had a special relationship with wells. Indeed, apart from the episodes of his near sacrifice as a boy and the blessing he gave to his son Jacob as an old man, Isaac is cited in the Bible exclusively in connection with wells – the well by which he met his future wife, Rebecca; the wells of Abraham, sabotaged by the Philistines, which Isaac unblocked; and others still that he dug himself later on (Genesis 26: 18).

The wells dug by Isaac were special, different from all the others. The philosopher Philo of Alexandria reminds us that each of the patriarchs travelled a personal path to the knowledge of God: Abraham through love and reflection; Jacob through the study of the Laws. Isaac, son of the former and father of the latter, sought God by observing and meditating on nature, much like a scientist.

In his research, Isaac realized that underground waters possess virtues that rainwater could never have, intuiting then what biochemistry would learn later – subterranean waters that have completed the hydrological cycle are richer in active and beneficial substances. The Bible puts it in spiritual terms: underground waters, like the human soul, work in silence and darkness and are thus enriched.

The secret of water resides in the slow silence with which it transforms all other substances. Similarly, Isaac, the patriarch on whom the Bible lingers least, and who does not seem to have performed many particularly newsworthy feats, is the man who knew how to build the most durable and plentiful wells, who was able to transform himself, the world and others in the process. Isaac correponds to the ideal man of Taoism, who prefers not to show off. Isaac is the paragon of humility, which in the Christian tradition would be akin to figures like Saint Francis of Assisi.

Digging a well means passing from superficial knowledge to a deeper awareness through study and experience. It is the attitude of the mature scientist, who is not perturbed but rather intrigued by the apparent incongruencies of his data, and with an open mind explores that which contradicts his preconceptions and established theories.

But there is even more to water than that, something more profound than an underground spring and more elevated than atmospheric vapour, and that is its connection to the soul. According to the Kabbalists, Isaac's wells were bottomless and could not be obstructed – they penetrated the abyss of the infinite consciousness, the water that the Divine Spirit had conjured up at the dawn of time.

In kabbalistic terms, opening a well allows the lower waters to emerge and the cosmic consciousness of the upper waters to descend and penetrate the universe of our interior. Through the unity of the waters there is formed a unity of the unconcious interior forces and intelligences that permeate the micro- and macroscopic reality of the universe – that which physicist David Bohm would call holomovement, the intrinsic consciousness of matter.

In order for a word to be creative, to be a benediction (from the Latin *bene* 'well' + *dicere* 'to speak'), it must be able to connect particulars, integrate differences and counter idolatry, superstition and tribalism, for every entity has its place in a holistic vision that encompasses all things. The visions of the monotheistic faiths and the quest of physics to construct a 'theory of everything' are expressions of those who consider the universe an integrated whole, which not only encompasses all differences, but exists precisely because of them.

It is remarkable that the Hebrew word for well, *beer*, also means 'to comment, explain'. According to the medieval commentator Rashi, this word also means 'to explain in seventy languages', as many nations as on the Earth. Through the water of the well, the word becomes generative; it creates good things or bad things, transforms reality, unveils the secrets hidden within the text of the Book of the Cosmos, explaining them in a language comprehensible to all human beings.

It is the doorway to understanding the mystery of the immense void that separates the nucleus of an atom from its electrons; to grasping the untold billions of those voids that separate the vibrating molecules of a single drop of water; to fathoming the meanings closed in the silence of the spaces between the letters that compose the Book of the Cosmos.

The word that is nourished by living waters transcends the barriers of language and silence and becomes accessible to all, beyond any differences in culture, race, gender or creed, beyond the life on this tiny planet.

~

CHAPTER 20

ENERGY FROM HEAVY WATER

It is no longer possible to cast the reality of cold fusion lightly aside.

JULIAN SCHWINGER (1918–94), winner of the 1965 Nobel Prize for Physics

Tens of thousands of years ago, human beings learned to manipulate fire in order to produce heat and energy, and while the technology and applications of controlled combustion have expanded enormously from the days of heated cooking stones and flaming arrows, the principle remains the same: our world, like theirs, is largely powered by fire, by the burning of combustible materials.

But not entirely. For our epoch has made significant inroads into the utilization of water as a source of energy. Fully 15 per cent of the electrical energy we use is generated by water, though unfortunately most of that comes from hydroelectric dams which, as we'll recall from earlier on in the book, can create serious environmental problems in themselves.

The energy of water can be exploited in other, cleaner ways, using the massive power of the ocean's tides, waves and currents as well as the energy of its biomass – marine algae produce immense quantities of carbon and methane. Hydrogen fuel-cell technology that uses solar energy to split the water molecule into oxygen and hydrogen to generate electricity is at an advanced stage of development and could one day power our automobiles and homes.

The abundance of hydrogen in water is the key to another energy revolution that could take place in the not-too-distant future, and that is nuclear fusion (not to be confused with fission). When two isotopes of the hydrogen atom, deuterium and tritium, fuse together, they release an enormous amount of energy. And while we've yet to learn how to control that energy in a practicable way, nuclear fusion is our principle hope for a clean supply of perpetually renewable energy for the future, and numerous physicists around the world are working toward making this dream into reality.

Hot nuclear fusion occurs naturally in the Sun at a temperature of about 100 million degrees C, which is how it produces light and heat. The nuclei of the Sun's hydrogen atoms fuse to form helium, releasing huge amounts of energy. For decades, physicists have been trying to reproduce this process on Earth, the main obstacles being the difficulty in achieving such temperatures and in controlling nuclear reactions. Recently, scientists have demonstrated that hot fusion can be contained by an electromagnetic field, so there is hope that within a few years it will be possible to sustain it in a reactor for more than a couple of seconds. At the moment, fusion can only be achieved in the uncontrolled and devastating form known as the hydrogen bomb.

Another possibility emerged in the late 1980s when scientists began working with the idea that water could supply unlimited energy at normal temperatures through the process of cold fusion. Like Schauberger and Benveniste, the first proponents of cold fusion were quickly dismissed, but small teams of researchers around the world have continued to pursue it, achieving results that are above reproach.

The central component for this process is known as 'heavy water' (D_2O), chemically identical to normal H_2O but whose hydrogen molecules are the isotopes deuterium and tritium, which have 'heavier' nuclei. Cold fusion offers the possibility of continuing research on fusion at manageable temperatures and with relatively simple equipment. To give an idea of why it might be worth doing so, the heavy water present in one cubic kilometre of seawater has more potential energy than all the world's known petroleum reserves.

In March 1989, Stanley Pons and Martin Fleischmann announced their discovery of a procedure for generating energy through cold fusion in a simple apparatus immersed in heavy water (figure 20.1). The news unleashed a long series of confirmations, retractions and condemnations which led in the end to the official censure of the two scientists and the near total marginalization of cold fusion research. Once again, we find water at the centre of a scientific scandal, about which there remains, as usual, more mystery than certainty.

Martin Fleischmann is one of the greatest living experts in electro-chemistry. A professor at Southampton University, he worked for a number of years with Stanley Pons at the University of Utah. Fliesch-mann is not just some run-of-the-mill scientist. It was he who discovered surface-enhanced Raman scattering (SERS), one of the most important nonlinear effects in the field of laser spectroscopy. In 1986 he became a member of the British Royal Society for his work in electrochemistry and thermodynamics, an honour bestowed upon only the most res-pected scientists.

But that all changed when Fleischmann and Pons communicated that they'd succeeded in producing energy through cold fusion in their Salt Lake City laboratory. They had passed electrical current with a low-voltage battery through two electrodes – the negative one made of palladium and the positive one of platinum – contained in a glass ampule immersed in a solution of heavy water and lithium salts.

To all appearances, this is a simple apparatus that would normally generate a certain amount of heat. But what the two scientists found was that it generated far more than expected, to the extent that the

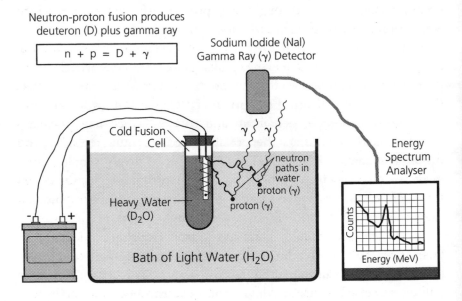

Figure 20.1 Fleischmann and Pons's experiment

metals were affected. They also found nuclear by-products such as helium, a small number of excess neutrons, and in some cases tritium. The conclusion was inescapable: some form of nuclear fusion must have been occurring in that simple cell.

The excess energy produced was measured at 5 MJ (megajoules) per cubic centimetre of palladium, equivalent to 1.4 kWh/cm³, a quantity of energy 100 times higher than what would have been produced by any purely chemical reaction. Indeed, one of the cells continuously produced for more than 100 hours 4.5 W for every watt of incoming current.

The implications are, to put it mildly, mind-boggling. Even at these primitive levels of output, cold fusion applied on a large scale could pro- vide huge quantities of transformable heat energy, without the lethal ionizing radiation of hot fusion. Moreover, no fusion cell built until now has ever shown signs of running out of power, suggesting that more advanced versions could potentially generate energy for years, even decades.

But even if we side with those who consider these results valid, we still need to explain its central mystery: why doesn't cold fusion emit dangerous ionizing radiation like other fusion processes? This has puzzled scientists for years, and has been used as an argument against its validity. For it is precisely because of its harmlessness that cold fusion would be like manna from heaven from an economic standpoint – a clean, inexhaustible, healthy energy source that would require no complex and costly safety measures.

Fleischmann and Pons went into that first press conference a bit pre- cipitously, due to the enormous economic and strategic implications of their discovery. By their own admission, they wanted to announce it as soon as possible for fear of news leaks and patent complications. But let's not forget that this 'haste' was the result of five and a half long years of intensive research, for which each of them paid at least 100,000 dollars out of their own pockets.

Many physicists, accustomed to the basic equation of hot fusion (production of neutrons = successful experiment), based their judgment of cold fusion as being unfounded, solely on the absence of neutrons.

Nevertheless, a frantic race to prove cold fusion was underway. A laboratory at the Massachusetts Institute of Technology tried replicat- ing the experiment just four days after the press conference, though without the exact 'recipe' used by Fleischmann and Pons. In those early weeks, no laboratory was able to produce anything like cold fusion – the

332 | WATER, PURE AND SIMPLE

experiments at Duke, the University of Michigan and the University of North Carolina all failed. Some scientists concluded that this was because Fleischmann and Pons's claims were bogus, others had the impression that they were reluctant to share the details of their procedure, others still attributed it to a problem with the materials being used.

Elsewhere, Uziel Landau of Case Western University, and John Appleby and Kevin Wolf of Texas A&M obtained positive heat readings at more or less the same levels found by Fleischmann and Pons, though only after 60 hours from the onset of the experiment.

Wolf demonstrated unequivocally the presence of neutrons, as did the Oak Ridge National Laboratory in Tennessee, where levels were four times higher than normal background levels. Meanwhile, researchers at Los Alamos supplied the strongest proof yet in support of cold fusion, and Robert Huggins of Stanford University showed that excess heat was produced using heavy water, while normal water remained unaffected.

A Tempest in a Glass of Water

The experiments were difficult to reproduce, they remained inexplicable in the light of existing theories, and above all even the positive results were inconsistent. It seemed as though every experiment gave different results – there were either too many or two few neutrons to justify the excess heat; Caltech's negative results were probably due to a calorimetry problem; the team at the University of Texas, who'd confirmed the original claim after just two weeks, later had to retract their findings when it was discovered their sample was contaminated. It was later determined that there were three principal reasons for these failures and inconsistencies:

- insufficient quantity of deuterium in the palladium lattice;

- insufficient voltage;

- difficulty in eliminating hydrogen from the palladium lattice to allow the deuterium to enter.

Other prestigious universities leapt headlong into cold fusion experiments, without necessarily knowing the details of the materials or methodology. Unfortunately, time was tight: the US Congress would be deliberating in just a few weeks as to how to distribute funding for physics research.

From feverish excitement, the atmosphere degraded into one of impatience. In the meantime, confirmations of the Fleischmann-Pons discovery were coming in from other parts of the world, specifically the University of Nagoya in Japan (November 1989) and India's Atomic Research Centre, headed by P K Iyengar (January 1990).

Another crucial factor for verifying cold fusion was time. The first results worthy of consideration might not appear for weeks after the initiation of the experiment, which posed a problem for the American laboratories, over whose heads hung the Congressional funding deadline.

In April of that first year, Italian physicist Francesco Scaramuzzi and his team at ENEA (National Agency for Alternative Energy) in Frascati announced that they had measured neutron emission from a cold fusion process using a pressurized metal chamber with heavy water and fragments of titanium. Another Italian, Antonio Bertin of Brigham Young University, had also recorded the presence of neutrons in the fusion between titanium electrodes and deuterium.

John Maddox, the director of *Nature* magazine who had fought so hard just a year before to squash Benveniste's 'impossible' discovery, was fiercely opposed to cold fusion from the outset. The attacks from Maddox and the magazine became increasingly vicious, and in the months following the historic discovery, *Nature* saw fit to reject any and every study from other laboratories that confirmed Fleischmann and Pons's findings. During that period, *Nature* received more articles on cold fusion than on any other subject which, by the editorial staff's admission, were divided equally between positive and negative results. *Nature* favoured neither camp, choosing to publish nothing at all.

The other scientific journals took a similar tack. Nobel Prize winner Julian Schwinger and Richard Feynman submitted a proposal for a theoretical study of cold fusion to the American Physical Society's *Physical Review Letters*, which was rejected without explanation. Outraged, Schwinger made a conspicuous show of resigning from the prestigious APS (American Physical Society).

Cold fusion is an inherently 'hot' issue, insofar as proof of its validity would render obsolete much of the world's existing economic infrastructure, so the media latched onto it eagerly. Pons and Fleischmann began taking brutal hits from the majority of both the specialized and the mainstream press, with the result that all that most scientists knew about cold fusion came from newspapers. They formulated their opinions on the basis of the largely negative views of the physicists who were interviewed, without considering that those views may have been conditioned by the concrete threat that fusion research posed to public and private funding for their own projects.

When Eugene F Mallove, then chief scientific editor at MIT Press, discovered that the graphs illustrating the study conducted by MIT had been manipulated in order to debunk cold fusion, he promptly resigned. Mallove then set out to write an extremely detailed chronological and analytical account of the first two years of cold fusion entitled *Fire from Ice*, and until his death in 2004, he published the journal *Cold Fusion*, which continues to exist today in both print and web form, communicating the latest developments in the field of cold fusion research.

The *coup de grâce* for the supporters of cold fusion came in November of 1989, when a jury composed of 23 eminent scientists chosen by the US Department of Energy advised against the use of federal funding for cold fusion research. The jury was headed by John R Huizenga, professor of chemistry and physics at the University of Rochester and outspoken sceptic with regard to cold fusion since day one. The two million dollars that had been initially set aside were promptly withdrawn.

During the deliberations, one of the members of the panel, Norman F Ramsey of Harvard (who had won the Nobel Prize for Physics that year), clashed with Huizenga, objecting to the hostile disposition of the jury. In the end, however, all he was able to do was get them to add a preamble and soften the language of the conclusions. This, alas, did not change the fact that the jury's final verdict was that cold fusion, in the absence of a supporting theory, did not merit any scientific attention.

Physicist Paul Chu, an expert in superconductors from the University of Houston, and Edward Teller, father of the H-bomb, expressed positive views on the potential of cold fusion, but their voices went unheard. In October of 1989, Chu, Teller and 50 other scientists formally proposed that believers and sceptics should work together in the interest of a greater understanding of cold fusion. No one took them up on it.

In Search of a Theory

Those who believed in the feasibility of cold fusion began looking for ways to explain it, while the sceptics sought to find every possible reason why it couldn't be explained. The latter maintained that the process was not credible because existing theories, based on hot fusion, required that there be a final product: helium-4. The former asserted that the mechanism of cold fusion was different from that which occurred in the plasma of hot fusion, and that other by-products were to be expected, as demonstrated by the positive results of the experiments conducted thus far.

Peter L Hagelstein, professor of electrical and computer engineering at MIT, drafted the first theoretical model in 1989, fusing deuterium nuclei with the palladium lattice, forming a helium-4 nucleus, which would determine the transfer of energy liberated by the fusion in the coherent vibrations of the lattice, which in turn would become heat. This model explains, among other things, the absence of harmful gamma rays in cold fusion.

Hagelstein reworked the original theory as he continued with his experiments. Inspired by the coherent flux of lasers, he coined the term 'coherent fusion', by which the theory is now known, recalling the theory of electrodynamic coherence developed by Del Giudice and Preparata which locates water memory in the coherent vibrations of H_2O molecules. It shouldn't be surprising that the two Italian physicists, captivated like so many others by the mysteries of water, have also been working for many years on promising cold fusion research.

Cold fusion in heavy water gave rise to a new field of research that straddles the boundaries between physics and chemistry, insofar as the latter, which traditionally works with the reconfiguration of electrons, stepped into the territory of the former when it became clear that electrochemical processes could also generate reconfigurations of the atomic nucleus, producing either small quantities of neutrons or none at all (aneutronic fusion).

In recent years, increased financial support for cold fusion research has been keeping Japanese universities and industry in the game, while in the US only a handful of wealthy independent scientists continue to pursue it. In Europe, cold fusion is greeted with either attacks or total indifference, with the exception of Francesco Scaramuzzi's team at ENEA's Energy Research Centre.

Today the metals most often used in cold fusion research are palladium, titanium, nickel and certain ceramic superconductors. Some electrochemical systems have managed to produce as many as 400–500 watts for every incoming watt. There now exists a range of methods for cold fusion – immersing nickel and other metals in an atmosphere of deuterium gas; bombarding metals with ultrasound (or instead of metal, ceramic compounds such as strontium-cerium oxide and lanthanum aluminium oxide).

In 2002 an announcement came out of the US Office of Naval Research that looked like it might reverse the unfortunate destiny of cold fusion. After years of research, a team from the ONR published a report confirming that cold fusion is a verifiable nuclear event. The importance of this acknowledgment cannot be underestimated – the ONR, apart from having produced 50 Nobel laureates, has given the world radar, lasers, GPS technology and thousands of other innovations. As with everything, they innovated as well in their approach to cold fusion, passing an electrical current through a solution of palladium dichloride in deuterium-enriched water. After 30 minutes, the temperature of the palladium cathode rose approximately 3 °C with respect to the surrounding liquid, demonstrating a clear energy gain.

One of the reasons that cold fusion is so difficult to reproduce is that the electrolytes and hydrogen and deuterium gases must be free of all impurities. Moreover, in order to maximize the charge of the metal lattices they are subjected to extremely high pressure, which often causes them to fracture, thus compromising the fusion process.

These problems can and should be resolved. But, as we've seen, when the discovery of an anomalous phenomenon – be it dowsing, lasers, water memory or cold fusion – proves to be difficult to reproduce and contrary to expectations, scientists tend to dismiss it out of hand and pursue it no further. The most common reaction is to ignore the new data. If they are obligated to consider it, rather than attempting to understand it, they prefer attacking the colleague who is causing the disturbance. Their strategy usually consists in asserting that the experiment was conducted incorrectly, or descending into accusations of fraud. The resistance of many scientists to reconsider their own theories is understandable, at least so long as there is no conclusive evidence to the contrary. Unfortunately, however, it is all too easy for healthy scepticism to transform into an irrational and prejudicial rejection of the new, the uncertain, the possible.

In 2004 the US Department of Energy began assembling all the studies that demonstrated in some way or other the existence of cold fusion, with the aim of financing new research and reviving the promising results that have been buried for years beneath the weight of ill will and preconception.

Hopefully, this chronicle of the history of cold fusion research has served to reinforce a fact we've already seen proven many times during the course of this book: despite its apparent innocuousness, water has a unique capacity to challenge, even shatter the rigid mental schema that impede us from looking at the world with minds as ductile as the world itself.

APPENDIX

~

WATER AS MEDICINE

Medicine is an art that straddles pure science and accumulated wisdom, with the aim of healing people through the use of both. Knowledge of the role played by water is essential for anyone who wishes to cultivate physical, mental and spiritual health.

In recent years there has been an increased awareness of the issues relative to the water that flows both within us and outside of us. The consumption of mineral water is climbing vertiginously, and the threat of a worldwide shortage of drinkable water has entered the public forum. Words like 'special', 'precious', 'indispensable', even 'amazing' roll off the tongues of anyone who has truly thought about water, be they scientist, mystic, beneficiary of divine intervention, or lay reader of a book like this one.

Well before germs and bacteria were recognized as carriers of disease, all the world's civilizations understood the importance of water for health and hygiene. Indeed, the populations that live at high altitudes – Tibet, Peru, Ecuador, Mongolia, the Caucasus – attribute their extraordinary longevity to the purity of the water they drink.

Archaeological excavations in Pakistan have brought to light the remains of the ancient city of Mohenjo Daro, where in c.5000 BC there existed an enormous public bath of some 350 square metres and where every home had its own well – an indication, if not necessarily of an awareness of hygiene as we know it, then at least of a deep appreciation for water. Ablutions have been central to Indian medicine since its ancient origins, and the Chinese would use waters from certain sources towards therapeutic and preventive ends, many of which were famed for fostering greater longevity.

In the West, the Phoenicians were the first to practise thermal bathing in the Mediterranean basin, leading to the construction of thermal baths in Crete as early as the 14th century BC. The Hittites, Egyptians, Macedonians and Greeks all exploited the curative powers of water and built innumerable bathing facilities around hot springs. Hippocrates himself believed firmly in the benefits of bathing, writing in the 4th century BC that 'The way to health is to have an aromatic bath and scented massage every day'.

The practice of bathing reached its peak in Roman times. Roman baths emerged during the Republican period around the 2nd century BC, and by the Imperial era they had become veritable entertainment complexes, often elaborately decorated, places for people to meet and relax and enjoy their prosperity. Between the fall of the Empire and the Renaissance, this tradition faded from social and hygienic practices in the West, while further east, in the Byzantine world and subsequently the Ottoman empire, bathing caught on and blossomed – it is no accident that the two principle schools of steam bathing are known as 'Turkish' and 'Russian' baths. Similar cleansing rituals had developed contemporaneously in North America and the Far East.

While no longer nearly as widespread in Europe, the ruling classes continued nevertheless to maintain the ancient tradition of 'the water cure', eventually producing the first scientific treatises on thermal waters in the 13th century. In 1571, the Venetian Andrea Bacci published a monumental seven-volume work on curative waters and thermal baths entitled *De thermis lacubus fontibus fluminibus, de balneis totius orbis et de methodo medendi per balneas.* Since that time, water cures both internal and external have become increasingly recognized and appreciated, such that today thermalism is an accredited subject of university study.

Medical hydrology is a scientific specialty that examines and applies the biological action and therapeutic effects of water, particularly naturally occurring thermal mineral waters.

We might do well to review a few terms relative to the salutary uses of water:

- **Hydrotherapy** (from the Greek *ùdor*, 'water') is a general term that refers to the therapeutic use of water of any origin, property or method (ocean, river, lake, spring, aqueduct, hot, cold, etc.) experienced in any way (bath, shower, swimming, drinking, etc.).

- **Crenotherapy** (from the Greek *krène*, 'source') is a method using water and its manifestations (i.e. mud, vapour) from a specific natural source.

- **Thalassotherapy** (from the Greek *thàlassa*, 'sea') refers to cures involving seawater and the marine climate.

All waters, including seawater, can be employed externally and orally with proper medical supervision.

Water is what gives us life, what makes it possible. It goes to follow that our very existence depends on its quality. Unfortunately, 35 per cent of the world's population does not even have ready access to drinkable water, never mind *good* water, while in the so-called developed countries much of the water provided to the population has become a toxic threat to human health, thanks to the myriad pollutants it contains.

The available fresh water on the Earth, above and below its surface, amounts to less than 1 per cent of the total: 99.3 per cent of the planet's water takes the form of oceans, glaciers and ice caps, a further indication of its preciousness. Yet we waste it as if the supply were infinte: in the Western world, the average per capita consumption of fresh water is about 130 litres a day.

Public hygiene is a rather recent phenomenon, historically speaking, and unfortunately still not very widespread. Over the course of their development, the majority of the world's major cities prioritized rail lines and gas lighting over public health; it was only in the 19th century that the construction of sewage systems was initiated, to remove bacteria and other dangerous sources of infection from people's homes. But in doing so, these cities established a precedent that has since transformed our lakes, rivers and oceans into enormous cesspools.

Thanks to technological 'progress', water, quintessential life-giving nutrient, has mutated into its opposite: the world's waters are becoming ever filthier and more poisonous. Industrial civilization has granted us the luxury of running water in our homes, though at the expense of its quality. The water that flows from our taps is by no means secure from contact with toxic compounds such as pesticides, herbicides, nitrates and nitrogenous fertilizers that seep into waterways and the water table from farmland and industrial areas. In the United States, the EPA

(Environmental Protection Agency) officially regulates safety levels for only 60 substances, yet there are many hundreds of known pollutants.

Water is the the chief component in virtually all the chemical reactions that take place in our bodies, and it is therefore essential that we ensure its quality, not just its quantity. It should be, in a word, pure. Accustomed as we are to draw it from our taps without a thought, we're no longer able to understand its real value, nor to distinguish between healthy water and inert, even harmful water. When water is treated, it can perhaps be said to be 'purified', but it is by no means *pure*, for it lacks the substances and ionic balance that give it its life-sustaining and organoleptic properties.

Technology has bequeathed to us aseptic but impoverished water. The drinking water of the developed world may no longer be a vehicle of infection, but it is one of the factors that contributes most to the general weakening of our constitution, making us more vulnerable to chronic, even lethal long-term disease. Aluminium, chlorine and fluoride are often deliberately added to water; copper can be released from the plumbing it travels through; heavy metals like lead, mercury, cadmium and arsenic are often present. Several of these substances are documented as being carcinogenic.

For decades, water was transported to our homes by lead pipes. In 1995, the annual report of the Drinking Water Inspectorate of Great Britain disclosed that the water of one in five homes was over the allowable limit of 10 µg of lead per litre, established in 1992 by the World Health Organization. The report warns that prolonged exposure to lead can cause 'serious neurological damage, particularly in infants, children and pregnant women'. Yet according to the very organization that established these levels, we're supposed to drink two litres of water a day – which in many parts of the world, even England, might paradoxically constitute an invitation to poison ourselves.

Aluminium, still widely used to line water pipes, is also found in the acid rains that feed the water supplies of our cities. The common disinfecting agent chlorine, once ingested, forms a variety of acidic halogen compounds such as trialomethanes that can damage living organisms over time. Yet there are still precious few systematic studies that analyse the full implications and real risk of these substances for our health – though some research points to a correlation with bladder and colon cancer.[69]

The other critical issue regarding the potability of water is that of nitrates, which mainly originate from the chemical fertilizers produced by industry and used indiscriminately in agriculture. Nitrates destroy vitamins A and E in our bodies, transforming them into toxic nitrites. For people whose stomachs secrete lower quantities of hydrochloric acid, these nitrites further decompose into nitrosamines, the carcinogenic properties of which are well known.

The limits established in 1985 by the European Community for nitrate concentrations (50 mg/l) are widely ignored throughout Europe. In the Italian region of Lombardy, for example, to avoid the risk of water supply cuts, the governing bodies have continued to cleverly manipulate (i.e. raise) the threshold of allowable nitrate concentrations in direct violation of EEC directives. The institutions of the EU should actively and aggressively encourage organic farming methods and impede, indeed penalize the use of these substances in both industry and agriculture. Unfortunately, the citizenry remains either indifferent or uninformed with regard to this serious health issue. In an Italian referendum held in the summer of 1991 that challenged the heedless use of pesticides, the necessary quorum was not reached, for voters heeded instead the political establishment's vested exhortations to 'go to the beach' rather than to the ballot box.

A detailed study of the chemical composition of drinking water conducted by Jan de Vries and Kitty Campion revealed that approximately one third of our water supply comes from underground. Given that water can be stored there for more than 20 years before re-entering the hydrological cycle, most of what we're presently consuming could predate the era of intensive farming with nitrate fertilizers. And this means that we can expect even further deterioration of the quality of the water we drink in the future.

In addition to water, two other life-sustaining elements are also at risk: food and air. While public awareness of and social mobilization against carbon emissions and genetically modified, hormonally inflated and nutrient-depleted food are relatively high, the only real measure people take with regard to water is to buy it at the supermarket. Meanwhile, we continue to make our coffee and cook our food with tap water.

The energetic properties of water vary. As we learned in earlier chapters, by absorbing, transporting and emitting energy, water renews and reinforces itself. The way it is stored and transported can therefore subject it to beneficial or harmful influences – indeed, certain mineral waters, if drunk directly from the source, must be ingested gradually, a quarter or half a cup at a time, so as not to provoke adverse reactions that can approach shock. Conversely, after weeks in a bottle these very same waters can be drunk by the litre.

Water and Diet

Our bodies, like the planet we live on, are about 70 per cent water. Our diet should reflect this same percentage. This doesn't mean one must drink massive quantities of mineral water. One and a half or two litres a day will be just right. Main sources should be vegetables and fruit, eating the latter as a meal in itself (particularly in the morning) or between meals. Carbohydrates and meat provide water as well, though in lesser quantities.

Some Important Parameters for Drinking Water

The quality of the water we drink can be evaluated according to three main bioelectronic principles: its 'power of hydrogen' (pH), oxido-reduction value (rH2) and resistivity (represented by the Greek letter ρ, which corresponds to 'r').

- pH is the measure of the concentration of hydrogen ions and the number of protons present in a substance, an expression of its relative acidity or alkalinity. Waters treated with chlorine, which include almost all those transported by aqueduct and/or contaminated by bacteria, are highly alkaline and therefore to be avoided.

- rH2 value reflects the number of electrons present in a liquid. When it loses electrons, oxidation occurs; if instead that number increases, this is called reduction. Waters with higher reduction values are of higher quality.

- Resistivity is an indication of the quantity of electrolytes, or free mineral ions in solution. Ions are atoms which, having either taken on or lost electrons, acquire a positive charge (cations) or negative charge (anions). The more electrolytes present in water, the lower its r-value. When this value is greater than 6,000 ohms, the water is usually of excellent quality.

Research suggests that populations that consume water with low resistivity values suffer a higher incidence of certain illnesses. This is due to the fact that only those mineral salts that refract polarized light through the cell membrane are utilized by our bodies, while all the others remain outside the cells, increasing osmotic pressure and thus depriving them of significant quantities of water. This osmotic process can weaken cells, compromising their proper functioning and thereby causing disease.

Purifying Filters

Water can be filtered and purified in nine different ways, with activated carbon and osmotic filters being the most widely used. Before fitting a filter, one should ascertain the problems specific to the water in question, since water quality and content can vary radically from one town to the next. It is also wise to get detailed information on a given filter's effective purification capacity as well as its composition (it's best to avoid filters that contain silver and iodine, for example), and to figure all these factors into how much one is willing to spend.

- Activated carbon filters remove bacteria, chlorine and heavy metals without removing soluble minerals, thus improving the water's taste, colour and odour. Depending on consumption levels, they should be changed every one or two years to avoid the accumulated residue becoming a source of contamination. Activated carbon filters are more economical than reverse osmotic filters, costing in the neighbourhood of 200 euros. This type of filter requires that the water be allowed to run for a while before being used.

- Reverse osmotic filters, among the best on the market, can cost upwards of several thousand euros. They last about five years and require annual maintenance. Water is directed through a series of special membranes that allow only the water molecules to pass, making them ideal filters for eliminating all solid substances, heavy metals and organic matter.

If the problem is excessive chlorination, activated carbon filters are more than adequate. If instead there is a problem of germs, trace metals, nitrates and other chemical pollutants, one must upgrade at the very least to a multilayered carbon filter.

Purified water is ideal for cooking, and should not be confused with distilled water, which is obtained by boiling water and collecting the condensation. The resulting water is completely devoid of minerals.

Softeners

In areas where the water is especially 'hard' – that is, with a high calcium content – it's a good idea to install a device called a softener. The advantages are many: energy savings through improved functioning of household appliances, greater digestibility, cleaner tableware and bathroom fixtures, less wear and tear on plumbing. Maintenance is limited to periodically reloading with salt.

Hydrotherapy

External applications of water in the form of thermal and hydropinic therapies are quintessentially natural cures whose effectiveness is widely recognized, thanks to thousands of years of experience confirmed by the results of recent scientific research.

To fully appreciate the role of water in all fields of medicine, we must approach it from a holistic standpoint, one that involves the inseparable totality of mind and body. The schools of 'natural' medicine most solidly founded in tradition are effective in part because the forces acting upon the external environment influence our body's vibrational field, a concept that the official scientific community recognizes insofar as it corresponds with the principle of electromagnetic interaction.

Our body is programmed to be healed by water, particularly the water it contains. The mobile parts of our internal ocean are composed of blood and other organic liquids. These serve to eliminate all the toxins that enter the body in the form of bacteria, viruses and their metabolytes, or as by-products of chemical substances. Coinciding with this system of fluid distribution are, among other things, the acupuncture meridians, which we discussed in Chapter 12.

Im Wasser ist Heil ('Water is health') was the motto of Abbot Kneipp (1821–97), considered the father of modern hydrotherapy. Kneipp was the first to classify the various types of water therapy, both general and local, internal and external. Baths, showers, sponge baths, water massage, compresses and packs with water of different tempeatures, steam therapies, even walking barefoot in the morning dew are still successfully used today as proper medical treatments in many thermal centres, some of which can be easily practised at home – although the effects are most beneficial when administered directly at the source.

Simple immersion in water can have therapeutic benefits. Earlier on we discussed the positive effects of isolation tanks, but we need not be so exotic: just think of the feeling of regeneration, relaxation and renewed vitality that we get from an ordinary shower or bath.

Wellness Through Water at Home

There are countless remedies that exploit the therapeutic properties of water; readers are invited to consult the bibliography, which contains easily accessible books for anyone wishing to try compresses, showers, hot and cold sponge baths or steam treatments at home.

The first and best habit to adopt is drinking pure water first thing in the morning before eating. During sleep, we lose fluid through sweat and the formation of urine. Drinking water first thing in the morning is a genuine therapeutic act, in that it literally wakes up the body, encouraging blood circulation, activating the dormant metabolism and stimulating intestinal activity, which improves the efficacy of waste elimination.

Tap water is obviously not ideal for therapeutic purposes, but if it is all that's available, it's best to let it run a bit before filling one's glass.

Compresses can be made with a moistened cloth, while poultices can be prepared by mixing clay or plant substances with distilled water and then soaking it up with a soft cloth, ideally a flannel. In fact, what might appear to be our grandmother's folksy superstition – applying a cloth dampened with hot water to the chest, replacing it every half-hour to cure bronchial cough, is still as valid as ever.

Moist heat (compresses, sitz baths, soaking hands and feet) is preferable to the dry heat of a heating pad, for example, particulary for those suffering from muscle spasms, cramps or colic, for it relieves pain more effectively, penetrates more deeply and encourages the circulation of blood and other vital fluids. In the event of severe inflammation, heat should only be applied with moderation.

Nasal lavage, useful for afflictions of the nose and paranasal sinuses, should be done with physiological water, which has the same salinity as plasma. In the absence of that, pure water with the addition of a pinch of sea salt, preferably crystal, will serve the same purpose (*see* the section below on 'Water and crystal salt').

It is also best to avoid the use of metal receptacles, especially when preparing herbal teas, since traces of the metal can be released into the water, interfering with the active agents – Pyrex, enamelled or clay vessels are preferable.

Aromatherapy With Water and Steam

Everyone knows that a substance emits odour only if it is humid – the distinctive 'smell' of a summer thunderstorm is due to the scents that are released from plants and trees, and from the ozone produced by lightning. Water facilitates not only acoustic communication, as we've seen, but olfactory communication as well.

Both land and sea animals send sexual messages through pheromones, which are transmitted by water molecules, whether in bodies of salt or fresh water or by air vapour. Pheromones stimulate the cutaneous and mucous membranes of the respiratory and digestive apparatuses of the recipient, as well as the scent receptors in the nostrils, which are directly connected to the olfactory bulb in the limbic region of the brain.

Essential oils are considered the purest and 'finest' part of a plant, their most precious essence, and they are usually extracted through a process of steam distillation. The molecules of these essences are small enough to easily penetrate our water-based bodies. Their scents also have an immediate effect on our psychological and emotive state, instantly inducing sensations from wellbeing to discomfort without our necessarily knowing consciously why, for the olfactory apparatus stimulates the brain even more quickly than our eyesight. This is because the olfactory bulb is situated in direct contact with the brain's entire subcortical network, which is what governs our emotional, neurovegative and hormonal equilibrium. The effectiveness of some essential oils in alleviating certain psychological disorders, including depression, has been demonstrated.

By aromatherapy we mean the therapeutic use of essential oils. The term, however, is rather reductive inasmuch as a number of these essences have powerful curative effects when ingested orally. Just a few drops of these highly concentrated aromatic extracts can have such intense therapeutic effects that it is best if they're used under the supervision of a qualified expert, for excessive dosages can provoke toxic reactions.

Let us now examine a few ways that essential oils can be used in conjunction with water and steam.

- Inhalation is a method of assimilating essential oils or other medicinal substances through water vapour, a process which occurs naturally during a bath when we breathe the vapour released by the water. Another method involves boiling water in a pot, extinguishing the heat source, adding a few drops of essence and then breathing the resulting steam. This is rendered more effective by covering one's head with a towel; to avoid the potential unpleasantness of excessive heat on the face, fashion a simple cardboard cone that directs the steam only to the nose and mouth. If one's condition requires doing this often and in significant quantities, it's a good idea to acquire a spray inhaler. The best one on the market is made by Siegle, named after the German doctor who invented it in the 1860s. It is a simple device that nebulizes still mineral water combined with medicinal substances or essential oils and delivers the vapour comfortably to the nose and mouth. If the medication accumulates in the mouth, it should be spat out rather than swallowed.

- There are numerous essential – oil diffusers available on the market designed to saturate the air and environment with aromatic molecules. They have a less intensive therapeutic action than inhalers, but are nonetheless beneficial.

- Humidifiers are very useful for bringing the right degree of humidity to the dry, polluted and overheated spaces of our homes and workplaces, particularly during the winter. The dry indoor microclimates caused by heating can weaken the respiratory system and provoke colds, bronchitis and asthma. It is therefore advisable during the winter to always run a humidifier in enclosed, artificially heated spaces. The bactericidal and purifying properties of certain essential oils will also help stop the spread of infection from people afflicted with colds or bronchitis. Among the oils most effective in this regard are mugo pine, juniper, eucalyptus, thyme, lavender and mint, some of which have documented antiviral and decongestant properties.

Bathing at Home

One doesn't have to go to a spa to enjoy the benefits of hydrotherapy. Just as that morning glass of pure water is a highly effective form of hydrotherapy, so is a relaxing bath in the comfort of one's own home.

Water is an ideal medium for the transfer of heat and cold, and as such excites the billions of nerve endings in the skin. These cutaneous receptors are also stimulated by the 'massage' generated by the motion of water. Distributing its strength with the knowing sensitivity of an expert physiotherapist, water acts on the the entire surface of the body, pore by pore. Its touch can be delicate, yet it can also be firm, as in the case of widely available products like pulsating showerheads and bath jets.

The surface of water, the part in contact with the air, is effectively its 'skin', and behaves in many ways like a true sense organ. The rapport between our own skin and this most 'creative' aspect of water is highly beneficial for our physical and mental health. A study published in 1999 by the prestigious *New England Journal of Medicine* showed that a 30-minute warm bath taken six times a week can lower glycaemia levels in patients afflicted with adult-onset diabetes,[70] probably owed in part to the increased absorption of sugars induced by vasodilation.

All that's required for a revitalizing bath that tones and purifies the skin is a full tub of water and a few hundred grams of coarse sea salt, or even better, crystal salt. You can also prepare therapeutic baths by adding the active principles of medicinal plants in the form of powders, essential oils, tinctures or an infusion of herbs. To prepare the latter, simply wrap the herbs in gauze and boil them for 20 minutes in 2 to 3 litres of water, then add the resulting infusion to the tub along with a spoonful of bicarbonate of soda which softens the water. Once in the bath, use the gauze pack full of herbs to massage your entire body.

Water and Crystal Salt

The water in our body, like that of the ocean, is a hydrosaline solution. Salt water can help maintain health and even cure a number of illnesses. We're not talking here about the processed and bleached sodium chloride we know as table salt, which is also an aggressive food preservative, the abusive consumption of which is a contributing cause of oedema and other pathologies such as gout, arthrosis, arthritis and kidney and bile duct stones.

Many people are not aware that refined table salt can contain preservatives and other additives for improving sprinkleability that current laws do not require be declared: carbonates of calcium and magnesium, E535, E536, E540, E550, E551, E552, E553b, E570, E572 and aluminium hydroxide. Conversely, unadulterated whole salt, which contains traces of all the minerals and oligoelements found in the human body, is easily transformed and does not need to be metabolized in order to be assimilated by the body's cells.

The different concentrations of salt in our body make cellular osmosis possible – that is, the passage of liquids from cells with lower saline concentrations to those with higher ones, thereby achieving an optimal functional balance. Crystal salt has a regular and ordered geometric structure that makes the molecules it contains available for use by the body. Because of salt's high electrical conductivity, it is essential for providing the body with the proper supply of energy and to ensure that the body's water has the right frequency spectrum to perform its vital activities.

The best source of crystal salt is not the sea, nowadays at constant risk of yet further pollution, but the mountains that emerged millions of years ago with the drying up of the oceans. A crystal salt of particularly high quality is mined in the Himalayas: its mineral content gives it a pink hue, and the extremely high pressure under which it was formed gives its crystals a quite orderly reticulate structure. The first scientific studies on Himalayan salt, which have only recently appeared, confirm its unique biophysical characteristics.

An oral cure using Himalayan salt consists in preparing a heavily saturated hydrosaline solution and adding it to still, oligomineral water. A teaspoon of the resulting solution is then diluted in a glass of water, which one drinks every morning on an empty stomach for at least three months. During this period, common table salt should be substituted with whole sea salt, or even better, milled crystal salt. A preliminary double-blind study conducted by the biophysicist Peter Ferriera in Germany in collaboration with the University of Graz shows an improvement in the general health of subjects undergoing the treatment. The hydrosaline solution appears to have an equilibratory effect, regulating arterial pressure in cases of hyper- and hypotension as well as overall pH levels, and also facilitating detoxification, even from heavy metals.

Himalayan salts also seem to help curb rheumatism, gout, arthritis and the formation of calculi, though it should be said that in some cases, in the early phases of treatment, the dissolution of toxic build-up can actually aggravate undesired symptoms.

They can also be applied in the form of local compresses and baths to treat skin ailments (psoriasis, acne, eczema), allergies, colds and mycosis.

Nasal and ocular lavage and inhalation are useful in relieving inflammations involving the eyes, nose and throat.

Water and Clay

Clay has anti-inflammatory, anti-anaemic, detoxifying and remineralizing properties. Like other kinds of hydrotherapy, mixing clay with water and applying it to the body in the form of poultices and masks (known as fangotherapy) can be done at home. Ventilated green clay especially offers many therapeutic benefits and can also be taken orally for general systemic cleansing as well as internal lavages, rinses and irrigations.

A simple method of such cleansing involves dissolving a teaspoon of green clay in a glass of still mineral water, leaving it overnight, then mixing it and drinking it the following morning on an empty stomach. This should be done for at least three weeks without interruption.

In the event of a strong reaction, skip the mixing step and drink only the water, leaving the clay sediment in the bottom of the glass. In any case, it is best to consult a doctor or qualified expert.

Turkish and Russian Baths

Over the centuries, Arab and Near Eastern populations have developed variations on the ancient Roman bath. The Turkish bath, or *hammam*, involves a steam room and a sweat room heated to temperatures upwards of 50 °C, after which the bather cools down with water and receives a massage. This is followed by washing with soap and warm water, then a final rest period in an unheated room.

The Russian bath most likely originates from the Turkish bath, and with a few modifications can be practised at home, starting with the placement of a wooden grate about 50 cm from the bottom of the bathtub. After heating the room, the tub is filled to just below the wooden grate with extremely hot water and infusions made from herbs or aromatic essences with medicinal properties. After lying for 15 to 20 minutes on the grate, suspended above the hot water, the bather takes a cold shower and then lies down wrapped in a warm, dry towel.

Steam bathing is especially good for those suffering from chronic rheumatism of the joints and muscles, gout, obesity and excess water retention. It can also stop a cold, even flu before it starts, and relieves sharp localized pain such as pinched nerves and backache. Steam bathing is not advisable, on the other hand, for people with kidney disorders or hypertension.

Mineral and Thermal Waters

Thermalism is a branch of medical hydrology concerning waters with proven therapeutic virtues. In Europe, their distribution and consumption are governed by EC-wide regulations.

All mineral waters, in different measures and ways, have therapeutic effects. The kinds and quantities of mineral salts they contain give each source its own specific curative properties, and for this reason they cannot be used indiscriminately for any type of pathology or in any season.

Only waters from very deep underground aquifers can ensure adequate potability and hygiene. Because they flow beneath the ground, they contain significant amounts of electrolytes, which give these waters varying degrees of electrical and sometimes radioactive properties. These, along with the complexities of their chemical composition, often make it difficult to thoroughly assess their relative bioactive efficacy. Nor are these physical characteristics the only factors responsible for a water's therapeutic value – the time that passes between extraction from the source, bottling and consumption can compromise the vitality and curative potential of the water.

Other factors demonstrate how mineral waters tend to elude standard chemical and physical analysis. For example, no one has come up with a satisfactory explanation as to why waters known for their capacity to break down calculi lose that capacity when boiled. We must also take into account that some of the hydrogen atoms in water are slightly radioactive. These atoms, along with other trace elements, play an important role in human health, though we still don't know exactly what it is.

These waters are vehicles of oligoelements, minerals which even at low concentrations are essential to the life of cells and the overall health and biostatic equilibrium of our body, functioning as regulators and as fundamental components of enzymatic processes. Among the most important oligoelements are zinc, iron, fluoride, copper, manganese, selenium, iodine and vanadium.

Mineral waters come from untainted underground springs and take their minerals from the surrounding rock, sands and clays. Waters from the deepest basins have been there for tens of thousands of years, soaking up ions as a result of extremely high temperatures and pressure.

The main constituents of natural spring waters (more than 5 mg/litre) are carbonic acid, bicarbonate, calcium, chorine, magnesium, silicic acid and sulphate ions. Minor constituents (0.01-0.1 mg/L) are boron, carbonate, iron, fluoride ions, nitrate, potassium and strontium. Trace constituents (less than 0.01 mg/L) number more than 50.

A child's body has a greater percentage of water (75 to 80 per cent) than an adult's. The consumption of water of the right quality and in the right quantities is essential to their development, which is why parents would do well to consult a paediatrician for advice in this regard. This is especially important for the preparation of infant formula and after weaning.

To grow up healthy, children need oligominerals like fluoride, iron, iodine, zinc, copper and selenium. Mineral salts, while necessary, should not be consumed in excessive amounts – too much sodium, for example, leads to weight gain and water retention, and an excess of sulphur will cause diarrhoea. Flouride is important for the prevention of tooth decay, but the correct dosages are not far from toxic levels. In countries where public water supplies are artificially flourated, great care must be taken not to exceed 2 mg/L, in which case the very teeth it is intended to protect will develop stains or mottling of the enamel.

Classifying Mineral Waters

The classification of mineral waters is determined by parameters that include source temperature, acidity, chemical composition, molecular concentration and therapeutic properties. Those that come from volcanic zones are generally hot – thus the name thermal waters – while many mineral waters come from cold springs.

The mineral waters one finds on the market are distinguished by degree of mineralization, otherwise known as the fixed residue, the components of which are printed on the label. The fixed residue is the minimum quantity of minerals left by water evaporated at 180 °C and has nothing to do with the limescale residues (calcium and magnesium salts) we find in tap water. Using this criterion, mineral waters are divided into four basic categories: minimally mineralized (fixed residue less than 50 mg/L), oligomineral (50–500 mg/L), mineral (500–1500 mg/L) and hypermineral (500–1500 mg/L).

The majority of mineral waters on the market are oligomineral – that is, relatively low in mineral content. They are not therapeutically intensive, but consumed along with a healthy diet they help detoxify the body, facilitate diuresis and contribute to one's mineral needs. Their diuretic action is due to the fact that they are rapidly absorbed by the body, especially the colon, and are likewise rapidly excreted by the kidneys because of their high ion content. Increased diuresis means elimination of electrolytes, thereby constituting a sort of internal micro-lavage. If the water is radioactive as well, it contributes to a greater number of inter- and intracellular exchanges in the blood and interstitial fluids.

Oligomineral waters help the body eliminate numerous substances such as ossalic and uric acid and sodium chloride, the accumulation of which can cause calculi, inflammation and toxic states. The water eliminated as urine can be upwards of 50 per cent of that consumed, a demonstration of the intense micro-lavage that oligomineral waters can provide, cleansing the urinary apparatus of calculi, sand, germs and bacteria.

While there are no strict limitations on the quantity of oligomineral water one can drink, ideally it should not exceed 250 cc (about a glassful) every half-hour, since greater quantities cannot be absorbed by the intestine and would cause diarrhoea. They are particularly unadvisable for those with intestinal atony, certain malformations, serious kidney disorders and some liver ailments.

People on a low-sodium diet for reasons of hypertension or water retention should only drink oligomineral waters with a sodium content of less than 20 mg per litre.

Waters that are ultra-rich in mineral salts invariably come from thermal springs. These must be consumed with caution and in very small quantities – especially when drunk at the source – for only short periods, usually not more than a couple of weeks and always under medical supervision. Taken in excessive quantities, hypermineral waters can aggravate the very pathologies they're prescribed to remedy. They are organized by their main ingredients: calcic, calcic-sulfurous, sodic-sulfurous, calcic-sulfate-magnesic, cloruro-sodic and sodic-bicarbonate. Those with high calcium content are useful for preventing osteoporosis.

Thermal Therapies

Hydropinic Treatments

Hydropinic treatment is a fancy way of saying drinking mineral water at the source, where its therapeutic effects are greatest (and continuing to drink it at home, if necessary). It is especially beneficial for people undergoing diuretic treatments and for those on low-sodium diets.

'As simple as drinking a glass of water' is a misleading phrase, insofar as one needs to know which water to drink and how and when to drink it in order to maximize benefits and avoid unpleasant side effects. One must be careful, for example, not to ingest air while drinking, which causes swelling and stomach ache. It is important when drinking to always keep the upper lip immersed in the water. Failing to do so, one takes in roughly equal volumes of air and water, such that people who drink three to four litres per day incorrectly, risk severely stretching their stomachs.

Mineral waters should generally be drunk in the morning on an empty stomach, starting with one glass per day. Breakfast should be kept to a minimum – tea, toasted bread and honey or jam. The dosage is then gradually increased, eventually reaching two to three litres a day at a pace of one glass every half hour.

A wide range of common ailments can be alleviated, in some cases eliminated, by drinking the right water with the right mineral balance. Metabolic disorders such as gout, diabetes, obesity and hypercholesterolaemia have been shown to respond positively, along with a proper diet, to certain mineral waters. Disorders of the urinary apparatus, digestive system, liver and blood can also be effectively treated with hydropinic therapy. To choose the right commercial mineral water, it is advisable to consult a physician as to which minerals to favour and which to avoid, then carefully read the information that most countries require by law to be printed on every label.

Balneotherapy

Balneotherapy is a form of hydrotherapy practised in tubs or pools, sometimes equipped with pressure jets. In a pool, the benefits of the water itself are compounded by the opportunity for physical exercise. A mineral water bath can last from 5 to 20 minutes, depending on the properties of the water.

The ideal temperature varies according to the pathology being treated: 37–39 °C for osteoarticular and metabolic ailments; 35–36 °C for vascular disorders (varicose veins, phlebitis, arterial ailments); 32–35 °C for skin disorders. Water is sprayed onto the patient's body, which is partially immersed in a tub, following a daily cycle of anywhere between 10 and 20 sessions.

Mud Therapy

Mud therapy, also known as fangotherapy, consists in the application to the body of clay-based mud that has been 'aged' for at least a year in tubs or natural pools through which thermal waters flow, thereby endowing the mud with specific chemicophysical and curative properties. The maturation of the mud allows complete transmineralization and ensures its therapeutic efficacy.

Muds are classified in three types: radioactive (sedative), salso-sulphuric (stimulant) and salso-bromo-iodic (resolvent). These can be applied in the form of compresses or directly on the skin. The main reason for its effectiveness is that mud packs, once removed, induce a sweating reaction that transports as much as 10 to 15 times the quantity of uric acid from the body as other forms of induced sweating.

Application can be local or total (except the head and chest); in the latter case, the therapy must be done on an empty stomach. A single session lasts between 20 and 30 minutes, with the temperature of the mud at approximately 47 °C. At the end of the session, the patient enters a bath of thermal water just over body temperature (38–39 °C), washes off, then lies down on a warm bed until the purgative sweating reaction has concluded.

A full mud therapy cycle runs from 12 to 20 days, with applications each day and a rest every four days. A temporary increase in congestion and inflammation of the parts of the body being treated is rather common. However, if during the treatment these symptoms persist for several hours (or in rare cases, days, usually with polyarthritic rheumatic ailments), the therapy should be interrupted until the symptoms return to their normally brief duration. The powerful effects of mud therapy, like anything powerful, can be negative as well as positive. It should therefore be undertaken only under strict medical supervision.

Mud therapy is widely used for all the disorders of the locomotory system (arthrosis, arthritis, traumatic injury, arthropathy, rheumatism) and is highly effective in the prevention of rheumatic pathologies – though its value in alleviating an acute existing condition is contested. It is also useful for treating gynaecological inflammations and post-menopausal disorders.

The most renowned mud therapy spas in Europe are Piestany in Slovakia, Dax and Saint-Amand-les-Eaux in France, Bath in England, along with Acqui, Abano, Agnano, Casamicciola, Sciacca, Porto d'Ischia, Sirmione, Salsomaggiore and Montecatini in Italy.

Irrigation

Irrigation, or lavage, refers to the introduction of mineral water into the body's orifices with the exception of the mouth.

- **Vaginal irrigation** is useful for inflammation of the genital apparatus and for post-surgical treatment.

- **Nasal irrigation** is used to treat atrophy of the mucous membrane of the nose and sinuses.

- **Colonic irrigation** is effective against chronic constipation and irritable bowel syndrome. It can be effectuated in several ways: drop by drop (which ensures rapid absorption of the water), enema (200 to 400 cl of water) and high colonics (filling the entire colon and lower intestine with water for a complete lavage, discussed further below).

Inhalation

We've already extensively discussed the techniques and benefits of inhalation in the section on steam and aromatherapy, which can be practised in normal spas, even at home. Suffice it to say, aerosol therapies that deliver mineral water in nebulized form are offered by many thermal spas as well. One variation worth mentioning is endotympanic insufflation, which consists of the introduction of a mist of warm mineral water into the Eustachian tube, which connects the ear to the pharynx, in order to inhibit the formation of catarrh and the potential deafness it can cause.

Thalassotherapy

Modern thalassotherapy makes use of all the natural agents native to marine environments, foremost among which is seawater – whether ingesting, inhaling it, injecting it or simply swimming in it (this latter optionally combined with alternating warm and cold tub sessions). Other integral components of thalassotherapy are climate, sand, seaweed, marine muds and hot water hydromassage.

Just being near the sea vitalizes the body and spirit, so anything on top of that is all the more salutary. Seawater has a composition similar to that of plasma, such that contact with the skin promotes the transfer of oligoelements into the circulatory system, resulting in muscular and psychic relaxation and stimulation of blood flow.

As with thermal spas, before choosing the thalassotherapy spa that is best suited to the condition one intends to treat, it's a good idea to inform oneself of the specific properties of the water and air beforehand, for these factors can vary significantly. To obtain the best results, one should plan on a stay of at least seven to ten days.

Many of the benefits of thalassotherapy come from plankton, which acts as an antibacterial agent, and from salt. Saline content in most marine locales averages around 35 grams per litre, rising to 42 in the Red Sea and much higher in the Dead Sea.

Modern thalassotherapy spas are equipped with pools of various depths and temperatures, tubs for deambulation and soaking, and areas for mud baths. Hygienic standards are rigorous, because in order to ensure the biochemical and therefore the therapeutic integrity of the water, it cannot be purified or sterilized. For this reason it is collected only from the increasingly rare areas where it remains in its pure, uncontaminated state, at least 50 to 60 kilometres from the coast at a minimum depth of 15 metres. Bacterial values, radioactivity and salinity are regularly monitored.

Treatments are usually based on the transmission of heat to the body through water, mud or sand, often alternating between hot and cold.

Some thalassotherapy centres prescribe the drinking of seawater – diluted, of course, and sweetened with fruit juice. Unlike mineral waters, seawater contains many living organisms and a significant quantity of other organic matter. Its curative virtues are numerous: it stimulates the metabolism, facilitates gastric and intestinal secretions, and reconstitutes and remineralizes the entire organism. It is also useful in promoting water retention in dehydrated individuals and maintaining calcium homeostasis.

The ailments for which people most often seek relief are skin and circulatory disorders, along with joint stiffness and the various forms of arthritis. The composition of the water or mud is modified by the addition of dried or fresh seaweed, depending on the condition.

Thalassotherapeutic treatments must be conducted under medical supervision. One should never drink seawater that has not been analysed and diluted by a healthcare professional. Thalassotherapy can also be extremely tiring for pregnant women and individuals in a particularly weakened state. This type of cure demands a strong constitution, especially in colder climates.

France has more than 50 thalassotherapy spas, many of which are on the northern and western coasts of Brittany and Normandy, with a number of new ones opening on the Côte d'Azur. The best known are at Biarritz, Quiberon, La Baule, Belle-Ile-en-Mer and St Malo in the north, while the main spas on the Riviera are at Antibes and Baie des Anges Biovimer, the latter being the largest thalassotherapy centre in Europe. Elsewhere on the continent: Sylt (Germany), Ostend (Belgium), Scheveningen (Netherlands), and Santampelio di Bordighera (Italy).

In Israel, along the Dead Sea, a special form of thalassotherapy is practised. The extremely high concentration of salts, the desert climate and the high atmospheric pressure of this region make it ideal for treating a wide range of pathologies, particularly arthrosis and psoriasis.

Some pharmacies sell a product called Quinton Isotonic, named after the French physician who devised the treatment, which can be taken intravenously, orally or as a nasal spray. Composed of cold-sterilized seawater, it is an excellent remineralizer, ideal for children and dehydrated patients. However, like bottled mineral waters, the vitality of products like this cannot be compared to that of waters taken fresh from the source.

Colonic Irrigation

This detoxifying therapy has been widely used in the Anglophone world for more than a century. Colonic irrigation is essentially the cleaning of the colon with pressurized water enemas. Since it can have a very powerful effect, it should first be authorized by a physician, and in any case administered by a healthcare professional with the proper equipment in an aseptic environment. An extended therapy cycle will flush out intestinal faecal residue that contributes to auto-intoxication of the body.

It is effective in treating intestinal disorders such as ulcerous colitis and Crohn's disease (except in the acute stages); food allergies; disturbances of the mucous linings of different parts of the body (asthma, constipation, diarrhoea, yeast infections); joint ailments; immune system disorders (multiple sclerosis, Bechterew's disease, and the various immunodeficiency pathologies). It should not be undertaken by individuals who have had recent intestinal or colon surgery, or those afflicted with diverticulitis or terminal-stage intestinal cancer. For those with chronic ailments, several consecutive treatment cycles are recommended. It is possible that during the cycle certain symptoms will actually worsen, then improve as the sessions proceed.

For healthy people who wish to do a detoxification treatment, colonic irrigation can be combined with a liquid vegetarian diet and a regular intake of milk-free intestinal probiotics. With a physician's permission, it can also be combined with a brief period of water fasting.

ENDNOTES

1   Alexandersson O, *Living Water. V Schauberger and the Secrets of Natural Energy*, Gateway, Bath 1990, pp 129 *et seq*.

2   Frank LA, Sigwarth JQ, 'Detections of small comets with ground-based telescope', *Journal of Geophysical Research and Space Physics,* vol 106, no 3, 2001.

3   Isaacs E, *et al, Physical Review Letters,* vol 82, p 600, 1998.

4   *See* for example, Keutsch FN and Saykally RJ, 'Water clusters: untangling the mysteries of the liquid, one molecule at a time', *Proceedings of the National Academy of Sciences USA,* vol 98, no 19, pp 10533–40, 2001.

5   Clary D, 'Chemical Physics: interfering with water', *Science,* vol 285, pp 1218–19, 1999.

6   Gregory JK, Clary DC, Liu K, Brown MG and Saykally RJ, 'The water dipole moment in water clusters', *Science,* vol 275, pp 814–17, 1997.

7   Alexandersson O, *Living Water: V Schauberger and the Secrets of Natural Energy, op cit* p 114.

8   Shah I, *The Way of the Sufi,* p 185, Penguin, London, 1990.

9   Aubrey D, *et al,* 'Distribution of phytoplankton in the southern Black Sea in summer', *Nature,* vol 386, pp 385–8, 1996.

10 Feynman R and Leighton RB, *The Feynman Lectures on Physics*, Addison-Wesley, Reading 1963, I, 3, 10.

11 Fung Yu-Lan, *A History of Chinese Philosophy*, Princeton University Press, Princeton, vol I, p 167, 1983.

12 Rohr J, *et al,* 'Experimental approaches towards interpreting dolphin-stimulated bioluminescence', *Journal of Experimental Biology,* vol 201, p 1447, 1998.

13 Rutgers M, *Physical Review Letters,* vol 81, pp 121–40, 1998.

14 Gharib M, Rambod E and Sharrif K, 'A universal timescale for vortex ring formation', *Journal of Fluids Mechanics*, vol 360, pp 121–40, 1998.

15 Eggers J and Dupont TF, 'Drop formation in a one-dimensional approximation of the Navers-Stokes equation', *Journal of Fluids Mechanics*, vol 262, pp 205–21, 1994.

16 Shi XD, Brenner MP and Nagel SR, 'A cascade of structure in a drop falling from a faucet', *Science*, vol 265, p 219, 1994.

17 Folsome C, *Life: Origin and Evolution*, Scientific American Special Publication, 1979.

18 Watson L, *Beyond Supernature*, p 70, Bantam, New York, 1987.

19 Greene B, *The Elegant Universe. Superstrings, hidden dimensions and the quest for the ultimate theory*, p 332, Jonathan Cape, London, 1999.

20 Terzani T, *Un indovino mi disse*, pp 342–3, Longanesi, Milano, 1995.

21 Schwenk T, *Sensitive Chaos*, p 39, Schocken, New York, 1976.

22 Emai E, Honda H, Hatori K, Brack A and Matsuno K, 'Elongation of Oligopeptides in a simulated submarine hydrothermal system', *Science*, vol 283, pp 831–3, 1999.

23 Carson R, *The Sea Around Us*, Staples Press, London, 1951. *See* also Watson, L, *Supernature*, pp 34–52, Hodder & Stoughton, London, 1973.

24 Piccardi G, *The Chemical Basis of Medical Climatology*, Thomas, Springfield (IL), 1962.

25 Capel-Boute C, *Observations sur les tests chimiques de Piccardi*, Presses Acadédemiques Européennes, Brussels 1960; Fisher, W, Sturdy, G, Ryan, M and Pugh, R, 'Some laboratory studies of fluctuating phenomena' in Gauquelin, M, *The Cosmic Clocks*, Peter Owen, London, 1969.

26 Cousteau JY, in Schwenk T, *Sensitive Chaos, op cit*, p 7.

27 Mayol J, *Homo Delphinus: The Dolphin Within Man*, Idelson-Gnocchi Ltd Publishing, 2001.

28 Scott EJ, *Dowsing: One Man's Way*, Neville Spearman, Jersey, 1977.

29 Baker RR, Mather JG and Kennaugh JH, 'Magnetic bones in human sinuses', *Nature*, vol 301, pp 79–80, 1983.

30 Rocard Y, *La Science et les sourciers*, p 133, Bordas, Paris, 1989.

31 Associazione Louis Turenne: www.momosturenne.it and www.turenne.it

32 Grof S, *Beyond the Brain*, pp 55 et seq, State University of New York Press, 1985.

33 Hooper J, Teresi D, *The Three-pound Universe*, Macmillan, 1986.

34 Valli M, *La saggezza folle. Meditazione e vita quotidiana*, p 84, Astrolabio-Ubaldini, Rome, 1971.

35 Yogananda P, *Autobiography of a Yogi*, Self-Realization Fellowship, 1998.

36 Personal communication in Capra F, *The Turning point*, p 422, HarperCollins, London, 1983.

37 Lilly JC, *The Scientist: A Metaphysical Autobiography*, p 90, Ronin Publishing, Berkely, CA, 1997.

38 *See* Schmidt S, Schneider R, Utts J and Walach H, 'Distant intentionality and the feeling of being stared at: two meta-analyses', in *British Journal of Psychology*, vol 95, no 2, pp 235–47, 2004.

39 Benveniste J, *et al*, 'Human basophil degranulation triggered by very dilute antiserum against IgE', *Nature*, vol 333, pp 816–18, 1988.

40 Maddox J, Randi J and Stewart WW, '"High-dilution" experiments a delusion', *Nature*, vol 334, pp 287–90; Benveniste, J, 'Dr. Jacques Benveniste replies', *Nature*, vol 334, p 291, 1988.

41 Benveniste J, *et al*, 'L'agitation de solutions hautement diluées n'induit pas d'activité biologique spécifique', *Comptes Rendus de l'Academie des Sciences*, vol 312, s ii, pp 461–6, 1991.

42 Schulte J and Endler PC (eds), *Fundamental Research in Ultra High Dilution and Homeopathy*, Kluver Academic, Dordrecht 1998; Belon P, Cumps J, Ennis M, *et al*, 'Histamine dliutions modulate basophil activation', *Inflammation Research*, vol 53, no 5, pp 181–8, 2003.

43 Rey L, 'Thermoluminescence of ultra-high dilutions of lithium chloride and sodium chloride', *Physica A*, vol 323, pp 67–74, 2003.

44 Elia V, Napoli E, Niccoli M, Nonatelli L, Ramaglia A, Ventimiglia E, 'New Physico-Chemical Properties of Extremely Diluted Aqueous Solutions. A calorimetric and conductivity study at 25 °C.' *Journal of Thermal Analysis and Calorimetry*, 78, 331–42, 2004.

45 Elia V, Napoli E and Germano R, 'The "Memory of Water": an almost deciphered enigma. Dissipative structures in the extremely diluted aqueous solutions', *Homeopathy*, vol 96, no 3, pp 163–9, 2007.

46 Reilly DT *et al*, 'Is evidence for homoeopathy reproducible?', *The Lancet*, no 8937, p 1601, 1994.

47 Del Giudice E, Preparata G, Vitiello G, *Physical Review Letters*, 61, pp 1085–88, 1988.

48 Del Giudice E and Preparata G, 'Coherent electrodynamics in water', in Schulte J and Endler PC (eds), *Fundamental Research in Ultra High Dilution and Homeopathy, ibid*, p 169.

49 Lu SY, Lo A, Chong LW, Tianshang L, Hua LH and Geng X, *Modern Physics Letters*, B19, pp 921–30, 1996.

50 Nagnostatos GS, 'Small water clusters (clathrates) in the homeopathic preparation process', in Endler, PC and Schulte, J (eds), *Ultra High Dilution – Physics and Physiology*, Kluver Academic, Dordrecht, p 128, 1994.

51 Garczarek F and Gerwert K, *Nature*, 'Functional waters in intraprotein proton transfer monitored by FTIR difference spectroscopy', vol 439, pp 109–112, 2006.

52 Eriksson PS, Perfilieva E, Bjork-Eriksson T *et al*, 'Neurogenesis in the adult human hippocampus', *Nature Medicine*, vol 4, pp 1313–17, 1998.

53 Chopra D, *Quantum Healing*, Bantam, New York, p 87, 1990.

54 Thellier M *et al*, 'Do memory processes also occur in plants?', *Physiologia Plantarum*, vol 56, p 281, 1982.

55 Davis P and Gribbins J, *The Matter Myth*, p 142, Simon and Schuster-Touchstone, New York, 1992.

56 Florito G, Biederman GB, Davey VA and Gherardi F, 'The role of stimulus pre-exposure in problem solving by *Octopus vulgaris*', *Animal Cognition*, no 1, pp 107–12, 1998.

57 Herman LM and Uyeyama RU, 'The dolphin's grammatical competency: comments on Kako (1999)', *Animal Learning and Behavior*, vol 27, no 1, pp 18–23, 1999

58 *See* for example: Schusterman RJ, Thomas JA and Wood FG (eds), *Dolphin Cognition and Behavior: a comparative approach*, Lawrence Erlbaum, Hillsdale, London 1996; Herman LM, *et al*, 'Dolphins (*Tursiops truncatus*) comprehend the referential character of the human pointing gesture', *Journal of Comparative Psychology*, vol 113, no 4, pp 347–64, 1999; Mercado E, Murray SO, Uyeyama RK, Pack AA and Herman LM, 'Memory for recent actions in the bottlenosed dolphin (*Tursiops truncatus*): repetition of arbitrary behaviors using an abstract rule', *Animal Learning and Behavior*, vol 26, no 2, pp 210–18, 1998; Mercado E, Uyeyama RK, Pack AA and Herman LM, 'Memory for action events in the bottlenosed dolphin', *Animal Cognition*, vol 2, pp 17–25, 1999; Wexler M, 'Thinking about dolphins', *National Wildlife*, vol 32, no 3, pp 5–9, 1994.

59 Sun P, *et al*, 'The spectrum analysis on the propagation of sound information along meridians', *Abstracts on Acupuncture and Moxibustion*, China Association of Acupuncture Moxi, p 337, 1987.

60 Bechara A, Damasio H, Tranel D and Damasio AR, 'Deciding advantageously before knowing the advantageous strategy', *Science*, vol 275, pp 1293–5, 1997.

61 Chatwin T, *The Songlines*, p 267, Jonathan Cape, 1987.

62 *Ibid*, p 33.

63 Rhie J and Romanowicz B, 'Excitation of Earth's continuous free oscillations by atmosphere-ocean-seafloor', *Nature*, vol 431, pp 552–6, 2004.

64 Rees M, Ruffini R and Wheelter JA, *Black Holes, Gravitational Waves and Cosmology*, Gordon and Breach, New York, 1974.

65 Koestler A, *The Ghost in the Machine*, p 166, Arkana, London, 1989.

66 Robins D, *The Secret Language of Stone*, Rider, London, 1988.

67 Watson L, *The Nature of Things: The secret life of inanimate objects*, Destiny Books, Rochester (VT), 1992.

68 Ni Hua-Ching, *I Ching. The Book of Changes*, p 503, Sevenstar, Santa Monica (CA), 1994.

69 Cantor KP, Lynch CF, Hildesheim ME *et al*, 'Drinking water source and chlorination by-products: risk of bladder cancer', *Epydemiology*, vol 9, no 1,

p 21–8, 1998; Freedman DM, Cantor KP, Lee NC *et al*, 'Bladder cancer and drinking water: a population-based case-control study in Washington County, Maryland', *Cancer Causes Control*, vol 9, no 1, pp 738–44, 1997; King WD and Marrett LD, 'Case-control study of bladder cancer and chlorinated by-products in treated water' *Cancer Causes Control*, vol 7, no 6, pp 591–604, 1996.

70 *The New England Journal of Medicine*, vol 341, p 924, 1999.

BIBLIOGRAPHY

Alexandersson O, *Living Water: V. Schauberger and the Secrets of Natural Energy*, Gateway, Bath, 1990.

Ann TK, *Cracking the Chinese Puzzles*, 5 vols, Stockflows, Hong Kong, 1982.

Bailey NTJ, *The Mathematical Approach to Biology and Medicine*, John Wiley & Sons, London, 1967.

Banuk AE, *Your Water and Your Health*, Keats Publishing, New Canaan (CT) 1990.

Belon P, Cumps J, Ennis M, Mannaioni PF, Robertfroid M, Sainte-Laudy J and Wiegant FAC, 'Histamine dilutions modulate basophil activation,' *Inflamm. Res.* 53 pp 181–88, 2004.

Belon P, Cumps J, Ennis M, Mannaioni PF, Sainte-Laudy J, Roberfroid M and Wiegant FAC, 'Inhibition of human basophil degranulation by successive histamine dilutions: Results of a European multi-centre trial', *Inflamm. Res.* 48 Suppl. 1 s17–S18, 1999.

Belon P, Elia V, Elia L, Montanino M, Napoli E, Niccoli M, 'Conductometric and Calorimetric studies of Diluted and Agitated Solutions on the Combined Anomalous Effect of Time and Volume Parameters', *Journal of Thermal Analysis and Calorimetry*, 2007.

Benveniste J, 'Dr. Jacques Benveniste replies', *Nature*, vol 334, p 291, 1988.

—— et al, 'Human basophil degranulation triggered by very dilute antiserum against IgE', *Nature*, vol 333, pp 816–18, 1988.

—— et al, 'L'agitation de solutions hautement diluées n'induit pas d'activité biologique spécifique', *Comptes Rendus de l'Académie des Sciences*, vol 312, s ii, pp 461–6, 1991.

Bird C, *The Divining Hand: The 500-year-old Mystery of Dowsing*, Whitford Press, New York, 1979.

Bohm D, *Wholeness and the Implicate Order*, Routledge and Kegan Paul, London, 1980.

Briggs J, *Fractals: The Patterns of Chaos*, Simon & Schuster, New York, 1992.

Brin A, *Océan et energie*, Editions Technip, Paris 1979.

Cahill T, *Dolphins*, National Geographic, Washington DC, 2000.

Cairns-Smith AG, *Genetic Takeover*, Cambridge University Press, Cambridge, 1980.

—— *Evolving the Mind*, Cambridge University Press, Cambridge, 1998.

Capel-Boute C, *Observations sur les tests chimiques de Piccardi*, Presses Académiques Européennes, Brussels, 1960.

Capra F, *The Turning Point*, Harper Collins, London, 1983.

—— *The Web of Life*, Doubleday, New York, 1996.

Carson R, *The Sea Around Us*, Staples Press, London, 1951.

Chaitow L, *Water Therapy*, Thorsons, London, 1994.

Chang C-Y, *Original Teachings of Ch'an Buddhism*, Random House, New York, 1994.

Chaplin M (ed), *Homeopathy*, 'The Memory of Water', Vol 96, 3, pp 191–230, July 2007.

Chatwin B, *The Songlines*, Jonathan Cape, London, 1987.

Chopra D, *Quantum Healing*, Bantam, New York, 1990.

Coats C, *Living Energies*, Gateway Books, Bath, 1990.

Crivelli N, *La sapienza della verità*, Original Researches, Milano, 1992.

Consigli P, *Agopuntura*, Fabbri Editori, Milano, 2000.

Coomaraswamy AK, *Traditional Art and Symbolism*, Princeton University Press, Princeton, 1989.

Cowan J, *Mysteries of the Dream-time*, Prism Press, Bridport, 1989.

Davis, P, Gribbin J, *The Matter Myth*, Simon & Schuster/Touchstone, New York, 1992.

De Meyer F, Capel-Boute C, 'Statistical Analysis of Piccardi chemical Tests', *International Journal Biometeor*, 31, pp 301-322, 1987.

Del Giudice E, Preparata G, 'A new QED Picture of Water: understanding a few fascinating phenomena', in Sassaroli E, *et al* (editors), *Macroscopic Quantum Coherence*, World Scientific, pp 49–64, Singapore 1998.

—— 'Coherent electrodynamics in water', in Schulte J, Endler PC (eds), *Fundamental Research in Ultra High Dilution and Homeopathy*, Kluver Academic, Dordrecht, 1998.

Dennett DC, *Darwin's Dangerous Idea: evolution and the meaning of life*, Simon & Schuster, New York, 1995.

De Vries J, *Water*, Mainstream, Edinburgh, 1990.

Dirac P, *Directions in Physics*, Wiley, London, 1978.

Dobbs H, *Tale of Two Dolphins*, Jonathan Cape, London, 1987.

Eberhard W, *A Dictionary of Chinese Symbols*, Routledge, London, 1988.

Elia V, Elia L, Cacace P, Napoli E, Piccoli M, Bavarese F, 'Extremely dilute solutions as multi-variable systems. A study of calorimetric and conductometric behaviour as function of the parameter time', *J. Therm. Anal. Calor.*, 84(2), pp 317–323, 2006.

Elia V, Elia L, Marchese M, Montanino M, Napoli E, Piccoli M, Nonatelli L, Bavarese F, 'Interaction of "extremely diluted solutions" with aqueous solutions of hydrochloric acid and sodium hydroxide. A calorimetric study', *J. Mol. Liq.*, yet to be published.

Elia V, Marchese M, Montanino M, Napoli E, Niccoli M, Nonatelli L, Ramaglia A, 'Hydrohysteretic phenomena of "extremely diluted solutions" induced by mechanical treatments. A calorimetric and conductometric study at 25 degrees C', *Journal of Solution Chemistry*, 34(8), pp 947–960, 2005.

Elia V, Elia L, Montanino M, Napoli E, Niccoli M, Nonatelli L, 'Conductive Studies of Serially Diluted and Agitated Solutions on an Anomalous Effect that Depends on the Dilution Process', *J. Mol. Liq.*, 158–65, 2007.

Elia V, Elia L, Napoli E, Niccoli M, 'Conductometric and Calorimetric Studies of Serially Diluted and Agitated Solutions: the dependence of intensive parameters on volume', *Internatonal Journal of Ecodynamics*, vol. 1, no.4, 2007

Elia V, Niccoli M, 'Thermodynamics of Extremely Diluted Aqueous Solutions', *Annals of the New York Academy of Sciences*, 879, p 241, 1999.

Elia V, Napoli E, Germano R, 'The "Memory of Water" – an almost deciphered enigma. Dissipative Stuctures in Extremely Diluted Aqueous Solutions'. *Homeopathy*, Vol 96, 3, pp 163–9, 2007

Emoto, M, *La risposta dell'acqua*, Mediterranee, Roma 2004.

Endler PC, Schulte J (eds), *Ultra High Dilution – Physics and Physiology*, p. 128, Kluver Academic, Dordrecht, 1994.

Erickson MH, *The Collected Papers of Milton H. Erickson on Hypnosis*, Irvington, New York, 1980.

Ferenczi S, *Thalassa. Saggio sulla teoria della genitalità*, Raffaello Cortina, Milano, 1993.

Feuchtwang SDR, *An Anthropological Analysis of Chinese Geomancy*, Southern Materials Center, Taipei, 1974.

Feynman, R, Leighton, RB, *The Feynman Lectures on Physics*, Addison-Wesley, Reading, 1963.

Folsome C, *Life: origin and evolution*, Scientific American Special Publication, 1979.

Freedman DM, Cantor KP, Lee NC *et al*, 'Bladder cancer and drinking water: a population-based case-control study in Washington County, Maryland', *Cancer Causes Control*, vol. 9, no 1, pp 738–44,1997.

Fung Y-L, *A History of Chinese Philosophy*, Princeton University Press, Princeton, 1983.

Gauquelin M, *The Cosmic Clocks*, Peter Owen, London, 1969.

Germano R, *Aqua*, Bibliopolis, Napoli, 2007.

Gleick J, *Chaos: making a new science*, Penguin Books, New York, 1988.

Goldin A, *Oceans of Energy*, Harcourt Brace Jovanovic, New York, 1980.

Goleman D, *The Meditative Mind*, Putnam, New York, 1988.

Golubitsky M, Stewart I, *Fearful Symmetry*, Penguin, London, 1992.

Greene B, *The Elegant Universe: Superstrings, hidden dimensions and the quest for the ultimate theory*, Jonathan Cape, London, 1999.

Grof S, *Beyond the Brain*, State University of New York Press, New York, 1985.

—— *The Holotropic Mind*, HarperSanFrancisco, 1992.

Hall N (ed) *Exploring Chaos: A guide to the new science of disorder*, WW Norton, 1994.

Havecker C, *Understanding Aboriginal Culture*, Cosmos, Sydney, 1987.

Hendel B, Ferreira P, *Acqua e sale*, Ina Verlags, Baar, 2004.

Hesse H, *Siddhartha*, New Directions Publishing Corporation, USA, 1951.

Higo J, Sasai M, Shirai H, Nakamura H, and Kugimiya T, 'Large vortex-like structure of dipole field in computer models of liquid water and dipole-bridge between biomolecules', *Proc Natl Acad Sci USA.*, 98(11), pp 5961–5964, 2001.

Hirst SJ, Hayes MA, Burridge J, Pearce FL, Foreman JC, 'Human basophil degranulation is not triggered by very dilute antiserum against IgE', *Nature*, vol 36, pp 525–7, 1993.

Hoyle F, *The Intelligent Universe*, Michael Joseph, London, 1983.

Hunt CA, Garrels RM, *Water: the web of life*, Norton, New York, 1972.

Huxley A, *The Art of Seeing* [1942], Creative Arts Book, Berkeley 1982.

Illich I, H_2O *and the Waters of Forgetfulness*, Boyars, London, 1986.

Institute of History of Natural Sciences, Chinese Academy of Sciences, *Ancient Chinese Technology and Science*, Foreign Languages Press, Beijing, 1987.

Istituto Paracelso, *Esperienza e progresso: l'agopuntura, la farmacologia, l'igiene nella Medicina Cinese*, Paracelso, Roma, 1987.

Kaplan A, *The Bahir*, Weiser, York Beach 1989.

—— *Sefer Yetzirah*, Weiser, York Beach, 1991.

—— *Immortality, Resurrection, and the Age of the Universe: A kabbalistic view*, Ktav Publication House, Haboken, 1993.

Keegan L, Keegan GT, *Healing Waters*, Berkley Books, New York, 1998.

Kirk R, *Snow*, William Morrow, New York, 1977.

Kneipp S, *My Water-Cure: Tested for More Than 35 years, and Published for the Cure of Diseases and the Preservation of Health*, London, Grevel, 1892.

Koestler A, *The Ghost in the Machine*, Arkana, London, 1989.

La Maya J, *La médecine de l'habitat*, Dangles, St Jeanne De Braye, 1995.

Lao Tzu, *Tao Teh Ching*, Shambala, Boston, 1989.

—— *Wen Tzu: Understanding the Mysteries*, Shambala, Boston, 1991.

Leboyer, F, *Birth Without Violence*, Healing Arts Press, New York, 1974.

Le Lann R, *Ces ondes qui nous soignent: La géobiologie*, Editions du Rocher, Monaco, 1994.

Leonardo da Vinci, *Il codice Leicester*, Giunti Barbera, Firenze, 1980.

Leopold LB, *A View of the River*, Harvard University Press, Harvard, 1994.

Leopold LB, Davis KS, *Water*, Time, New York, 1966.

Lichy R, Herzberg E, *The Waterbirth Handbook*, Gateway, Bath, 1993.

Lilly JC, *Communication Between Man and Dolphin*, Crown Publishers, New York, 1979.

—— *The Scientist: A metaphysical autobiography*, Ronin Publishing, Berkeley (CA) 1997.

Lilly JC, Gold EJ, *Tanks for the Memories: Flotation tank talks*, Gateways, Nevada City (CA), 1995.

Livio M, *The Golden Ratio*, Headline, London, 2002.

Lovelock J, *The Ages of Gaia*, Oxford University Press, Oxford, 1989.

Luk C, *The Secrets of Chinese Meditation*, Weiser, York Beach (Maine), 1991.

McCrone J, *The Ape that Spoke*, Picador, London, 1990.

Mallove EF, *Fire from Ice: Searching for the truth behind the cold fusion furore*, John Wiley & Sons, New York, 1991.

Mandelbrot B, *The New Scientist's Guide to Chaos*, Penguin, London 1991.

Maneglier H, *L'Histoire de l'eau*, Bourin, Paris 1991.

Man-Ho K, O'Brien J, *The Elements of Feng-Shui*, Element, Shaftesbury, 1992.

Matt DC, *God and the Big Bang*, Jewish Lights, Woodstock (VT), 1996.

Mayol J, *Homo delphinus: The dolphin within man*, Idelson-Gnocchi Ltd, 2000.

Meier L, *Ancient Secrets*, Villard, New York, 1996.

Mermet A, *Principles and Practice of Radiesthesia*, Element, Shaftesbury, 1987.

Meschia M, *Stazioni di quieto esilio*, Castel Maggiore, 2004.

Milton R, *Forbidden Science*, Fourth Estate, London, 1995.

Mopsik C, *Le Zohar*, French trans, Verdier, Paris, 1981.

Morgan E., *The Aquatic Ape*, Souvenir Press, London 1982.

—— *The Scars of Evolution*, Penguin, London, 1991.

—— *The Aquatic Ape Hypothesis*, Souvenir Press, London, 1997.

Mullin T, 'Turbulent Time for Fluids' in N Hall (ed) *Exploring Chaos: A guide to the new science of disorder*, WW Norton, 1994.

Ni, Hua-Ching, *I Ching. The Book of Changes*, Sevenstar, Santa Monica (CA), 1994.

Ni, M, *The Yellow Emperor's Classic of Medicine: A New Translation of the Neijing Suwen with Commentary* Shambhala, Boston, 1995.

Nollman J, *Dolphin's Dreamtime*, Bantam Books, New York, 1990.

Norris KS, *Dolphin Days*, Northon, London, 1991.

Odent M, *Water and Sexuality*, Arkana, London, 1990.

Payne R, *Among Whales*, Scribner, New York, 1995.

Peat DF, *Superstrings and the Search for the Theory of Everything*, Abacus, London, 1992.

Piccardi G, *The Chemical Basis of Medical Climatology*, Thomas, Springfield (IL), 1962.

Pielou EC, *Fresh Water*, University of Chicago Press, Chicago, 1998.

Prigogine I, *From Being to Becoming. Time and Complexity in the Physical Sciences*, Freeman, San Francisco, 1980.

Prigogine I, Stengers I, *Order out of Chaos: Man's New Dialogue with Nature*, Bantam, New York, 1984.

Radin D, *Entangled Minds: Extrasensory Experiences in a Quantum Reality*, Paraview Pocket Books, 2006

—— *The Conscious Universe: The scientific truth of psychic phenomena*, HarperCollins, New York, 1997.

Ramban, *Commentary on the Torah*, translated by Rabbi Charles B Chavel, Shilo Publishing House, New York, 1971.

Rees M, *Just Six Numbers: The Deep Forces That Shape the Universe*, Weidenfeld & Nicolson, 1999.

Rees M, Ruffini R, Wheeler JA, *Black Holes, Gravitational Waves and Cosmology*, Gordon and Breach, New York, 1974.

Rey L, 'Thermoluminescence of ultra-high dilutions of lithium chloride and sodium chloride', *Physica A*, vol 323, pp 67–74, 2003.

Ricci Lucchi, F, *I ritmi del mare*, La Nuova Italia Scientifica, Roma 1992.

Robins D, *The Secret Language of Stone*, Rider, London, 1988.

Rocard Y, *La science et les sourciers*, Bordas, Paris, 1989.

Rosner F, *Medicine in the Bible and the Talmud*, Ktav Publishing House, New York, 1977.

Rossbach S, *Feng Shui: The Chinese art of placement*, EP Dutton, New York, 1983.

Rousselet-Blanc V, Mangez C, *Les animaux guerisseurs*, Lattès, Paris, 1992.

Sainte-Laudy J, and Belon P, 'Use of four different flow cytometric protocols for the analysis of human basophil activation. Application to the study of the biological activity of high dilutions of histamine', *Inflamm*. Res. 55, Suppl. 1, s23–S24, 2006.

Schauberger V, *The Water Wizard*, ed. by C Coats, Gateway Books, Bath, 1998.

Schiff M, *Un cas de censure dans la science*, Albin Michel, Paris, 1994.

Schroeder GL, *The Science of God*, Broadway Books, New York, 1998.

—— *Genesis and Big Bang*, Bantam Books, New York, 1990.

—— *The Hidden Face of God*, Free Press, New York, 2001.

Schulte J, Endler PC (eds), *Fundamental Research in Ultra High Dilution and Homeopathy*, Kluver Academic, Dordrecht, 1998.

Schusterman RJ, Thomas JA, Wood FG (eds), *Dolphin Cognition and Behaviour: a comparative approach*, Lawrence Erlbaum, Hillsdale, London, 1986.

Schwartz G, Russek L, *The Living Energy Universe*, Hampton Roads, Charlotteslville (VA), 1999.

Schwenk T, *Sensitive Chaos*, Schocken, New York 1976.

Scott EJ, *Dowsing: one man's way*, Neville Spearman, Jersey, 1977.

Scott KS, *Chemical Chaos*, Oxford University Press, Oxford, 1991.

Shah I, *The Way of the Sufi*, Penguin, London, 1990.

Shaw RS, 'Strange attractors, chaotic behavior, and information flow', *Zeitschrift für Naturforschung*, vol 36a, n 80, 1981.

Sheldrake R, *A New Science of Life: the hypothesis of formative causation*, JP Tarcher, Los Angeles, 1981.

—— *The Presence of the Past*, HarperCollins, London, 1988.

—— *Seven Experiments that Could Change the World: a do-it-yourself guide to revolutionary science*, Inner Traditions, London, 2002.

Skinner S, *The Living Earth Manual of Feng-Shui*, Graham Brash, Singapore, 1983.

Stewart I, *Life's Other Secret: The new mathematics of the living world*, John Wiley, New York, 1998.

Stewart I, Golubitsky M, *Fearful Symmetry*, Penguin, London 1992.

Summerhayes CP, Thorpe SA, *Oceanography*, Manson, London, 1996.

Ki S, and Yunkyo L, *The Canon of Acupuncture: Huang Ti Nei Ching Ling Shu*, Korea Acupuncture Society, Seoul, Korea, 1985.

Talbot M, *The Holographic Universe*, HarperCollins, New York 1992.

Terzani T, *Un indovino mi disse*, Longanesi, Milano, 1995.

Thompson DW, *On Growth and Form*, ed. by JT Bonner, Cambridge University Press, Cambridge, 1961.

Tritton D, 'Chaos in the Swing of a Pendulum' in N Hall (ed) *Exploring Chaos: A guide to the new science of disorder*, WW Norton, 1994.

Tucci G (ed), *Il libro tibetano dei morti*, Editori Associati, Milano, 1988.

Turenne L, *De la baguette de coudrier aux détecteurs du prospecteur*, 10 vols, Desforges et Omnium Littéraire.

Valli M, *La saggezza folle: Meditazione e vita quotidiana*, Promolibri, Torino, 1995.

Venturini N, *Le acque, le fonti*, Muzzio, Padova, 1995.

Vinas F, *Idroterapia*, Red, Como, 1992.

Waters D, *Chinese Geomancy*, Element Books, Shaftesbury, 1989.

Watson L, *Beyond Supernature*, Bantam, New York, 1987.

—— *Gifts of Unknown Things: A True Story of Nature, Healing and Initiation from Indonesia's 'Dancing island'*, Inner Traditions, 1992.

—— *Supernature*, Hodder and Stoughton, London, 1992.

—— *The Dreams of Dragons*, Destiny Books, Rochester (VT), 1992.

—— *The Nature of Things: The secret life of inanimate objects*, Destiny Books, Rochester (VT), 1992.

Weber R, *Dialogues with Scientists and Sages: The search for unity*, Routledge and Kegan Paul, New York, 1986.

Wilkens A, Jacobi M, Schwenk W, *Understanding Water*, Floris Books, 2005.

Wolf FA, *Mind into Matter: A new alchemy of science and spirit*, Moment Point Press, Portsmouth (NH), 2001.

Wong E, *Feng-Shui*, Shambhala, Boston, 1996.

Wyllie T, *Dolphins: Telepathy and Underwater Birthing*, Bear, Santa Fe, 1993.

Yogananda P, *Autobiography of a Yogi*, Self-Realization Fellowship, 1974 and 1998.

Zhadin MN, Novikoff VV, Barnes FS, Pergola MF, 'Combined Action of Static and Alternating Magnetic Fields on Ionic Current in Aqueous glutamic acid Solution', *Bioelectromagnetics*, 19, pp 279–92 (1998).

INDEX